FLORIDA STATE
UNIVERSITY LIBRARIES

JUL 2 2 1999

TALLAHASSEE, FLORIDA

Processes of the World-System

POLITICAL ECONOMY OF THE WORLD-SYSTEM ANNUALS

Series Editor: IMMANUEL WALLERSTEIN

Published in cooperation with the Section on the Political Economy of the World-System of the American Sociological Association.

About the Series

The intent of this series of annuals is to reflect and inform the intense theoretical and empirical debates about the "political economy of the world-system." These debates assume that the phenomena of the real world cannot be separated into three (or more) categories—political, economic, and social—which can be studied by different methods and in closed spheres. The economy is "institutionally" rooted; the polity is the expression of socioeconomic forces; and "societal" structures are a consequence of politico-economic pressures. The phrase "world-system" also tells us that we believe there is a working social system larger than any state whose operations are themselves a focus of social analysis. How states and parties, firms and classes, status groups and social institutions operate within the framework and constraints of the world-system is precisely what is debated.

These theme-focused annuals will be the outlet for original theoretical and empirical findings of social scientists coming from all the traditional "disciplines." The series will draw upon papers presented at meetings and conferences, as well as papers from those who share in these concerns.

Volumes in this series:

Volume 1: *Social Change in the Capitalist World Economy* (1978)
Barbara Hockey Kaplan, *Editor*

Volume 2: *The World-System of Capitalism: Past and Present* (1979)
Walter L. Goldfrank, *Editor*

Volume 3: *Processes of the World-System* (1980)
Terence K. Hopkins and Immanuel Wallerstein, *Editors*

Processes of the World-System

Edited by **Terence K. Hopkins**
and **Immanuel Wallerstein**

Volume 3, **Political Economy of the World-System Annuals**
Series Editor: Immanuel Wallerstein

SAGE PUBLICATIONS   Beverly Hills   London

Copyright © 1980 by Sage Publications, Inc.

All rights reserved. No part of this book may be reproduced or utilized in any form or by any means, electronic or mechanical, including photocopying, recording, or by any information storage and retrieval system, without permission in writing from the publisher.

For information address:

    SAGE Publications, Inc.   SAGE Publications Ltd
    275 South Beverly Drive   28 Banner Street
    Beverly Hills, California 90212   London EC1Y 8QE, England

Printed in the United States of America

Library of Congress Cataloging in Publication Data

Main entry under title:

Processes of the world-system.

   (Political economy of the world-system annuals ; v. 3)
   Papers presented at the third annual PEWS conference, held at the State University of New York at Binghamton, May 1979.
   Includes bibliographies.
   1. Economic history--Congresses. 2. Capitalism--Congresses. 3. Business cycles--Congresses.
4. Social classes--Congresses. I. Hopkins, Terence K.
II. Wallerstein, Immanuel Maurice, 1930-
III. American Sociological Association. Section on Political Economy of the World-System. IV. Series

HC13.P77   330.9   79-27385
ISBN 0-8039-1378-8
ISBN 0-8039-1379-6 pbk.

FIRST PRINTING

CONTENTS

Preface
TERENCE K. HOPKINS
IMMANUEL WALLERSTEIN 7

PART 1: THE WORLD SOCIAL ECONOMY: CYCLES AND TRENDS

1. Stages of Accumulation and Long Economic Cycles
   DAVID M. GORDON 9
2. From Hegemony to Competition: Cycles of the Core?
   NICOLE BOUSQUET 46
3. Long Waves and the Cotton-Spinning Enterprise, 1789-1849
   KENNETH BARR 84
4. Stages, Cycles, and Insurgencies: The Economics of Unrest
   JAMES E. CRONIN 101
5. Cycles of Formal Colonial Rule
   ALBERT BERGESEN 119

PART 2: THE WORLD CLASS STRUCTURE: PROLETARIANIZATION AND BOURGEOISIFICATION

SECTION A: PERIPHERALIZATION AND CLASS FORMATION

6. Class Development in Rural Egypt, 1945-1979
   JAMES F. TOTH 127
7. Agriculture and Social Organization: Brazil's Agreste, 1845-1978
   JASON W. CLAY 148
8. Capitalism and South African Agriculture, 1890-1920
   MARTIN J. MURRAY 158

SECTION B: SOCIAL MOVEMENTS AND THE POLITICS OF THE CAPITALIST WORLD-ECONOMY

9. The Future of the World-Economy
   IMMANUEL WALLERSTEIN — 167
10. Maoist Conceptualizations of the Capitalist World-System
    EDWARD FRIEDMAN — 181
11. Proletarianization and Class Alliances in the Americas
    SUSANNE JONAS
    MARLENE DIXON — 224
12. Celtic Nationalism in Britain: Political and Structural Bases
    CHARLES C. RAGIN — 249
13. State-Building and Ethnic Structures: Dependence on International Capitalist Penetration
    CYNTHIA H. ENLOE — 266

PART 3: WORLD-SYSTEMS ANALYSIS: PROBLEMS OF METHOD

14. On the Holism of a World-Systems Perspective
    ROBERT L. BACH — 289

Commentary
   CHRISTOPHER CHASE-DUNN — 311
   RAMKRISHNA MUKHERJEE — 314
   TERENCE K. HOPKINS — 316

Notes on the Contributors — 319

PREFACE

The papers collected here were given at the Third Annual Conference of the Political Economy of the World-System (PEWS), held at the State University of New York at Binghamton, May, 1979, under the auspices of the Fernand Braudel Center for the Study of Economies, Historical Systems, and Civilizations, in conjunction with the PEWS Section of the American Sociological Association.

In preparing for this year's PEWS conference, we thought we could discern three central issues, in the study of the capitalist world-economy as an historical system, each of which would make an appropriate general subject for a set of papers reporting to the conference on work in progress. For each, there was a quite broad array of scholars here and abroad who had been addressing the subject and the issues it raises for world-system studies, and doing so, we believed, in ways that were at once inventive, reasoned, and clarifying of earlier efforts. Yet they were not for the most part in touch with one another. Nor were the commonalities we thought would be evident in their respective inquiries recognized by, let alone familiar to, the far wider body of historical and social scientists devoting their scholarly efforts to the disciplined study of the capitalist development of the modern world-system.

The papers on each of the three central topics comprise the respective parts of this volume. The periodicities of the accumulation process on a world scale—a "world" continually formed and reformed by "the process" itself—and, in particular, the *theoretical* place and *interpretative* importance of "long waves," form the focus and subject matter of the papers in Part I. The relocation of "class struggle" into a wider setting than it has conventionally been given—here as the theoretical mediation between the world-system processes of peripheralization and proletarianization, in one direction, and of transformations of that system's relational networks or social structures, in another—inform the interpretative accounts in the papers comprising Part II. And the implications for the conduct of inquiry of the claim about the "singularity" of the capitalist developmental processes taken as a whole, and thus of the discernible different understandings (or constructions) of "part-whole" relations in world-systems studies, form the subject of the lead paper and the commentaries it elicited in Part III.

Our original hope, to editorialize briefly, was we believe more than realized. For not only do the reports of work-in-progress that are gathered in each part bear on one another in ways neither intended nor foreseen by their authors—or, for that matter, by the editors, but of even more significance, in our judgment—as a manifest indication of the intellectual scope and internal coherence of what has come to be known as the "world-historical" or "world-system" perspective in the definition and study of modern social change—is the quite remarkable array of mutual implications and common understandings which the papers in one part have for or share with the papers in the other parts. This is a preface, not an introduction, and so extended comment on these implications and understandings is inappropriate. At the same time, it is a preface and not an introduction precisely because we believe extended comment along these lines is neither necessary nor desirable. It is unnecessary because the papers so clearly speak to one another, as it were, without for the most part even addressing one another, that to sketch their mutual implications and common understandings here would be gratuitous and, as a result, patronizing. It is undesirable because it would require presuming that the framework-in-becoming, evidence in the multiple levels of relevance the papers here have for one another, is already sufficiently formed for a particular version of it to command broad acceptance—and that we do not believe is true, yet.

Our thanks to those who prepared papers for the conference; to those whose attention to amenities and details made it succeed as an occasion, in particular, Donna M. DeVoist, Administrative Assistant of the Center; and to those whose support of the Fernand Braudel Center and its research programs made possible the Center's being host to the conference.

—Terence K. Hopkins
—Immanuel Wallerstein

PART 1
THE WORLD SOCIAL ECONOMY: CYCLES AND TRENDS

Chapter 1

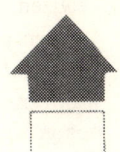

STAGES OF ACCUMULATION AND LONG ECONOMIC CYCLES

David M. Gordon

> [A crisis is] the manifestation of *all* the contradictions of the bourgeois economy.... [But] permanent crises do not exist.
> —Karl Marx (1968: 507, 497n)

> Kondratyev Swings: A myth perpetuated by people who—sharing the apocalyptic visions of Plato, Marx, Toynbee and others—believe that there is a mystical pattern of history that permits true believers to divine the future.
> —*Citibank Monthly Economic Letter* (January 1978: 16)

Not surprisingly, the current crisis of the world capitalist economy has prompted a new wave of interest in long economic cycles.[1] Both mainstream and Marxian economists have joined in reviving a theoretical and empirical interest which many had buried in the 1940s.[2] The list of recent long cycle literature has already grown remarkably long.[3]

As before, long cycle analyses still have a vulnerable Achilles heel. The

---

AUTHOR'S NOTE: As with many projects like this which gestate over a period of years, I have received so many helpful criticisms and suggestions from so many friends and colleagues that I could not possibly take the space to thank them personally. The institutional debts are equally important and more tractable: I want to thank colleagues and students at the New School for Social Research and friends at the Union for Radical Political Economics for guidance and support. I was always grateful that they treated this quirkish interest of mine with nothing worse than bemusement. The teasing has only begun; they'll be quick to point out, of course, that all the errors remain mine.

earlier generation of long cycle analysts, from Kondratieff through Schumpeter and the secular stagnationists of the 1940s, largely failed to elaborate a coherent (much less a unified) theoretical foundation for their interpretations of long cycles.[4] This weakness has plagued the more recent work as well. The analytic problems of long cycle analysis are complex, and it does not yet appear that the recent work has begun to solve some of the most vexing questions which previously plagued long cycle theorists: Why should long cycles recur? Why should they last roughly fifty years? What determines their amplitude? What is the connection between the sources of stagnation in one cycle and the innovations or events which stimulate recovery and a new burst of accumulation in the next?

This essay builds upon a central criticism of earlier mainstream *and* Marxist analyses of the rhythms of capitalist development. Despite many differences among those analyses, all have suffered, in my view, because they have taken the basic structure of social relationships in capitalist societies for granted. They have attempted to account for alternating periods of economic prosperity and stagnation without properly considering the connections between the structure and contradictions of the social relationships conditioning capital accumulation and the "purely" economic dynamics through which long cycles appear to manifest themselves. As I try to argue in this essay, a careful analysis of the structural requirements of capital accumulation in capitalist societies casts the problems of long cycle analysis in a somewhat different theoretical light. It begins to point, I think, toward some promising provisional resolutions of many (though certainly not all) of the theoretical problems which long cycle analysis must resolve.

In general, I argue, a conceptual reformulation of the Marxian notion of "stages of capital accumulation" constitutes both a necessary condition for clarifying our understanding of long economic cycles and a suggestive foundation upon which to base more narrowly "economic" hypotheses about the origin, character, shape, and period of long cycles themselves.[5]

Do long cycles even exist? Are we wasting our time puzzling over imaginary phenomena or relics of earlier stages of capitalist development? I do not have the space in this essay to review the current state of the empirical evidence for or against long cycles.[6] I am content to agree with the cautious conclusion of the Research Working Group on Cyclical Rhythms and Secular Trends (1979: 487): "[The] data are beset by technical inadequacies. Nevertheless, there certainly exists a *prima facie* case for the existence of Kondratieff cycles worthy of further investigation."

I agree with that tentative opinion for two reasons. First, I think that sufficient regularity in the empirical pattern of capitalist growth and stagnation has been demonstrated to warrant the plausibility of the empirical hypothesis that long economic cycles have occurred.[7] Second, to propose an analogue with Pascal's wager about the existence of God, it seems prudent to make what I'll call "Kondratieff's Wager" about the existence of long economic cycles.[8] If long cycles *do* exist and we *ignore* them, particularly from a political perspective, we run the risk of basing our analytic observations and strategic planning upon completely misplaced conceptions of the trajectory of capital accumulation; it could only be likened, on a much more cosmic political-economic scale, to pissing in the wind. If, on the other hand, long cycles *don't* exist and we devote a certain amount of intellectual attention to their investigation, all we've wasted is a little time and energy. Posing the alternate hypothesis that long cycles *exist* makes much more sense, in this light, than eliding that possibility altogether.[9]

I have drafted this essay with that kind of skeptical intention. The essay has two major sections. The first seeks a theoretical clarification of the Marxian theory of stages of accumulation. The second builds upon that "theory of stages" to advance some tentative hypotheses toward a political-economic theory of long cycles. A concluding section highlights the differences between this analysis and other positions in the literature.[10]

TOWARD A MARXIAN THEORY OF STAGES OF ACCUMULATION

At least since Lenin's classic work (1917) on imperialism and monopoly capitalism, Marxists have typically presumed that capitalist development passes through successive "stages of accumulation," (Thus the pervasive reference to the modern stage of "monopoly capitalism.") Neither in Lenin nor in more recent arguments, however, do we find more than a distant resemblance to a rigorous theory of stages.[11]

I provide in this section an outline of what I hope provides a rigorous theoretical foundation for a theory of stages of accumulation. The analysis moves through a sequence of derived hypotheses. Each of the hypotheses outlined in this section is *necessary* for the derivation of a theory of stages of accumulation but none is *sufficient* by itself.[12] The analysis begins by accepting the Marxian premise that capital accumulation dominates the structure and dynamics of capitalist society and therefore that the requirements for capital accumulation provide the most promising starting point for an examination of the structures shaping concrete life in capitalist societies.

(1) THE NECESSITY OF STRUCTURAL STABILITY FOR CAPITAL ACCUMULATION

The accumulation of capital through capitalist production cannot take place either in a vacuum or in chaos. Individual capitalists will not invest in production if they are unable to make reasonably determinate calculations of their expected rates of return. Failing the possibility of such calculations, they will leave their money to the financial and commercial spheres, earning the "financial rate of return."[13] The expectations of capitalists and their calculations of potential (relative) profitability hinge not only on variables over which they have some influence but also upon a complex of social relationships in the broader environment which they are individually powerless to transform. These environmental conditions include not only "economic" factors like the availability of credit and the level of expected demand, but also social and political factors like the reliability of a potential labor force, the hospitality and stability of governments in foreign countries where resource extraction and basic production take place, and the supportiveness of domestic government policy for accumulation in general. The more unstable these economic, social, and political elements of the general climate affecting accumulation, the less likely it will be that capitalists seek accumulation through production. The greater the stability of the social environment, the more likely it will be that individual capitalists respond to their "werewolf hunger" for accumulation by seeking to produce as much surplus value as possible.

These observations lead directly to a simple and straightforward hypothesis: relative stability in the general social and economic environment affecting the possibilities for capital accumulation is a necessary condition for sustained and rapid accumulation; without such structural stability, the pace of capital accumulation in a capitalist economy is likely to slacken.[14]

(2) THE DETERMINACY OF THE SOCIAL STRUCTURE OF ACCUMULATION

If the first hypothesis is to have any operational meaning, one obviously requires a specification of the "general social environment affecting the possibilities for capital accumulation." We can derive this specification directly from the general Marxian analysis of the process of capital accumulation.

(2a) THE INSTITUTIONS NECESSARY FOR STABLE ACCUMULATION

The following paragraphs outline a list of the institutions whose stability is necessary for a stable environment for accumulation.[15] I have organized the list into four logical categories. The logical categories are identified by roman numerals, while the names of the institutions are preceded by an asterick and printed in italics.

I. Agents of Accumulation

Corporate Structure. Individual units of accumulation are not automata; they have an internal life and internal problems. As the concentration and centralization of capital produces continually larger units of accumulation, firms must periodically resolve problems of internal organization arising out of the conflict between their habitual modes of internal organization and their new size and scope of operation. Without such periodic resolution, the firm's capacity to make rational investment decisions will be severely limited. A relatively stable internal corporate structure is therefore necessary in order to permit capitalist decision-making.[16]

II. Motors of Accumulation

Two intrinsic contradictions in the capitalist mode of production provide the continuing "motor force" or "drive" to accumulation—*inter capitalist competition* and *the class struggle*.[17] Each of these contradictions requires some moderation before sustained and rapid accumulation is possible.

The Structure of Competition. Elements of both competition and monopoly are always present in capitalist economies, and individual capitalists have always sought to establish a margin of protection from the relentlessness of unmitigated competitive pressure. The moderation of competition requires a set of structured social relationships among capitalists; it cannot be achieved through the actions of a single firm alone.[18] Some moderation of competition is necessary to prevent the kind of economic instability which would undermine accumulation.

The Structure of the Class Struggle. While the basic conflict between capitalists and workers is intrinsic in capitalist economies, the intensity of that opposition can vary, ranging from the spreading brushfires of periods like the 1880s and 1930s in the United States to periods of attenuated and contained class struggle, like the 1950s and 1960s in the United States. As with intercapitalist competition, the intensity of the class struggle depends on a complex of structured social relationships affecting the relative consciousness and strength of both capitalists and workers. These social relationships constitute the structure of the class struggle; the stability of that institution is also a necessary condition for rapid accumulation.

III. Systemic Requirements for Accumulation

Two important requirements for accumulation are established at the level of the economy as a whole, either in the entire world-economy or, at the least, at the level of a national economy. If *any* individual capitalist is able to take advantage of these elements of the social structure of accumulation, *all* will be able to do so.[19]

The Structure of the Monetary System. Capital accumulation requires exchange. Exchange requires a standard unit of equivalence, one of the several functions of money in capitalist economies. The reliability of currency exchange ratios can vary. (The stability of a national currency can dissolve, as in the Weimar Republic in the 1920s, for example, or the relative exchange ratios of national currencies in the world market can begin to fluctuate rapidly and contribute to explosive instability in the patterns of world trade, as seemed increasingly characteristic of the world-economy in the late 1920s.) This kind of instability in the monetary system poses significant barriers to accumulation. Relative stability in the structure of the monetary system is therefore a decisive systemic requirement for capital accumulation.

The Structure of the State. Capitalist societies have historically generated "liberal" notions of individual freedom from "absolutist" state rule. These notions of individual freedom have created intrinsic contradictions in capitalist societies between the "rights of property" and the "rights of person" or the "rights of citizenship."[20] (This conflict is simplistically expressed by the conflict between two political algorithms: "one person, one vote" and "one dollar, one vote.") If masses of citizens begin to seek the imposition of their political rights of person on capitalists' rights of property, as with the Populists in the United States in the early 1890s, these movements can begin to threaten the pace and possibility of capital accumulation. The structure of the state constitutes the set of social relationships which determines the relative stability of this contradictory political relationship; its stability therefore comprises another necessary condition for rapid and sustained accumulation.

IV. Requirements for Individual Capital Accumulation

Given the fulfillment of these (prior) conditions for capital accumulation, individual capitalists can potentially pursue the augmentation of their stocks of money through the circuit of capital accumulation. Their journey along this circuit meets many potential obstacles, posing some additional conditions for successful accumulation. As long as a significant number of capitalists can share in the satisfaction of these conditions for accumulation, then a rapid rate of accumulation in the economy as a whole is at least possible. If any one or more of these conditions is not satisfied, rapid accumulation is problematic. The "social" character of these institutions is manifold. On the one hand, an individual capitalist cannot achieve a fundamental transformation of these institutions on his/her own; in this sense, these institutions are structured through a *social* process which frames the activities of *individual* capitalists. On the other hand, it is not necessary that *all* firms in a capitalist economy share access to all these institutions for rapid accumulation to take place. As long as a significant number of capitalists can secure the satisfaction of this subset of necessary conditions, rapid accumulation is possible. This consideration differentiates these "requirements for individual capital accumulation" from the "systemic requirements" outlined above.[21]

A. Access to the Means of Production

The Structure of Natural Supply. Capitalists who use substantial amounts of raw materials, like energy, must be able to secure stable access to the quantities they need at predictable prices. If the supply of raw materials is threatened or prices begin to fluctuate rapidly, the basis for accumulation will be threatened.[22]

The Structure of Intermediate Supply. Capitalists must also be able to secure access to the machine goods and finished goods which comprise the other principal components of constant capital.[23] This requires that bottlenecks not develop in the machine goods industries and other industries, like steel, of critical importance in the supply of intermediate goods. As Marx pointed out (1968: 497ff.), sudden disruptions in the supply of intermediate products can generate a sustained stagnation reverberating throughout the economy. Without a stable structure of intermediate supply, the rate of capital accumulation can quickly slacken.[24]

Individual capitalists must also be able to secure access to reliable supplies of labor power. Since the *Production and reproduction of labor power* in capitalist societies have been mediated in one sphere and the *exchange of labor power* has been transacted in another, this requirement frames the necessity of two interconnected institutional conditions.

The Social Family Structure. The family, the schools, and other institutions must perform in such a way that a steady and appropriate supply of labor is available to the labor market. The quality and quantity of the supply of labor power cannot be taken for granted; recurrent changes in the structured relationship between these institutions and the capitalist economy have occurred.[25] The composite of these institutions securing the production and reproduction of labor power—what I am calling the "social family structure" for ease of reference—must be organized in a coherent fashion in order for sufficient quantities and appropriate qualities of labor power to be available to the individual unit of accumulation.

The Labor Market Structure. If the price of labor power fluctuates rapidly or sufficient quantities are not available at the prevailing wage, capital accumulation may also be threatened. The structure of labor market institutions mediating the exchange of labor power has changed dramatically through the history of capitalist development.[26] Those changes have had dramatic effects on the pace and character of capital accumulation; a stable labor market structure is demonstrably necessary for stable accumulation.

B. The Production of Surplus Value

The Structure of Labor Management. It is not sufficient for rapid capital accumulation that the structure of the class struggle effect a general moderation of class conflict. It is also necessary that capitalists be able to count on steady and reliable methods of securing the greatest possible surplus labor time out of the labor power they have purchased on the market. "To the capitalist," as Braverman puts it (1974: 58), "[this] presents itself as the problem of [labor] *management.*" Like others of the institutions outlined here, the structure of labor management has changed periodically through the history of capitalist development.[27] As with the corporate structure, moreover, the ideas and techniques underlying innovations in the structure of labor management derive in large part from the general context within which capitalists pursue production and are not uniquely and singularly determined by the actions of individual capitalists by themselves. Successive transformations in the structure of labor management have played a critical role in reconstituting the possibilities for capital accumulation. (See Gordon, et al., 1980, for this argument for the United States.)

C. The Realization of Surplus Value

The Structure of Final Consumer Demand. Capitalists must sell their products in order to be able to realize the full value of the surplus value they have generated in production. Individual consumer demand does not exist solely as the simple collection of households' preferences and is not affected by the macroeconomic determinations of "effective demand" alone. Social structures provide the basis for and help shape individual consumer demand. (Highways must exist, for instance, in order for consumers to be able to pursue and effectively satisfy their demand for automobiles. Urban electrical systems must also exist, similarly, for consumers to be able to consume modern electrical appliances.) This structured social foundation for final consumer demand must be in place for capitalists to be able to expect full realization.[28]

D. The Turnover of Capital

As Marx suggested at great length (1967: Vol. II), the capitalist's journey around the circuit of capital accumulation does not occur instantaneously. Both money and commodities must be advanced and stored to facilitate efficient utilization of resources during the entire period of the "turnover" of capital. Institutional structures must help ensure that the turnover of capital proceeds steadily and smoothly.

The Financial Structure. Capitalists must be able to gain access to the cash flow necessary to finance investment, acquisition of the means of production, and inventory management. If their internal retained earnings are insufficient, they must be able to secure external funding. Wildly fluctuating interest rates or unreliable sources of external capital can damage their prospects. Once again, a reliable resolution of these potential problems is a necessary condition for rapid accumulation.[29]

The Structure of Administrative Management. Corporations must effect the circulation of commodities—both the "factors of production" and finished products—to facilitate accumulation. To the capitalist, to paraphrase the earlier quote from Braverman, this has presented itself as the problem of administrative management. Through capitalist development, this problem has generated systems of computerized record-keeping, market research, advertising, and many other administrative innovations. These systems, like the corporate structure and the structure of labor management, depend upon external as well as internal relationships. This organized structure of administrative management must be compatible with other institutions required for accumulation and must not be changing too rapidly if capitalists are to be able to manage the circulation of commodities effectively.

(2b) THE UNITY OF THE SOCIAL STRUCTURE OF ACCUMULATION

Given this catalogue of individual institutions, we can further hypothesize that the social composite of these individual structures must exist and function reliably in order for capital accumulation to proceed smoothly. This institutional composite comprises the "social environment" whose stability is postulated in the first hypothesis above. I call this composite the *social structure of accumulation*. There are two possible versions of this hypothesis on the unity of the social structure of accumulation, a weak and a strong formulation.

The weak version of the hypothesis proposes that the social structure of accumulation is the simple social aggregation of the structures of the constituent institutions necessary for rapid accumulation, nothing more than the composite sum of the individual parts of that structure. This formulation implies that the dissolution of the structure of any individual institution would potentially threaten the stability of accumulation but that it would *not* necessarily generate a progressive instability in the structure of any other (one or more) constituent institutions of the social structure.

The strong version of the hypothesis proposes that the interdependencies among the individual institutions create a combined social structure with a *unified* internal structure of its own—a composite whole, in effect, whose intrinsic structure amounts to more than the sum of the individual institutional relationships. This stronger hypothesis suggests (a) that the social environment affecting the pace and possibilities for capital accumulation acquires an integrated structural form at a social level; and (b) that changes in any one constituent institution are very likely to reverberate throughout the entire structure, creating instability in all of the other constituent institutions.[30]

Although one might assume at first blush that a stronger hypothesis would require more extended justification than a weaker version, I would argue that some basic presuppositions of Marxian theory suggest much greater plausibility and relevance for the strong hypothesis about the unity of the social structure of accumulation. The Marxian theory of accumulation, in its most complete version, places critical emphasis on the interdependent connections among the spheres of production and circulation (Marx, 1967: Vols. II, III; Shaikh, 1977: 108-121). The historical materialist method, particularly as it has developed since the 1960s, similarly underscores the "totality" of the process of historical development in concrete social formations (Fleischer, 1973: 64-103). Both of these perspectives—one at a more abstract level, one much more concrete—suggest that the social relationships in any set of institutions within a social structure of accumulation would be extremely likely to exercise mutually interdependent influence and, through those interactions, assume a form which is *inseparable* from the complex of relationships within the unified social structure of accumulation as a whole—which is, in a logical sense, nondecomposable.[31]

These observations lead to a final suggestion about the unity of the social structure of accumulation. Just as many Marxists hypothesize that the "forces" and "relations" of production acquire a unified interdependence within the structured relationships of a "mode of production" and that the mode of production itself has a certain unified (dialectical) logic, so may we also hypothesize, at a somewhat lower level of abstraction, that a given social structure of accumulation acquires a specific internal unified (dialectical) form with an integrated internal structure and a determinate set of internal contradictions.[32] This points toward two critical implications for Marxian analyses of capitalist development. First, the outline above of the constituent institutions of a social structure of accumulation underscores the necessity of studying the *full* set of relationships within a social structure of accumulation, not simply the relations of exploitation in production or the variations in the degree of relative competition and monopoly in the corporate structure or the structure of final consumer demand.[33] Secondly, if it does make sense to hypothesize an integrated, internally unified set of structured social relationships within a given social structure of accumulation, then Marxists must accept the analytic responsibility of studying the logic of those relationships alongside studies of the logic and dynamics of the mode of production and the concrete totality of history itself. The social structure of accumulation must become an object of full and legitimate analytic inquiry, in this sense, if we are to understand the forces shaping historical development and the political possibilities for social change.

(3) THE RELATIONSHIP BETWEEN ECONOMIC CRISIS AND THE SOCIAL STRUCTURE OF ACCUMULATION

Marxian economic theory proposes that economic crisis is extremely likely, if not inevitable, in capitalist economies. (See Bell, 1977; Wright, 1977; Shaikh, 1978; and Weisskopf, 1978, for recent reviews of Marxian crisis theory.) The theory of stages of accumulation depends upon a set of important hypotheses about the relationship between economic crisis tendencies and the social structure of accumulation.

(3a) CRISES ⟶ THE SOCIAL STRUCTURE OF ACCUMULATION

Let us assume the validity of the Marxian hypothesis about the general tendencies toward economic crisis. As a crisis tendency becomes increasingly manifest, one would also hypothesize that stagnation will increasingly undermine the stability of the social structure of accumulation. This seems likely for both *financial* and *social* reasons. First, many of the constituent institutions of the social structure of accumulation have tangible structured relationships whose maintenance requires a flow of funds. (Government programs to legitimate the system and contain potential protest among the unemployed, for example, require continuing and often increasing financial commitments.) The costs of financial maintenance are analogous, indeed, to the allocation of funds for the depreciation of structures and equipment in investment planning. If the pace of accumulation slackens, then less surplus will be available for the maintenance of the institutions of the social structure of accumulation. More and more poorly maintained, these institutions are obviously likely to work less well and experience increasingly severe friction in their operations. Second, it seems likely that the spreading competition and conflict which crisis generates will also threaten the internal integrity of the *social* relationships within the social structure of accumulation. (As narrowing margins generate more and more pressure on corporate/union wage bargaining, for example, the structure of labor management is likely to experience social strain.) These two considerations suggest an obvious general hypothesis: economic crisis at the level of the economic system as a whole is likely to generate corresponding crisis tendencies in the social structure of accumulation.

(3b) THE SOCIAL STRUCTURE OF ACCUMULATION ⟶ CRISES

Social structures of accumulation, as I suggested above, are likely to have their own internal contradictions. One would naturally expect that these contradictions, in one or more constituent institutions, would eventually become more and more manifest through a relatively independent dynamic at the level of the social structure of accumulation.[3,4] If and when this occurs, the spreading instability which these contradictions generate is likely to reinforce or perhaps even to help trigger more fundamental tendencies toward economic crisis at the level of the accumulation process in general. This points toward a second obvious hypothesis: instability in the social structure of accumulation may potentially contribute to the likelihood and development of economic crisis in the capitalist world-economy.[35]

(3c) THE MUTUAL INTERDEPENDENCE OF ACCUMULATION IN GENERAL AND THE SOCIAL STRUCTURE OF ACCUMULATION

These first two hypotheses combine to frame a more formal hypothesis about the mutual interdependence of the "laws" of accumulation (at the level of abstraction of the capitalist mode of production) and the internal logic and dynamics of a specific social structure of accumulation. Economic crisis can threaten the stability of a social structure of accumulation and, correspondingly, instability in the social structure of accumulation can undermine the possibilities for accumulation in general. Hypothesis: When either the economy begins to stagnate or institutional contradictions within the social structure of accumulation begin to "erupt," accumulation in general *and* the social structure of accumulation are *both* likely to begin to dissolve.

(3d) A FORMAL DEFINITION OF ECONOMIC CRISIS

These first three hypotheses permit the derivation of a formal definition of the Marxian notion of economic crisis, of what Marx frequently called "universal crisis."[36] If a stable social structure of accumulation is necessary for rapid accumulation and if tendencies toward economic stagnation tend to erode the stability of a social structure of accumulation, then an economic crisis can be defined as a period of economic instability in capitalist economies whose resolution depends upon the *reconstruction* of a social structure of accumulation. This permits a formal definition of the difference between an economic crisis and a periodic business cycle. While the capitalist economy tends endogenously to generate both business cycles and economic crises, normal economic activity, within the context of prevailing social relationships, is sufficient to restore prosperity during a business cycle recession. Normal economic activity is *not* sufficient, on the other hand, to generate a resolution of an economic crisis and a restoration of a rapid rate of accumulation; changes in the *prevailing social relationships,* with the ultimate effect of reconstituting the environmental stability necessary for rapid and sustained accumulation, are necessary for crisis to come to an end.[37]

(4) THE NECESSITY OF A NEW SOCIAL STRUCTURE OF ACCUMULATION FOR THE RESOLUTION OF ECONOMIC CRISIS

Earlier generations of Marxists frequently mistook crisis for "breakdown" and expected that capitalist accumulation would not revive. We now know better. The evolution of economic crisis can itself provide the conditions necessary for the resolution of economic crisis and the restoration of sustained and rapid accumulation.[38] Three hypotheses about this process provide the final building stones for a formal theory of stages of accumulation.

(4a) THE STRUCTURAL ORIENTATION OF STRUGGLE DURING CRISIS

As economic crisis deepens and the social structure of accumulation begins to dissolve, capitalists are increasingly likely to orient their policies and practices toward structurally effective solutions to crisis.[39] As this transition in the focus of capitalists' activities occurs, working people are also likely to shape their activities of resistance with an increasingly structural focus simply because previous forms of struggle become more and more untenable. This means that at least two major economic classes (and, potentially, other socioeconomic groupings as well) are likely to turn increasingly to activities which have some promise of affecting the structural composition and stability of capitalist social formations.[40]

(4b) THE NECESSITY OF A NEW SOCIAL STRUCTURE OF ACCUMULATION

Given the relatively integrated structure of relationships in the previous period of rapid accumulation, it seems safe to hypothesize that the combined effect of class struggle in crisis will preclude a simple return to and restoration of that (largely dissolved) social structure of accumulation.[41] Hypothesis: Given the virtual impossibility of restoring the former social structure of accumulation and given the necessity of a stable structure of accumulation for sustained and rapid accumulation, a *new* social structure of accumulation is a necessary condition for the restoration of the possibility of sustained and rapid capital accumulation after a period of economic crisis.[42]

(4c) THE ENDOGENOUS DETERMINATION OF THE RELATIONSHIPS OF THE NEW SOCIAL STRUCTURE OF ACCUMULATION

Both capitalists and workers (as well as other socioeconomic groupings), as I have already argued, wage struggle during economic crisis with increasingly structural orientation. If and when a new social structure of accumulation becomes possible, the social transformation embodied in that new structure of accumulation will depend upon the relative power and objectives of those economically active classes and groupings, and the evolution of crisis will have played a fundamental role in affecting that relative power and those respective objectives. It seems fairly clear, therefore, that the trajectory of the class struggle during an economic crisis will play a fundamentally determinate role in shaping the internal content of the new social structure of accumulation. The content of a new social structure of accumulation, in short, will not fall from the sky but will be generated, to a substantial degree, by forces *endogenous* to the general process of capital accumulation.[43]

(5) A DERIVED THEORY OF STAGES OF ACCUMULATION

This sequence of hypotheses provides the necessary analytic ingredients for a formal theory of stages of capital accumulation. As long as the capitalist mode of production continues to dominate a society and as long as tendencies toward economic crisis constitute an intrinsic contradiction of the general process of capital accumulation, then we can hypothesize that the alternating rhythm of rapid accumulation and economic stagnation will require a *succession* of qualitatively differentiable social structures of accumulation. In order to highlight this notion of succession, we can refer to the respective social structures of accumulation through the history of capitalist development as *stages of accumulation*.[44] Table 1.1 provides a formal and skeletal review of the sequence of hypotheses permitting the formal derivation of this theory of stages of accumulation. The logic of this theory also permits a conceptualization of five determinate phases within any given stage of accumulation.[45]

Phase A: *Establishment of the Social Structure of the Accumulation.* The new constituent institutions acquire shape through a process involving both heavy investment in those new institutional forms and a consolidation of the social stability and capitalist hegemony necessary for the reconstitution of rapid and sustained accumulation.

Phase B: *Expanded Reproduction Within the New Stage of Accumulation.* Individual capitalist accumulation takes off, permitting steady growth, and continuing infrastructural investment helps accelerate the rate of growth. The constituent institutions of the new stage of accumulation work smoothly.

Phase C: *Deceleration of the Rate of Accumulation.* Crisis tendencies begin to slow the general rate of investment and, potentially, the manifestation of contradictions in the social structure of accumulation also contributes to stagnation. Capitalists will seek to postpone stagnation by maintaining production and borrowing to supplement internally retained earnings, but the narrowing margin of (produced and realized) surplus value also shrinks the margin of flexibility for maintenance and reproduction of the social relationships within the social structure of accumulation.

TABLE 1.1 Component Hypotheses of the Theory of Stages of Accumulation

---

(1) The Necessity of Structural Stability for Capital Accumulation

   A stable economic environment is necessary for rapid and sustained accumulation.

(2) The Determinancy of the Social Structure of Accumulation

   (a) The Institutions Necessary for Stable Accumulation

   There are thirteen specific institutions which comprise the full set of institutions whose stability is necessary for rapid capital accumulation. (The stability of each institution is necessary but not sufficient by itself.)

   (b) The Unity of the Social Structure of Accumulation

   These specific institutions comprise the social structure of accumulation.

   (i) Weak Hypothesis. The social structure of accumulation consists of the simple structural composite of these individual institutions. Changes in one institution do not necessarily force changes in others.

   (ii) Strong Hypothesis. The social structure of accumulation acquires an internally unified and integrated structure of its own. Changes in any one or more constituent institution(s) will force changes in others through the dissolution of the social structure of accumulation itself.

(3) Economic Crisis and the Social Structure of Accumulation

   (a) Crises ⟶ the Social Structure of Accumulation

   General tendencies toward economic crisis are likely to generate corresponding crisis in the social structure of accumulation.

   (b) Social Structure of Accumulation ⟶ Crises

   Internal contradictions of the social structure of accumulation, if and when they become increasingly manifest, are likely to reinforce or perhaps even trigger general tendencies toward economic crisis.

   (c) The Mutual Independence of Accumulation in General and the Social Structure of Accumulation

   The rhythm of development and dissolution of both accumulation in general and social structures of accumulation are therefore likely to develop synchronously.

   (d) A Formal Definition of Economic Crisis

   An economic crisis is a period of economic instability whose resolution requires the reconstruction of a social structure of accumulation.

(4) The Necessity of a New Social Structure of Accumulation for the Resolution of Economic Crisis

   (a) The Structural Orientation of Struggle During Crisis

   Capitalists, workers, and other socioeconomic groupings will acquire an increasingly *structural* orientation in their activities and struggles as crisis continues and deepens.

TABLE 1.1 Component Hypotheses of the Theory of
            Stages of Accumulation (continued)

   (b) The Necessity of a New Social Structure of Accumulation

This makes it virtually inconceivable that a return to the old social structure of accumulation is possible; a *new* social structure of accumulation will therefore be necessary if and when a restoration of accumulation takes place.

   (c) The Endogenous Determination of the Relationships of the New Social Structure of Accumulation

The trajectory of struggle during a period of crisis will *endogenously* shape the internal content of the new social structure of accumulation after the resolution of crisis.

(5) A Theory of Stages of Accumulation

As long as the capitalist mode of production continues to dominate a social formation and as long as crisis tendencies recurrently impede capital accumulation, therefore, the history of capitalist development will feature a *succession* of social structures of accumulation, each successive structure differentiable from the others. These successive social structures of accumulation comprise a series of *stages of accumulation*.

Phase D: *Acceleration of Institutional Instability.* Investment expectations falter. The continually shrinking margin of surplus begins to create spreading instability in the social structure of accumulation, reinforcing expectations of instability. Individual actors continue to seek "normal" solutions to problems of accumulation, and the spreading instability therefore creates intensifying competition both within and between economic classes (and other socioeconomic groupings).

Phase E: *Economic Crisis Unfolds.* The institutional fabric begins to unravel, with international and domestic instability spreading rapidly. The futility of "normal" solutions begins to prompt more structurally oriented activity, and these struggles begin to shape the terms of resolution of crisis.

(Phase A': *Establishment of a New Social Structure of Accumulation and Accession of New Stage of Accumulation. . . .*)

Several concluding comments about the theory of stages of accumulation seem important.

First, it should be clear that this analysis involves a formal methodological premise for Marxian analysis. In order to understand (and also to change) reality, the theory of stages suggests that one must analyze social relationships in capitalist societies at least *three* different levels of abstraction. At the most abstract level, one must analyze the internal relationships of the capitalist mode of production. At an intermediate level of analysis, one must analyze the internal relationships of successive stages of accumulation in order to understand how the force of the mode of production and the effectivity of concrete activities are mediated. At the most concrete level, one must study the historical totality of people's activity within the limits imposed by these more fundamental determinations.[46]

Secondly, the theory of stages is not in any way a semantic reformulation of more traditional Marxian hypotheses about the general tendencies in capitalism toward mechanization, concentration, and centralization of capital, and the reproduction of the reserve army of labor. These general tendencies help create and condition the laws of accumulation producing crises and framing the possibilities for the resolution of crisis, but they are conceived at a different level of abstraction from the determinate analysis of the internal structure and contradictions of any particular stage of accumulation.[47] Analyses of the former cannot be substituted for the latter.

Thirdly, one cannot take the theory of stages or leave it according to one's tastes. The *necessity* of the succession of stages of accumulation is highlighted by two related ideas which lie at the core of Marxian theory. First, capital accumulation involves the dialectical unity between the *social* environment affecting the possibilities for accumulation and the *individual* activities mediating that process of accumulation. Insofar as that dialectical relationship cannot be dissolved, one cannot presume to understand the process of capital accumulation without fundamental attention to the *social* relationships conditioning the individual activities mediating accumulation. Secondly, the inherent instability of the accumulation process involves, among other contradictions, a fundamental conflict between the social requirements of accumulation and the private objectives and activities of individual capitalists and workers. Combining these two theoretical observations, one can conclude that the succession of stages of accumulation is a logically necessary feature of capitalist development because of the fundamental contradiction in capitalist societies between the social character of accumulation and its dependence upon essentially "private" activities. When this contradiction erupts and crisis results, individual accumulation cannot resume until the social basis for accumulation is reconstituted.[48]

TOWARD A MARXIAN THEORY OF LONG ECONOMIC CYCLES

The theory of stages of accumulation, as we have already noted, intrinsically generates a hypothesis of the likelihood of alternating periods of rapid and stagnant capital accumulation. While this helps make the phenomenon of long economic cycles not only unsurprising but also quite expectable—at least from the Marxian perspective—the theory of stages of accumulation as elaborated to this point is hardly sufficient to provide a full explanation of the apparent contours of long economic cycles.

I argue in this part of the essay that careful consideration of the logic of capital accumulation highlighted by the theory of stages can also provide some suggestive (and very provisional) clues to the character of long economic cycles.[49] I develop those suggestions in two separate sections—first considering what I call the "infrastructural investment dynamic" of long economic cycles; and then considering, taking off from suggestions by the Research Working Group (1979), what I call the "world-market control dynamic" of long cycles.

(1) THE INFRASTRUCTURAL INVESTMENT DYNAMIC

I hypothesize that stages of accumulation generate a bunching of investments in social infrastructure and that this infrastructural investment dynamic conditions the contours of long economic cycles. As with the theory of stages of accumulation, this argument can be developed through a sequence of hypotheses.

(1a) THE NECESSITY OF INFRASTRUCTURAL INVESTMENT

I have already argued that periodic construction of a new social structure of accumulation will recur in capitalist societies. Although part of this social structure of accumulation involves relatively intangible social relationships like systems of labor management, part of it also involves tangible structures and equipment. In particular, the new social structure of accumulation, in order to facilitate access to both factors of production and final consumer demand, will necessarily involve new systems of natural and intermediate supply, transportation, and communication.[50] These systems will require substantial financial expenditure on design and construction. This kind of expenditure can be called, in general, *infrastructural investment*—investment in the tangible physical facilities which permit the circulation of commodities *among* individual units of accumulation. Without such infrastructural investment, there will be no physical foundation for the new stage of accumulation.

(1b) THE "BUNCHING" OF INFRASTRUCTURAL INVESTMENT

Because this infrastructural investment will be concentrated at the beginning of a stage of accumulation, the flow of infrastructural investment expenditures will not be continuous over that stage of accumulation. Infrastructural investment expenditures will be "bunched," to use the economic phrase for this phenomenon, at the beginning of each stage of accumulation. Apart from continuing maintenance expenditures (or "infrastructural depreciation"), new infrastructural investment will decline after the first period of construction of the social structure of accumulation.[51]

Economists have long recognized that a bunching of investment expenditures will endogenously generate a cycle of economic activity. When the first wave of investment begins, the economy begins to expand rapidly as a result of the multiplier and accelerator effects of investment. Once the rate of investment begins to slow (as a result of the saturation of the demand for that particular investment good), then the economy not only loses the economic boost which those investment expenditures themselves provide but also begins to experience a decelerating impact from the loss of business to those sectors *supplying* the investment goods sector.[52] If there is a bunching of infrastructural investment at the beginning of a stage of accumulation, therefore, we can hypothesize that economic activity in that stage of accumulation will be influenced by an *infrastructural investment cycle*. The economy will receive a strong boost at the beginning of the stage of accumulation and will experience considerable economic drag after the need for infrastructural investment has dried up. The economy would only get another comparable boost if and when new infrastructural investment was needed *and* it became possible to finance it.

Earlier long cycle theorists, particularly Schumpeter (1939) and Hansen (1941), paid considerable attention to the bunching of infrastructural investment as a potential source of the shape and period of long economic cycles but did not ultimately develop that idea. Schumpeter explicitly argued (1939: 74-84, 187-192) that investment in durables, which for him would have included what I am calling infrastructural investment, will not be "bunched" and that such bunching cannot be considered as an independent endogenous source of economic cycles—insisting, indeed, on the "absurdity" of such ideas (1939: 191). Schumpeter's analysis began with the provisional assumption of competitive equilibrium and sought to inquire whether individual capitalists (separately or aggregatively) would, for any reason, cluster their investments; "such sudden jerks [of investment] are not likely to occur," he concluded, "except in consequence of innovation."[53] If we start with the social context affecting investment and the presumption of automatic tendencies toward disequilibrium, however, it would be astonishing if we assumed anything *but* the clustering of infrastructural investment at the beginning of a stage of accumulation.[54]

(1c) SOURCES OF THE AMPLITUDE AND LENGTH OF INFRASTRUCTURAL INVESTMENT CYCLES

There are several reasons for expecting that the infrastructural investment cycle will have wide amplitude and considerable length from trough to trough.

We would naturally expect, first of all, that the infrastructural investment cycle would generate strong forces for overall *expansion* and that the infrastructural investment boost would last for many years. We can safely assume that the social infrastructure constitutes a very large portion of the total capital stock of any given economy. If much of this investment is clustered at the beginning of a new stage of accumulation, then the ratio of investment demand to total economic activity in that period will be unusually large, giving rise to an unusually large multiplier-accelerator effect.[55] The sources of the length of this expansionary period are two-fold. First, the magnitude of the investment required for reconstituting the infrastructure undoubtedly requires that this investment be spread out over a period of years, since it is unlikely that immediate financing for the entire new infrastructure would be available.[56] Secondly, no matter how much financing is available, the infrastructure undoubtedly requires a long lag between initial conception and final completion simply because of the complexity of the construction tasks and the magnitude of the projects involved.[57]

There are also several important reasons for expecting that the period of infrastructural investment *contraction* would last for many years:

*First, the infrastructure involves many extremely durable structures which would presumably last for decades before physically requiring replacement.

*Secondly, assuming that much of the financing of the initial infrastructural investment was accomplished through borrowing, the amortization of that debt (including interest charges) would constitute a continuing drain on total surplus potentially available for new infrastructural investment well past the final completion of the infrastructure itself.[58]

*Thirdly, the calculus of investment planning itself suggests that capitalists would be very slow to move toward huge new infrastructural investment projects until the economic crisis has already taken hold. Unless we assume that all individual capitalists have strong risk preference, we can safely hypothesize that the risks of individuals' entrepreneurs *not* being able to control the full returns from investments in infrastructural investments (as a result of their character as partly public goods[59]) will deter individuals from considering infrastructural projects until the deepening of crisis forces them to the realization that they have little choice. Furthermore, capitalists are likely to prefer investment projects with short periods of amortization when the financial rate of return is high and are likely to prefer investment projects like infrastructural investments with very long payoff periods only when the rate of interest has fallen to (relatively) much lower levels. Since it is likely that the real financial rate of return, to the degree that it revolves around the average rate of profit, will fall to its lowest point during a period of economic crisis, capitalists are more likely to find infrastructural investment projects relatively less *un*attractive as the crisis nears its trough.[60]

*Fourthly and finally, infrastructural investment requires relatively coordinated activity among capitalists with increasingly structural orientation. As the "new public choice" theorists have also emphasized, there are significant financial and organizational costs to political coalition-building for coordinated projects. It seems plausible to hypothesize that individual capitalists will seek to avoid investment projects carrying this extra cost of coalition-building until the exigencies of economic crisis leave them virtually no other alternative.

(1d) THE SPECIFIC PERIOD OF INFRASTRUCTURAL INVESTMENT CYCLES

The preceding hypotheses serve only to suggest that the infrastructural investment cycle would have a long period. They are not sufficient to suggest that this "long period" would have any specific determinate length. It appears that Kondratieff cycles, if they exist, have covered a period of roughly forty-sixty years. Is it possible that the infrastructural investment cycle has a period of approximately this length and that its shape and period therefore help explain the apparent length and regularity of long economic cycles themselves?

I am inclined to answer those questions affirmatively, to suspect that the period of the infrastructural investment cycle is, indeed, roughly forty-sixty years. Although much more work will be necessary before I would be willing to advance this argument with anything more than halting confidence, I would hypothesize that the infrastructural investment cycle lasts roughly 50 years because of the relationship between the *scale of investment* required at the beginning of that cycle and the *supply of potentially investable funds* available to finance that investment.

However tentative, that hypothesis obviously requires some elaboration and justification. I have found it most convenient to argue the plausibility of this hypothesis by comparing four different kinds of investment: investments in inventories, business equipment, residential structures, and infrastructure. Although there is considerable debate on these issues, economists have argued at one point or another that each of these kinds of investment generates an investment cycle of specific length—with inventory cycles (the Kitchin or "minor" cycle) lasting two-three years; business equipment cycles (the Juglar or "major" cycle) lasting six-ten years; residential building cycles (the Kuznets cycle) lasting fifteen-twenty years; and what I am calling the infrastructural investment cycle (otherwise the Kondratieff or long cycle) for roughly forty-sixty years.[61] Few have carefully examined, however, the sources of these differences in cycle period.

Let us assume a bunching of any particular kind of investment. Let us further assume that a determinate portion of the total stock of that investment good will be replaced by new (bunched) investment.[62] There is no reason to assume that the supply of funds for such new investment is highly (much less infinitely) elastic. There are fixed and continuing claims on huge portions of gross domestic product (GDP) at any point in a economic cycle. A large portion of GDP must be devoted to the basic consumption costs of subsistence. Another large portion must cover the continuing costs of depreciation for all four kinds of investment goods. The remaining portion of total surplus, a kind of net investment fund, will be distributed among all four kinds of investments with respect to current cyclically generated investment demands. All of that surplus would be available for any one kind of investment—say business equipment—only if all three other investment cycles were simultaneously at their respective troughs. Since the four cycles are more likely to move together than to move countercyclically, this means that only a *portion* of the net investment fund would be available to finance the net new replacement demand for any one or more of the four kinds of investment goods. This supply of potential investment funds will not vary with the scale of investment required for the respective investment goods but will be a function of the rate of growth in the economy, the relative congruence of the respective investment goods cycles, and the relative elasticity of credit markets.[63]

The effect on the *period* of the respective cycles follows directly: the *larger the scale of investment* required for net replacement of a particular kind of investment good, given the relative inelasticity of total net investment funds available for that (bunched) investment demand, the *longer will be the period* necessary to execute the full set of projects required to fulfill that net replacement demand.[64]

Although I have taken no more than a passing glance at the relevant data, I am inclined to suspect that these considerations can account for the apparent differences in length of the three shorter investment goods cycles and are consistent with the hypothesis of a roughly fifty-year period for the infrastructural investment cycle.[65]

(1e) THE INFRASTRUCTURAL INVESTMENT DYNAMIC AND THE LONG ECONOMIC CYCLE

This sequence of hypotheses culminates directly in some derived hypotheses about the relationship between the infrastructural investment dynamic and the long economic cycle. The theory of stages of accumulation suggests the necessity of substantial infrastructural investment at the beginning of a stage of accumulation, leading to the bunching of infrastructural investment. The character of infrastructural investment itself leads us to expect a wide amplitude and substantial length to that investment cycle. The particular scale of investment required, given the relatively inelastic supply of funds available for those investment projects, seems consistent with the observed (roughly fifty-year) period of long economic cycles. These hypotheses jointly suggest that the dynamics of accumulation in general, mediated by successive stages of accumulation, "cause" long economic cycles and that the particular character of the infrastructural investment required at the beginning of a new stage of accumulation influences the specific length of the periods of expansion and contraction associated with that long economic cycle.[66]

(2) THE WORLD-MARKET CONTROL DYNAMIC

Recent work by Wallerstein (1973, 1979), the Research Working Group (1979), and Frank (1978) suggests another essentially parallel line of investigation about long economic cycles. Within the context of the world-economic system, they suggest that the capitalists of particular nation-states will struggle for relative control over the structure of the world market. (Hegemony is desirable, of course, because the possibilities for rapid commercial and industrial accumulation are greatest if an individual group of capitalists has a relative advantage in gaining access to commodities and capital at relatively low prices.) There are several important reasons for suspecting that this national competition for world-market control would generate a cyclical dynamic consistent with observations of long economic cycles (and complementary to the preceding hypotheses about "infrastructural investment dynamics").

There are infrastructural costs to the pursuit and creation of world-market control which require financing and amortization. Control requires both government and private expenditures on modernized transportation facilities, resource exploration, colonial conquest and expansion, and military force for the protection of trade channels and colonies. Because these world-market control investments involve large scale and many of these control structures have relative durability, these investments would be just as likely as infrastructural investments in general to require long periods for installation and repayment.

Would we expect a bunching of world-market control investments? Let us assume the existence of tendencies toward economic crisis in the world capitalist economy. As crisis develops, world trade begins to slacken and protectionist rivalries begin to intensify. This disolution of traditional trading patterns, along with the protectionism it presumably tends to generate, is likely to create some room for maneuver for previously dominated nations, allowing them to seek new power within the context of the world market. During the previous period of rapid expansion, the hegemonic national power was able to prevent such incursions and the subordinate powers had much to lose by eschewing the trade channels constituted within the structure of the established world-economic system. As crisis develops, the power of the hegemonic nation declines and the subordinate nations have much less to lose by moving outside traditional trading paths. Toward the end of a crisis, this is likely to spur intense national investment in the infrastructure necessary for increases in relative world-market control. There is likely, in short, to be a bunching of world-market control investments at the beginning of a new stage of accumulation for exactly the same reasons as I earlier advanced for infrastructural investment in general.[67]

Wallerstein et al. also advance the further suggestion that the world-market control dynamic may generate a *pairing* of long economic cycles, with a first cycle involving a single nation's hegemony in the world market and a subsequent cycle featuring multination rivalry within the world market. While this additional hypothesis does seem to work well for at least the nineteenth and twentieth centuries (see Research Working Group [1979: 497-499]; and Kindelberger [1974: chs. 1,2]), I am not yet persuaded that a period of hegemony must *necessarily* be followed by a period of rivalry. It seems theoretically consistent with (at least my version of) the world-market control dynamic that a formerly hegemonic power might emerge from crisis with its hegemony restored or that a new nation might be capable of creating hegemony for itself in the process of the construction of a new social structure of accumulation. (See also Bousquet, 1979.)

In any case, the world-market control dynamic seems compatible with the infrastructural investment dynamic. Taken together, they provide a reasonably coherent and consistent set of hypotheses about long economic cycles which can help explain why cycles recur, why they feature wide amplitudes and long periods, and why they feature some of the particular historical patterns commonly observed over recent centuries. If one builds upon a determinate set of hypotheses about the structured social relationships conditioning capitalist development, the phenomenon of long economic cycles seems much less mysterious than many have previously concluded.

A CONCLUDING NOTE

While the analysis developed in this essay draws on many strands of both earlier and more recent long cycle analyses, it has also sought to overcome many problems in those analyses by seeking a more integrated and comprehensive approach to the explanation of long economic cycles. I have provided in this section a brief concluding review of the major differences between the analysis developed in this essay and other major positions in the available literature.

(1) Some analyses, like Schumpeter's, begin from the vantage point of the individual capitalist (or entrepreneur). This starting point provides no logical reason for one to expect a bunching of investments. That forces one to assume, as does Schumpeter, that the source of long cycles is autonomous or exogenous events like "epoch-making innovations." If one begins, as I have tried to do, from a more careful consideration of the social context of capital accumulation and works through that analysis to a theory of stages of accumulation, then one naturally inclines toward an analysis which emphasizes the *connections* between endogenously generated investment cycles—through both the infrastructural investment dynamic and the world-market control dynamic—and the general contours of long economic cycles. One is not forced to invent an exogenous source of the long cycle dynamic precisely because a more comprehensive analysis of capitalist development points fairly inexorably to a plausible set of hypotheses about endogenous determinants.

(2) Some analyses, particularly Kondratieff's original investigations and the recent explorations by Forrester et al.,[68] have suffered from the opposite weakness. They have built from a relatively mechanical model of endogenously generated investment cycles without any social content to those analyses. Their analyses provide no indication either of how infrastructural investment relates to the general institutional characteristics of respective stages of development or of how specific social and political struggles would (or would not) affect the trajectory of the long cycle dynamic. By locating long cycle analysis within the framework of a theory of stages of accumulation, I have tried to emphasize the connections between the general context of capitalist development and the specific mechanisms which lend shape and period to long cycles *and* to underscore the necessity of developing determinate analyses of the successive social structures of accumulation which give meaning to those connections.

(3) Some mainstream economists, working within a framework which presumes the probability of equilibrium growth in capitalist economies, have been content to settle for very partial theories of the determinants of long economic cycles. Rostow (1978) places great emphasis on the movements of relative commodity prices, for example, while Dupriez (1947, 1978) places similar emphasis on the dynamics of credit markets. If we begin, in contrast, with a perspective which emphasizes the full social context conditioning capital accumulation and the interdependencies of the accumulation process, there is no reason to expect that single-factor theories of the origins of long economic cycles are sufficient. In developing the links between stages of accumulation and long economic cycles, I have tried to suggest a framework which highlights the multiple forces giving rise to an alternating rhythm of expansion and contraction in capitalist economies.

(4) Schumpeter, Baran and Sweezy, and Mandel have stressed the exogeneity of the sources of stimuli to restored capital accumulation; all emphasize, in one way or another, the critical importance of exogenous technical innovations. I think that stress derives from a common failure to appreciate the critical importance of the increasingly *structural orientation* of economic struggles as economic crisis deepens. Because the stages of accumulation framework emphasizes the endogenous process through which capitalists, workers, and others begin to contest the terms of resolution of crisis, I am also led to emphasize the endogenous determinants of the specific "innovations" which seem to permit the restoration of the rate of accumulation. Just as I do not believe that new social structures of accumulation fall from the sky, my analysis of the dynamics of economic crisis leads me to doubt the celestial origins of technical innovation as well. I think that others' emphasis on exogenous technical innovation derives in part from the technological determinism which Braverman and others have recently challenged. The political danger, of course, is that we may waste precious political opportunities while we wait for Godot to arrive with his epoch-making ideas.[69]

(5) Wallerstein and others have focused on the structure of the world-economy as an entry point to hypotheses about long economic cycles. Their analyses complement mine in many ways, but there seem to be two important differences which deserve mention. First, the hypotheses advanced by the Research Working Group (1979) about the relative demand for and supply of high and low-wage goods between core and periphery do not seem to me particularly promising as bases for a theory of long cycles; I think that the stages of accumulation framework, with its derived hypotheses about infrastructural investment, can provide a more coherent and consistent provisional explanation of long cycles.[70] Second, Wallerstein in particular has placed great emphasis on the continuities of the structure and contradictions of the world-economic system from the fifteenth century to the present; this leads him to place far less emphasis on the critical importance of exploitation in production and the dynamics of surplus-value production than my analytic framework would suggest. While it would require an essay at least double the length of this one to explore the full implications of these differences in substance and/or emphasis, I remain inclined to a somewhat more classically Marxian argument that the inauguration of fully "capitalist production" at the beginning of the nineteenth century had critical impact on the general dynamics of capitalist development but also on the specific character of the political economic forces generating long economic cycles.[71]

These concluding comments, let alone this entire essay, undoubtedly sound self-confident and more than a little self-serving. I would like to end on a much more modest and tentative note. I think that some of the ideas advanced in this essay may help advance our investigation of both stages of accumulation and long economic cycles, but they remain little more than guidelines for further investigation. I am awed by the complexity of the problem and the enormity of the theoretical, historical, and empirical questions which still await us. At the least, I hope that this essay will help persuade others to join in this challenging and critical analytic project.

NOTES

1. Throughout this essay, I shall use the term "long economic cycle" to refer to the observed phenomenon of alternating periods of expansion and contraction in the world capitalist economy which, together, last roughly fifty years and which have also been labeled "Kondratieff cycles" and "long waves." Particularly for neoclassical economists, this usage courts a little confusion, since many have also called the "Kuznets cycle" of fifteen-twenty years the "long cycle." When I'm referring to the Kuznets cycle, I call it by that name.

2. As R. A. Gordon wrote in a standard macroeconomics textbook in 1961 (238, 239), for instance; "In the last 10 or 15 years, however, the existence of these 'Kondratieff' waves has been increasingly questioned. . . . The existence of the long swings in prices has already been recognized, though . . . there is reason to doubt that they should be viewed as cycles." The most influential critique of Kondratieff and his long cycles was written by Garvy (1943).

3. See the enormously useful annotated bibliography prepared by Barr (1979).

4. See Garvy (1943) for a detailed critique of Kondratieff, whose standard 1926 article was first published in English in 1935 and has recently been reprinted in a convenient form (1979). See Mandel (1975: ch. 4) for detailed critiques of Kondratieff and other earlier proponents of long wave theory.

5. This essay takes off from some themes first presented in Gordon (1978a). Throughout this essay, I build from a methodological skepticism of the traditional Marxian separation between the economic sphere and other domains of social life. See Bowles and Gintis (1980) for more on this theme.

6. Rostow (1978) and Maddison (1977) provide some detail on the empirical evidence. From the earlier generation see, for example, Dupriez (1947) and Burns and Mitchell (1946).

7. There are three important weaknesses in the mainstream argument that the book was closed on long cycles. First, one should begin with the qualitative evidence on alternating rhythms of capitalist development, first, and then frame quantitative investigations within that evidence (see Gordon, 1978a). Secondly, one should study the dynamics of the world capitalist economy as a whole, not just for any one or a few countries. Thirdly, until Frank (1978) and the Research Working Group (1979), there had been far too little attention paid in the English-language literature to the possibility that long cycles have dated from the fourteenth or fifteenth centuries instead of the nineteenth century. See the bibliographic selections in Barr (1979: section V).

8. I doubt that Kondratieff ever made this argument, but I feel much more comfortable passing the wager off on him than I do calling it "Gordon's Wager" or the "Fool's Paradox."

9. I should add that I do not yet consider myself even a proponent of long cycles. I am very interested in the possibility and consider the questions they raise of

critical importance, but I remain skeptical about the empirical evidence and the theoretical arguments. I might explain this essay in the following way: *If* long cycles *do* exist, I think that the theoretical hypotheses advanced in this essay offer a more promising provisional explanation of long cycles than others I have seen in the literature.

10. To anticipate the general themes of that conclusion, I have written this essay from the Marxian perspective; its arguments therefore have few points of contact with neoclassical analyses of capitalist growth. I have focused most of my comments on analyses by nonneoclassical mainstream economists, like Schumpeter and Rostow, and the variants among the Marxian analyses, including Mandel, Baran and Sweezy, and, if we may call him a Marxist, Wallerstein.

11. Neither Lenin (1917) nor Hilferding (1920), for example, clearly articulated the methodological premises necessary for their arguments that capitalism had moved into a new stage of development. Nor do Baran and Sweezy (1966) provide much help in understanding exactly what has changed or has not changed about capitalist development in the period of "monopoly capitalism." After working on this material for a while, I was finally able to find an English translation of a text by the eminent Japanese Marxist Kōzō Uno, who, as I gathered from Sekine (1975), had formalized a "theory of stages" of capitalist development. Uno (1975) argues, as I do in this essay, that we must formalize three levels of abstraction in Marxian theory and that we must explicitly analyze the structure and dynamics of the respective stages of development. But, at least in the one work I have read, he provides no articulated theory of the process through which stages succeed each other or of the internal institutional articulation of each stage of accumulation.

12. These hypotheses were formulated in this way in order to facilitate their exposition. None of the separate hypotheses is intended to be examined entirely on its own, out of this general context; each is meaningful, as currently formulated, *only* in terms of its connections with the other hypotheses in this sequence.

13. Even these simple assertions are threaded with complexities, of course, but it appears that even Marxists can remain content with the proposition that capitalists measure their expected rates of return from production against the financial rate of return. For a discussion which takes us a bit beyond this first level of approximation, see Shaikh (1979).

14. This proposition is noncontroversial to Marxists but poorly appreciated. Its most accessible dimension is the notion, best developed by Koshimura (1977), that instability can quickly spread throughout capitalist economies like a chain reaction. Its less appreciated dimension is the recognition that the fabric interweaving the activities and expectations of individual capitalists is actually a set of structured *social* relationships in the broader social environment, not simply a marketplace or the "sphere of circulation." (This leads to some important considerations about the relations of priority among the "economic" and "political" domains; see Bowles and Gintis, 1980.) From the neoclassical perspective, of course, this first hypothesis makes little sense unless it is recast in the language of growth theory; then, the threat of instability bears resemblance to the "knife-edge" conditions of stability and instability derived from the relationships between warranted and optimal growth paths.

15. I define an "institution" as a set of social relationships whose relative stability and reproducibility permit the repeated fulfillment of an important socioeconomic function. This definition immediately stresses the *social* character of the context within which accumulation takes place. For an interesting critique of the neoclassical perspective for its failure to take account of this social setting, see Ganssmann (1979).

16. Chandler (1962) provides a useful analysis of one such transformation in internal corporate structure in the early twentieth century in the Unites States.

17. I do not believe, as some Marxists do, that one or the other of these contradictions has logical priority over the others. Both contradictions are intrinsic, in my mind, to the logic of the relationships of the capitalist mode of production—a combined reflection, indeed, of the unity of production and circulation of which Marx frequently wrote.

18. In the late nineteenth century in the United States, for example, local and regional monopolies provided firms with some measure of protection from the intensity of competition, while price leadership and government regulation in the twentieth century have served somewhat similar functions.

19. It seems important to emphasize, at this stage, that these hypotheses are intended to apply to the totality of the world capitalist economy and not simply to any single national economy. (See Wallerstein, 1979.)

20. This historically generated process creating "liberal ideas" was politically necessary, in the initial period of original accumulation, to free the bourgeoisie from the restraints of the absolutist state. Once that initial liberation had been accomplished, the "liberal" ideas acquired a "relatively autonomous" life of their own. For further discussions of this conflict, see Wolfe (1977).

21. Part of the history of capitalist development, of course, involves fractional capitalist efforts to exclude other capitalist units from equal access to some of these requirements for accumulation. To the extent that this process has created a structural differentiation among kinds of capitalist corporations, it raises the possibility of barriers to the full equalization of the rate of profit. See Mandel (1975: ch. 3).

22. The current energy crisis obviously dramatizes the importance of this structural requirement. On other periods of transformation in the structure of natural supply, see Mandel (1975: ch. 2).

23. This distinction between "natural supply" and "intermediate supply" is not the same as the traditional Marxian distinction between the fixed and circulating components of constant capital. I have chosen this terminology simply in order to emphasize the historical importance of the quest for stable structures of "natural supply."

24. The recent analytic innovations pioneered by Leontief and Sraffa further emphasize the importance of these intermediate connections. See Koshimura (1977) on their implications for the possibility of instability and crisis.

25. Women and children have moved in and out of the family, for example, and the functional relationship of the schools to the economy has changed several times. See Zaretsky (1973) on the family and Bowles and Gintis (1976) on the schools.

26. One can hardly compare, for example, the labor market structure of a nineteenth-century economy without labor unions and the late twentieth-century economy with well-developed collective bargaining institutions.

27. Braverman (1974) discusses some of this development, while Gordon et al. (1980) provide a somewhat more systematic historical account of these changes.

28. This hypothesis highlights one of the weaknesses of neoclassical theory, which takes individual preferences in the market as exogenously determined (see Gintis, 1972).

29. Itoh (1975) places special emphasis on the importance of credit instability in the development of a Marxian theory of crisis.

30. This would mean, concretely, that increasing instability in the world market would erode the margins which helped maintain stability in collective bargaining relationships, or that changes in the relative prices of energy would begin to force

changes in the structure of final consumer demand (away from automobiles toward other forms of mass transit).

31. It is interesting to note that the weaker hypothesis of the separability of institutions would represent a much more *structuralist* approach to the functional fulfillment of individual institutional requirements, without regard for the interconnections which coexistence could be expected to create.

32. I hope that this emphasis on the *dialectical* form of this internal structure will help protect me from misplaced charges of excessive structuralism. There is nothing about the analysis developed in this section which suggests that these social structures of accumulation, once established, are unlikely to disappear.

33. Some Marxists, overcome with their efforts to differentiate Marxian analyses of production from neoclassical foci on circulation through markets, emphasize exploitation in production to the virtual exclusion of any other relationships in capitalist economies. Others, like Lenin (1917) and Baran and Sweezy (1966), ascribe changes in the structure of capitalism to simple and singular changes in the degree of product market competition, manifested by the change from "competitive" to "monopoly" capitalism.

34. One obvious example of this possibility is the erosion of U.S. imperialist hegemony in many parts of the world during the 1950s and 1960s.

35. This hypothesis helps situate crisis theory, I think, and helps point toward useful analyses of the various ways in which crisis tendencies have become manifest through the respective stages of capitalist development.

36. There is surprisingly little careful definition in the literature of the Marxian concept of crisis and its differences from a business cycle recession. Part of this neglect undoubtedly stems from the earlier tradition of Marxist theories of "breakdown" which, in presuming that capitalism would never recover from crisis, obviated the necessity of distinguishing between a crisis, from which there would be no escape, and a recession, from which escape was ordained (see Sweezy, 1942: ch. XI).

37. This helps clarify, in particular, the relationship of political struggle in crisis to the economic dynamics which underlie both crisis and recovery from crisis. Struggle matters, according to the perspective developed here, precisely because it constitutes part of the soil in which new conditions of life in capitalist societies will germinate—and not simply because it may increase the possibilities for socialist revolution.

38. In order to avoid misunderstanding, I am speaking in this section about situations in which the capitalist system does, indeed, succeed in reestablishing itself. There is always the possibility in crisis, of course, that capitalists' efforts at reconstitution will fail and that some new system, perhaps through a socialist revolution, will replace the capitalist mode of production.

39. As my discussion of the *phases* of a stage of accumulation below suggests, the continuation of crisis is likely to force at least some capitalists out of a period of intensive competition into a period of cooperative quest for "structural" solutions to crisis. Many of these cooperative solutions may involve only private-sector cooperation, like oil companies' joint ventures; that is why I speak here of "structural orientation" rather than demands for state intervention.

40. This hypothesis does not imply any particular teleology of the objectives of particular economic classes. The course of struggle during crisis provides sufficient guidance to individual strategies and objectives that we do not need recourse to Hegelian notions of predestined political development.

41. This hypothesis seems so obvious that it is, in fact, difficult to defend rigorously. We can say, at the least, that the synergy of class interaction and objective

conflicts would render a return to the precise structure of a previous social structure of accumulation a veritable coincidence.

42. One of the implications of this hypothesis is that there will be costs of construction and that one dimension of the struggle in the late stages of crisis will focus on the *incidence* of payment (through taxes and otherwise) for these costs of construction. Another implication is that a transition from instability to stability is necessary; some appeals to common destiny, as with patriotic appeals during wartime, seem necessary as part of this process. I have not yet systematically explored the relationship between this version of the stages analysis and the recurrence of major wars.

43. I have developed one example which illustrates this general point: I argue (1978b) that firms began moving out of central cities in the United States at the turn of the century (around 1900) because increasingly turbulent class struggle had been concentrated in downtown factory and working-class housing districts. Decentralization, an important component of the new social structure of accumulation, was shaped by the character of struggle in the previous period of crisis. This point carries critical implications about the character of political struggle during crisis. As people fight in crisis to protect their working and living conditions, the positions they take on issues affecting the content of a new social structure of accumulation will make an enormous difference. For this reason, we must pay critical attention to the ways in which the endogenous dynamic of accumulation and crisis affects and places limits upon our options for struggle. Mandel and others in the Trotskyist tradition react suspiciously to this kind of argument, since they traditionally emphasize the separability of economic forces and political strategy and since their historic political battles leave them particularly suspicious of arguments like mine, which smell to them of "economism." Private communication with Mandel convinces me, however, that there is far less incompatibility on this issue than first impressions would suggest.

44. Mandel (1975) comes closest to something like this theory of stages, for he pays full attention to all the strands of transformation from one stage to another; he falls short, nonetheless, because he fails to articulate a full methodological foundation for his interesting analysis of successive stages in the world capitalist economy.

45. Despite differences in elaboration of the character of stages of accumulation, Schumpeter (1939) actually came fairly close to sketching this kind of contour within the period of a given long cycle. These phases have important implications for social and political (and not simply "economic") analyses; it appears that the timing of bursts of political struggle like strikes and movements for civil rights, for example, are clustered in Phases C and E of the long cycle. See Cronin (this volume) for hints of this kind of connection.

46. Uno (1975) also makes exactly this point. I might add that it is possible that we could profitably apply something like the stages framework to an analysis of societies dominated by other modes of production as well. I have found it useful, for example, to treat the feudal period in Western Europe as consisting of two stages of development, each with its own internal logic and contradictions, the first extending from the ninth century to about 1000 A.D. and the second covering the period through roughly 1350.

47. This point cannot be further developed, of course, until we have completed a careful analysis of the internal logic and dynamics of respective stages of accumulation; see Mandel (1975) for a start in this direction. It is important in that project to remember the distinction between national economies and the world-economy; some elements of the social structure of accumulation in any given stage will be common to the world-economy and others will vary from one country to the next.

48. Marx frequently noted this kind of contradiction, noting in the *Grundrisse* (1973: 749), for example: "The growing incompatibility between the productive development of society and its hitherto existing relations of production expresses itself in bitter contradictions, crises, spasms." Schumpeter also makes some similar comments (1939: 130-145).

49. In presenting the ideas contained in this section to various audiences, I have learned to try to anticipate a misimpression which the argument frequently prompts. I argue that long cycles are fundamentally *caused* by the logic of capital accumulation and its movement through stages of accumulation. I do *not* argue that the infrastructural investment dynamic causes long cycles but much more simply that the infrastructural dynamic provides a kind of center of gravity to their specific amplitude and period. I am *not* advancing, therefore, an "effective (investment) demand" theory of long cycles and have not abandoned the labor theory of value. The presuppositions of the labor theory of value frame my analysis of the accumulation process and that analysis provides the ultimate explanation for long cycles. In developing an analysis of the implications of infrastructural investment for the timing of long cycles, I am abandoning the labor theory of value no more than Marx does in Volume II of *Capital* when he studies the turnover period of capital and the possibility of the bunching of machine-goods investment.

50. The text does not develop one important strand of this hypothesis—that these transformations requiring infrastructural investment have geographic dimensions which dramatize the need for *new* infrastructure. (If plants move to the U.S. South because of the power of unions in the North, then new infrastructure is needed.) I am beginning to explore the implications of these geographic dimensions for the process of constructing a new stage of accumulation (Gordon, 1980).

51. The middle of the nineteenth century witnessed "bunched" investment in railroads, for example; the turn to the twentieth century involved colonial expansion, urban infrastructure (resulting from decentralization of manufacturing), and electrical power; while the post-Second World War period involved heavy investments in highways, air travel, the petro-chemical complex of industries, and new systems of communications.

52. See R. A. Gordon (1961: chs. 5-6) for an elaboration of this process for the business cycle in general.

53. It was for this reason that Schumpeter hinged his theory of long cycles around the occurrence of exogenously generated innovations. His argument led him to criticize both Marx and Kalecki for their "bunched" investment models of cycles (Schumpeter, 1939: 185-192).

54. This argument would also apply to the initial bunching of investment in business equipment and residential construction, since we would expect that new waves of investment would be set off at the beginning of the new stage of accumulation by the construction of new structures of natural supply, intermediate supply, and final consumer demand. Mandel (1975: ch. 4) makes some of this argument; since I had not been able to read his new work on long waves (1980) at the time of writing, I do not know how much further he develops these arguments in that set of lectures.

55. In 1949, for example, investment in plant and equipment in transportation, public utilities, communication, and commercial sectors accounted for 53% of total *private* expenditures for new plant and equipment in the United States (U.S. Bureau of the Census, 1975: Series 306-332).

56. Both Mandel (1975) and Forrester (1976) emphasize that liquid capital funds for investment are likely to be available in unusually large proportions at the trough

of the crisis, but it remains unlikely nonetheless that these funds would be sufficient for full financing of necessary infrastructural investment.

57. Kalecki (1937) built a model of investment dynamics explicitly around the lag between investment orders and the delivery of investment goods.

58. Suppose we assume a twenty-five-year amortization period on large-scale financing and that infrastructural investment projects require a full twenty years for final completion (e.g., the railroads). This means that repayment on the funds borrowed to finance infrastructural investment in the twentieth year will continue into the forty-fifth year after the beginning of the new stage of accumulation; the economy will not be free from this drain on potentially investable surplus until forty-five years after the beginning of the infrastructural investment cycle.

59. Infrastructural investments are likely to be "public goods" in the sense that individuals cannot be excluded from their use for, at least two reasons. First, the scale of financing required undoubtedly means that either the government or large financial consortia will fund many infrastructural projects, implying that a relatively wide range of users would be permitted to gain access to that infrastructure. Secondly, although this argument could be extended too far, it is likely that the character of infrastructure as such, with its facilitation of the general network of commodity exchange, tends to "benefit" everyone because it makes possible the universal flow of commodities.

60. This proposition about the relationship between interest rates and payoff periods is formally true as a result of the calculus of the present valuation of a stream of benefits from an investment project. The present value of two alternative investment projects can be compared with the following equation:

$$\text{Present value} = \frac{\sum_i B_{1_i}}{(1+r)^{n_1}} = \frac{\sum_i B_{2_i}}{(1+r)^{n_2}}, \quad i = 1, \ldots, n_1, n_2,$$

where B_{j_i} = the annual revenues from the respective investment projects, r = the going rate of interest, and n_j = the payoff period over which benefits will be realized. If $n_1 > n_2$ and $\sum_i B_{1_i} = \sum_i B_{2_i}$, then the first project (with the longer payoff period) will be preferred to the second if and only if funds can be raised during a period when the rate of interest falls sufficiently below previous levels that the denominator of the left-hand side of the equation equals the value of the right-hand side at previous rates of interest. (If the two projects are being compared at the same rates of interest, then the difference in the present value streams between the two projects will be lower, the lower the market rate of interest.)

61. See Schumpeter (1939: 161-174) and R. A. Gordon (1961: chs. 9, 11).

62. Although the assumption of bunching makes sense, there is no reason to assume that *all* of the investment in a particular investment good will be concentrated in the period of greatest bunching. (For example, there is no reason to assume that all infrastructural investment will be replaced at the beginning of a new stage of accumulation.)

63. The assumption of the inelasticity of available funds is obviously critical to this model. A dynamic version would obviously incorporate the growth of savings with the growth of the economy (fueled by growing investment), but the basic premise that there are determinate limits to the flow of funds available for investment would not be affected. In this sense, a Marxian approach to theories of investment would begin to depart dramatically from theories in the Keynesian tradition which view effective demand as the ultimate determinant of the rate of growth and investment demand as an exogenous determinant of the level of econom-

ic activity. Within the Marxian perspective, the funds available for investment are ultimately limited by total (produced and realized) aggregate surplus value (and its distribution); the process which determines the limits to that aggregate magnitude cannot easily be reduced to an "exogenous" process and we cannot easily assume that sufficient funds will be available to finance any warranted or desired level of investment demand.

64. The hypothesis can be expressed algebraically:

$$A_i = \frac{\Delta K_i}{\varphi Q}, \quad i = 1, \ldots, 4,$$

where A_i = the full period (in years) across which an investment project will take place; ΔK_i = the warranted (stock) value of the replacement demand for any given component of the total capital stock; φ = the proportion of total GDP available for net investment in any given year; and Q = the annual (flow) value of the gross domestic product. The value of φQ will not vary among kinds of investment projects but the (stock) value of ΔK_i will vary with the total size of that component of the capital stock and the contours of its particular investment cycle. The larger the component of total K and the greater the bunching of investment in a particular investment good, *ceteris paribus*, the greater will be ΔK_i and, as a consequence, A_i. Although I have not seen the underlying equations of their model, I assume that a dynamic version of these relationships frames the models generating simulated long cycles in capital formation in Forrester (1976) and the System Dynamics Group (1977).

65. The following simple calculations illustrate the consistency of this approach to the determinants of the length of the cycle with aggregate data on the total value of respective components of the capital stock. Suppose we take the *midpoints* of the customary estimates of the length of the respective cycles (inventory cycles, 2-3 years; business equipment cycles, 6-10 years; residential building cycles, 15-20 years): inventory cycles, 2.5 years; business equipment cycles, 8 years; and residential building cycles, 17.5 years. These values are in the relative proportions of 1 : 3.2 : 7. Suppose we then take estimates of the replaceable stock of those components of the capital stock. Not all inventory is considered replaceable; let us take Fabricant's estimate (1950: 323) that about 60% of the total inventory stock varies in close conformity with the short-term "inventory cycle." We can then compute values for the value of these components of national wealth for, say, 1958, from U.S. Bureau of the Census (1975: Series 475-479). The (replaceable) value for inventories was .6 x $95.7 billion. The values for business equipment and residential structures were $199.8 billion and $385.0 billion respectively. These values stand in the relative proportions of 1 : 3.5 : 6.7. These extraordinarily primitive calculations suggest, in short, that the relative length of the respective cycles is in fairly close proportion to the relative sizes of the respective components of the capital stock. I have not yet even tackled the question of how to categorize the components of the infrastructure, since they would undoubtedly include elements of private nonresidential structures, public structures, and much of what is sometimes devoted to business equipment expenditures (as in phone equipment for communications systems). The fact that the simple hypothesis about the relationship between cycle length and replacement stocks is at least plausibly consistent with the data on inventories, business equipment, and residential structures arms me with the courage to propose that a proper valuation of the infrastructure capital stock might well turn out to be in hypothesized proportion to the values of the other (slightly recalculated) components of the capital stock.

66. Having reached the end of this argument, I would urge readers to look back at note 49 for a caution about what this analysis of the infrastructural investment dynamic does and does not involve.

67. This analysis also has interesting implications for the intrinsic contradictions of systems of world-market control. I assume that these systems acquire more and more friction and that it becomes more and more difficult to maintain them on their own terms. Think of some of the parellels, for instance, between British domination of the American colonies in the 1760s and 1770s and U.S. domination of countries like South Vietnam in the 1960s.

68. See Forrester (1976) and the Systems Dynamics Group (1977), as well as the interview with Forrester in *Fortune* (1978).

69. See note 43 for a discussion of the political roots of this difference. At the time of writing, I do not know how Mandel treats these issues in his new book (1980).

70. More specifically, I do not find any reason for one to expect the kinds of movements in relative costs and prices which would be necessary to generate a model of (not just one, but two paired) long economic cycles out of this analysis. The model seems as stretched as Rostow's model (1978) of relative commodity prices.

71. I do not mean to suggest that I would rule out the possibility of long cycles before the nineteenth century. I simply mean to suggest that the mechanisms and dynamics of successions of stages of accumulation are likely to be affected significantly by the advent after the Industrial Revolution of "fully" capitalist production. This discussion will have to await another forum.

REFERENCES

BARAN, P. and P. SWEEZY (1966) Monopoly Capital. New York: Monthly Review Press.

BARR, K. (1979) "Long waves: a selective, annotated bibliography." Review II, 4: 675-718.

BELL, P. (1977) "Marxist theory, class struggle, and the crisis of capitalism," pp. 170-194 in J. Schwartz (ed.) The Subtle Anatomy of Capitalism. Santa Monica, CA: Goodyear.

BOUSQUET, N. (1979) 'Esquisse d'une théorie de l'alternance de périodes de concurrence et d'hégémonie au centre de l'économie-monde capitaliste." Review II, 4: 501-518.

BOWLES, S. and H. GINTIS (1976) Schooling in Capitalist America. New York: Basic Books.

------ (1980) Marxist Method and the Theory of Politics. Unpublished manuscript in progress.

BRAVERMAN, H. (1974) Labor and Monopoly Capital. New York: Monthly Review Press.

BURNS, A. and W. MITCHELL (1946) Measuring Business Cycles. New York: National Bureau of Economic Research.

CHANDLER, A. (1962) Strategy and Structure: Chapters in the History of the Industrial Enterprise. Cambridge, MA: MIT.

Citibank (1978) "Long swings I: Kondratyev invents history." Monthly Economics Newsletter (January): 12-16.

CRONIN, J. E. (1980) 'Stages, cycles, and insurgencies: the economics of unrest." This volume.

DUPRIEZ, L. (1947) Des mouvements économiques généraux. Louvain: Institut de Recherches économique et sociales.
——— (1978) "1974 a downturn of the long wave?" Banca Nazionale del Lavoro, Quarterly Review 126 (September): 199-210.
FABRICANT, S. (1950) Inventories and Business Cycles. New York: National Bureau of Economic Research.
FLEISCHER, H. (1973) Marxism and History. New York: Harper & Row.
FORRESTER, J. W. (1976) "Business structure, economic cycles, and national policy." Futures (June): 195-214.
Fortune (1978) "We're headed for another depression: interview with Jay Forrester.' January 16: 145-148.
FRANK, A. G. (1978) World Accumulation, 1492-1789. New York: Monthly Review Press.
GANSSMANN, H. (1979) "On the reconstruction of economics as a social science." Unpublished manuscript, New School for Social Research.
GARVY, G. (1943) "Kondratieff's theory of long cycles." Review of Economics and Statistics (November): 203-220.
GORDON, D. M. (1978a) "Up and down the long roller coaster," pp. 22-35 in Union for Radical Political Economics (ed.) U.S. Capitalism in Crisis. New York: Union for Radical Political Economics.
——— (1978b) "Capitalist development and the history of American cities," in W. Tabb and L. Sawers (eds.) Marxism and the Metropolis. New York: Oxford University Press.
——— (1980) Toward the Critique of CAPITAlopolis. Unpublished manuscript in progress.
———, R. C. EDWARDS, and M. REICH (1980) "The historical development of labor segmentation in the United States." Forthcoming in M. REICH et al., The Segmentation of Labor in U.S. Capitalism.
GORDON, R. A. (1961) Business Fluctuations. New York: Harper & Row.
GINTIS, H. (1972) "Alienation and power." Review of Radical Political Economics IV, 5: 1-34.
HANSEN, A. (1941) Fiscal Policy and Business Cycles. New York: W. W. Norton.
HILFERDING, R. (1920) Das Finanzkapital. 2nd ed. Vienna: Wiener Volksbuchhandlung.
ITOH, M. (1975) "The formation of Marx's theory of Crisis." Bulletin of the Conference of Socialist Economists IV, 1: 1-19.
KALECKI, M. (1937) "A theory of the business cycle." Review of Economic Studies (February): 77-97.
KINDELBERGER, C. (1974) The World in Depression, 1929-1939. Berkeley: University of California Press.
KONDRATIEFF, N. D. (1979) "The long waves in economic life." Review of Economics and Statistics LVI, 3: 573-609. Reprinted in Review II, 4: 519-562.
KOSHIMURA, S. (1977) "Equations of chain bankruptcy: from sectoral to general crises," pp. 255-282 in J. Schwartz (ed.) The Subtle Anatomy of Capitalism. Santa Monica, CA: Goodyear.
LENIN, V. I. (1917) Imperialism. Modern edition published 1967. New York: International Publishers.
MADDISON, A. (1977) "Phases of capitalist development." Banca Nazionale del Lavoro Quarterly Review 121 (June): 103-137.
MANDEL, E. (1975) Late Capitalism. London: New Left Books.
——— (1980) Long Waves in Capitalist Development. Cambridge, England: Cambridge University Press.

MARX, K. (1967) Capital (3 volumes). New York: International Publishers.
––– (1968) Theories of Surplus Value (Part II). Moscow: Progress Publishers.
––– (1973) The Grundrisse. London: Penguin.
REICH, M., D. M. GORDON, and R. C. EDWARDS (1980) The Segmentation of Labor in U.S. Capitalism. Forthcoming.
Research Working Group on Cyclical Rhythms and Secular Trends (1979) "Cyclical rhythms and secular trends of the capitalist world-economy: some premises, hypotheses, and questions." Review II, 4: 483-500.
ROSTOW, W. W. (1978) The World Economy: History and Prospect. Austin: University of Texas Press.
SCHUMPETER, J. A. (1939) Business Cycles (2 volumes). New York: McGraw-Hill.
SEKINE, T. (1975) "Uno-Riron: a Japanese contribution to Marxian political economy." Journal of Economic Literature (September): 847-877.
SHAIKH, A. (1977) "Marx's theory of value and the 'transformation problem'," pp. 106-139 in J. Schwartz (ed.) The Subtle Anatomy of Capitalism. Santa Monica, CA: Goodyear.
––– (1978) "An Introduction to the history of crisis theories," pp. 219-241 in Union for Radical Political Economics (ed.) U.S. Capitalism in Crisis. New York: Union for Radical Political Economics.
––– (1979) "Notes on the Marxian notion of competition." Forthcoming in Cambridge Journal of Economics.
SWEEZY, P. (1942) The Theory of Capitalist Development. New York: Monthly Review Press.
System Dynamics Group (1977) "Capital formation and the long wave in economic activity." Printed report. Cambridge, MA: System Dynamics Group, Sloan School of Management, MIT.
U.S. Bureau of the Census (1975) Historical Statistics of the United States, Colonial Times to 1970. Washington, DC: U.S. Government Printing Office.
UNO, K. (1975) Principles of Political Economy. Translated by T. Sekine. Unpublished manuscript.
WALLERSTEIN, I. (1973) The Modern World-System. New York: Academic Press.
––– (1979) The Capitalist World-Economy. Cambridge, England: Cambridge University Press.
WEISSKOPF, T. (1978) "Marxist perspectives on cyclical crisis," pp. 241-260 in Union for Radical Political Economics (ed.) U.S. Capitalism in Crisis. New York: Union for Radical Political Economics.
WOLFE, A. (1977) The Limits of Legitimacy: Political Contradictions of Contemporary Capitalism. New York: Free Press.
WRIGHT, E. O. (1977) "Alternative perspectives in Marxist theory of accumulation and crisis," pp. 195-231 in J. Schwartz (ed.) The Subtle Anatomy of Capitalism. Santa Monica, CA: Goodyear.
ZARETSKY, E. (1973) 'Capitalism, the family, and personal life." Socialist Revolution 1-2.

Chapter 2

FROM HEGEMONY TO COMPETITION: CYCLES OF THE CORE?

Nicole Bousquet

Any change of perspective on history entails the reconceptualization of many well-studied phenomena. Such is the case with the world-system perspective, the first premise of which is the existence, since the beginning of the sixteenth century, of a concrete spatio-temporal entity, the world-economy. It is a well-known fact that since the sixteenth century, three Western countries, Holland, England, and the United States, have glittered at certain moments of their history for their accomplishments in the realm of material civilization, and drawn the rest of the world in their nets. Up to now, the Dutch, British, and American hegemonies have been understood as being unique and discrete phenomena. Viewed in the context of a single spatial and temporal entity, a world-system, what was until now seen as unique and disjunct, becomes continuous, relative, and comparable. A new field of study is born: the changing pattern at the center of the world-system, i.e., the alternation of periods of hegemony and of competition among core powers. We now find ourselves in the most complete theoretical vacuum. And who likes a vacuum?

Since both patterns at the center have repeated themselves since the sixteenth century, it is natural to wonder whether we are faced with a cyclical phenomenon. It is an old notion that civilizations, empires, and hegemonic powers are bound to the fatality of a life cycle from birth and growth to decay and death. Now that the phenomenon takes place in a broader context, the world-economy, the idea that it is a cycle can be understood in at least two ways: either the changes of politico-economic pattern at the center stem from the internal dynamic of a single core power, or they somehow are the manifestation of cyclical activity encom-

AUTHOR'S NOTE: We are grateful to Mr. Pierre Meurice, interpreter, for his precious help in translating this chapter from French to English.

passing the whole of the center. The idea that changes at the center could be cyclical is extremely attractive from a world-system perspective, for these changes appear essential to the very survival of the system through history. Let us imagine for a moment that competition at the center would persist indefinitely; then the world-system would face the imminent danger of breaking into many separate empires. If, on the other hand, hegemony were to last, then predictable insubordination at the periphery of the system would call for the use of force and for the setting up of a repressive apparatus by the hegemonic power, and the world-economy would eventually mutate into a world-empire. The succession of hegemonic and competitive situations at the core breaks two opposite trends, each equally harmful to the survival of the world-economy. Moreover, to conclude hastily that a sequence which has repeated itself only three times and in such an irregular fashion is cyclical would be somewhat presumptuous. It would be like saying that the changes of relative position of runners in a race was cyclical. So, it is best to enquire first about the concrete relationship between changes of configuration at the core and already-known cycles within the world-economy.

Our hope is to find a clear temporal coincidence between a given pattern at the core and a given phase of known cycle within the world-economy. Since situations of hegemony and competition are lasting ones we should look for a correlation with either secular trends or long cycles (such as the Kondratieff wave) which would repeat themselves throughout the whole history of the world-economy. But here is the first stumbling block. In general, historians agree on the existence of secular trends for the sixteenth through eighteenth centuries but not afterwards, and on the incidence of Kondratieff waves since the beginning of the nineteenth century but not before. It is true that a few studies have indicated the existence of Kondratieff-like cycles in certain regions of the world-economy before the nineteenth century, but it has not as yet been established whether these are so contemporary as to lead to the conclusion that a general conjuncture exists. On the other hand, finding secular trends for the nineteenth and twentieth centuries should be an easier task given the availability of better data. However, such is not the case. As is well known, the indices of economic activity are numerous: prices, wages, production, productivity, investment, etc. The problem is that, viewed in terms of secular trends, these indices do not show a common turning point; consequently, any proposed periodization for the nineteenth and twentieth centuries depends on a somewhat arbitrary choice of index. Moreover, it is not enough to rely on the behavior of one single indicator if one wishes to establish the existence of secular trends; a rationale has to be found, an intelligible correlation of many indicators of economic activity has to be discovered—just as it has been done in the case of the already known secular trends and cycles (business cycles, Kitchin, Kondratieff, etc.). It is only when the long-term variation of any given indicator is understood in terms of the others, when a pattern of simultaneous variation emerges, that the existence of secular trends for the nineteenth and twentieth centuries could be credibly asserted. For the moment it is preferable to plot the conjuncture since the sixteenth century on the basis of secular trends from the beginning of the sixteenth century to the end of the eighteenth, and of Kondratieff cycles from then on. This is not totally artificial since there is a possibility that the secular trends of the first centuries of the world-economy gave way to Kondratieff cycles at the end of the eighteenth century. We thus propose the following sketch of the conjuncture:

Early 16th century to 1620-1650:	A-phase
1620-1650 to 1720-1750:	B-phase
1720-1750 to 1814:	A-phase
1814 to 1849:	B-phase
1849 to 1873:	A-phase
1873 to 1896:	B-phase
1896 to 1929:	A-phase
1929 to 1938-1945:	B-phase
1938-1945 to circa 1970:	A-phase
1970-:	B-phase

Let us draw roughly the relationship between this particular plotting of the conjuncture and the changing configuration at the center of the world-economy. It is at the end of a long A-phase, the sixteenth century, that Holland accedes to an hegemonic position within the world-economy. She looses this status toward the end of the seventeenth century, that is, in the course of a secular trend of stagnation. Britain rises to hegemony at the end of the eighteenth century and the first two decades of the nineteenth century, that is at the end of a secular trend of growth. She looses, if not hegemony, at least supremacy in the realm of production (we will define the term later) in the last quarter of the nineteenth century, that is during the B-phase of a Kondratieff cycle according to some, or in the first decades of the twentieth century that is during the A-phase of a Kondratieff cycle according to others. The United States became the hegemonic power within the world-economy in the era of prosperity following the Second World War. Finally U.S. hegemony has been faltering since the beginning of the 1970s, that is, during what many acknowledge to be the B-phase of a Kondratieff cycle. So as we can see there appears to be a relationship between the rise to hegemony and an A-phase (be it secular or part of a Kondratieff cycle) on the one hand, and a B-phase and the return to a situation of competition on the other. But let us add immediately that this relationship is not systematic enough (all A-phases do not lead to a situation of hegemony, and all B-phases do not end up in a situation of competition) and that it is too loose (secular trends *end up* in one or the other of the two situations) to be satisfactory. Were the correlation perfect, we still would have to explain why a given general conjuncture of growth (an A-phase) should produce different results in different regions of the center and end up in the *differentiation* of the center into a hegemonic and nonhegemonic entities. In the same vein we would still have to explain why a B-phase should level out differences and bring the center back to a situation of competition.

As conjuncture alone does not constitute a viable explanation of the changes of politico-economic configuration of the center (although it should remain an important dimension of our analysis), it is time we looked for something else. We have thought it convenient to set the problem within the theoretical framework of existing theories of development in the field of economic history and reformulate it in the terms of their most familiar key concepts. What follows should be taken not as a tight set of proven propositions but rather as a model of explanation to be checked later. Space does not allow us to lay out all the relevant empirical data, but it should be stressed that what follows is based on familiarization with much empirical and theoretical material and lengthy efforts at conceptualization and synthesis.

Our object of study will thus be the succession of periods of hegemony and periods of competition at the center of the world-economy. These changes should be conceived as multidimensional. Indeed we can always ascribe economic, political, and ideological dimensions to phenomena both of hegemony and competition. Nor should another important dimension, core-periphery relations, be forgotten.

There is a hegemonic situation within the world-system when one country of the center simultaneously enjoys supremacy in the realms of production, commerce, and finance, and occupies a position of political leadership. Indeed there is hegemony when the products of one core power predominate in the world-market over those of other nonhegemonic powers; when its merchants or equivalent economic institutions carve for themselves a large part of the world network of exchange; when it controls and owns the largest part in relative terms of the world production apparatus. Thanks to the lion's share in world trade and investments, the currency of the predominant power becomes the universal medium of exchange and its metropolis becomes the financial center of the world. Provided it acquires the necessary deterrents, the predominant power will take upon itself the mission of keeping order in the world-system and impose, by means of threats and rewards, convenient solutions to existing conflicts. Consequently, long periods of peace, the *Pax Britannica* and the *Pax Americana* (the Dutch hegemony is an exception), are typical of hegemonic situations. The official ideology of the hegemonic power claims universal validity. Equating what is good for the hegemonic power with what is good for the whole world-system, this ideology erects into universal principles rules of the game whose true function is to consolidate the hegemonic power's domination over the world-system: the freedom to sail of the Dutch (*mare liberum*), the freedom to trade of the British, and the freedom to invest of the Americans. On the other hand, the beginning of the hegemonic period will be the occasion for the shifting of relationships between the core and the periphery. Economic relations between the two regions of the world-system become focused on the hegemonic power. Such a reorientation, in the case of the colonized periphery, will require decolonization. This is why the rise of British and later American hegemony has been accompanied by a wave of decolonization. At the beginning of the hegemonic period, mainly while the decolonization process is going on, the predominant power champions the cause of colonized and oppressed peoples. At the periphery, nationalism takes on a new meaning and is felt as the legitimate expression of a genuine liberation movement. As long as the hegemonic power enjoys a measure of legitimacy, it can rely mostly on economic mechanisms to extract the surplus-value from the periphery and thus behaves in a relatively civilized fashion. This kind of mostly economic domination has been termed "economic imperialism." Over the duration of the hegemonic situation, the legitimacy of the dominant power is eroded, and given the fact that its political power is yet unchecked by that of the nonhegemonic center, its behavior toward the periphery becomes arrogant and its political interventions more blatant. Understandably, the terms of trade then turn clearly against the periphery.

Competition can also be described in the same terms as hegemony. Competition means that nonhegemonic core powers strive to regain or increase their share of the world-market. Economic rivalry can take various forms: free competition of products on the world-market, enclosing national economic areas behind tariff barriers or other more disguised forms of protectionism, or extending political control over the periphery (be it by the creation of empires or zones of political influence). Nonhegemonic core countries, who have carved for themselves a part of the world network of production and distribution, will at the same time use their national currencies in a growing volume of transactions. Monetary zones will emerge and this will contribute to the creation of tensions within the monetary system which, until then, had revolved around the predominant power's currency. The political leadership will falter—the unthinkable starts to happen: rebellions at the periphery or breaches of "due" respect on the part of nonhegemonic powers. Without a strong leadership within the world-economy, political tensions arise and often develop into armed conflicts. On the other hand, the economic links between the periphery and the core tend to become multilateral, and economic transactions with the nonhegemonic center become more frequent. This will be the case even for the still colonized periphery. Thus Spanish colonies at the end of the seventeenth century traded illegally with the three competing core powers of the day, France, England, and Holland, to such an extent that trade with the Spanish metropolis came practically to a standstill.

Political relations between the core and the periphery are also altered with the return of competition. This is a time when land-hungry core countries conquer and divide among themselves large territories not yet integrated into the world-economy (when there were still such regions) and parts of the already integrated periphery where local political power is particularly weak. Waves of colonization have thus accompanied the return to competition at the center. The effects of competition for the uncolonized periphery (Latin America at the end of the nineteenth century, and most of the periphery nowadays) are not as well-known. It could very well be that competition at the center tends to provide such areas of the periphery with more elbowroom and to increase their bargaining power. This could explain why in such periods terms of trade between the core and the periphery tend to favor the periphery.

Since hegemony and competition move along many dimensions, it is to be expected that the transition from one to the other will be gradual rather than sudden. Of all these possible dimensions of change we have chosen to study one, the realm of production. Isolating one dimension and researching systematically the independent impact of one single factor is a perfectly sound methodology. Far from being an oversimplification, it is a legitimate and necessary step toward a broader, multifactorial, more complex analysis of a phenomenon. If we choose here to examine the sole dimension of production, it is both for practical considerations—we cannot do everything at the same time—and heuristic reasons—to see how much one given factor can explain. It is also because this dimension appears at first glance more important than the others. Wallerstein (1980) has observed that production supremacy occurs first in the transition from competition to hegemony and is the first to disappear in the transition from hegemony to competition. So let us consider here the changes of politico-economic configuration of the center as a kind of epiphemonenon, as a transformation of a superstructure stemming from an underlying economic process, i.e., development at the center.

Historically the center of the world-economy has been host to a process of growth and development both in terms of the diversification of production and improvements in the methods of production. Growth and development are subject to conjuncture, i.e., to phases of acceleration and phases of deceleration. Just as the development process is irregular in time, it is uneven in space. Indeed the history of the center is characterized by the incidence of technological gaps and disparities in terms of efficiency between the productive apparatuses situated in the various countries of the core. There are times in the history of the center when the gap between core countries is widest, and others when most disparities seem to disappear. Between these two extreme situations we observe two trends: one toward differentiation, i.e., polarization of the center into hegemonic and nonhegemonic powers, and another of indifferentiation, i.e., a return to a certain homogeneity of the center. Production supremacy marks the end of the former, and competition in production marks the end of the latter. Strictly speaking, these trends are not processes (for they are the result of more than one dynamic) but just a straight line drawn between two extreme situations which will serve us as a dummy variable. The usefulness of such a dummy variable is to illustrate what we want to explain—the appearance and disappearance of gaps—and to facilitate the task of establishing the sequence of the various factors coming into play at one time or another.

The process of development is the result of the reallocation of human and material resources and of innovation. It is precisely the uneven distribution of innovation at the core that causes temporary gaps between different countries. But here the term innovation needs precision. In the vast body of economic history literature, the concept of innovation has been broken up into a variety of subcategories. As will be obvious later, these qualifications of the term have proved useful for the purpose of describing the gaps that can now and then be found between core powers in the course of history. So it is appropriate to review them briefly here. A first distinction has been made between product and process innovations on the one hand, and innovations in the methods of production on the other. The word "process" usually refers to a theoretical method of manufacture, while "methods of production" is the application of this process through different combinations of the factors of production (labor, capital, land, and raw materials). Changes in the methods of production may be gradual and take place within a known technology; these are referred to as improvements. Or they may be radical and change drastically the existing combination of factors of production, thus shifting the "technological frontiers." These are innovations proper. To the effect of establishing such a distinction Milward and Saul (1973: 172) propose that

> we ought to differentiate between a shift of technology within the present range of knowledge, that is to say, adjustments of the

combination of factors used in a known process according to the dictates of the relative price of those factors and the finding of a new technology, so that land, labour, capital and materials are combined in a different way altogether.

Among innovations likely to improve or change drastically the methods of production J. D. Goulds makes the distinction between "physical and engineering" and "organizational and managerial" types, the latter being as likely to improve productivity as the former. Gould (1972: 363) defines management improvements in the following way:

> Such functions of management as promoting the motivation on the part of workers, to seek higher productivity; planning factory layout, the logistics of material flow, and the integration of sequential processes to minimize delays; intra-firm allocation of resources and selection of output-mix to maximize profit, and the like.

It is the uneven distribution of radical innovations in the methods of production of whatever type that generates the kind of disparities at the center upon which production supremacy will rest. On the other hand, product and process *innovations* and mere *improvements* of products, processes and methods of production, have historically been more equitably distributed within the center. In our view, the diversification of products and processes is in itself a single centerwide process which is otherwise subject to conjuncture, i.e., to phases of acceleration and deceleration. In the course of this transhistorical process, there are periods during which a particular entity of the center, while participating to the process as do other core entities, continues to choose among known methods of production those that are most efficient in terms of labor, and ends up finding radically new methods of production in one or more sectors. It is when such innovations take place that the seeds of production supremacy (that is, the exclusive domination of the products of the innovative sectors over the world-economy)—and hegemony—are sown.

It is the resilience of particular conditions affecting the "national economic area"[1] of the future hegemonic power that will systematically bias the choice of methods of production toward more capital-intensive and labor-saving methods, i.e., most efficient methods in terms of volume of production per man-hour. National economic areas are in fact different environments within which the process of diversification of products and processes unfolds and takes different forms in terms of methods of production. The first of these conditions is a particular combination or state of the factors of production. For one reason or another, labor will be more scarce and more expensive in terms of real wages than in other core countries, to such an extent that further growth of production entails the risk of a disproportionately steep increase of labor costs. The cost of labor is also higher in relation to the cost of another factor of production, namely capital. It is the well-known proposition of Habakkuk in *American and British Technology in the Nineteenth Century* that the choice of methods of production is at least in part determined by the relative costs of labor and capital. As reported by Gould (1972: 361), Habakkuk proposes that

> American entrepreneurs adopted more capital intensive methods than the British because the ratio of American wage rates to British wage rates was higher than the ratio of the product of the cost of capital goods times the rate of interest in America to that of the corresponding product in Britain. . . . Further, the American labour supply was not only dearer but less elastic.

Crouzet (1967: 171-172) makes a similar point when he discusses the peculiarities of English development in the eighteenth century compared to that of France:

> during the first half of the eighteenth century, industrial growth in England has reached limits not to be crossed without a technological breakthrough which the increase in population and in demand from the 1740's made imperative. In France on the other hand, there was no shortage of labour, output could be increased to meet demand without looking for drastic innovations. This may rank as the most important of the differences to be observed between England and France, but it was in part due to England s earlier and more intensive industrialization, and hence to the situation in the seventeenth century.
>
> There remains the question of capital resources. In eighteenth century England, capital was relatively abundant, as is shown by the fall of interest rates in France. . . . However, in England capital accumulation was at a faster rate than the growth of other factors especially labour supplies and this was a powerful incentive to innovation.

It is also the argument of North and Thomas (1973: 142) for the Low Countries in the sixteenth century:

> [Between 1500 and the beginning of the seventeenth century] the cost of capital fell substantially relative to the prices of the other factors of production. No sector of the economy of the Netherlands was immune from the influence of this dramatic change in relative factor prices. Capital, financial and physical, was increasingly substituted for other productive factors in agriculture and industry as well as commerce. Agriculture became more capital-intensive, wastes

were drained and cleaned, fencing was improved and fertilizers were extensively employed. Credit was increasingly utilized to finance all business activity and more roundabout, specialized means of production were employed. Industrial production became at once larger in scope and more specialized.

The other set of conditions affecting the future hegemonic power and biasing the choice of methods of production is a particularly intense or a differently structured demand. There is a well-known debate between Saul and Habakkuk around the explanation of the emergence of more capital-intensive methods of production in the United States during the second half of the nineteenth century. Against Habakkuk, Saul (1972: 37) argues that the choice of techniques is determined more by demand than by the availability and cost of the factors of production:

> The mass production techniques which emerged in the United States after 1850 were relevant [elsewhere] only where there were a mass demand for a homogeneous product.

It is somewhat astonishing to find that Habakkuk takes Saul's position on the subject of technological changes in England at the end of the eighteenth and the beginning of the nineteenth century:

> Most of the economically important inventions of the Industrial Revolution period can more plausibly be ascribed to the pressure of increasing demand rather than to the random operation of the human instinct of contrivance, changes in factors prices or the Schumpeterian innovation [Habakkuk, 1968: 34].

The main factors behind this demand are, always according to Habakkuk, internal and external trade and the size and the structure of the English market with its characteristic large middle-income strata. As we know, demand entails both a conjunctural and a structural dimension. It is of course to the latter that Habakkuk refers.

In brief, we are faced with two hypotheses regarding the choice of capital-intensive techniques: demand, and the particular state or combination of the factors of production. Nonetheless, we must not forget that a consensus exists on the following facts: the high cost and scarcity of labor, the particular demand structure and intensity, and the adoption of capital-intensive techniques in our three cases: the Low Countries in the sixteenth century, England in the eighteenth century, and the United States in the latter part of the nineteenth and the twentieth centuries. It is not indispensable to choose between the two theories for these are not necessarily mutually exclusive; indeed, it could very well be that they complement each other. For instance, it is plausible that the scarcity and the high cost of labor spurs the adoption of capital-intensive techniques, which in turn contribute to increasing the volume of production and by the same token, the per capita income, hence demand. It is equally plausible that a growing demand acts as a stimulus for the growth of production which increases manpower requirements. If labor availability remains inelastic in the short term, a rise in real wages would then occur, which in turn would lead to the adoption of more capital-intensive methods of production.

Particular conditions of labor supply and of demand lead, as far as the future hegemonic power is concerned, to the generalization of the "best practice" in the context of known technology and methods of management in all sectors of economic activity so much so that they eventually operate close to the technological frontier of the day. Before supremacy proper, the future predominant power's productivity per capita and even more so per man-hour of work will be higher than that of the rest of the center. This prior relative superiority of the methods of production of the future hegemonic power is, by the way, recognized by its contemporaries. Thus, sixteenth-century Flanders (before the Dutch hegemony) was the pole of attraction for the rest of Europe. In the eighteenth century, England attracted visitors and was admired by most eminent continental observers. By the middle of the nineteenth century, the resourcefulness and know-how of the American labor force had already been noticed by Europeans. The ingenious improvements of methods of production within the limits of known technology along with a higher overall productivity, i.e., superiority in the methods of production, is not what we mean by supremacy in the realm of production. Within a known technology various combinations of the factors of production are likely to produce similar results in terms of costs and product quality. It is for this reason that, despite the greater general efficiency of the methods of production of the future hegemonic power, the center remains in a situation of competition. For production supremacy to take place, new methods of production have to be invented in one or more sectors. Production *superiority* remains a necessary condition of production *supremacy*, for major innovations in production methods are much more likely to happen in a national economic area operating at the limit of known technology than in those where the best practice has not been generally adopted. Such major innovations (technological or managerial) will take place, as we have already suggested, in a given sector of production of the future hegemonic power: shipbuilding in the Dutch case, textile (spinning devices) and mining (the steam engine) in the English case, and electronics in the American case. It is a characteristic of major innovations that they will cause numerous multiplying effects in other sectors of production. Thus in

Holland, management innovations in shipbuilding and sea transport provided a model of low profit margin operations in an era when profits, obtained mostly in the trade of luxury products, were high. In the case of England, mechanization was extended, along with the steam engine, to a variety of processes of production. In the United States, progress in the electronics sector (namely the invention of computers) revolutionized the management of enterprises across the board.

Thus supremacy in the realm of production rests upon radical innovations of methods of production. Once these take place, the gap between the hegemonic power and the rest of the center becomes technological as well. Besides, disparities in terms of productivity per hour of work and income per capita, an indicator of demand, become more pronounced. Let us go back one step at this point. These disparities result from the spreading of the best practice prior to the achievement of supremacy in the realm of production; the increased productivity in the innovative sector(s) further stimulated by success on the world market; the interaction of the new technology with other sectors of production; and finally the further increase in productivity in traditional sectors under the pressure of brisk demand in the innovative sectors. Thanks to the multiplying effects of radical innovations in one or several sectors, the pendulum of differentiation of the center will be pushed farther still.

Before considering the second characteristic tendency of development at the center, indifferentiation, it may be useful to see at what times these tendencies occurred concretely, in order to make our paradigm clearer. From the beginning of the sixteenth century up to approximately 1580, the Low Countries distinguished themselves from other regions of the core by a higher productivity in all sectors of economic activity, including agriculture. This occurred at a time when in other regions of Europe, agricultural per capita production was decreasing as an effect of demographic growth coupled with stationary agriculture technology. In the following period, from 1580 to about 1620, the United Provinces witnessed important technological and managerial innovations. According to de Vries (1976: 92-93) industry in the Dutch Republic attained an entirely new level of importance within a few decades after 1580. It is in shipbuilding that most major innovations took place: the *fluitship* (product innovation), the wind-powered sawing mill, the crane (technological innovations), concentration of industry, economies of scale, precut timber stockpiles (managerial innovations). Some of these had important multiplying effects which must have contributed to reduce operating costs in many sectors. From 1620 until 1650 at least, Dutch production keeps diversifying. To this effect, de Vries suggests that "by the second half of the seventeenth century, the Republic achieved a position of international importance in each of those industries (brick-making, ceramics, linen bleaching, brewing, distilling, salt boiling, and sugar refining)." Thus from the beginning of the sixteenth century to approximately 1650-1675 the center went through a period of differentiation.

During the last decades of the seventeenth century, England spared no effort to bridge the gap with Holland by adopting Dutch methods of production, diversifying production, and increasing productivity. These changes have been described most vividly by a contemporary, a Bristol merchant, John Cary who wrote in 1695:

> it proceeds from the ingenuity of the manufacturer, and the improvement he makes in his ways of working: thus the refiner of sugars goes through that operation in a month, which our forefathers required four months to effect; thus the distillers draw more spirits, and in less time than those formerly did who taught them the art. The glass maker hath found a quicker way of making it out of things which cost him little of nothing. Silk stockings are wove instead of knit. Tobacco is cut by engines instead of knives. Books are printed instead of written, deal board are sawn with a mill instead of men's labour. Lead is smelted by wind furnaces instead of blowing with bellows; all of which save the labour of many hands, so the wages of those employed need not be lessened [Coleman, 1977: 157].

D. C. Coleman (1977: 159), who wishes to corroborate these changes, suggests that, if all the relevant statistics existed, they would show that the latter decades of the seventeenth century were marked by brisk industrial advance (followed by slower growth in the early eighteenth century). Up to 1750, not only England but also France and other regions of the center like the Rhine valley and Hamburg developed these very sectors of production—textiles and shipbuilding—in which the Dutch had excelled in the seventeenth century. After 1750, even semiperipheral political units, like Spain, Prussia, and Austria, made attempts to develop some of these sectors of production. Thus it can be said that, during the last decades of the seventeenth century and the whole of the eighteenth century, the center of the world-economy was going through a period of *indifferentiation*. It can also be argued, if we take not Holland but England as our point of reference, that the same period was one of *differentiation*. What was so peculiar to England then was that it was alone to witness a productivity jump at the end of the seventeenth century. Indeed it has been Crouzet's (1967: 171-172) argument that despite the fact that rates of production and productivity growth were about the same in France and England during most of the eighteenth century, different effects would be obtained in England by the end of the century because at the start, in the seventeenth century, it had a higher productivity level. In relation to England then, the center was in a phase of differentiation since the last decades of the seventeenth century. England would subsequently accede to supremacy in the realm of production at the end of the eighteenth century thanks to radical innovations in methods of production, i.e., the mechanization of the spinning and later of the weaving processes and the application of the steam engine to many production processes. The pendulum of differentiation would be pushed further—until about 1850—by the application of these major inventions to other sectors, by the productivity improvements of traditional sectors under the pressure of demand from the innovative sectors, and finally by improvements of existing products and processes. According to Landes (1969: 193), it was toward the middle of the nineteenth century that the Continent tried to catch up with England:

> The period from 1850 to 1873 was Continental industry's coming-of-age. It was a period of unprecedented rapid growth. These years were also years of technological maturation. They were marked in essence by the working-out on the Continent of those innovations that constitute the heart of the Industrial Revolution and had developed and diffused in Britain a generation or more earlier.

This particular tendency toward indifferentiation would last until at least 1913. By then, most West European countries, as well as the United States, had already attained (or even surpassed in the case of the United States) the technological sophistication, levels of productivity, and per capita income of England (see Figures 2.1 and 2.2). It was also between 1890 approximately and 1913 that countries such as Holland, Sweden, and Denmark came to equal British levels of productivity and approximate British average per capita income, i.e., overall demand. This period reminds us somewhat of the last half of the eighteenth century when production and technological sophistication typical of the core spread to the semiperiphery. From 1913 on, the United States set itself clearly apart from Western Europe in per capita income and even more clearly in terms of productivity (see Figures 2.3 and 2.4). The tendency of U.S. differentiation lasted until the end of the Second World War, when the gap between the United States and the rest of the center in terms of productivity and per capita income was the widest. It is, oddly perhaps, when these disparities began to disappear in the 1950s and early 1960s that major innovations occurred, and that electronics, thanks mainly to the computer, became the most advanced sector in the United States. It was a peculiarity of U.S. hegemony that what had been previously a sequence in the case of Holland and England—production supremacy in the world-economy preceeding and being followed by a process of emulation in the nonhegemonic center—here took place concurrently, in the 1950s and 1960s. For their importance and numerous multiplying effects, innova-

(text continued p. 62)

FIGURE 2.1 Output per Man-Hour (calculated at 1955 U.S. dollars relative prices as a proportion of the United Kingdom, selected years between 1870 and 1913 [U.K. = 100])

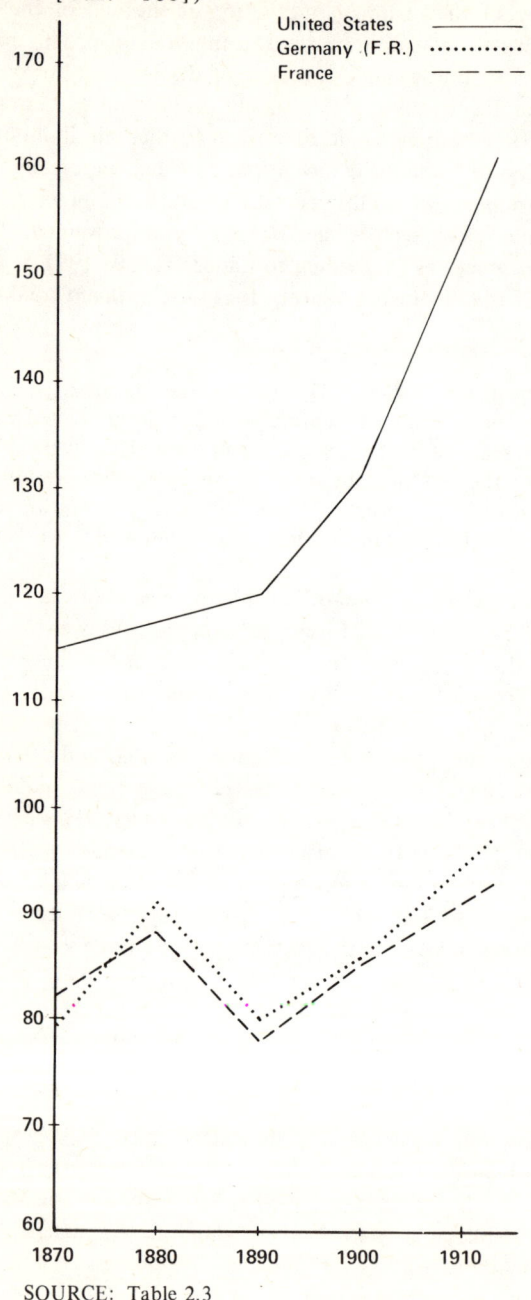

SOURCE: Table 2.3

FIGURE 2.2 Output per Capita (calculated at 1955 U.S. dollars relative prices as a proportion of the United Kingdom, selected years between 1870 and 1913 [U.K. = 100])

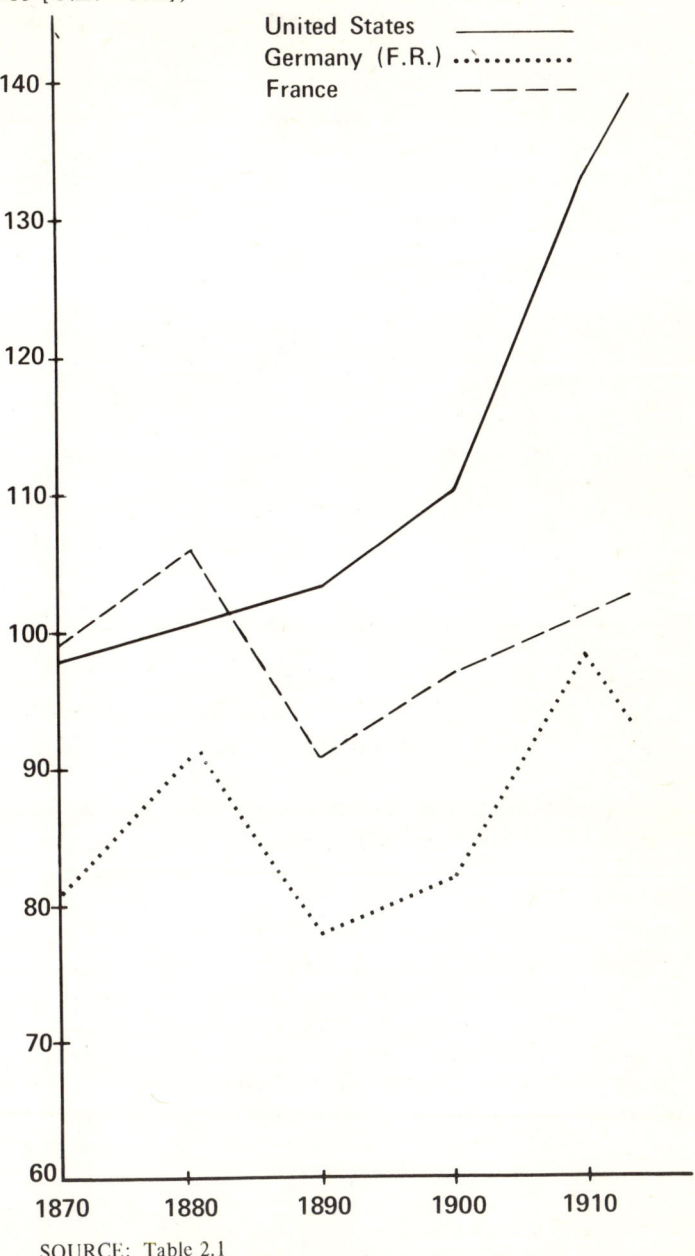

SOURCE: Table 2.1

FIGURE 2.3 Output per Capita (calculated at 1955 U.S. dollars relative prices as a proportion of the United States, selected years between 1870 and 1960 [U.S. = 100])

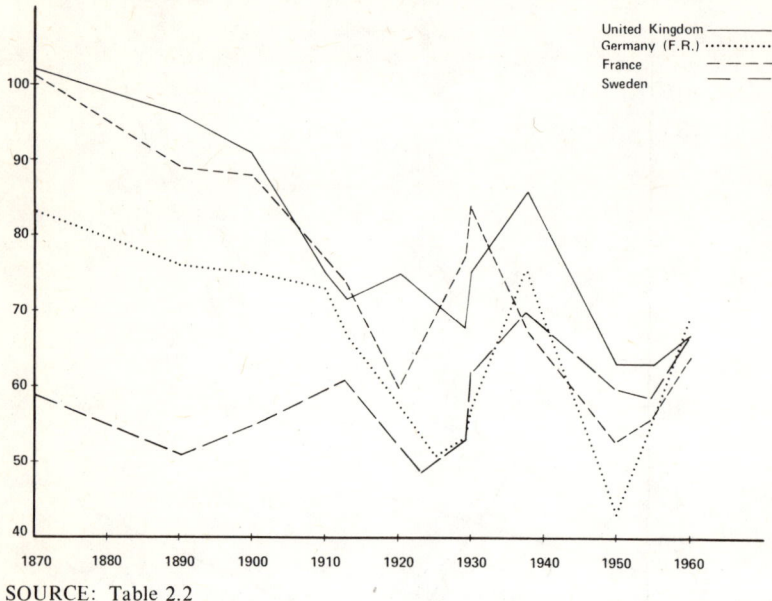

SOURCE: Table 2.2

tions in the field of electronics can best be compared to the mechanization of textile production and the broad application of the steam engine in England at the end of the eighteenth century and the beginning of the nineteenth, and equally, to the innovations in shipbuilding in Holland at the end of the sixteenth century. According to Christopher Freeman (1974: 108-109):

> The introduction of reliable and relatively low-cost electronic computers is perhaps the most revolutionary of the post-war period, influencing almost every other industry and service. They increased enormously the efficiency with which large quantities of data could be processed, such as pay-roll calculations, invoicing, insurance premiums, design calculations and so forth . . . it is electronics which made it possible to "automate" a much greater variety of operations and processes than was hitherto possible.

The production supremacy of the United States within the world-economy after the end of the Second World War rested upon the export of technology of the electronics sector as well as the export of technology

FIGURE 2.4 Output per Man-Hour (calculated at 1955 U.S. relative prices as a proportion of the United States, selected years between 1870 and 1977 [U.S. = 100])

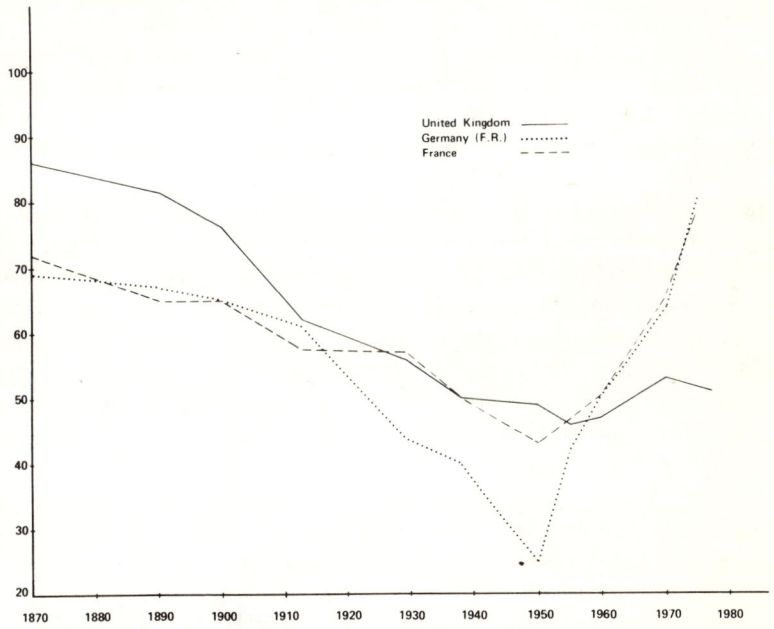

SOURCE: Table 2.4

from sectors where original methods of production had been developed before the Second World War. Despite such a massive export of technology, the United States maintained a clear technological edge until the end of the 1960s, thanks to the fact that U.S. industries had the greatest and most developed research and development infrastructure in the world. While technological development in the advanced sectors went on in the United States, a process of emulation unfolded in Western Europe and Japan from the early 1950s. In effect, from then on, productivity and per capita income rates of increase were consistently greater in Western Europe and Japan than in the United States. American production supremacy (and hegemony) was now coming to an end. The productivity and per capita income gaps between the United States and the rest of the center were now being bridged, and West Germany and Japan in particular were now close seconds to the United States in the most advanced sectors of technology.

Let us now return to the analysis of the second trend in the development of the center, indifferentiation. Sooner or later, the gaps between the hegemonic power and the nonhegemonic center will start to narrow. We will now attempt to explain how and why this happens, at what stage the center returns to a situation of competition, and what exactly is meant by "competition."

It is logical to think that the reversal of the trend toward differentiation is a function of both developments in the hegemonic country and occurrences in the nonhegemonic center. Let us look first at the hegemonic power. In our opinion the most crucial change to take place here is the alteration of the innovative process. This consists in a shift away from radical innovations in the methods of production to less dramatic, minor innovations aiming at improving *existing* products, processes, and methods of production. Innovation altogether comes to a standstill when a phase of recession (a B-phase) eventually hits the center. This is seemingly what happened in the case of Holland. Great innovations took place approximately between 1580 and 1620. Then, from 1620 to the middle of the seventeenth century, came a period of diversification and improvements of production. And then the seventeenth-century depression finally affected Holland, we like to think (for this has yet to be proven) that innovation stopped altogether. In the case of Britain, it was in the third decade of the nineteenth century that radical innovations in methods of production came to an end. Crouzet (1978) suggests this effect:

> It is generally believed that the period 1815-1847 marked the end in Great Britain of the Industrial Revolution in the strict sense of the term. Most of the technical innovations that characterized it had been put into effect before 1830, and it only remained to exploit and improve them.

Furthermore, according to Crouzet, Britain lost its leadership in technology in the 1860s:

> It appears that the most advanced countries on the Continent (as well as the United States) had reached the technological level of England by the 1860's, and after 1870 at the latest the latter was certainly no longer the dominant center of technical innovation. To be sure, inventive genius had not dried up there, and Britons still made numerous and important inventions. But some of them were adopted more rapidly, and on a larger scale, outside their country of origin. Furthermore, in the new and decisive domains of future industrial growth—chemicals, electricity, internal combustion engines, machine-tools—almost all the important inventions were being made elsewhere [Crouzet, 1978: 336].

It is to be expected and remains to be proven that the next period, 1873-1896 (a B-phase) slowed down what was left of the innovation process in Britain. In the case of the United States we believe that there were also three distinct phases of innovation during the hegemonic period: a first phase, in the 1950s, when radical innovations in the methods of production took place; a second in the 1960s, marked by the improvements of products, processes, and methods of production; and a last one, beginning in the 1970s, when the innovation process came to a stop. Research at the Stanford Research Institute, the results of which were reported by *Newsweek* (1974) magazine, established that, in the 1950s, 82% of the major innovations marketed in the world originated in the United States. At the end of the 1960s this proportion was reduced to 55%. According to the same study, during the recession years of the 1970s, inflation swelled the costs of research and development, undermined profitability, and deterred entrepreneurs from investing in the field as earnestly as before. In the same vein, *Business Week* (1979) reports:

> During the past decade [the 1970s], the concentration of the chief executive officer of most big corporations on financial matters has kept him focused almost exclusively on the short run, on next quarter's earnings of this year's profits.... Using the excuse of applying the techniques of professional management, a lot of chief executives have turned timid in the area of product and process innovation.... In big companies, there is a bureaucracy designed to accomplish the opposite. It slows down innovation to the point that the bright people who are best at this kind of work leave or give up in frustration. And too often bureaucracies in companies have vested interests in the products or the old way of doing things and are imaginative only in devising reasons why new-product or new-process work should be killed.

Why should the innovative process within the confines of the hegemonic power be subjected to such alterations? There is a school of thought which seeks the roots of the phenomenon in an aging process, a growing rigidity toward change plaguing the whole productive apparatus of the "mature" hegemonic power. Thus de Vries (1976: 251), a keen student of Holland, believes to have diagnosed the latter's difficulties at the end of the seventeenth century as symptomatic of "high-level traditionalism." According to some, Great Britain also was going through a climacteric at the end of the nineteenth century. The same is being said now of the United States. Another school explains the loss of technological leadership (the argument has been made mostly in the case of Great Britain) by overspecialization in certain sectors of production and the corresponding commitment to a certain infrastructure, which would act as a deterrent to the start of new sectors of production. According to yet another hypothesis, the phenomenon happens because circumstances surrounding the appearance of major innovations, mostly scarcity of labor, no longer prevail. As the hegemonic situation proceeds, the labor supply of the hegemonic power becomes, for one reason or another, more elastic. Demographic growth, immigration of foreign labor, and the forming of new social strata educated to meet the new requirements of the production process, are all possible responses to the rapid growth and high wages prevailing at the beginning of the hegemonic period. Also, labor tends to become relatively more abundant with the spreading of the new methods of production. Indeed, it is only in relation to the old methods of production that labor can be said to be scarce. Once the methods of production are radically transformed, labor is not necessarily scarce anymore. For instance, it was in the context of the putting-out system that labor was scarce in England at the end of the eighteenth century. Mechanization of spinning and weaving, along with concentration of production, freed for factory work large numbers of rural spinners and weavers. Drastic changes in the methods of production seemingly altered not only the supply but also the demand for labor. Observing the striking changes of the industrial structure in Europe after the Second World War, Gould (1972: 312) suggests that the effects of such changes

> may [therefore] have been to "polarize" demand for skills, greatly increasing the demand for highly-trained scientists, engineers, managers, accountants, lawyers and clerks, and at the other end, demand for workers capable of carrying out routine, repetitive tasks or tasks involving physical effort with only the minimum skill, capable of being acquired on the spot.

A last hypothesis bearing on the eventual drying up of the hegemonic power's innovative capacity is that demand for her long successful products within the world-economy shrinks or collapses under an unfavorable conjuncture or the closing up of important markets behind protectionist barriers.

All these hypotheses have a measure of credibility and deserve a more extensive treatment than the few passing comments that can be offered here. Since the last hypothesis—that of diminished demand—involves factors or processes at play elsewhere in the world-economy and particularly at the core (the protectionist response for instance), it will be discussed later along with the occurrences at the nonhegemonic center in the return to a situation of competition.

The proposition that the loss of innovative capacity by an "aging" hegemonic power, besides requiring elaboration, proves somewhat difficult to verify. The first and most obvious way to measure the overall capacity of the hegemonic power's productive apparatus to reproduce and renew itself is the productivity index (i.e., the average product per man-hour). A first difficulty is that productivity indexes for core countries (not to mention the periphery) do not go back beyond 1870. A second problem with such overall indexes is that we never quite know if we are measuring structural changes in the relative importance of different sectors (which all have different rates of growth) within the national economic area or what we hope to measure, that is, general across-the-board productivity changes. In order to conclude that our hegemonic powers go through a climacteric, we ought to know: (1) if each of their individual sectors of economic activity were eventually affected by slower rates of productivity growth; (2) if these were due to the abandonment of the best practice and the failure to reinvest, rather than to the fact that rates of growth were slower in situations where the best practice prevailed; (3) if a slower multisectoral rate of productivity growth was due to an internal process or was rather associated with an unfavorable conjuncture within the world-economy. It is indeed important to disentangle conjunctural effects from productivity changes specific to the hegemonic power. The two are often confused; it is often during a recession that contemporary observers and later students of the evolution of the hegemonic power come up with the idea of a general decline, of a climacteric. Finally, it is crucial to observe the performance of the most advanced sector(s), for if these lose their dynamism and inventiveness, one can imagine what might happen to other less dynamic sectors. All we can conclude here is that the story of the concrete modalities of the decline of our three hegemonic powers has not been told yet, and that a great deal more sectoral and microeconomic research is needed. This does not mean that we should ignore indexes of general productivity in our analysis. They remain a useful if gross measure of emerging and disappearing gaps between core countries.

Let us now turn to the hypothesis of a more abundant labor force as a deterrent to drastic changes in methods of production and even the keeping up with the best practice as the situation of hegemony goes on. We have already seen that, in the period preceding hegemony, special conditions of scarcity of labor coupled with a particular demand situation systematically biased the future hegemonic power's selection of production techniques in favor of those most likely to save labor. At that time, then, the impact of labor scarcity was general. But when labor becomes more abundant, is the impact equally general within the hegemonic power's national economic area? If such were the case, we would have found here a plausible explanation for an assumed, apparently generalized decline. But it is far from certain that the impact of an abundant labor force is general in the short term. We know that oversupply of labor tends to be confined to particular sectors of the economy like services (and agriculture, in the case of peripheral countries). There would be nothing surprising if, in the short term, the impact of abundant manpower were confined to a few sectors, and did not impede the adoption of the best practice in other sectors. This is what seemingly happens today in peripheral countries, where often the very latest technology is imported. In the long run, however, it is difficult to imagine that a situation of abundant labor would have no impact whatsoever on the choice of technology. For the moment, our impression is that changes toward the adoption of the best practice occur before and at the beginning of the hegemonic period in reaction to the demand of rapidly growing advanced sectors, but that as the rate of growth of that demand peaks and settles at lower and more even rates, the incentive to keep up with the best practice in other sectors becomes less and the fact that labor is now relatively more abundant reinforces this trend.

However, the hypothesis we find most attractive from our world-system perspective is that of overspecialization of the hegemonic power. Precisely that which made it so successful at first in the world-economy acts as a deterrent to drastic innovative changes later. It is as though the hegemony carries the seeds of its own destruction. In our view, the very success of the hegemonic power's advanced sectors within the world-economy contributes, at some half-way stage in its hegemonic life, to shifting the innovative process away from major changes in the methods of production, and toward merely repeating and improving what had been so successful. As long as the advanced sectors on which supremacy rests are profitable, they remain the privileged sectors for capital accumulation. Entrepreneurs will be lured into the fullest exploitation of existing markets and will keep investing in the improvement and diversification of existing products, processes, and methods of production. So, the growth of key advanced sectors is simultaneous with a technological lull in terms of major innovations. As we know, technological lulls are dangerous; they allow others to buy time.

The alteration of the innovative process of the hegemonic power midway in its career is not, however, the sole condition for narrowing the gap between the hegemonic power and the rest of the center. If the nonhegemonic center did not engage into a catching-up process, the existing gap with the hegemonic power would perhaps not widen, but would not narrow either. Catching up is a complex process. It is not enough to borrow a few advanced techniques; the gap must also be bridged in terms of productivity and per capita income, i.e., in terms of demand. The Dutch "challenge" to late seventeenth- and early eighteenth-century Europe consisted not in the mere borrowing of techniques but also in duplicating the diversity, productivity, and "general wealth" of the Dutch. The "British challenge" to mid-nineteenth-century Europe was equally complex: Western Europe had to "industrialize." And it has long been a cliché of popular literature on the subject that the American challenge consists in "automation." All these changes are required not only in order to bridge the existing disparities, but also and more importantly in order to create in other regions of the center the conditions of autonomous innovation which ultimately undo the maintenance of hegemony.

But why should the nonhegemonic center (and those countries aspiring to this status) engage in an emulative process in the first place? The question has been both a challenge and a source of frustration for the best minds. After attempting in vain to explain why some countries eventually caught up with Britain at the end of the nineteenth century, Peter Mathias (n.d.) concluded somewhat impatiently that it had to be so. There could be after all a grain of truth to this. We are here confronted with what some would call a law: At the core of the world-economy, uneven development does not last forever; the tendency toward inequality *always* comes to an end; and eventually inequalities themselves will *always* disappear. This may seem obvious but things might have happened differently. For instance, one hegemonic power might have been displaced by another which had attained a superior technological sophistication and higher levels of productivity and average per capita income, without the general lift in technological sophistication, productivity, and per capita income we observe in that part of the center that has not been and will not be hegemonic. Of course if such had been the case, large regions would, with time, fade away from the center. The history of disparities between the core and the periphery is totally different. Here unequal development is a constant. There is no remission to the growing gap between the core and the periphery, other than the occasional slowing down of the process during phases of recession. The explanation of such fundamental differences in the development at the core and that of the periphery is of course the key to the yet incomplete theory of development within the capitalist world-economy.

On the topic of innovation and diffusion of technology at the center, there are two sets of propositions: those emphasizing the importance of demand, and others insisting rather on the combination, or the current situation, of factors of production. Technological innovation and diffusion are either a function of a particular situation of factors of production or a function of demand. One of the proponents of the latter is W. N. Parker (1972: 65) who states that

> more often ... inventors have been attracted not so much by relative factor scarcities as by the state of production in relation to the whole stage of technology. It is important to consider then not so much relative factor supplies as the general level of wealth, its distribution and demand in the economy.

Moreover, he proposes that factors of production have to adapt themselves to existing technology other than the other way around:

> The problem for population growth and for saving has been to adjust factor supplies to the relationship between technology and resources on the one hand and demand on the other. It is these, I would insist, and not technology which are adjustable and adjusting elements [Parker, 1972: 77].

Inadvertently perhaps, Parker touches a crucial difference between development at the center and at the periphery of the world-economy. When new technology is adopted by a core country, it is either adapted and modified on the basis of the immediate situation of factors of production, or it is adopted *in toto* without modification, and the factors of production have to adapt over a period of time to the new technology. This is particularly true of the labor supply. By means of different mechanisms (slower demographic growth, emigration or control over immigration, education), core countries ultimately control the labor supply in terms both of the numbers and quality required by the production process. Things are very different at the periphery. Here technology is imported without regard to the prevalent situation of the factors of production. Labor, which is mainly unskilled, will never succeed, barring a demographic catastrophe, in adjusting its numbers to the diminished labor requirements occasioned by the importation of core technology. Indeed, the importation of core technology seriously worsens the already existing problem of excess labor. When such technology is applied to sectors in which redundant labor is concentrated, particularly agriculture, the negative impact is greater still. The adoption of core technology at the periphery might increase productivity per man-hour, but it hardly has any effect on per capita income and therefore on demand. The demand end of the feedback mechanism that we find at the center where, in phases of prosperity, increased productivity increases per capita income, i.e., demand which in turn stimulates further productivity growth is absent at the periphery. This is one of the reasons why the core-periphery gap is ever widening. It must also be emphasized that the core-periphery gap is always greater than those that can be found at the center in period of maximum differentiation. In such periods existing data from 1870 on indicate that the gap between the hegemonic power and the poorest country of the core does not exceed 60% in terms of per capita income—the only exceptions being Italy in the 1950s and possibly Japan as can be seen in Tables 2.1 and 2.2. In terms of productivity per man-hour, the gap is a little wider, but it never goes beyond the 70% mark, the only exception being for obvious reasons, Germany in the early 1950s, as can be seen in Tables 2.3 and 2.4.

(text continued p. 75)

TABLE 2.1 Output per Capita (calculated at 1955 U.S. relative prices as a proportion of the United Kingdom)

	U.K.	U.S.A.	Canada	Norway	Sweden	Denmark	Netherlands	Switzerland	Belgium	Germany*	France	Italy
1870	100	98	98	77	56	70	–	–	94	81	99	77
1880	100	–	107	–	65	79	–	–	–	91	106	76
1890	100	103	87	–	53	69	–	72	–	78	91	52
1900	100	110	90	63	61	75	88	–	–	82	97	49
1910	100	133	113	71	78	90	90	–	–	98	–	56
1913	100	138	117	72	84	97	91	81	110	93	102	59

*1950 and after: Federal Republic of Germany.
SOURCE: Calculated from Table A.1 (see Appendix).

TABLE 2.2 Output per Capita (calculated at 1955 U.S. relative prices as a proportion of the United States)

Year	U.S.A.	U.K.	Canada	Norway	Sweden	Denmark	Netherlands	Switzerland	Belgium	Germany*	France	Italy
1870	100	102	100	78	58	72	–	–	96	83	101	78
1890	100	97	85	–	51	67	–	70	–	76	89	51
1900	100	91	82	57	55	68	80	–	–	75	88	44
1910	100	75	85	53	58	67	68	–	–	73	–	42
1913	100	72	85	52	61	70	66	59	80	67	74	43
1920	100	75	76	61	49[1]	64[2]	69	60[3]	–	51[4]	60	44
1929	100	68	75	58	53	64	70	69	76	53	77	41
1930	100	75	79	69	62	74	76	75	83	57	84	43
1938	100	86	71	77	70	75	67	73	75	75	68	47
1950	100	63	76	56	60	60	48	54	57	43	53	30
1955	100	63	76	60	59	54	49	59	58	55	56	34
1960	100	67	74	64	67	65	59	67	61	69	64	43

*1950 and after: Federal Republic of Germany.
1. 1923
2. 1921
3. 1924
4. 1925
SOURCE: Table A.1 (See Appendix).

TABLE 2.3 Output per Man-Hour (calculated at 1955 U.S. relative prices as a proportion of the United Kingdom)

Year	U.K.	U.S.A.	Canada	Norway	Sweden	Denmark	Netherlands	Switzerland	Belgium	Germany*	France	Italy
1870	100	115	114	74	58	66	–	–	98	79	82	75
1880	100	–	131	–	66	75	–	–	–	91	88	74
1890	100	120	103	–	57	69	–	66	–	80	78	52
1900	100	131	110	67	68	77	102	–	–	86	85	52
1913	100	161	144	81	95	102	110	78	122	98	93	66

*1950 and after: Federal Republic of Germany.
SOURCE: Table A.2 (see Appendix).

TABLE 2.4 Output per Man-Hour (calculated at 1955 U.S. relative prices as a proportion of the United States)

Year	U.S.A.	U.K.	Canada	Norway	Sweden	Denmark	Netherlands	Switzerland	Belgium	Germany*	France	Italy
1870	100	86	99	64	51	58	–	–	85	69	72	62
1890	100	84	87	–	48	57	–	55	–	67	65	44
1900	100	76	84	51	52	59	78	–	–	65	65	40
1913	100	62	89	50	59	64	68	48	76	61	58	41
1929	100	56	70	52	44	54	70	52	67	44	57	38
1938	100	50	52	47	43	42	48	42	52	40	50	38
1950	100	49	81	50	50	46	43	40	53	25	43	34
1955	100	46	84	52	51	42	46	44	52	42	46	36
1960	100	47	82	58	56	48	49	40	54	50	50	40
1970	100	53	90	–	78	66	68	–	70	64	65	57
1977	100	51	95	–	84	86	89	–	100	80	78	71

*1950 and after: Federal Republic of Germany.
SOURCE: Table A.2 (see Appendix).

Let us return to the dynamic of disparities at the center. Parker's hypothesis (meant for the core) involves three sets of factors: technological change, demand, and factors of production. According to Parker, demand is the independent variable, technological change is the dependent variable, and factors of production are a function of technological changes to which they are supposed to adjust eventually. In our opinion, Parker is right as regards the nonhegemonic center. What happens in the case of the future hegemonic power, however, is an exception to the rule. Here the relationship between the three phenomena is not as postulated by Parker. Major innovations in the methods of production are a response to two interacting phenomena: a particularly favorable demand, *and* the current situation of factors of production (scarcity and high cost of labor). On the other hand, in the nonhegemonic entities, the state and structure of demand and the current situation of the factors of production is not the same as those surrounding the emergence of the major innovations occurring in the confines of the future hegemonic power. These entities are confronted with new methods of production that are not suited to their structure or level of demand or the prevalent situation of their factors of production. Nonhegemonic core countries (and countries aspiring to this status) may react to such a situation in many ways. One way, more inward-looking, consists in adopting innovations to the current situation of the factors of production, possibly by means of intermediary technology, while protecting with tariffs the somewhat uncompetitive new sectors from the competition of foreign products. This seemingly has been the traditional path of France throughout history. Another way, more outward-looking, is to adopt the new methods of production as they are and capitalize on cheaper labor so as to compete effectively on the world market with the product of the hegemonic power. This strategy has been adopted possibly by England at the end of the seventeenth century and most certainly by Germany at the end of the nineteenth century and Japan after the Second World War. Finally, nonhegemonic entities can defer the adoption of innovation until proper conditions of demand and of the factors of production prevail. This was probably the case of the whole of Western Europe between the two wars. Thus there are a variety of strategies for bridging the gaps with the current hegemonic power, but what triggers the emulation process itself remains obscure. All we know for sure is that there is a limit, a threshold, to the decline of the nonhegemonic center.

Could conjuncture be the answer? A summary review of the facts show that this is not the case. The process of emulation was triggered in England at the end of the seventeenth century, that is, in a B-phase. More often though the phenomenon occurs in an A-phase. In core countries of Western Europe the process of emulation of hegemonic Great Britain began in an A-phase, that is, around 1850. It was equally in an A-phase between 1950 and the 1970s that Western Europe and Japan gradually bridged the gap with the United States. Our general impression is that conjuncture, good or bad, is not responsible for triggering off the process of emulation, but that it speeds it up in an A-phase and slows it down in a B-phase. This was true at least for the period between 1870 and 1913 when the rest of the center was catching up with Britain. The bridging of the gap in terms of productivity and per capita income occurred not between 1870 and 1890, a B-phase (in some cases, the trend was even reversed) but between 1890 and 1913, an A-phase (see Tables 2.1 and 2.3). If we take the United States as a point of reference and look at the modalities of the differentiation process between 1870 and the Second World War, we see that the gap in per capita income (see Table 2.2) increased mainly between 1890 and 1929, a long A-phase. For some countries the gap widened mostly between 1890 and 1913, and for others between 1913 and 1929, but nonetheless always in a phase of prosperity. During the 1929-1938 depression, the trend toward differentiation slowed down and was even reversed in some cases. The curve of productivity per man-hour is the only one to behave differently than expected: the productivity gap between the United States and the rest of the center kept widening during the depression years. This reflects the fact that unemployment during the depression was much higher in United States (and Canada and the U.K.) than in Western Continental Europe. Another test to which the proposition that A-phases speed up and B-phases slow down the trend toward indifferentiation can be submitted is to look at the ways the gap was bridged between Western Europe and Japan on the one hand and the United States on the other, first in the A-phase between 1950 and circa 1970, and the B-phase from 1970 on. For the time being, unfortunately, comparison can only be made in terms of productivity per man-hour for want of data on the evolution of per capita income after the 1950s. Throughout the 1950-1977 period, the rates of productivity increase were higher in the rest of the center (excluding socialist countries) than in the United States. In the 1950s, the rate of differentiation of the nonhegemonic center in relation to the United States was slow. While the average (unweighted) annual growth of productivity was 3.43% for the whole of the nonhegemonic center, it was 2.4% for the United States, the difference being a mere 1%. In the 1960s, growth of productivity sped up both for the nonhegemonic center, where it became 6.8% as a yearly average, and the United States, where it stood at 3.4% a year on the average. The difference between the two regions of the center is then a full 3.4% a year. In the 1970s, rates of productivity increases were lower than those of the 1960s everywhere at the center except in Belgium. In the nonhegemonic center, the average (unweighted) rate of productivity growth was 4.9%, while in the United States it was only 2.3%. Thus the differential rate of growth between the United States and the rest of the nonhegenomic center was 2.6% lower per year than during the 1960s when it stood at 3.4% per year on the average. This confirms our impression that periods of growth accelerate the trend toward differentiation, and that B-phases slow it down.

Just as the trend toward differentiation ends up in situation of production supremacy, the trend toward indifferentiation leads to a situation of competition. At first sight there seems to be a link between a B-phase and the return to competition. In the seventeenth century, for instance, it was in a B-phase that the Navigation Acts were promulgated and that France adopted protectionist policies and forbade other core powers, especially Holland, to trade directly with her West Indian colonies. It was also in a B-phase, between 1873 and 1896, that the nonhegemonic center (Europe and the United States) fell back into protectionism and that European powers engaged in a struggle over Africa. Finally, in the recession years since 1970 core powers are reverting to protectionism albeit in an disguised fashion (like government subsidies for production and exports).[2] It is indeed true that the protectionist reflex is triggered off by a B-phase, but protectionism must not be mistaken for competition. Protectionism occurs each time the center goes through a phase of recession in situations of hegemony as well as in situation of competition. In fact, the center only loosens its protectionism in the course of an A-phase occurring in a situation of hegemony. Nonetheless one has to recognize that the protectionist reaction takes somewhat different modalities if it happens in an hegemonic situation or in a situation of competition. In a situation of hegemony, protectionism will be more defensive than offensive. It will limit itself exclusively to the enhancement of production processes unfolding within the confines of the national economic area, and will not involve the periphery which in any case has been practically abandoned to the hegemonic power. In a situation of competition, on the other hand, the protectionist reaction will be more aggressive, will involve political expansion at the periophery or tighter competition for its surplus-value, and will often end up in armed conflicts. (Thus far, the return to the situation of competition in the 1970s has not produced such dramatic and open confrontation between core powers but signs of a faltering American leadership within the world-economy are obvious.) In brief, an unfavorable conjuncture will always bring about a protectionist reaction. A B-phase triggers a return to clear-cut political competition only in the course of the trend toward indifferentiation. The arbitrary fashion with which protectionism occurs along a trend toward indifferentiation must also be noted. Protectionism does not happen at any given phase of some kind of national development process but occurs whenever there is a bad conjuncture. For instance the Navigation Acts and Colbertist protectionist policies occurred in England and France respectively before they started to emulate Holland—and in recession years in the latter half of the seventeenth century. The protectionist reaction in Europe and the United States toward Britain occurred at the end of the nineteenth century, i.e., more or less in the middle of an emulation process which started toward 1850 and lasted until 1913 approximately—and during a B-phase (1873-1896). Finally, the disguised protectionism we observe during the recession years of the 1970s comes in the course of a twenty-year trend toward indifferentiation. A last qualification should be added to the term competition. A protectionist reaction in the course of the return of the center toward relative equality between the core powers in terms of productivity and demand within national economic areas is to be sure a political form of economic competition. Nonetheless, in the cases where the emulation process originated before the protectionist reaction as in the case of Western Continental Europe in the last half of the nineteenth century, and Western Europe and Japan since the 1950s it is possible that economic competition on the world market between the products of core powers happens *before* the protectionist reaction. Such has been the case at the end of the 1960s, that is, before a subsequent return to protectionism when some Japanese and Western European products started to compete with those of the United States.

What we have suggested in these pages is that the changes of global politico-economic configuration at the center take place at the end of two lasting trends, differentiation and indifferentiation in terms of the production apparatuses located within the center's national economic areas. The alternation of these two trends is peculiar to the history of development at the center. The change of politico-economic configuration at the center is not a direct effect of the conjuncture but results rather from two trends both affected, in the same way, by conjuncture—acceleration in an A-phase and deceleration in a B-phase. What had to be explained in the last instance was not so much the overall politico-economic changes of configuration as the very trend which results in them. We saw that the trend toward differentiation is the result of a systematic bias leading, while the process of diversification of products and processes is unfolding in the entire center, to the adoption on the part of one particular political entity participating in the process, of methods of production characterized by their economy of labor. The effects of this bias manifest themselves first by the adoption in every sector of economic activity of the most efficient methods of production, in other words of the best practice within known technology. Once the best practice prevails within the national economic area of the future hegemonic power, any further growth threatens to increase the cost of manpower and thus causes a crisis of capitalist accumulation. Thereupon, drastic transformations of the methods of production take place in one or a few sectors. Thanks to these major innovations, the entity wherein they occur first finds itself in a position of production supremacy within the world-economy, and eventually obtains other dimensions characteristic of authentic hegemony, namely, commercial and financial supremacy, and political leadership coupled with military supremacy. The application within the hegemonic power of the new innovations in various sectors, as well as the stimulating effect on all other sectors of the rapid growth of advanced sectors will contribute to push farther the pendulum of differentiation at the center. The gaps between the hegemonic entity and the nonhegemonic center will consist in technological sophistication and disparities in terms of per capita income (demand) and productivity per man-hour. Two sets of factors will contribute to the final reversal of the trend toward differentiation, those which concern the hegemonic power and those concerning the nonhegemonic center. We suggested that it is the success of the advanced sectors of the hegemonic power within the world-economy which alters the process of innovation, turning it away from major changes in the methods of production, and toward the mere improvement of existing methods of production and the diversification of products and processes. An unfavorable conjuncture will eventually slow down the process of minor innovations altogether. Unfortunately, we have not succeeded in finding a similar mechanism which would explain the beginning of the process of emulation by nonhegemonic core countries. All we could observe is the presence of a threshold, of a limit to the decline of the nonhegemonic center in terms of per capita income (demand) and productivity. We noted also that as the trend toward differentiation ends up in an hegemonic situation, the tendency toward indifferentiation brings the center back into a situation of economic competition, which may sometimes coincide with the return of protectionism. The protectionist reaction itself is strictly conjunctural and does not happen at any specific stage of the trend toward indifferentiation.

Let us come back at last to our original question, i.e., whether politico-economic changes of configuration at the center are cyclical. In a nutshell: these changes are not cyclical in themselves, nor are they the direct result of economic fluctuations. Rather, they are the end result of two trends which are affected by conjuncture but are in reality structural effects. The tendency toward differentiation results from the presence in one particular core entity of a bias toward the adoption of capital-intensive methods of production. And the tendency toward indifferentiation is the result of, on the one hand, a mechanism inherent to the hegemonic situation (overspecialization) and on the other, of the presence of a threshold acting as a limit to the decline of the nonhegemonic center and as a triggering point of the process of emulation.

The fact that the core of the world-economy is made up of *various* political entities is a fundamental aspect of the changes of politico-economic configuration at the center. It is obvious that without the geo-political division of the center there would be no competition and no hegemony. But more is involved here: the very dynamic of the phenemonon rests upon the division of the core into "national economic areas" since in the short term, the existence of national barriers prevents both the homogenization of the situation of the factors of production and the leveling of demand throughout the center. Indeed, these barriers prevent the full mobility of factors of production, mostly labor, and allow the appearance and persistence of shortages of manpower in certain areas of the center. Similarly, on account of the geo-political division of the center, new demands in a particular part of the core cannot be quickly spread over the whole, so that a more intense pressure can be exercised on a single production apparatus. Labor scarcity and demand pressure on a given production apparatus favors a "technological response" to a local problem, i.e., a radical transformation of methods of production. The heterogeneity of national economic areas is responsible for the fact that the process of development unfolding over the entire center produces locally (i.e., nationally) different results. This is not to say that each core country is an "economy" endowed with a dynamic of development of its own. It means rather that the unfolding of a centerwide process in the idiosyncracy of national economic areas is responsible for the uneven development that can be observed at certain times in the history of the core. And may we add, on a more speculative note, that without the division of the center into national economic areas, the process of development of methods of production since the sixteenth century might have been slower. On the other hand, without a centerwide process of diversification of products and processes, there would have been no need for drastic changes in the methods of production.

APPENDIX

TABLE 2.5 Output Per Capita (calculated at 1955 U.S. relative prices in thousand dollars, selected years between 1870 and 1960)

Year	U.S.A.	U.K.	Canada	Norway	Sweden	Denmark	Netherlands	Switzerland	Belgium	Germany*	France	Italy
1870	.4510	.4604	.4529	.3535	.2595	.3232	–	–	.4316	.3727	.4574	.3525
1880	–	.4787	.5136	–	.3109	.3786	–	–	–	.4376	.5067	.3639
1890	.6995	.6795	.5918	–	.3583	.4652	–	.4867	–	.5302	.6203	.3533
1900	.8443	.7671	.6927	.4818	.4667	.5731	.6745	–	–	.6296	.7458	.3717
1910	1.025	.7682	.8712	.5458	.5964	.6897	.6932	–	–	.7504	–	.4335
1913	1.129	.8158	.9538	.588	.6821	.7933	.7403	.6632	.8987	.7610	.8300	.4848
					1923	1921		1924		1925		
1920	1.144	.8579	.8692	.6923	.62	.7	.7912	.7692	–	.6557	.6891	.5058
1929	1.4282	.9654	1.0760	.8214	.7689	.9114	.9936	.9725	1.0914	.7524	1.0956	.5843
1930	1.2873	.9669	1.0123	.8821	.7951	.9514	.9810	.9675	1.069	.7394	1.0767	.5485
1938	1.3358	1.1501	.9530	1.0726	.9380	1.0050	.8989	.9762	1.0048	1.0053	.9036	.6298
1950	2.0547	1.2990	1.5526	1.15	1.2286	1.2238	.9852	1.1	1.1609	.8749	1.0816	.6095
1955	2.3228	1.4719	1.7541	1.3706	1.3780	1.2477	1.1259	1.36	1.3348	1.2868	1.2974	.7886
1960	2.3839	1.6028	1.7528	1.5278	1.5867	1.5435	1.4	1.6038	1.4565	1.6342	1.5189	1.0239

* Federal Republic of Germany.
SOURCES: A. Maddison, *Economic Growth in the West, Comparative Experience in Europe and North America* (New York, 1964). Maddison reports in Table I-8, p. 40, the comparative levels of output in 1960 at 1955 prices in U.S. dollars for the countries, here-above mentioned. We have regressed the data up to 1870 with the help of Table A-2, p. 201, movement in total volume of output (1913 = 100) and divided the results by those of the translated index of population of Table B-1 into absolute numbers.

TABLE 2.6 Output per Man-Hour (calculated at 1955 U.S. relative price [U.S. = 100], selected years between 1870 and 1977)

Years	U.S.A.	U.K.	Canada	Norway	Sweden	Denmark	Netherlands	Switzerland	Belgium	Germany*	France	Italy
1870	12.23	10.65	12.16	7.854	6.22	7.04	–	–	10.42	8.45	8.76	7.98
1880	–	11.59	15.12	–	7.62	8.72	–	–	–	10.57	10.20	8.52
1890	20.07	16.80	17.38	–	9.55	11.51	–	11.06	–	13.41	13.02	8.77
1900	24.86	18.98	20.78	12.64	12.85	14.66	19.43	–	–	16.22	16.16	9.86
1913	32.80	20.36	29.31	16.5	19.3	20.82	22.36	15.78	24.76	19.98	18.92	13.44
1929	51.00	28.57	35.62	26.47	22.33	27.59	35.59	26.24	33.92	22.62	29.25	19.31
1938	68.49	34.18	35.52	32.142	29.16	28.54	32.51	28.89	35.72	27.39	33.77	25.68
1950	79.11	38.66	63.78	39.44	39.58	36.08	33.94	31.86	42.04	20.05	34.09	26.88
1955	90.62	41.9	76.1	47.	46.6	38.	41.5	39.6	47.4	37.6	41.8	32.78
1960	100.	47.	82.	58.	56.	48.	49.	48.	54.	50.	50.	40.
1970	139.7	72.67	126.14	–	108.87	91.79	94.61	–	97.62	88.65	90.4	80.18
1977	163.5	84.05	154.70	–	136.6	139.84	145.9	–	164.08	130.68	127.31	115.68

*1950 and after: Federal Republic of Germany.

SOURCES: A Maddison, *Economic Growth in the West, Comparative Experience in Europe and North America* (New York, 1964). Maddison reports in Table I-8, p. 40 the comparative output per man-hour in U.S. relative prices of 1955, for the year 1960. We assigned the absolute percentage to the 1960 figure of the index of output per man, Table H-1, 1870–1960. For the years 1970 and 1977 we have calculated from 1960 on the levels of productivity reached in 1970 and 1977 with the known annual rates of increase of productivity between 1960–1969 and 1970–1977 from the Bureau of Labor Statistics reported by *Newsweek Magazine*, p. 61, June 4, 1979.

NOTES

1. We prefer the term "national economic area" to that of "national economy" for the latter has been associated with the idea that each country is endowed with its own dynamic of development. Our premise is that "national economic areas" are idiosyncratic in terms of the situation of the factors of production, the organization of production, and so on, but that the dynamic of development is located at the level of the center if not of the world-economy.

2. In an article entitled "La fausse querelle du protectionism," in the August 4, 1979, *Le Monde Diplomatique*, Alain Weil wonders if: "In a context of acute international competition, is not any national policy intended to reinforce the national economy in fact protectionist? Protectionism in the narrow sense is merely the most directly perceptible segment of the larger policy."

REFERENCES

Business Week (1979) "To revive research and development." September 17.
COLEMAN, D. C. (1977) The Economy of England 1450-1750. Oxford: Oxford University Press.
CROUZET, F. (1967) "England and France in the eighteenth century: a comparative analysis of two economic growths," in E. M. Hartwell (ed.) The Causes of the Industrial Revolution in England. London: Methuen.
――― (1978) L'Economie de la Grande-Bretagne Victorienne. Paris.
de VRIES, J. (1976) The Economy of Europe in an Age of Crisis, 1600-1750. Cambridge: Cambridge University Press.
FREEMAN, C. (1974) The Economics of Industrial Innovation. Harmondsworth: Penguin.
GOULD, J. D. (1972) Economic Growth in History: Survey and Analysis. London: Methuen.
HABAKKUK, H. J. (1968) "The historical experience on the basic conditions of economic progress," in M. E. Falkus (ed.) Readings in the History of Economic Growth. London: Oxford University Press.
LANDES, D. S. (1969) The Unbound Prometheus: Technological Change and Industrial Development in Western Europe from 1750 to the Present. Cambridge: Cambridge University Press.
MATHIAS, P. (n.d.) "British industrialisation: unique or not?" L'Industrialisation en Europe au XIXe siècle. Colloques Internaux de C.N.R.S. 540.
McCLOSKEY, D. N. (1970) "Did Victorial Britain fail?" Economic History Review XXIII (December).
MILWARD, A. S. and S. B. SAUL (1973) The Economic Development of Continental Europe 1780-1870. Totowa, NJ: Rowman & Littlefield.
Newsweek (1974) "Innovation: has America lost its edge?" June 4.
NORTH, D. C. and R. P. THOMAS (1973) The Rise of the Western World: A New Economic History. Cambridge, England: Cambridge University Press.
PARKER, W. N. (1972) "Technology, resources, and economic change in the West," in A. J. Youngson (ed.) Economic Development in the Long Run. London: Allen & Unwin.
SAUL, S. B. (1972) "The nature and diffusion of technology," in A. J. Youngson (ed.) Economic Development in the Long Run. London: Allen & Unwin.
WALLERSTEIN, I. (1980) The Modern World-System: II. Mercantilism and the Consolidation of the European World-Economy, 1600-1750. New York: Academic Press.

Chapter 3

LONG WAVES AND THE COTTON-SPINNING ENTERPRISE, 1789-1849

Kenneth Barr

INTRODUCTION

I offer two propositions. On the one hand, long waves constitute a fundamental momement of global capitalist development. The rhythmic pattern of that movement is characterized by alternating periods of expansive growth and then of forced growth totaling roughly fifty to sixty years in duration. This proposition is assumed for the purposes of this paper, and thus serves as a premise.[1] On the other hand, the capitalist enterprise, which is the primary unit of social action within the capitalist world-economy, operates and is continually restructured in conjunction with the rhythmic pattern of long waves. What follows is but a contribution to the latter of these propositions. I have selected one long wave, dating from 1789 to 1849. The focus is enterprises engaged in the manufacture of cotton goods, though I am especially interested in those producing yarn. And the specific geographical region under consideration is south-east Lancashire and adjoining areas, England.

The format of the paper is straightforward. First a working model appropriate to the study of the capitalist enterprise functioning in conjunction with long waves is sketched. Then the historicity of the 1789-1849 long wave in terms of the profitability and organization of cotton textile production is outlined. And finally a case study of how one cotton-spinning enterprise fared over the course of the long wave is summarized.

THEORETICAL FRAMEWORK

The point of departure is a model of the capitalist enterprise,[2] hereafter referred to as the *enterprise*. The model is abstracted from a comparative

FIGURE 3.1 Phases of Business Activity Within the Capitalist Enterprise

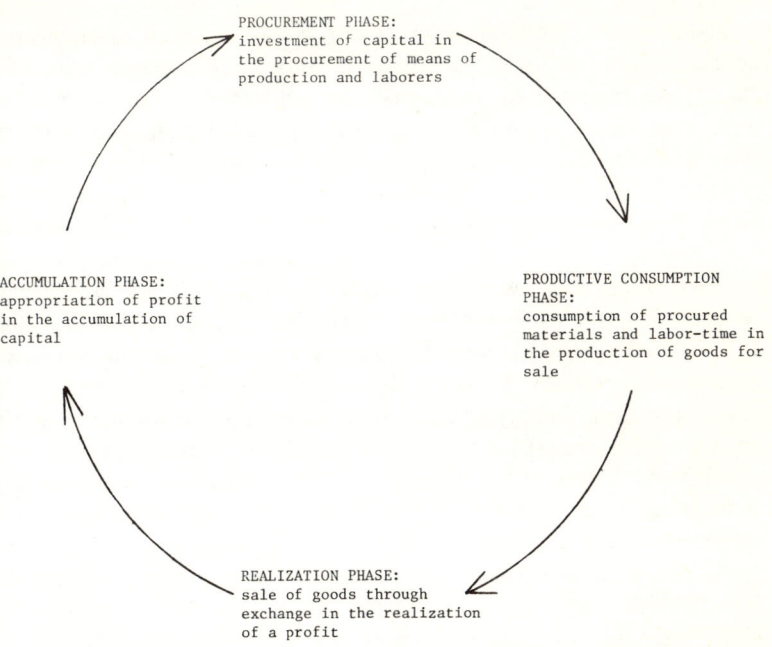

study of different kinds of enterprise over the history of the capitalist world-economy. As a construct, the enterprise is conceived as a profit-seeking commodity-producing, capital-accumulating business entity. If you like, it is a unit of capital—which means, therefore, that the capital-labor relation is reproduced within the confines of the enterprise.

The enterprise integrates four sets of activities, designated as phases within the model. These are the procurement, productive consumption, realization, and accumulation phases. The concept *business activity* refers to the complex of activities pertaining to these four phases. Figure 3.1 schematically illustrates the sequential nature of the phases within the model.

In the *procurement* phase, money-capital is invested in the acquisition of means of production (raw materials, tools and machinery, energy, etc.) and laborers. A prerequisite is, given the need, the existence of readily expandable markets for capital, commodities, land, and labor. The procurement phase draws the enterprise into contact with other institutions such as banks furnishing capital, enterprises or commercial concerns supplying raw materials or even possibly labor, and so on. Remuneration for labor services, if at all provided, need not necessarily be in the form of wages. Laborers, which may or may not possess their own means of production, need only be procured and accordingly made available for exploitation by capitalists.

In the *productive consumption* phase, laborers expend human energy on the transformation of raw materials into products which are subsequently appropriated by capitalists. The productive consumption phase requires at least one production process (e.g., the manufacture of yarn), wherein there is at least one though probably a series of labor processes (e.g., cleaning, carding, roving, spinning, etc., within the manufacture of yarn). The various labor processes within the production process are conjoined by an internal circulation of materials (e.g., between the converted dwelling house where the cotton is cleaned and the carding mill; between the carding mill and the spinning mill; between the spinning room and the sorting room within the spinning mill; etc.). An administrative apparatus coordinates the labor processes without, however, necessarily controlling them directly (e.g., weaving by cottage out-workers within a putting-out enterprise).

In the *realization* phase, material products are marketed and thus sold through exchange. This realizes the products as commodities, and hence potentially realizes a profit. The exchange process may of course be mediated by commercial concerns, such as brokerage houses or commission agencies, and bolstered by credit. The purchased commodities may either enter the procurement phase of another enterprise or, as consumption goods, enter directly into the reproduction cycle of given households. Transportation, as the physical movement of goods, is not of the realization phase, even though it facilitates exchange. It is instead of the productive consumption phase, and may itself constitute the sole production process of a single enterprise.

And finally, in the *accumulation* phase, various forms of revenue (personal income, interest, ground-rent) are extracted in providing subsistence for the capitalist class. A portion of the realized profit is potentially accumulated into a capital fund, the calculation of which is determined by the principles and procedures of accounting. This capital may be subsequently invested in the procurement of means of production and laborers. Reinvestment fosters the maintenance and extension of the enterprise's business activities.

In light of the above formulation, the argument runs as follows. On the one hand, variation of business activity—in terms of both the magnitude and rate of change as well as the organization and structure of that activity—conform to the rhythmic pattern of long waves. The mechanisms of global capitalist development operate through the enterprise. As such, the enterprise's business activities reflect the movement of that development.

On the other hand, long waves of capitalist development (in reference to the world economy) and variation of business activity (in reference to the enterprise) do not adhere to a mere cause and effect logic. The enterprise while operating in its competitive milieu fosters its own existence vis-a-vis those institutional units of the world economy with which it interacts over its life span. As such, the individual enterprise influences long waves of capitalist development by affecting, however limited the specificity of its impact, the activities of various institutions. And it is the composite totality of those institutions which forms the basis of the developmental process.

The business activity of an enterprise is, then, both a *manifestation* and a *motor force* of long waves. The process of making profits, which presumes the exploitation of labor and posits the accumulation of capital, mediates this connection between the world economy, with its long waves of development, and the enterprise, with its variation of business activity. For the drive to make profits determines the character of the enterprise's interactions with other institutions, and simultaneously is conditioned by the enterprise's specific location within the world-economy.

HISTORICAL CONTEXT

I now want to turn to the historicity of the long wave from 1789 to 1849 in order to delineate the varying profitability and changing organization of cotton textile production. This will provide the historical context for the case study laid out in the next section. Three distinct periods of the long wave can be discerned: the *A-phase,* or period of expansive growth, 1789-1810; the *T-phase,* or period of transition, 1811-1817; and the *B-phase,* or the period of forced growth, 1818-1849. However, since the case study is of an English enterprise, only the patterns located specifically in England (namely, south-east Lancashire, but also adjacent regions of Cheshire) are to be explicated. These patterns are not, of course, generalizable to the level of the world-economy.

A-PHASE

The period from 1789 to 1810 was generally one of expansion in a sea of wars, blockades, and embargoes. Years of prosperity stood out relative to those of crisis and depression. The overall economic climate was in the main conducive to brisk business activity. Credit extended. Investment stabilized. Prices inflated. Labor worked. Management relaxed. And markets widened.

Concerning the cotton textile industry, empirical evidence supports the thesis that enterprises engaged in the manufacture of cotton goods realized higher rates of profit over the course of the A-phase than they did during the subsequent T- and B-phases. Mechanization greatly reduced the cost of labor per unit of output (Hobsbawm, 1962: 59). The cost of raw materials very gradually declined, especially with the diffusion of Whitney's cotton-gin during the 1790s (Edwards, 1967: 253; Mitchell and Deane, 1972: 490). Wartime conditions generally inflated the prices of cotton goods, above all on the European Continent where exporters sold commodities at prices greater than what could be retrieved in the home markets (Lee, 1972: 142). And if Hamilton's (1942) thesis is correct, one can add that at least for the early part of the A-phase there was a surplus profit boost given the lag of wages behind that of sale prices (cf., Shapiro, 1967: 214-229).

It is also possible to chart a distinct path toward *specialization* in the manufacture and trade of cotton goods during the A-phase. The period immediately prior to this A-phase, a B-phase (1763-1789),[3] was a time of reconstitution and diversification of the cotton textile industry (Mantoux, 1961; Wadsworth and Mann, 1931). It was quite common for the capitalist to be at once investor, machine-maker, manager, merchant, salesman, and accountant. Gradually, from the 1790s, diversification was reversed. In the procurement of raw cotton, the chain of commodity exchange linking the cotton producers with the yarn manufacturers, and especially that between the importers and the yarn manufacturers, became increasingly dense. Merchant dealers, already widespread, grew in numbers as the industry expanded; but they also began to specialize in a smaller range of goods and markets (Edwards, 1967: 180-181). At the same time, brokers concerned primarily or wholly with cotton—both selling brokers, acting on behalf of the importers, and buying brokers, acting on behalf of either merchant dealers or yarn manufacturers—squeezed into the chain of commodity exchange (Dumbell, 1923; Edwards, 1967; Hyde et al., 1955; cf., however, Buck, 1925; Ellison, 1968). Whereas machine-making had been combined with spinning, it was slowly disassociated from the capitalist's functions (Edwards, 1967: 199-204). Independent weaving manufactories, "quite a few" with as many as fifty to one-hundred handlooms, cropped up as well (Bythell, 1969: 33). Yarn and cloth manufacturers engaged merchant dealers or agents, who either directly purchased the goods or undertook to sell them for an agreed rate of commission, thereby relieving the manufacturers from marketing activities. And the warehousing business also developed rapidly during this period (Chapman, 1972: 47-48).

T-PHASE

The time-span from say 1811, or even as early as the fall of 1810, through the winter of 1817 marks a transition from the A- to the B-phase. Initiated by the slump of 1811, the transition period was one of uneven, often stagnant growth—that is, of growth continually interrupted by glutted markets and overproduction, culminating in yet a second slump, that of 1816/1817. Although growth can be said to have continued throughout the transition period, there was, especially for the cotton textile industry, a contraction of profitable business activity. An immediate response on the part of capital was to cut back production; and, to be sure, idle capacity proved the norm. And on the part of labor, the reaction was an explosion of working class political action which was to condition the whole of the subsequent period: the Luddite movement (1811-1813), and, following an interval of riots and strikes, the Pentridge Rising (1817); and following Peterloo (1819), three decades of increasing radicalism and working-class organization (Thompson, 1966).

The T-phase is best conceptualized as a temporary break on industrialization, or more generally on capitalist development, in turn creating an impetus for the reorganization of business activity and forced industrialization. Major tendencies characteristic of the B-phase, in contradisdiction to those of the A-phase, have their roots in the T-phase. And by 1815 these were already in motion.

B-PHASE

The period from the 1816/1817 slump to roughly 1849, as opposed to that of 1789-1810, was marred by the periodicity of boom and collapse, culminating in the structural crisis of global capitalism beginning in the 1830s (roughly 1836-1849). The overall economic climate was at best conducive to risky business activity. Credit contracted. Investment destabilized. Competition magnified. Prices deflated. Bankruptcies swelled. Unemployment multiplied. The working-class rebelled. And the ruling-class attacked.

During the B-phase, profit margins entered a sharp and persistent decline.[4] This was, if you will, "impelled onward" by the continual fall of sale prices due to growing competition. One estimate puts it that for a typical count of yarn the sum left for expenses, wages, and profits—being the yarn price less the cotton price—fell 72% betwen 1815 and 1832 (Collier, 1965: 5). So too was the case with cloth. This led Edward Baines (1966), foremost nineteenth-century historian of the cotton textile industry, to state in 1835 that, given the nearly 75% decline in the price of one piece of warp between 1814 and 1833, "it is certain that in every branch of the trade profits of the capitalists have been greatly reduced within the last twenty years" (p. 356). Furthermore, studies of company records reveal that heavy losses were absorbed by enterprises during the latter years of the B-phase (Boyson, 1970: 27-33; Lee, 1972: 138-143; Foster, 1974: 83, 296). The cutting of wages and the procuring of cheaper labor were an immediate response by capitalists to contracted profit margins. And indeed wages did tend to fall and attempts were made to replace the relatively well-paid skilled mule-spinners with the self-acting mule. Wage cuts and mechanization were of course limited by the ability of laborers to force stoppage of production. At the same time, wages, already at a minimal level (Collier, 1965), could only be retrenched so far, and the self-acting mule was not necessarily seen as economical. Thus, on the one hand, capitalists directed their energies against working-class living standards. But the repeal of the Corn Laws, which aimed at decreasing the price of food and, ipso facto, the price of labor, did not come until 1846. And, on the other hand, since the cost-price of power machinery did not noticeably shrink until the 1850s, there was a speed-up in the flow of production (Von Tunzelmann, 1978: ch. 7). By the early 1850s, however, with a depoliticized working-class movement and, along with diminished costs, a stabilized profit rate, the situation changed (Foster, 1974: esp. ch. 7). A new, expansive period of capitalist development was initiated.[5]

A trend toward *integration* and *consolidation* of business activities, certainly begun by 1815, can also be observed (Rodgers, 1960; Smith, 1953; Taylor, 1949). The integration tendency was vertical, through the combination of two mechanized production processes—yarn and cloth manufacture. Concomitant with integration was the concentration of capital. According to estimates, fixed capital invested in the cotton textile industry rose steadily over the duration of the B-phase (Blaug, 1961). Much of this capital was employed in expanding and rebuilding or adding new factories, more so than in merely multiplying the numbers of new enterprises (Chapman, 1972: 32-33). The point of entry therefore grew substantially over what it had been in the 1790s, when little fixed capital investment was required to initiate a business endeavor. This must surely have created the conditions for the "relative" reduction in the number of small-scale enterprises (cf., however, Chapman, 1979; and Gatrell, 1977). On the marketing end, some of the larger more established enterprises attempted to consolidate their markets, in an oligopolistic fashion, by arranging minimum prices in key markets, by decreasing the number of agents employed in each market, and hence by creating a "more uniform selling policy" (Edwards, 1967: 236). Furthermore, in Manchester, some enterprises extended the scope of their marketing activities by conducting warehousing and merchanting of goods at the same location (Smith, 1953).

In sum, then, specialization and inflated profit margins were associated with the A-phase (1789-1810), designated as a period of expansive growth of the capitalist world-economy. By the slump of 1811, however, radically uneven prosperity dampened the expansive tendency, and as a result the disruptive situation during the T-phase (1811-1817) set forth the conditions for a reorganization of the cotton textile industry. Integration and concentration of business activities, along with contracted profit margins, which further propelled the integration/consolidation movement, were characteristic of the B-phase (1818-1849), a period of forced growth of the world-economy.

CASE STUDY

I can now move on to the case study, which, it seems, fits well with its historical context spelled out above. The case selected for examination is the McConnel & Kennedy fine cotton spinning enterprise (hereafter referred to as M&K), based in Manchester, England.[6] Information is of sufficient quality and quantity to reconstruct with reasonable clarity M&K's history over the course of the long wave from 1789 to 1849.[7] The aim here is to articulate the manner in which this enterprise's business activities aligned with the general rhythmic pattern of the long wave. The model of the capitalist enterprise—with its procurement, productive consumption, realization, and accumulation phases—is herein implicitely utilized as a tool in organizing the case study.

A-PHASE

The A-phase was, for M&K, a period of rapid growth and expansion coupled with increasing specialization in its activities. The enterprise was begun in 1795 by James McConnel and John Kennedy, both Scots originally apprenticed as machine-makers, with an initial capital investment of £1,770. At first premises were rented. But soon after the business commenced, there was sustained investment in land, mill construction, and steam engines. By 1806 there appears to have been two factories, one of which was a magnificent seven story fireproof building (Tann, 1970: 19), along with five converted dwelling houses wherein various labor processes were situated. Gas lighting was installed in 1809. After 1806 no further building was undertaken until 1818-1820, and after that not again until the 1860s. By the end of the A-phase, 1810, the capital stock was valued at £88,375 (a nearly fifty-fold increase over the initial capital investment in 1795); and 269 mule jennies were in operation (Lee, 1972: 162, 167; McConnel & Co., 1906: 8-13).

During this period of massive investment there seems to have been no difficulty in recruiting labor. Free wage-laborers were seen as most desirable. This freed McConnel and Kennedy from having to house, clothe, and feed indentured apprentices, a practice quite common among the rural manufacturers. In 1802, 312 workers were employed; and by 1816, the next date for which data are available, there were over 1000 workers, with 41% under the age of 16 (Lee, 1972: 114). In procuring raw cotton, the costly long-stapled Sea Island variety was preferred. Grown along the South Carolinian and Georgian coasts, this cotton is particularly suited to the manufacture of fine yarns. The cotton was acquired in small quantities from Manchester merchant dealers through public auction or private deal during the enterprise's early years of existence. By the 1800s, however, cotton was primarily procured in large quantities via private deal through Liverpool buying brokers.

In the manufacture of goods for sale, there was initially combined within M&K two production processes—yarn manufacture and machine-making. M&K quickly came to specialize in yarn manufacture, and specifically in the finer counts of yarn. Rarely were counts under 80 produced, and orders for counts in the upper 200s were common. The average was around 170. In contrast, the average count produced in England at that time was no more than 40, a relatively coarse yarn (Lee, 1968: 90). Machine-making was relegated to the enterprise's own productive uses, and thus, by 1800 or so, no longer for sale.

In order to increase the volume of output in spinning, and simultaneously to lower the cost of labor per unit of output, technical advancements in productivity were a continual process. Between 1800 and 1810 alone there was a nearly 40% augmentation in spindleage per mule jenny (Lee, 1972: 162). As for exploitation of labor, James McConnel himself put it aptly when he said that "without the employment of children, spinning would be unprofitable" (quoted in Smith, 1953: 57). Laborers worked 74.5 hours per week, with Sundays off. It has also been claimed that M&K introduced into Manchester the practice of replacing adult male spinners with women, who operated the smaller mules and received only half the wages of the male spinners (see Collier, 1965: 17).

The primary yarn market for M&K was Scotland, where the textile industry, centered in the Clyde Valley, was oriented toward the export (or reexport) of yarn and piece goods, principally to Europe and in spite of wartime conditions. A number of agents were employed in Scotland by M&K. They received 5% commission with the risk for payment of all debts. Six months credit was allowed, whereby a bill was drawn on a London discount house which matured in three months and was paid three months after delivery. Because of the incentive of large-scale selling at inflated prices, the European export market, although risky given the possibility of consfication of goods, became an important outlet as well. Sales were made either with domestic exporters or through foreign agents (usually German or Swiss). Northern Ireland, namely Belfast and the Lagan Valley, was another market. But the immediate hinterland—Lancashire and adjacent regions—was insignificant. Throughout the A-phase markets continued to expand for the yarns produced by M&K.

The result of, and indeed the stimulus for the growth and expansion of the enterprise during the A-phase was the ability to realize profits. Data on profits are, however, rather patchy. The data that exist cover the years

1798-1810, after which there are no relatively comparable figures until the 1830s. The peak for profits during the A-phase was the year 1804, calculated at £18,773, or 30.1% of the total capital in the enterprise. After 1804, the profit rate dropped and then stabilized; only once, with the 1809 crisis, did profits fall below a 10% annual return on capital investment (Lee, 1972: 167; see also Shapiro, 1967: 252). Compared with other enterprises, whether from the textile industry or from the metal or brewing industries, M&K's growth rate was quite high (Crouzet, 1972: 198-199). The capital for reinvestment and expansion was due to the practice of plowing back profits into the enterprise. Revenues extracted from realized profits were minimal, with the personal incomes absorbed by McConnel and Kennedy's respective households being the only revenue of any significance.

T-PHASE

From the slump of 1811 through the slump of 1816-1817, business activity was continually disrupted, and times of relatively continuous prosperity thus altered. The initial stage of restructuration of M&K's business activities can also be observed during this period of transition.

The procurement of Sea Island cotton became difficult. This impelled M&K to enter into direct transactions with American brokers in Charleston. But this in turn was undermined by U.S.-imposed trade embargoes, which forced a considerable decline in cotton exports to England, with Sea Island registering no imports for 1813-1814 (Edwards, 1967: 252). M&K was therefore pushed into temporarily producing coarser yarns, for which cotton was available from Brazil and elsewhere.

Mills were often run on short time, and at one point were shut down due to contracted markets. Strikes also closed down the mills for short durations. Factory operatives thus were underemployed, if at all employed, and even then in the face of diminished wages. For male spinners, the decrease in average weekly earnings was from 40-45s in 1810 to 30-34s by the end of the T-phase (McConnel & Co., 1906: 51). Stretchers, reelers, and pickers also witnessed substantial wage curtailments. As it was, the payment of wages compelled McConnel and Kennedy to retrieve cash loans from their agents. And when mills were in operation, productivity levels, as indicated by average spindleage per mule jenny, interestingly remained the same throughout this period except for a slight less than 1% increment in the year 1815 (Lee, 1972: 162).

The death rate of firms swelled over the course of the T-phase. The correspondence of McConnel and Kennedy reveals that they constantly pressured their agents to turn all debts into cash to avoid potential losses. Credit terms were reduced, from six to four months, and commission rates were cut. In one instance, prior to the 1811 slump, in 1808, all agents in

Scotland save for one were dismissed, thus enabling M&K to concentrate its marketing activities for this particular market in the hands of one man (Daniels, 1915: 184). This practice was maintained throughout the transition period and subsequent B-phase.

To be sure, the T-phase was marked by decelerated capital accumulation due to contracted profits. However, M&K did not integrate weaving with spinning in order to retrieve or ward off potential losses, a trend that otherwise was to become common amongst cotton-spinning enterprises during the B-phase. John Kennedy doubted whether the labor costs saved by the introduction of power looms would offset the capital outlays on power machinery and the disadvantage of being required to run a complex of power looms at full capacity (cited in Wadsworth and Mann, 1931: 405). The decision was not based on the fact that there was lacking capital for investment. On the contrary, by 1817 there was if anything a surplus of capital; and besides what reinvestments took place, McConnel and Kennedy searched out the possibility of investment opportunities beyond the confines of their cotton-spinning enterprise (Lee, 1972: 108-112).

B-PHASE

The period of transition set the stage for M&K during the post-1817 B-phase: a time of adaptation and modification to new conditions of the world-economy; a period of concentration and consolidation of business activities. It was, without a doubt, a time of growth—but of increasingly difficult, or, if you will, of *forced* growth. There was initially sustained investment in the construction of a new factory, built between 1818 and 1820, and in corresponding additions of mule jennies. By 1826 these numbered 400, a substantial increase over the 269 mule jennies in 1820—which is the same as it was in 1810 when 100 new jennies were added (Lee, 1972: 102, 162).

In the procurement of cotton, a practice was established, initially tried during the 1811 slump, whereby cotton was purchased in bulk direct from Charleston and Savannah brokers. Such a practice was especially important since the overall demand for Sea Island cotton was continually rising while its supply remained constant, or even declined (Baines, 1966: 297-298, 302; Bruchey, 1967: 28). As for the procurement of labor, its supply seems to have been maintained. The labor force of M&K grew only slowly through this period, leveling off in the 1830s around 1,500 or so employees (Lee, 1972: 172-173).

In order to retain an adequate level of exploitation, McConnel and Kennedy were openly opposed to factory legislation that might have lessened their control over the labor processes. They were particularly antithetical to the Factory Bill of 1833, which proposed to limit the work week to 69 hours. Productivity was increased, but *only* gradually. What producitivity gains there were seem to have been at least partially offset by the increased expenditures on improvements necessary to reach the level of quality in technique enabling a boost in output (see H. Houldworth's testimony to the Committee on Factory employment in 1833, cited in Lee, 1972: 135). More important was the policy firmly established in the 1820s of sustaining a full level of capacity in an effort to sell large quantities of yarn at reduced prices. And if M&K fit the general pattern during this period, and it appears that it did, there was coupled with that an emphasis on intensifying the exploitation of labor (see Von Tunzelmann, 1978). That is to say, through increases in machine speeds laborers were induced to manufacture more products, and therefore potentially to create more in profit, per unit of labor time. This policy of forced output surely propelled the turnover of capital within the enterprise. Strikes, however, such as those in 1818, 1826, and 1844, often hindered the policy's implementation.

The most pronounced change in the structure of business activity during the B-phase was an alteration in markets. The Scottish and Irish markets, as well as the European export market, declined in relative importance beginning in the early 1820s. A shift in focus occurred, then, from the Clyde Valley, Scotland, to the Midlands, England, where the Nottinghamshire lace and hosiery industry attracted McConnel and Kennedy's attention. The enterprise began doubling yarn, and even began producing some lace thread, and sold either direct or via an agent to hosiers and lace manufacturers, thereby gradually consolidating its activities in this particular market. And M&K certainly attempted to monopolize the Nottinghamshire market as well (Lee, 1972: 80-86).

Given the nature of these various changes in the structure and organization of M&K's business activities, it would seem that the realization of profits after 1815 became increasingly difficult. And it appears that it did. Between 1815 and 1830 the sale price of one lb of 100 count yarn produced by M&K fell over 51%; but its cost price (composed here of the price of cotton, including waste, plus the cost of labor per lb of yarn) lessened only 36.5% between 1812 and 1830, which are the only dates for which data on cost price exist (see, for sale price, Ashton, 1948: 230; and for cost price, Baines, 1966: 253). Calculations made for the relatively prosperous years, 1834-1836, show an average profit of roughly 10% per annum on total capital (less liquid assets), which was much less than the calculations made for 1798-1810 (Lee, 1972: 139-140). And between 1837 and 1839, a period of acute worldwide depression, a loss of at least £33,712 was recorded (Lee, 1972: 140). After that, descriptive information, although sketchy, suggests that times were difficult until the 1850s. The extent to which the diminishing rate of profit was counterbalanced by the policy of forced output, which, by propelling the turnover of capital, might have augmented the mass of profits, remains an open question. In any case, there appears to have been a heavy burden on the rate of accumulation; but except for the 1837-1839 depression, the mass of profits accumulated as capital most likely attained a satisfactory level. After all M&K survived the B-phase, and indeed survived the whole of the nineteenth century.

M&K AND THE LONG WAVE

In sum, the most expansive period of growth for M&K was from its beginnings in 1795 through the boom of 1810, clearly within the bounds of the A-phase. The rate of profit, though peaking early in the century, was of a sufficient level to sustain that pace of growth through the practice of plowing back profits. At the same time, both as the basis for and as the consequence of that level of profit, M&K came to specialize in its business activities. It dispensed with machine-making as a commodity-producing activity and focused on the manufacture of the finer counts of yarn.

However, between 1811 and 1817, the time-span of the T-phase, M&K confronted a period of stagnation. Expansion was abated. There was for the whole of the T-phase no enlargement of plant nor any signficant technical advances in productivity; and on occasion production was run at less than full capacity. The result seems to have been not so much a cut into the total capital of the enterprise, but instead an accumulation of a surplus of temporarily noninvestable capital.

Following the transition period, over the course of the B-phase, 1818-1849, M&K's history was basically one of adjustment and restructuration of business activities. This was, I have argued, an immediate response to declining profit margins. Fundamental changes took place in purchasing, production, marketing, and reinvestment policies, which of course affected other institutions besides M&K itself. Most important of these policy changes was the stress on realizing a high volume of profit through forced output. However, M&K did not integrate weaving with spinning, and instead pursued an oligopolistic strategy by concentrating on key markets for fine yarns and, by the 1820s, lace thread. Expansion during the B-phase fostered the conditions for accumulating a mass of capital apparently due to the appropriation of an adequate volume of profit rather than a high rate of profit. This in turn not only sustained the heavy fixed capital investment from 1818 through the 1820s, which was necessary in order to secure a volume of profit that would potentially counter the rapidly contracting rate of profit. It also continually replenished the supply of circulating capital, the turnover of which was accelerated because of the policy of forced output.

It appears, then, that variation and change in the business activities of M&K occurred in *conjunction* with the rhythmic pattern of the 1789-1849 long wave, with its A-, T-, and B-phases. On the one hand, M&K flowed with and adapted to the altering conditions of capitalist development. As such, M&K's business activities reflected the long-wave movement of that development. On the other hand, the changing structure of M&K's business activities affected to varying extents the actions of other institutional units of the world-economy, including cotton plantations, brokerage houses, transportation enterprises, commission agencies, exporting concerns, other fine cotton-spinning enterprises, textile-weaving enterprises, and so on. As M&K responded to the fluctuations of the rate of profit, itself determined by the vicissitudes of capitalist development, so too did M&K's actions influence that process of making profits and hence, as well, mold the course of capitalist development especially as it pertained to the cotton textile industry.

CONCLUSION

One case study of one enterprise from one industry for one geographical region over the course of one long wave proves nothing. Nevertheless, the study should persuade one to accept a simple conclusion: namely, that there is reason to pursue the examination of long waves in the manner herein proposed. A partial approach to the subject matter has been presented. It stresses the import of the capitalist enterprise not only within the process of capitalist development as such, but as an essential unit of analysis in the scrutiny of that developmental process. For by initially assuming the occurrence of long waves, the focus on the altering structure and profitability of the enterprise's business activities allows one to move from a given institutional unit of the capitalist world-economy to the macrostructure and global processes of that economy. In short, by analyzing how the mechanisms of capitalist development operate through the enterprise, and how in turn the actions of the enterprise influence the pattern of development, one can begin exploring the nature of the capitalist world-economy and its long-wave character of growth. What is needed, therefore, is a comprehensive comparative study of individual enterprises, in light of their respective historical contexts, juxtaposed to tentatively periodized long waves over the history of the capitalist world-economy. Maybe then we'll be able to formulate a coherent theory of capitalist development.

NOTES

1. For the presentation or review of data relevant to the study of long waves, see especially Dupriez (1947), Gayer et al. (1953), Imbert (1959), Kondratieff (1979), Rostow (1978), and Schumpeter (1939).

2. I have elaborated this model at length in an unpublished paper, "On the Capitalist Enterprise."

3. Frank (1978) has correctly characterized the period from 1763 to 1789 as a long crisis of global capital accumulation marked by widespread economic depressions. The primary reactions to this B-phase were, first, an extensive colonial expansion (e.g., India) combined with a superexploitation of colonial possessions, and secondly, within the more advanced economic regions of the world, the accumulation of idle capital and the clustering of mechanical inventions and scientific discoveries. A more detailed account of the expansive A-phase, 1789-1810, would of course have to consider the 1763-89 B-phase insofar as it created the conditions for the post-1789 expansion.

4. Deane and Cole (1962) disagree. For them, the English cotton textile industry of the 1830s and 1840s witnessed a "marked increase in the share of profit in net output" (p. 189). This argument stresses that increases in productivity produced high profit margins. The evidence, however, seems to point to the contrary: productivity did not grow rapidly enough to offset the narrowing margin between cost price and sale price. See especially Foster (1974), Lee (1972), and Von Tunzelmann (1978).

5. Evidence buried in Blaug (1961), for instance, indicates that the growth rate between 1850 and 1856 was much greater than that between 1834 and 1850.

6. In 1826, John Kennedy retired from M&K. Soon after, M&K became McConnel & Co. And in 1898 McConnel & Co. was amalgamated into the Fine Cotton Spinners and Doublers Association. However, in order to avoid confusion I shall retain the name McConnel & Kennedy (M&K) throughout the chapter.

7. For the history of McConnel & Kennedy, see especially the enterprise's "autohistory" (McConnel & Co., 1906), and also Daniels (1915) and Lee (1972), which are based on the company records. See as well, for particular aspects of M&K, Collier (1965), Edwards (1967), Lee (1968), and Smith (1953). An article by Kennedy (1819) is also revealing.

REFERENCES

ASHTON, T. S. (1948) "Some statistics of the Industrial Revolution in Britain." Manchester School of Economics and Social Studies XVI (May): 214-234.

BAINES, E. (1966) History of the Cotton Manufacture in Great Britain. New York: A.M. Kelley. Originally published in 1835.

BLAUG, M. (1961) "The productivity of capital in the Lancashire cotton industry during the nineteenth century." Economic History Review XIII (April): 358-381.

BOYSON, R. (1970) The Ashworth Cotton Enterprise: The Rise and Fall of a Family Firm, 1818-1880. Oxford: Clarendon.

BRUCHEY, S. W. (1967) Cotton and the Growth of the American Economy, 1790-1860. New York: Harcourt Brace Jovanovich.

BUCK, N. S. (1925) The Development of the Organisation of the Anglo-American Trade, 1800-1850. New Haven, CT: Yale University Press.

BYTHELL, D. (1969) The Handloom Weavers: A Study in the English Cotton Industry During the Industrial Revolution. Cambridge: Cambridge University Press.

CHAPMAN, S. D. (1972) The Cotton Industry in the Industrial Revolution. London: Macmillan.

--- (1979) "Financial restraints on the growth of firms in the cotton industry, 1790-1850." Economic History Review XXXII (Feb.): 50-69.

COLLIER, F. (1965) The Family Economy of the Working Classes in the Cotton Industry, 1784-1833. Manchester: Manchester University Press.
CROUZET, F. (1972) "Capital formation in Great Britain during the Industrial Revolution," pp. 162-220 in F. Crouzet (ed.) Capital Formation in the Industrial Revolution. London: Methuen.
DANIELS, G. W. (1915) "The early records of a great Manchester cotton-spinning firm." Economic Journal XXV (June): 175-188.
DEANE, P. and W. A. COLE (1962) British Economic Growth, 1688-1959. Cambridge: Cambridge University Press.
DUMBELL, S. (1923) "Early Liverpool cotton imports and the organisation of the cotton market in the eighteenth century." Economic Journal XXXIII (Sept.): 362-373.
DUPRIEZ, L. (1947) Des mouvements économiques généraux. 2 vols. Louvain: Institut de Recherches Economiques et Sociales de l'Université de Louvain.
EDWARDS, M. M. (1967) The Growth of the British Cotton Trade, 1780-1815. New York: A. M. Kelley.
ELLISON, T. (1968) The Cotton Trade of Great Britain. New York: A. M. Kelley. Originally published in 1886.
FOSTER, J. (1974) Class Struggle and the Industrial Revolution: Early Industrial Capitalism in Three English Towns. London: Methuen.
FRANK, A. G. (1978) World Accumulation, 1492-1789. New York: Monthly Review Press.
GATRELL, V.A.C. (1977) "Labour, power, and the size of firms in Lancashire in the second quarter of the nineteenth century." Economic History Review XXX, 1: 95-139.
GAYER, A. D., W. W. ROSTOW, and A. J. SCHWARTZ (1953) The Growth and Fluctuation of the British Economy, 1790-1850. Oxford: Clarendon.
HAMILTON, E. J. (1942) "Profit inflation and the Industrial Revolution, 1751-1800." Quarterly Journal of Economics LVI: 256-73.
HOBSBAWM, E. J. (1962) The Age of Revolution, 1789-1848. New York: Mentor.
HYDE, F. E., B. B. PARKINSON, and S. MARRINER (1955) "The cotton broker and the rise of the Liverpool cotton market." Economic History Review VIII, 1: 75-83.
IMBERT, G. (1959) Des mouvements de longue durée Kondratieff. Aix-en-Provence: La Pensée.
LEE, C. H. (1968) "Marketing organisation and policy in the cotton trade: M'Connel & Kennedy of Manchester, 1795-1835." Business History X (July): 89-100.
——— (1972) A Cotton Enterprise, 1795-1840: A History of M'Connel & Kennedy Fine Cotton Spinners. Manchester: Manchester University Press.
KENNEDY, J. (1819) "Observations on the rise and progress of the cotton trade in Great Britain: particularly in Lancashire and the adjoining counties." Memoirs and Proceedings of the Literary and Philosophical Society of Manchester III: 115-137.
KONDRATIEFF, N. D. (1979) "The long waves in economic life." Review II, 4 (Spring): 519-562. Originally published in Russian in 1925.
MANTOUX, P. (1961) The Industrial Revolution in the Eighteenth Century. London: Jonathan Cape. Originally published in French in 1907.
McConnel & Co. Ltd. (1906) A Century of Fine Cotton Spinning. Manchester: Falkner.
MITCHELL, B. R. and P. DEANE (1962) Abstract of British Historical Statistics. Cambridge: Cambridge University Press.

RODGERS, H. B. (1960) "The Lancashire Cotton Industry in 1840." Transactions of the Institute of British Geographers XXVIII: 135-153.

ROSTOW, W. W. (1978) The World Economy: History and Prospects. Austin: University of Texas Press.

SCHUMPETER, J. A. (1939) Business Cycles: A Theoretical, Historical and Statistical Analysis of the Capitalist Process. 2 vols. New York: McGraw-Hill.

SHAPIRO, S. (1967) Capital and the Cotton Industry in the Industrial Revolution. Ithaca, NY: Cornell University Press.

SMITH, R. (1953) "Manchester as a centre for the manufacture and merchanting of cotton goods, 1820-30." University of Birmingham Historical Journal IV, 1: 47-65.

TANN, J. (1970) The Development of the Factory. London: Cornmarket.

TAYLOR, A. J. (1949) "Concentration and specialisation in the Lancashire cotton industry, 1825-1850." Economic History Review I: 114-122.

THOMPSON, E. P. (1966) The Making of the English Working Class. New York: Vintage.

VON TUNZELMANN, G. N. (1978) Steam Power and British Industrialisation to 1860. Oxford: Clarendon.

WADSWORTH, A. P. and J. de L. MANN (1941) The Cotton Trade and Industrial Lancashire, 1600-1780. Manchester: Manchester University Press.

Chapter 4

STAGES, CYCLES, AND INSURGENCIES: THE ECONOMICS OF UNREST

James E. Cronin

The revolution in human understanding that we associate with the names of Marx and Engels, but that also informs much of what is useful in modern social science, is in essence a recognition of the link between the conditions of man's existence and his thought and action.[1] Unfortunately, however, the assertion of this connection has often been twisted or degenerated into a claim about the primacy of material over mental life. The ensuing debate has not only been intellectually sterile and inevitably a stalemate, but has diverted attention from the analysis of the precise mechanisms by which the baser aspects of things, the social relations and techniques surrounding production and reproduction, affect belief and behavior. Among contemporary Marxist historians, in fact, there is a tendency to treat economic forces like the Deists treated the creator: the divine presence set everything moving and then retired; in like manner, the mode of production calls forth an array of class forces that face each other and do battle through culture and politics, but with little further attention to economic considerations narrowly or broadly conceived.[2] What gets lost in such an approach is any sense of the continuing interactions that occur in real life and that must be allowed into a properly materialist rendering of the past.

The links between material reality and the affairs of ordinary people are perhaps most easily glimpsed by reviewing the impact of economic change on social and political movements. The concern here will be with such relationships during the era of industrial capitalism, and with movements of popular and democratic variety. Most of the examples, though not all, will be drawn from the British experience, not because it is typical or in any sense paradigmatic, but because no country has had a longer experience with industrial capitalism or a greater variety of social movements in response to it, and also because one does not have to reckon in this case with the complications introduced by major political discontinuities such as have occurred in France, Italy, and Germany. To be sure, such complicating political factors could themselves be subjected to analysis in social and economic terms—indeed they have been time and again (e.g., Goldfrank, 1978)—but the primary concern here is with the relatively undiluted effect of economic and technical change upon the outlook and actions of the working population.

To the extent that economic development is inherently a dynamic process, ubiquitous in its extent and persistent in its effects, one must begin by noting the general transformation, brought about by industrialization, from preindustrial varieties of protest, generally aimed at restoring an idealized older order, to modern styles of insurgency, whose vision is toward a future of shared and humane progress. Marx recognized this "modernization of protest" as it was occurring in mid-nineteenth-century France, and wrote eloquently of the tangled contradiction of archaic conceptions and modern realities in the *Eighteenth Brumaire:*

> The social revolution of the nineteenth century cannot draw its poetry from the past, but only from the future. It cannot begin with itself before it has stripped off all superstitutions in regard to the past. Earlier revolutions required recollections of past world history in order to drug themselves concerning their own content. In order to arrive at its own content, the revolution of the nineteenth century must let the dead bury their dead. There the phrase went beyond the content; here the content goes beyond the phrase.

Shedding the rhetoric of the past was a long, painful process; dropping the old forms of struggle was easier, because they lost relevance in an urban, industrial world. The shift has been much studied of late (see Tilly et al., 1975; Tilly, 1978; Stearns, 1976; Cronin, 1979 a, b), and though some resent the labeling of certain forms of struggle as primitive or backward-looking (e.g., Amsden, 1978), the reality of the transition seems incontrovertible.

Even if it is hard to pinpoint the precise moment when an old form of protest died and a new one came into its own, it is nevertheless clear that different styles of unrest and insurgency prevailed before and after the Industrial Revolution. In the seventeenth and eighteenth centuries, for example, Europe witnessed a high tide of food riots and other defensive forms of unrest, as ordinary people pressed into service the institutions of early modern society against the incursions and encroachments of the state and the market. These acts of resistance relied upon the old-fashioned networks of the village community and the organizations of artisans for mobilization, and upon theories of inherited corporate rights and responsibilities for their justification (Tilly, 1975; Thompson, 1971).

A sharp break occurred in the nineteenth century, as the dynamic of industrialization shattered the stable mental outlooks of the emerging working-class, destroyed their local communities, and forced through a restructuring of social bonds in an urban and industrial context. The transformation was highly traumatic, and led to that radicalization of traditional forms of protest that lay behind the revolutionary outbreaks of 1776-1848 (Hobsbawm, 1962; Gillis, 1977). Gradually, though, new types of social movements arose, the two most important being strikes and mass political (largely electoral) activity, the one based on the trade union, the other on the political party. Collective action of this sort is typically (though not universally) forward-looking and ideologically progressive, and is built upon the solidarities of the workplace and the local working-class community. It tends to be highly politicized, and organized on a larger scale—regional or national rather than local, industrial rather than craft, and so on—than previous varieties of protest and mobilization. It tends also to occur at very different times in terms of economic cycles and trends: earlier outbursts of protest tended to come at moments of extreme distress, at the bottom of the industrial cycle, the peak of grain prices; since the industrial revolution the peaks of unrest have coincided normally with peaks in the business cycle (Hobsbawm, 1963a; Bouvier, 1963; Perrot, 1974; Kaelble and Volkmann, 1972; Ashenfelter and Johnson, 1969; Bain and Elsheikh, 1976). Clearly, workers have learned to press their grievances at the hour most advantageous to themselves and are no longer governed by the cries of their bellies.

Though this transformation in patterns of opposition is never entirely complete, and despite the enduring and recurring quality of much of the rhetoric of social struggle, recognizing the transition is critical to an understanding of the link between economics and popular politics. It directs us to the existence of two separate modes and moments in the economic determination of social movements. There is, first, the process by which the logic of the market and of industrial organization is imposed on a population, and by which the pattern of capitalist development is superimposed upon, and ultimately displaces, the rhythms of rural life. During this stage, which lasted until about 1867 in England and still later in France and Germany, old and new economic cycles were intertwined, and old and new styles of protest interacted and reinforced one another, imparting to the era a particularly restive quality. Subsequent to this one finds a rather different process, which exhibits a logic of its own and a rhythm unique to the period of mature capitalist development, and upon which we shall concentrate for the remainder of this chapter.

The quickest and simplest survey of movements of protest and insurgency since the late nineteenth century reveals the fundamental problem to be analyzed. Whether one uses as an indicator the membership of trade unions, the incidence of strikes, the electoral support of socialist and labor parties or, as the Tillys have done, an index of violent protests, the curve of social movements is extremely "jumpy and discontinuous," as Eric Hobsbawm (1963a) noted in his seminal essay. Insurgency ordinarily explodes upon the scene, taking both left and right by surprise. Years of patient propaganda and diligent organizing may well have prepared the ground for mass mobilization, but the actual timing of strike waves and bursts of organization has born little relation to these prior efforts. Marx's metaphoric equation of "the revolution" with "the old mole" working away beneath the surface of events captures well the apparent unpredictability of insurgency, as does Lenin's argument that "real history" includes "both slow evolution and swift leaps, breaks in continuity." Writing from a quite different perspective, John Dunlop (1948) contended that the record of labor movements in America was also marked by major discontinuities, by periodic explosions of militancy, imparting a very distinctive rhythm to its history: "The process," he wrote "is like waves eating away at the base of a cliff, which eventually crashes into the sea."

For several reasons, these discontinuities have been largely ignored by the current generation of labor historians. The move away from institutional studies of trade unions and political formations, the focus upon working-class culture and daily life, and the general empiricist disdain for theory and analysis have all contributed to this historiographic neglect, though none of these circumstances justifies it.[3] In consequence, our appreciation of these crucial events and turning points in social history is very shallow, our understanding possibly less clear than when Hobsbawm and Dunlop first approached the topic. It is obviously time to reconsider the problem.

Let us begin by pairing down the issue a bit. What is not a problem, what is not at all mysterious, is the ending of waves of strikes and political agitation. Social movements seem to be inherently entropic—they either continue to grow and develop, or else become routinized and pessimistic, and ultimately decline. And what ordinarily guarantees that they will not grow indefinitely is repression. Repression unfortunately works, and a series of defeats does break the momentum of insurgency. British labor did not bounce back from the loss of 1926 until at least 1945; French trade unions were placed on the defensive from the disastrous railway strike of May 1920, the so-called "civic battle of the Marne," until 1936. Workers isolated in a particular industry are even more susceptible to suppression—the employers' rout of the British engineers in the lockout of 1897-1898 kept those workers quiescent throughout most of the ferment of

1910-1914; the bitter medicine wore off only during the war. Even where defeat is not so sharp and bitter, the failure to storm the heights at the peak of insurgency leads to apathy and cynicism, to in-fighting within the left, and ultimately to passivity or, at least, to a lowered plateau of struggle.

So, it is not difficult to comprehend the wave-like character of social movements looked at from the rear; what is difficult is to explain why explosions of popular activism occur in the first place. A brief chronology of the ups and downs of English labor might help us to sketch the outlines of an answer.[4] Beginning with the stabilization of politics in the mid-Victorian period, the first bout of labor militancy came in 1871-1873, at the height of the speculative boom that preceded the Great Depression of 1873-1896. The record of this upsurge is rather spotty, but we know for sure that the number of workers in the major trade unions quadrupled inside of four years. The agitation was led by recent recruits to the "new model unions," like the Amalgamated Society of Engineers, organizations built and sustained by the generation of craftsmen and artisans that created and maintained the machinery of the industrial revolution, fashioned the factories in which it was employed, and did the skilled work necessary for the construction of the road and bridges and other elements in the "built environment" of "the workshop of the world." It is no doubt an oversimplification to call these workers an "aristocracy of labor," for this implies a degree of cooptation and assimilation inconceivable (to me) before the twentieth century, but the designation does convey the great distance that separated this organized, or at least organizable, stratum from the mass of unskilled and quite degraded workers characterized at the time simply as "labourers" (Hobsbawm, 1963b; Shepherd, 1978; Field, 1978-1979).

Many of the gains of 1871-1873 were subsequently eroded by the shift in tactical leverage toward the employers during the depression, and wages followed union membership in a sharp plunge to 1880. The very blackest years of depression were probably the mid-1880s, after which a brief revival commenced. Short-lived and weak as it was, the upturn provided the spark for a wave of strikes and organizing of unprecedented dimensions, the "new unionism" of 1889-1890. Though a recent crop of revisionist historians (Duffy, 1961; Lovell, 1978) has arisen to argue the essential continuity between the old and new unions and the old and new styles of bargaining, the contrast remains striking. 1889-1890 marked the entry into trade union activity of a large group of hitherto unorganized, unskilled workers: dockers, gas workers, common laborers and even some scattered groups of agricultural workers. The entire tone of the labor movement changed as well, from one of pessimism and moderation to one of raucous optimism and daring militancy. Appeals became inclusive; previously exclusive groups of unionists in engineering and textiles, in the mines, and on the railways began to open their ranks; and a reorientation was wrought in the strategic thinking of labor's most advanced and active elements. The spirit of the entire venture was epitomized by the widespread support for the eight-hour day (Duffy, 1968)—a demand that spoke both to the recent experience of massive unemployment and to the expanded vision of the future that gripped many of the rank-and-file.

The bright prospects of the first years of the "new unionism" rather quickly faded. The employers began a coordinated counteroffensive, recruiting a strike-breaking "free labour" force and winning major tests of strength with the textile workers in 1893, the engineers in 1897, and the South Wales miners in 1898. The unions affiliated to the Trades Union Congress lost almost half a million members between 1890 and 1895 as the return of depression and the pattern of defeat sapped enthusiasm. Fortunately, though, the Great Depression came to an end in the mid-1890s, and trade union membership picked up again by 33% in the first five years of the so-called Edwardian boom. Still, as measured by the willingness to strike, labor remained cowed until 1910, when another dramatic expansion of both union membership and strikes commenced.

Between 1910 and 1913, unrest spread through most of the labor movement, engulfing miners and dockers, railwaymen, textile workers, and builders. The demands were again broad and inclusive, the organizing principles even more so. The rhetoric of syndicalism resonated strongly among a variety of groups, and served as a metaphor with multiple meanings: to some it meant a demand for total unionism; to others it was a protest against the impotence of the Labour party in Parliament; to others it implied a critique of bureaucratic conservatism in the unions and a call for industrial unionism; to a certain number of leaders, syndicalism and the sympathetic strike seemed the only counter to the increased concentration and collective strength of the bosses; and to some it was just an evocative phrase (Holton, 1976).

What brought this upsurge to a close is not absolutely clear. There were signs of life in the insurgency during the first half of 1914 and promises of major tests of strength in the autumn, but there were also indications of dissipation. In any event, the war replaced concerns over the future of labor with the immediacy of mobilization for battle. The effects of the war upon labor were contradictory; at first, it encouraged social peace and industrial conciliation, but as it dragged on, it stimulated further anger and collective activity. The upshot was the great wave of militancy of 1919-1920. In terms of goals and participation, this movement was largely of a piece with prewar events, but in strategic terms it threw up an entirely novel and useful device in the shop stewards' movement (Hinton, 1978).

The unrest was also broader and deeper after the war, and represented a more serious social crisis, particularly because it coincided with a sea-change in mass political affiliation. Between the "coupon election" of 1918 and the election of 1922, Labour replaced the Liberals as the major party of opposition, and the functioning of the British political system was transformed (Cowling, 1971). So, too, was the relationship between political and economic power, as the financial, conservative upper class sought to ensure that a victory for the Labour party would not lead to social revolution by shoring up the power of the Treasury, and behind it of the City, over the other organs of the state apparatus and over the industrial section of the bourgeoisie.[5] These developments within the elite circles of the polity helped to guarantee the impotency of the two interwar Labour governments; what determined the industrial impotency of labor was unemployment and defeat. Depression came to Britain in 1920, and it eroded the bases of workshop organization. Miners, textile workers, and engineers lost major strikes in the next three years, and the entire working class was defeated in the General Strike of 1926 (Phillips, 1975).

The interwar slump devastated Britain's old staple industries—mining, textiles, and shipbuilding especially—and when revival began after 1935, it was concentrated in new industries and quite new areas. The industrial center shifted southward, from Lancashire and Yorkshire in the north to a southern band running from London across to Oxford and then up toward Birmingham. The result was that no strike wave occurred in Britain during the 1930s comparable to those in France or the United States, for the workers in the new industries had yet to develop the "habit of solidarity," as Hobsbawm has called it, and the workers in the old sectors never regained the strength. Still, the depression worked on men's minds, effecting a profound transformation that in concrete terms meant a revulsion from massive unemployment and a resolve never to suffer its recurrence (Saville, 1977). This attitude, coupled with the general leftward movement of opinion, fueled the organizing drive that began with the declaration of war in 1939 and that led, ultimately, to the convincing Labour victory of 1945. Labour's triumph at the end of the war, when it deposed the man who had led the country through its severest military test, is poorly appreciated. We are all too aware of the failings of Labour's rule from 1945 to 1951, which were real enough, and insufficiently aware of its accomplishments and, most importantly, of the social movement its electoral triumph signified. This is not the place to set that record straight, but we may begin simply by situating it within the history of social movements, and by according it the place within British history that the organizing of the CIO in the United States and the strikes of 1936 in France occupy in those nations' social history.

The further explosions of strike militancy have occurred since 1945. The first, and smaller of the two, began about 1957 and lasted until 1962. This brief bout of industrial strife was associated with the rise of the "unofficial strike," a strike initiated by the rank-and-file of the unions without the approval of the leadership: the tactic was particularly effective in the engineering industry, especially in the car factories, and was accompanied by a marked growth in the organization of shop stewards. What actually triggered the outburst was one of those brief economic downturns that have been the manifestation of Britain's "stop-go" economic policy. The recession of 1956-1957 in Britain served to rekindle old fears of unemployment, and workers responded by a more insistent attitude toward pay increases and by a demand for government action to prevent what the British call "redundancies."

In these two areas British workers were surprisingly successful, and on the strength of this performance they responded forcefully to the problems of inflation after the devaluation of 1967. Thus, 1968-1972 witnessed a strike wave of massive proportions and enormous success: unionization jumped dramatically as groups of white-collar employees organized for the first time; wages shot up; and government attempts to curb "unofficial" action were thwarted. Moreover, the scope of wage demands since 1968 and the tone of the movement together suggest that the expectations of ordinary workers have been heightened and expanded for the first time since the heady years just after the Great War (Clements, 1978). The confrontation between the Heath government and the miners in 1974 and the rebellion against Callaghan's and Healy's wage policies in the winter of 1978-1979 reveal the depth and permanence of the transformation of workers' attitudes; and they suggest, too, the workers' much enhanced capacity for collective organization and action and the political stalemate that this new social balance has produced.

Before asking what resemblance this uneven pattern of militancy bears to the rhythms of economic evolution, a few points should be made regarding the events themselves. First, despite the formal similarities of the movements, each has been distinctive in its strategic orientation, its preferred organizational style, its slogans and demands, and its social composition. These explosions of activism are in this sense profoundly creative: they are responsible for stretching the boundaries of popular political thought, for launching innovations in union tactics and structure, and for bringing new groups within the orbit of organized labor. They represent, therefore, not only quantitative indicators of the intensity of social conflict, but also turning points in the history of society, moments of transition between qualitatively different stages of political and social development.

With this in mind, one may better approach the problem of how these events connect with the ups and downs of the economy. One fact is evident: none of these outbursts has occurred at the trough of the business cycle. The largest upheavals, 1910-1913, 1919-1920, 1968-1972, have come during the peaks of business activity that bring to an end periods of long-term expansion. The "new unionism" of 1889-1890 was, of course, the product of the Great Depression of 1873-1896, but its actual birthing came in the mild revival that separated the two dismal troughs of the mid-1880s and 1893. Similarly, the little strike wave of 1957-1962 may well have been sparked by the spectre of recession and redundancy, but unemployment was never a serious statistical problem during the 1950s and 1960s. The two upsurges of union growth unaccompanied by major strikes, 1895-1900 and 1938-1948, were even more clearly connected with periods of economic upswing. Both periods were years of rapid recovery from prolonged slumps.

It seems, though, that the need for a favorable short-term conjuncture for the launching of insurgency represents only a minor prerequisite for unrest, a factor more important in the timing than in the deeper causation of events. The distinctive character of successive explosions and their rather lengthy periodicity further suggest that the cause must be deeper and more fundamental than the seven-ten year business cycle, and must have qualitative as well as quantitative dimensions. Rather than proceed by a lengthy process of induction, let me instead offer a hypothesis and an argument: the force that seems to qualify as the critical determinant of the explosive character of social movements is the uneven character of economic development, conceived specifically in terms of the long waves of Kondratieff. These long waves lie behind the discontinuous course of social struggle; they determine its form and content, and guarantee its expression. Long waves impact upon strikes on two distinct levels. Most simply, each upswing or downswing of a long cycle poses novel problems and possibilities for workers and stimulates the learning process of the working class. In this way the particular climate of successive stages of economic change comes to inform collective action; workers are forced to reason about their conditions and prospects, to frame demands and justifications, to think through and finally to implement strategic alternatives. Ideological shifts, changes in the tactics and organizational forms used by workers, and extensions of activism are thus all linked to the peculiarities of each phase of a long wave. In terms of ideology, tactics and organization, there is a process of making, unmaking, and remaking the working class. Its culture and its patterns of collective expression thus take on a persistent dynamism that gives rise inevitably to debate, internal struggle, and change within the labor movement.

This continual remaking of the working class proceeds on an even deeper level, however, and concerns the very structure and composition of the class itself. To understand this, we might make a brief detour to consider the theory of long waves more closely. There have been, fittingly, two waves of theorizing about Kondratieff's notion of long waves: the first occurred between the wars and largely within the boundaries of the Soviet Union; the second has happened very recently in the West. The record of the earlier polemics reveals that discussion then centered not on the existence of long waves or Kondratieff's description but on their causes and, by implication, their place in the general process of capitalist development (Garvey, 1943; Day, 1976). Kondratieff (1926) himself said rather little about causation, but did suggest that the rhythm he discerned was "inherent in the essence of the capitalistic economy." His opponents, Trotsky among them, argued that long waves were real enough, but could not be labeled as cyclical, as Kondratieff had done. Rather, they were best understood as distinct stages in the evolution of capitalism. Trotsky argued further that these stages were caused not so much by the internal logic of capitalism but by shocks from the outside, like wars, revolutions, imperial conquest, or the discovery of natural resources, that shifted the terms and the climate of capital accumulation. Kondratieff retorted that these apparently external phenomena were themselves determined by the internal rhythm of capitalism, and what made that conform to the fifty-year pattern was the periodic exhaustion and replacement of capital stock. Kondratieff pointed out that, "Marx asserted that the material basis of crises, or of average cycles, repeating themselves each decade, is the wearing out, replacement and expansion of the mass of means of production in the form of machines lasting an average of ten years." By a similar logic, "it can be suggested that the material basis of long cycles is the wearing out, replacement and expansion of fixed capital goods which require a long period of time and enormous expenditures to produce" (cited in Day, 1976: 76). What Kondratieff meant by "fixed capital goods" is what we know of as infrastructure or social overhead capital—transport and communication systems, buildings, and so on.

Neither Kondratieff nor his theories fared well in the Soviet Union under Stalin, and in imitation Western Marxists ignored them as well. Curiously, a line much closer to Trotsky's, emphasizing the noncyclical nature of the phases of development delineated by Kondratieff, came to dominate discussion inside and outside the Soviet Union. The hypothesis of "long waves" met with equally stony silence from orthodox economists as well, with the notable exception of Schumpeter (1939). Even here, though, Kondratieff's arguments were quite effectively buried by Schumeter's stress upon bursts of heroic entrepreneurial activity. As a result of this near-universal neglect, Kondratieff's name is conspicuously absent from the key texts of bourgeois and Marxist economics alike, from Sweezy's (1942) *Theory of Capitalist Development* and from the first edition of Samuelson's *Economics* in 1948. Indeed, as late as 1970, Samuelson was boasting of the irrelevance of the study of cyclical behavior generally. In his opinion, the National Bureau of Economic Research, the official body charged with the monitoring and prediction of cycles and crises had long since "worked itself out of one of its first jobs, namely business cycles" (cited in Frank, 1978: 87).

The long neglect of "long waves" has ended in the 1970s, an obvious intellectual response to the entry of the world-economy into an era of stagnation and uncertainty. Of necessity, much of the recent literature has been an exercise in rediscovery, and it has often been marked by a "born again" enthusiasm that is slightly amusing (see especially Shuman and Rosenau, 1972; and Forrester, 1978). More serious analysts (Barraclough, 1974; Rostow, 1975, 1978) have been aware of the difficulties in applying Kondratieff's model to the current era, but have not resolved them. Two treatments have been more substantial and creative, those of Mandel (1975) and Gordon (1978). Mandel, to his credit, is more tolerant than his mentor, and he seeks to synthesize the ideas of Trotsky and Kondratieff. His major concern theoretically is to explain the mechanisms that produce the upsurges in investment and innovation that characterize the ascendant phase of the long wave. His answer is an increase in profits, which occur because of increased exploitation. Whether this adds up to a sufficient explanation or not, whether in particular his argument should not be augmented by a discussion of the market (Wallerstein, 1978), does not concern me as much as does Mandel's ignoring of the distinction between investments in machines and technology and infrastructural investment. Recognizing and elaborating this distinction is the great merit of David Gordon's recent contribution.

What Gordon has done is to place the analysis of long waves in the context of the qualitative evolution of capitalist society. Specifically, by combining a theory of stages closer to the Japanese Kozo Uno (Sekine, 1975) and much subtler than the more orthodox scheme of competitive, monopoly, and state monopoly capitalism, with Kondratieff's argument about waves of infrastructural innovation, Gordon has provided us with a more thoroughly materialist model of capitalist development. Moreover, he has endeavored to link analytically the processes of depletion and regeneration of infrastructure to the constitution and reconstitution of social structure. Upsderminings in growth are thus associated with clusters of technological innovations, as Kondratieff and after him Schumpeter insisted, with waves of construction of plant, transportation networks, and housing, with shifts in the concentration of capital, in styles of labor management and control, in the structure of labor markets and, by implication, in the level of wages and the extent of the domestic market, and a variety of other supporting institutions in the "social structure of accumulation." Downswings are marked by the thorough diffusion and exhaustion of innovation, the physical wearing down of the infrastructure, and often the breakup of the institutional matrix of social relations.

What this argument suggests is that long waves, specifically the upswings of long waves, do not simply produce prosperity and economic growth, but are profoundly innovative in terms of social relations as well. With each upturn of a long wave comes not only new machines and rising prices, but the recreation of the working class and much of the social environment. New sectors surge ahead economically, employing the latest technologies and restructuring the pace and organization of work; and characteristically employment in these sectors grows while it declines or stagnates in older industries. With such changes usually come geographical shifts, the building of new physical environments and the subsequent creation of new social networks, styles of life, communities, and subcultures. And all of these changes imply different possibilities and patterns of collective organization. Together they add up to a process through which the working class is reshaped, reconstituted, and recreated every half-century or so.

The implications for the analysis of the periodic explosions of working-class activism in Britain and elsewhere are clear: long waves serve not only to regularly reeducate the labor movement in its economic understanding and social and strategic orientation, but in addition to transform the composition of the working class, and to redraw the lines of class cleavage throughout society and the parameters of collective action. In theoretical terms, the course of labor history is not simply the trajectory through time, through ups and downs, victories and defeats, of the working class conceived as a stable social entity, but the quite complicated story of the social and political struggles of a class whose very make-up is constantly changing.

The remaking of the working class through the succession of long waves, in this view, is compounded—a matter of ideas and actions and of class constitution itself. In Britain the series of insurgencies described above reveals not merely the progress, and occasional regression, of the class but also its changing definition. The qualitative differences in the participants, the demands, and the strategies of each strike wave signal different stages in the evolution of the class. We may recall as examples certain features of the history of insurgency in Britain. The two explosions of militancy just before and after the First World War wrought two enormous achievements: the organization of the unskilled workers on the docks and the rails and the emergence of the metalworkers as pacesetters in strike action. The first reflected the long-term transformation, through regularization of the work process and some minimal mechanization, of unskilled and casual laborers into a modern, semiskilled workforce. The second testifies to the simultaneous process by which the metal industry, itself becoming rationalized and more modern through the degradation or replacement of skilled by semiskilled labor, supplanted textiles as the leading industrial sector. The emergence of these new workers, or new types of workers, fueled the militancy of the second decade of the century and altered the entire tone and content of the labor movement (Bauman, 1972; Cronin, 1980; Stearns, 1976).

This industrial transformation during the period before the war was paralleled by a reshaping of the social landscape within which ordinary men and women lived and toiled. It was the heroic age of city building —not just in England, of course, but throughout Europe and America—and in the expanding cities social classes had more room to sort themselves out by wealth and occupation. Distinct communities of workers, with an intense—some (Stedman Jones, 1974; Anderson, 1966) would say too intense and too inward-looking—network of institutions and a supportive—some would here add "incorporating"—subculture, grew up, reinforcing social allegiances and making solidarity a way of life. And because the transport revolution linked with the application of electricity to trams extended the city radially without effecting that divorce between workplace and residence, so obvious in contemporary cities, the web of associations running through the working-class neighborhoods became the underpinning for political and industrial mobilization. Union organization and strike activity were thus greatly abetted by the same forces that cemented the bond between the Labour party and the community, and at virtually the same moment.

It is evident that technological change since 1920 has fashioned a new collection of occupational groups into the present working class: the old industries, cotton and coal, have waned; growth now centers in the white-collar ranks of service sector employees who are being slowly but discernably proletarianized; and the metal and engineering industry has been again transformed with assembly lines and automation. Working-class communities have also changed. They have shifted physically out of Wales and the industrial north and out of the city core everywhere to new types of housing in suburban locations in the south of England. They have become less self-contained and insular, too, as mass communication and popular culture have penetrated the inner world and daily lives of working people.

The consequences for mobilization and activism have been contradictory. The development of technology and industrial organization has shifted the locus of power downward to the shop floor, enhancing the leverage of small cohesive work groups and negating the moderating predispositions of union leaders; hence the unofficial strike. The convergence of the terms and conditions of white-collar employment with those of manual workers has eroded the deference and passivity of the nonmanual labor force; hence the great jump in white-collar unionization since the mid-1960s. On the other hand, the slow disappearance of a distinctively working-class style of life has led to a greater overlapping between respectable, bourgeois public opinion and workers' own stated beliefs: hence the coexistence of an antilabor public opinion and massive strike waves. The increased role of the state in the economy, often presided over by Labour party politicians, and as an adversary in the setting of wages and in bargaining generally has also led to the disintegration of the links between the Labour party and the working class, and to the decline of labor as a political and cultural force. Hence the drifting apart of the political and industrial wings of the labor movement and the growing inability of either political party to handle specifically industrial unrest.

The strike wave of 1968-1972, therefore, much like that of 1919-1920, registered both an escalation in the demands and expectations of working people and the maturation of major alterations in social and economic structure. In both cases, the origins of structural changes can be traced back to painful economic slumps during the 1870s and 1880s or during the interwar years, but the basic agent propelling and at first smoothing the way for structural transformation was the powerful pressure of a Kondratieff upswing. And, also in both cases, the petering out of the boom allowed the contradictions of growth to surface in a massive insurgency.

The analogy should not be pushed further than this, for there are marked dissimilarities between the movements of 1919-1920 and 1968-1972 as well as elements of comparability. The point is simply that both explosions of militancy have been situated chronology at the end of a prolonged prosperity that served thoroughly to remake the working class, its thoughts and practices. That is the burden of my argument: that the sustained trends in economic history that we may call either Kondratieff waves or, following Hobsbawm, Garvy, and others, "qualitatively distinct phases of ecomomic evolution," set new tasks for labor and stimulate its ideological and political development and, on a still deeper level, recast the very lineaments of the social formation. In terms of the overall transformation from traditional to modern economies and societies and their attendant forms of protest, this means a gross asymmetry in the coherence and stability of the picture on either side of the divide of the industrial revolution. Insurgency in the earlier era was patterned and predictable, informed by minimal expectations and a stable world view. Since the coming of capitalist industrialization, mobilization and protest have manifested a discontinuity and variability that is the mirror image of capitalism itself, in all its complexity and dynamism. Finally, to conclude on a more pragmatic note, it is this dynamism, this incessant tendency to change, this refusal (to paraphrase Marx) of modern industry ever to look upon the existing form of production as final that makes capitalism revolutionary, and that makes revolutionaries optimistic.

NOTES

1. As Lukács (1971: 27) argued, "It is not the primacy of economic motives in historical explanation that constitutes the difference between Marxism and bourgeois thought, but the point of view of totality."
2. Richard Johnson (1978) has argued along similar lines, taking Marxist historians to task for having retreated too far and too fast from the damaging consequences of economic determinism. The result, according to Johnson, has been a reduction and simplification in the very definition of economics.
   Unfortunately, Johnson couples the argument with a rather unwarranted attack upon the work of Edward Thompson and Eugene Genovese. Though it is correct to note that material forces get relatively short shrift in *The Making of the English Working Class* and *Roll, Jordan, Roll*, neither of these books can be evaluated in an intellectual vacuum. Put in historiographical context, they in fact look quite different. Thompson's work, for example, can only be understood against the background of a large literature on the economics of the industrial revolution that requires no repetition, while Genovese's book must be situated as the last act of a trilogy that began, suitably enough, with *The Political Economy of Slavery*.
   Still, Johnson's points are worthy of careful consideration. The present writer has made a comparable argument using the work of Eric Hobsbawm as a positive example (Cronin, 1978-1979).
3. Many of the criticisms of the "new social history" by Elizabeth Fox Genovese and Eugene Genovese (1974-1975) are particularly appropriate here. They argue forcefully that the vogue for local studies of working-class culture—most of them demonstrating its vitality and viability—leads to a depoliticization of labor history and a neglect of the dimensions of oppression and resistance.
4. What follows is an account based upon the standard histories of British labor and upon my own separate researches. For citations to the former and a summary of the latter, see Cronin (1979b).
5. This development has been largely ignored by British historians, but it can be pieced together from various sources on administrative history, on interdepartmental rivalries after the war over "reconstruction," on the role of the Bank of England and the Treasury in securing the return to gold in 1925 (Moggridge, 1972), on the general relationship between the City of London and industry (Rubinstein, 1977), and on the attitude of the government and employers toward labor and strikes (Desmarais, 1970). One suspects that, when the story is eventually told, it will read much like that told by Charles Maier (1975) for the continent. An early indication that this will be so is Robert Scally's (1975) recent study of Lloyd George and social imperialism.

REFERENCES

AMSDEN, J. (1978) "Spanish Anarchism and the stages theory of history." Radical History Review 18 (Fall): 66-75.

ANDERSON, P. (1966) "Origins of the present crisis," in P. Anderson and R. Blackburn (eds.) Towards Socialism. Ithaca: Cornell University Press.

ASHENFELTER, O. and G. JOHNSON (1969) "Bargaining theory, trade unions, and strike activity." American Economic Review LIX: 35-49.

BAIN, G. S. and F. ELSHEIKH (1976) Union Growth and the Business Cycle: An Econometric Analysis. Oxford: Basil Blackwell.

BARRACLOUGH, G. (1974) "The end of an era." New York Review of Books XXI, 11: 14-20.

BAUMAN, Z. (1972) Between Class and Elite. Manchester: Manchester University Press.

BOUVIER, J. (1964) "Mouvement ouvrier et conjonctures économique." Le Mouvement Social 48: 3-30.

CLEMENTS, L. (1978) "Reference groups and trade union consciousness," pp. 309-332 in T. Clarke and L. Clements (eds.) Trade Unions under Capitalism. Hassocks, England: Harvester.

COWLING, M. (1971) The Impact of Labour. Cambridge: Cambridge University Press.

CRONIN, J. (1978-1979). "Creating a Marxist historiography: the impact of Hobsbawm." Radical History Review 19 (Winter): 87-109.

--- (1979a) "The peculiar pattern of British strikes since 1888." Journal of British Studies.

--- (1979b) Industrial Conflict in Modern Britain. London: Croom Helm.

--- (1980) "1917-20 as a Moment in Class Formation." Social Science History IV, 1.

DAY, R. B. (1976) "The theory of long waves: Kondratieff, Trotsky, Mandel." New Left Review 99 (September-October): 67-82.

DESMARAIS, R. (1970) "The supply and transport committee, 1919-26: a study of the British government's method of handling emergencies stemming from industrial disputes." Ph.D. dissertation, University of Wisconsin.

DUFFY, A.E.P. (1961) "New unionism in Britain, 1889-1890: a reappraisal." Economic History Review XIV: 306-319.

--- (1968). "The eight hours day movement in Britain, 1886-1893." Manchester School of Economic and Social Studies XXXVI: 203-223, 354-363.

DUNLOP, J. T. (1948) "The development of labor organization: a theoretical framework," in R. Lester and J. Shister (eds.) Insights into Labor Issues. New York: Macmillan.

FRANK, A. G. (1978) "The economics of crisis and the crisis of economics." Critique 9 (Spring-Summer): 85-112.

FIELD, J. (1978-1979) "British historians and the concept of the labor aristocracy." Radical History Review 19 (Winter): 61-85.

FORRESTER, J. W. (1978) "A great depression ahead?" Futurist XII (December): 379-385.

GARVY, G. (1943) "Kondratieff's theory of long cycles." Review of Economic Statistics XXV: 203-220.

GENOVESE, E. F. and E. GENOVESE (1976) "The political crisis of social history: a Marxian perspective." Journal of Social History X (Winter): 205-220.

GENOVESE, E. D. (1967) The Political Economy of Slavery. New York: Random House.
——— (1974). Roll, Jordan, Roll. New York: Random House.
GILLIS, J. (1977) The Development of European Society. Boston: Houghton-Mifflin.
GOLDFRANK, W. L. (1978) "Fascism and world economy," in B. H. Kaplan (ed.) Social Change in the Capitalist World Economy. Beverly Hills: Sage Publications.
GORDON, D. (1978) "Up and down the long roller coaster," in U.S. Capitalism in Crisis. Published by the Economics Education Project of the Union for Radical Political Economics.
HINTON, J. (1973) The First Shop Stewards' Movement. London: Allen & Unwin.
HOBSBAWM, E. J. (1962) The Age of Revolution. New York: Mentor.
——— (1963a) "Economic fluctuations and some social movements since 1800," pp. 149-184 in Labouring Men. Garden City, NY: Anchor.
——— (1963b) "The labour aristocracy in nineteenth-century Britain," pp. 321-370 in Labouring Men.
HOLTON, R. (1976) British Syndicalism. London: Pluto.
JOHNSON, R. (1978) "Thompson, Genovese, and socialist-humanism." History Workshop 6 (Autumn): 79-100.
KAELBLE, H. and H. VOLKMANN (1972) "Konjunktur und Streik während des Übergangs zum Organisierten Kapitalismus in Deutschland." Zeitschrift für Wirtschafts- und Sozialwissenschaften XCV: 513-544.
KONDRATIEFF, N. D. (1926) "Die langen Wellen der Konjunktur." Archiv für Sozialwissenschaft und Sozialpolitik LVI: 573-609.
LOVELL, J. (1978) "The new unions." Bulletin of the Society for the Study of Labour History 36 (Spring): 15-17.
LUKÁCS, G. (1971) History and Class Consciousness. Cambridge, MA: MIT.
MAIER, C. (1975) Recasting Bourgeois Europe. Stabilization in France, Germany, and Italy in the Decade after World War I. Princton, NJ: Princeton University Press.
MANDEL, E. (1975) Late Capitalism. London: New Left Books.
MOGGRIDGE, D. E. (1972) British Monetary Policy, 1924-1931: The Norman Conquest of $4.86. Cambridge: Cambridge University Press.
PERROT, M. (1974) Les ouvriers en grève. France, 1871-1890. 2 vols. Paris: Mouton.
PHILLIPS, G. A. (1976) The General Strike. London: Weidenfeld & Nicolson.
ROSTOW, W. W. (1975) "Kondratieff, Schumpeter, and Kuznets: trend periods revisited." Journal of Economic History XXXV (December): 719-754.
——— (1978) "Regional change in the fifth Kondratieff upswing," in D. C. Perry and A. J. Watkins (eds.) The Rise of the Sunbelt Cities. Beverly Hills: Sage Publications.
RUBINSTEIN, W. D. (1977) "Wealth, elites, and the class structure of modern Britain." Past and Present 76.
SAVILLE, J. (1960) "Trade unions and free labour: the background of the Taff Vale decision," pp. 317-350 in A. Briggs and J. Saville (eds.) Essays in Labour History. London: Macmillan.
——— (1977) "May Day 1937," pp. 232-284 in A. Briggs and J. Saville (eds.) Essays in Labour History. Vol. III. London: Croom Helm.
SCALLY, R. J. (1975) The origins of the Lloyd George Coalition: The Politics of Social-Imperialism, 1900-1918. Princeton, NJ: Princeton University Press.
SCHUMPETER, J. A. (1939) Business Cycles. New York: McGraw-Hill.
SEKINE, T. (1975) "*Uno-Riron:* a Japanese contribution to Marxian political economy." Journal of Economic Literature XIII (September): 847-877.

SHEPHERD, M. A. (1978) "The origins and incidence of the term 'labour aristocracy'." Bulletin of the Society for the Study of Labour History 37 (Autumn): 51-67.
SHUMAN, J. B. and D. ROSENAU (1972) The Kondratieff Wave. New York: Delta.
STEARNS, P. (1976) "The unskilled and industrialization: a transformation of consciousness." Archiv für Sozialgeschichte XVI: 249-282.
STEDMAN JONES, G. (1974) "Working-class culture and working-class politics in London, 1870-1900: note on the re-making of a working class." Journal of Social History VII (Summer): 460-508.
THOMPSON, E. P. (1963) The Making of the English Working Class. New York: Random House.
--- (1971) "The moral economy of the English crowd in the eighteenth century." Past and Present 50: 76-136.
TILLY, C. (1975) "Food supply and public order in modern Europe," in Tilly (ed.) The Formation of National States in Western Europe. Princeton, NJ: Princeton University Press.
--- (1979) "Collective violence in European perspective," in H. D. Graham and T. R. Gurr (eds.) Violence in America: Historical and Comparative Perspectives. Beverly Hills: Sage Publications.
---, L. TILLY, and R. TILLY (1975) The Rebellious Century. Cambridge, MA: Harvard University Press.
WALLERSTEIN, I. (1978) "World-system analysis: theoretical and interpretive issues," pp. 219-235 in B. H. Kaplan (ed.) Social Change in the Capitalist World Economy. Beverly Hills: Sage Publications.

Chapter 5

CYCLES OF FORMAL COLONIAL RULE

Albert Bergesen

Formal colonial rule by core states over peripheral areas has come in two waves or cycles. The first, centered in the Americas, lasted from the sixteenth through early nineteenth century. The second, centered in Africa, India, and Asia, lasted from the late nineteenth through the mid-twentieth century. These waves or cycles of colonialism can be clearly seen in Figure 5.1, which presents the total number of colonies for each year from 1415 through 1969. The data come from coding Henige's (1970) exhaustive study of the dates of colonial administrations, from the establishment of the first Portuguese colony in Ceuta in 1415 through the end of his study in 1969. The years during which a colonial governor was in office was used as an indicator of formal colonial rule, and the number of governors in office for all the colonial powers was totaled for each year.[1] The complete data set is presented in Bergesen and Schoenberg (1980). The presence of two cycles is quite clear. The question now is what do they mean, what processes do they reflect, and what do they tell us about the operation of the world-system?

CORE INSTABILITY AND FORMALIZED CORE–PERIPHERY RELATIONS: WORLD-SYSTEM BOUNDARY MAINTENANCE

If we assume there is a collective reality to the world-system above and beyond the realities of its constituent components of core, semiperiphery, and periphery, then it is possible to specify certain processes that belong solely to the world-system as a corporate actor. These collective properties or waves, or cycles, can only be seen from the perspective of the system as a whole, over the long duration of its existence.

The recurring establishment of more explicit political control over peripheral areas can be seen from the point of view of the world-system as a whole as a tightening or formalization of its basic social relations.

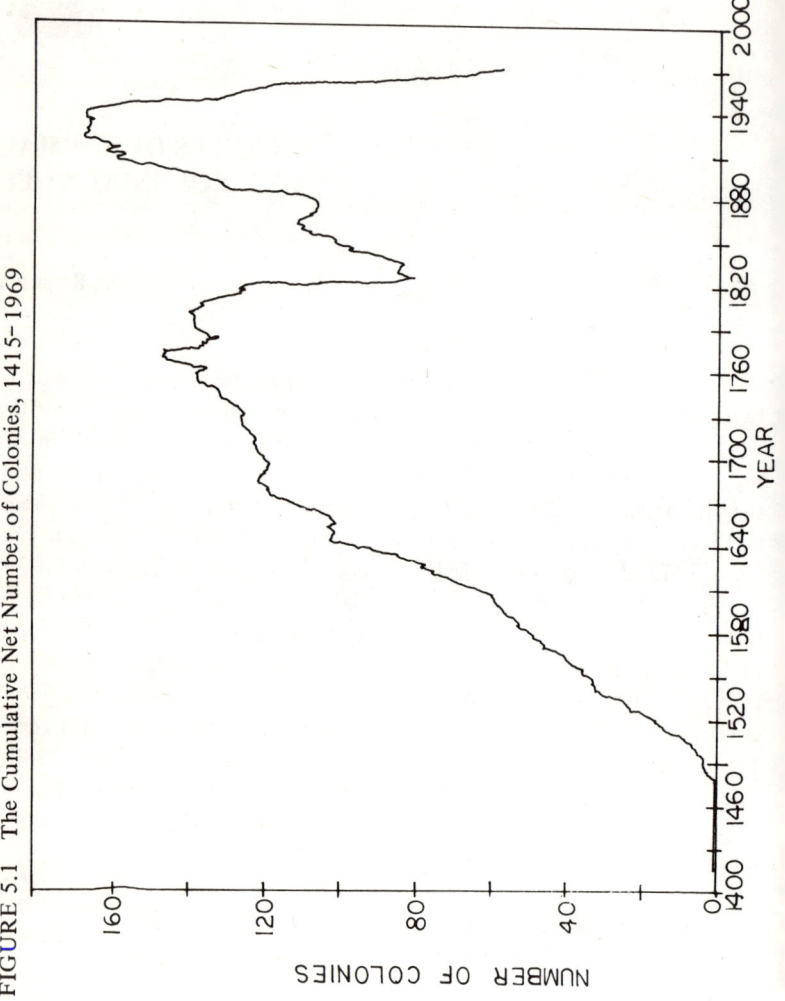

FIGURE 5.1 The Cumulative Net Number of Colonies, 1415–1969

Colonialism expands when there is instability within the core and contracts when there is stability. There is instability when there are multiple core powers of more or less equal strength, and there is stability when one hegemonic power dominates. From the sixteenth through the early nineteenth centuries the core was composed of competing rivalrous and warring states. It was the age of the Absolutist State, balance of power politics, and constant warfare. The core was unstable, and colonialism expanded to reaffirm and reset world social relations in response to problems within the center of the system. During the mid-nineteenth century there was a single hegemonic power, Britain, peace, and colonialism contracted as the first colonial wave in the Americas collapsed. During the last quarter of the nineteenth century Britain declined, Germany and the United States rose, power became more equally distributed across core states, and the core became increasingly more unstable, eventually decomposing into the second Thirty Years War of 1914-1945. With this core instability colonialism again expanded, this time in Africa, India, and Asia after 1870. Then after 1945, with the emergence of another hegemonic power, the United States, and resultant peace among the major powers, the core was again stable, and the overall system became more informally structured: the second wave of colonialism virtually collapsed in the short period between 1947 and 1962. Finally, with the power of the United States fading during the 1970s, with the rise of Japan, Europe, and the Soviet Union, the core is again becoming composed of more equal states rather than one dominant state, and once again core-periphery relations are formalizing as peripheral areas are being once again brought under the influence of the major powers.

A multicentric core and formal core-periphery relations; a unicentric core and informal core-periphery relations[2] —this is one identifiable dynamic of the world-system.

These are obviously very general and abstract ideas, and one sign of their generality is the fact that the more explicit political regulation of core-periphery relations is not limited to just colonialism. Trade relations also vary with the same cyclic rhythms. During the first wave (1500-1815) mercantile regulations formally controlled trade; during the first trough (1820-1870) trade was more informally structured with the era of free trade; during the second wave (1870-1945) tariffs rose, protectionism increased, and neo-mercantile policies were adopted by all the major core powers as trade again became more formally structured; during the second trough (1945-1973) free trade again appeared in the form of the General Agreement on Tariffs and Trade (GATT) and trade again became more informal. Finally, during the beginning of a possible third cycle (1973-) protectionism, import restrictions, quotas, and neo-mercantile policies in general are once again on the rise, as core-periphery trade is once again becoming more formally regulated.

This model is general in another sense. Even though formal colonial rule has virtually disappeared, political relations between core and periphery once again tightened the presence of core powers began to replace the free trade imperialism of the 1945-1973 American hegemony.

> Does the Third World still exist: In its poverty and under-development more than ever; in its "nonalignment" less and less. Most of Asia has already been divided into Soviet, American, and Chinese spheres of influence ... [and] now that Africa has entered the storm zone, its internal political and social conflicts are overshadowed by the politics of the great powers. The few years of relative national autonomy that followed decolonization are, for the weaker and more artificial of these new countries, now little more than a memory [Julliard, 1978:3].

The increased Soviet presence in Africa, South East Asia, and the Islamic Crescent and the coming struggle over global hegemony with the United States are reminiscent of struggles over colonial empires by the core powers during the last quarter of the nineteenth century.

LONG-TERM DEVELOPMENTAL TRENDS OF THE WORLD ECONOMY

The troughs of these cycles are also important, for the mid-nineteenth century and the 1945-1973 periods involved a dramatic expansion of the capitalist world-economy. The cycles, with the predominance of political factors like colonialism, and the troughs, with the emphasis upon the more purely economic elements of an expanding capitalist economy, alternate over time as the world-economy grows and expands. The cycles are becoming shorter: the first lasted 410 years (1415-1825), the second only 143 years (1826-1969), and if the trend holds, the third will be even shorter. The cycles are also becoming less severe, in that they involve less and less of the destruction and disruption of local social formations. The first wave involved the virtual annihilation of local Indian populations in the Americas to make way for the transplantation of core people and institutions, and the uprooting, enslavement, and transportation of Africans to the Americas as a coerced labor force. The second wave was much less a matter of displacing people and civilizations and more a question of domination and control through political occupation. Also, the neo-mercantilism after 1870 was less severe than before as no core state forbade foreign ships from its colonies, forced colonial trade through specific ports, or forbade manufactures which might compete with the home economy. Finally, the third wave, in that it doesn't involve formal colonial rule at all, but questions of arms dependence and the more subtle control through client states, is even less severe than the second wave. The "neo-neo-mercantilism" of the 1970s seems less severe than the high tariff barriers that were erected from the 1870s through the 1930s, although it must be noted that we are just beginning the third cycle, and the ultimate shape of trade relations is yet to be decided.

If the waves are becoming shorter and less severe, they will conceivably disappear in the future, and the more purely economic mode of integration present in the mid-nineteenth century and the 1945-1973 troughs will predominate. The extraeconomic mechanisms of colonial rule represent a form of primitive accumulation acting to initiate the system and then becoming progressively less important as the overall world economy grows and expands. Sometime in the future they will disappear altogether, leaving us with a pure capitalist world economy capable of accumulation and reproduction of its social relations without resorting to such extraeconomic mechanisms as colonialism. In some sense the movement from mechanical to organic solidarity Durkheim noted on the societal level is being reproduced on the world level, as the mechanical solidarity of political domination is gradually fading away and being replaced by the more organic solidarity of a self-perpetuating and self-reproducing capitalist world-economy.

WORLD CLASS RELATIONS

Finally, colonialism sheds some light on questions of class relations and class struggle in the world-system. It has been suggested (Brenner, 1977) that the present focus upon the core-periphery division of labor emphasizes exchange relations at the expense of relations of production and the class struggles they involve. In effect, half of the process of reproducing material existence is being left out of the present world-system perspective, and the most important half at that, since socio-productive relations are generally thought to determine exchange relations. In effect, something prior to trade and exchange determines and creates the world division of labor. Brenner has raised an important point. He wants to focus upon productive relations, class relations, and upon who controls the means of production and who is uprooted from their natural economy and proletarianized. Fine. The problem is that he sees class relations in the compartmentalized form of relations between particular groups nestled within national formations. For him there are class relations in sixteenth-century eastern and western Europe, class relations in colonial Virginia, and class relations in colonial Pennsylvania. It is not that there are no relations between the groups he identifies, there are. The problem is that these are the *only* class relations he articulates. There are also relations of production and class relations on a world scale, between the core and periphery as a whole. This tendency to see only exchange relations on a world scale, and productive relations on a national scale, reflects the early stages of our understanding of just how production is in fact organized and structured in a world-economy. Trade between nations seems so obvious and straightforward, it is no wonder that questions of unequal exchange, commodity sale on a world-market, and the core-periphery division of labor, would be the terms in which we would first conceptualize capitalism on a world scale. Brenner counterbalances class relations in the various sectors of the world-economy with exchange relations at the world level. He has the right set of social relations (production rather than exchange), but the wrong level of analysis (national rather than world). There is simply no reason why world social relations have to be *only* exchange relations. There can also be productive relations on a world scale (Bergesen, 1980).

Brenner is right: we need to talk about class relations. But, he is also wrong in thinking that these class relations exist only between groups nestled within national formations. The heart of the question becomes how we define a mode of production. Where Brenner, Laclau (1971), and others have problems is that they fail to see that the analytical notion of a mode of production has become synonymous with national societies, and more over the defining characteristic of the capitalist mode of production has become synonymous with the historically specific means of proleterianizing labor in the core, the wage relation. The idea that slavery, serfdom, and wage labor each constitutes the defining characteristics of a different mode of production is *only* a consequence of focusing upon core societies and tracing their developmental evolution over time. Then, yes, slavery, feudalism, and wage labor, are separable, and each can be considered an indicator of different modes of production which follow one upon the other. If, however, slavery in the Americas and wage labor in England coexist, and are obviously interconnected in a most fundamental way, then we must speak of them as part of one mode of production. To make the *slavery* that harvests cotton which is then spun into cloth by British *wage* earners into two modes of production denies the obvious connection between their labor activity.

The determining factor is the character of the mode of production as a whole, and if the world-economy is, as it must be, a singular mode of production, then it is the nature of *world relations of production* which in turn determines the relations between various classes within national formations. The separate class relations in each nook and cranny of the world-economy cannot, and do not, constitute determinate world relations of production.

COLONIALISM: CLASS STRUGGLE ON A WORLD SCALE

How, then, do we approach the question of class relations on a world scale? The central question in terms of class struggle is the way in which people are deprived of control over their means of production. Colonialism constitutes the historical form by which most of the world has lost control over their local economies, and been forced to participate in certain productive activities, like the export of raw materials, which in later centuries appears as a matter of market choice or as production for profit or a world-market. The sale of raw materials on a world-market, even for profit, is a necessity, much like the sale of labor power. The control of the world productive process is in the hands of the core, not the periphery, and what the latter sells and produces is determined not by its own needs (food, industrial diversification, accumulation of national capital, etc.) but by the needs of core capital. In this sense the sale of commodities for profit on a world-market is not the most fundamental social relation of world capitalism. Unequal exchange and the world division of labor do not occur in a vacuum, outside of world class forces which make their very operation historically possible. There is sale for profit in exporting raw materials, but there is profit in other activities, and the profit mechanism alone does not distinguish core economies which are diversified from peripheral economies which specialize in exporting cash crops. Without an understanding of the world class struggle involved in centuries of colonial expansion and plunder it is impossible to fully understand the seemingly self-generating core-periphery division of labor. The core-periphery division of labor and the process of unequal exchange are direct consequences of the class struggle between core and periphery that resulted in the loss of control by local economies over the shape and content of their productive activity. Since the sixteenth century the vast majority of the world's territory has been brought under colonial control. What we now call the periphery represents social formations and local modes of production that were either destroyed or significantly modified such that their productive activity came to be directed toward generating surplus value that was transferred—either directly as in the earlier centuries of colonial plunder, or indirectly through unequal exchange—to the core.

NOTES

1. Governors that were part of the *intendencia* reorganization of the Spanish colonies beginning in the 1780s, were not coded, as they represented more of an administrative reorganization rather than the advent of new colonial expansion. This left 390 colonies divided among the major powers as follows: Britain (172), France

(65), Spain (59), Portugal (38), the Netherlands (23), the United States (8), Germany (7), Italy (5), Denmark (3), Belgium (2), Sweden (2), Russia (1).

2. This model reflects a basically Durkheimian conceptualization of social process in which the organic quality of collective existence is seen as the determinate factor. This model is obviously shaped by Erikson's (1966) notion of the corporate community's (here the world-system as a global collectivity) response (here colonialism and mercantile trade relations) to social instabilities and boundary crises (here core instability and multipolarity).

REFERENCES

BERGESEN, A. (1980) "From utilitarianism to the world-system: the shift from the individual to the world as a whole as the primordial unit of analysis," in A. Bergesen (ed.) Studies of the Modern World-System. New York: Academic Press.
——— and R. SCHOENBERG (1980) "Long waves of colonial expansion and contraction, 1415-1969," in A. Bergesen (ed.) *Studies of the Modern World-System.* New York: Academic Press.
BRENNER, R. (1977) "The origins of capitalist development: a critique of neo-Smithian Marxism." New Left Review 104 (July/Aug.): 25-92.
ERIKSON, K. (1966) The Wayward Puritans. New York: John Wiley.
HENIGE, D. (1970) Colonial Governors. Madison: University of Wisconsin Press.
JULLIARD, J. (1978) "For a new 'Internationale.' " New York Review of Books (July 20).
LACLAU, E. (1971) "Feudalism and capitalism in Latin America." New Left Review 67 (May/June): 19-38.

PART 2
THE WORLD CLASS STRUCTURE: PROLETARIANIZATION AND BOURGEOISIFICATION

SECTION A
PERIPHERALIZATION AND CLASS FORMATION

Chapter 6

CLASS DEVELOPMENT IN RURAL EGYPT, 1945-1979

James F. Toth

The ruling class in Egypt has repeatedly experienced a structural schizophrenia in periods of crisis and capital contraction which then becomes only somewhat resolved when internal squabbles over capital disappear. An increased volume of capital has often produced an uneasy alliance among competing interests in the ruling class. When resources dip below the bare minimum, the alliance is again rent by internal conflict. Severe competition for capital between rival branches of the ruling class means increased exploitation of workers in order to produce the desired surplus. Such ruthless exploitation may explode into social violence precipitating the need for rivals to come together and forget their differences. The influx of new capital becomes the glue to cement yet another ruling coalition.

This is what happened in Egypt in the 1940s and early 1950s. The postwar economic decline fragmented the Egyptian ruling class, and only the revolution and an influx of new capital could bring it together again. But new landed proprietors were unable and/or unwilling to supply funds for economic development, and the state power itself became the major accumulator of surplus capital. In the 1960s, this capital dried up; private farmers increasingly circumvented stiff state regulations in order to make profits in any way possible. The new regime of 1970 was forced to recognize the supremacy of private landed capital, but still unable to find investment and development funds, had to align itself with Western capital—banks and corporations—merely to "break even," without putting undue pressure on those farmers whose support underwrote its power. Dependent peripheral development (or underdevelopment) thus had swung full circle.

THE CAST OF CHARACTERS

In the 1940s, the social structure in rural Egypt consisted of three groups: absentee landlords, peasants, and landless workers.

The big landlord was the mainstay of the Egyptian ruling class. Statistically defined as any owner possessing 50 feddans of land or more, this group contained only 11% of all landowners yet possessed 34.2% of all the land (see Table 6.1). Such landlords operated ^{c}ezba's—large rural factories which produced cotton, rice, and sugar cane, mostly for European markets. Europeans were noticeably absent from this group (only 5% of foreign individuals or corporations in Egypt owned land); they chose "merely" to retain financial control over agricultural production by dominating the credit banks (Baer, 1962: 79). This segment of the rural ruling class, consisting of the palace (King Faruq and his court) and other prominent Ottoman, Turkish, and Albanian families, was organically linked to the urban commercial and small industrial bourgeoisie and together the two were tied to foreign capital. During the late 1940s, despite world conditions which saw a proliferation of commodity markets replacing the former British monopoly, these landed aristocrats did not choose to improve and expand agricultural production. Instead, they kept their dominant and conservative class position by maintaining loyal ties to British merchants, controlling the palace and state apparatus, and blocking all attempts at agrarian reform (Hussein, 1973: 17-25; Abdel-Malek, 1962: 50-67).

TABLE 6.1 Distribution of Land Before 1952 Law

Size of Ownership (feddans)	Owners (thousands)	%	Area (feddans)	%	Average Holding Per Owner
Small ownerships:					
5	2,642	94.3	2,122	35.4	0.8
Medium ownerships:					
5–10	79	2.8	526	8.8	6.6
10–20	47	1.7	638	10.7	13.6
20–50	22	0.8	654	10.9	29.7
Large ownerships:					
50–100	6	0.2	430	7.2	71.7
100–200	3	0.1	437	7.3	145.7
200	2	0.1	1,177	19.7	588.6

SOURCE: Mahmoud Abdel Fadil, *Development, Income Distribution and Social Change in Rural Egypt (1952–1970)*. London: Cambridge University Press, p. 11.

The Egyptian peasantry consisted of those possessing less than fifty feddans of land. Quantitative variation in landholdings had qualitative consequences for rural production. Peasants owning more than twenty feddans were able to use technology which provided economies of scale in agricultural production; those with five feddans or more, according to a 1913 law, could, unlike poorer peasants, have access to mortgage loans to finance expanded production; and finally, owners with two feddans possessed the minimum amount of land required to support a small rural family (Abdel Fadil, 1975: 18, 31-34; Mayfield, 1971: 41). Those owning under five feddans led a precarious life indeed! Those with more were in a more viable and survivable position. These rich peasants varied considerably in their orientation toward market production, risk taking (which often meant an established access to capital and technology), and labor management. Many rich peasants—usually the wealthier ones owning more than twenty feddans—were entrepreneurial farmers ready to expand production by optimally combining the factors of production to maximize profits. Labor was hired directly at the lowest possible wage allowing the farmer to discharge labor without the burden of personal ties. However, other rich peasants—often those wealthy peasants suffering a decline in fortunes—were more conservative, producing for a precarious self-sufficiency, and seeking to maintain their position not by economic expansion but through political patronage. Patronage meant finding patrons among the landed aristocrats as well as retaining control over labor through complex ties of tenancy and sharecropping despite their impediments to greater flexibility and profits (Abdel Fadil, 1975: 42-43; Ibrahim ^{c}Amr, cited in Binder, 1978: 72).

In addition to owning land, rich peasants often managed land for absentee landlords, thus giving themselves access to the better land and a voice in the distribution of the rest. Since land holdings were fragmented and scattered, entrepreneurially minded peansants sought, thereby, to lease in neighboring plots and rent out distant plots in order to maximize the size of the production unit. They were particularly hard-hit, then, by the runaway rents of the 1940s. Between 1938 and 1950, rents increased five-fold. Speculators helped fuel these fires. Net revenues were often less than the rents themselves, clearly indicating the higher value rented land brought in, in contrast to cultivated land. With such high overhead costs, the expansion of production was impossible and profit margins lean. Such restrictions forced these rich peasants to oppose the conservative policies of the palace though still basically supporting the overall system from which they benefited. They alternatively confronted the palace and those landlords above them who blocked their way and allied themselves with the very same aristocrats in order to preserve their class position (Harik, 1972: chs. 2 and 3; Radwan, 1977: 74; Binder, 1978: 132).

It was not enough to just own land, regardless of the amount. In order to insure control over agricultural production, capital accumulation, and labor supply—in short, to reproduce the rural social formation—it was, of course, necessary to dominate the state political apparatus. At the national level, this consisted of a parliamentary facade occupied by aristocratic landlords, members of political parties loyal to or loyally opposed to the palace and its British allies. At the local level, the ^cumda or village headman represented the state in his capacity to maintain public order, collect taxes, settle disputes, allocate state land, and mediate between different interest groups. Before Muhammad Ali and Egypt's integration into the world capitalist market, the ^cumda had held much more control over local economic interests. But throughout the nineteenth century, this independent power declined, especially after the reign of Ismail (1863-1879), who created the first national parliament, and the beginning of the British occupation (1882). Landlords increasingly absent from the countryside and residing in Cairo or Alexandria merely continued their political domination of the countryside by giving up the headmanship for a seat in parliament. While the interests of the landlords and the state apparatus continued to coincide, they soon became administered locally by the one or two rich peasant families who now governed the village. While the office of headman appeared more and more as the bottom rung of the state apparatus, it would be a mistake to assume that the ^cumda had become nothing more than a manager for dominant class interests. The exclusive middleman position gave the rich peasant headman some leverage in directly controlling local affairs (Baer, 1969a).

By the 1940s, landlords could no longer assume that village headmen would deliver votes and represent their interests. These interests had begun to compete with those of the palace, now no longer controlled exclusively by big landlords but increasingly concerned with its own interests and those of the merchants and bankers benefiting from the war-time economic boom. Parties representing the landlords were increasingly forced actively to recruit headmen in order to insure their compliance, thus giving additional power to the ^cumda position and increasing its value to rich peasant competitors and, in turn, aristocratic politicians.

Beneath the rich peasants, both politically and economically, the poor peasants with five feddans of land or less represented the largest number of landowners: 94.3% of all owners possessing about one-third of the land. Here was Chayanov's ideal family farm, neither hiring in nor hiring out labor, producing sufficiently for both home consumption and the market place (Abdel Fadil, 1975: 11,27; Hussein, 1973: 23-37). But the ideal was seldom realized: changes in family composition, the annual season, but especially changes in the rural economy forced family members off the farm as direct producers. Some became owner-managers, attempting to rise to the level of the rich peasants; others were in the process of losing their land and selling their labor to landlords and farmers. The wealthier ones were too bound to the dominant ruling segment to upset the rural social structure. But at the same time, like their wealthier mentors, they too were frustrated in their attempts at reform and the pursuit of their own interests. This segment also could choose channels of the state bureaucracy, the mosque, and petty professional occupations (teachers, policemen, soldiers, peddlers) to pull themselves up the village social hierarchy (Abdel Fadi, 1975: 60). But in the 1940s, these channels were few. The bureaucracy was monopolized by Copts and Jews; merchandising was dominated by Greek and Levantine families—all those social elements lacking a substantial power base. Barriers against economic and professional expansion pushed the poor peasants, too, into political opposition.

The poor peasants at the other end of the scale—those owning less than two feddans—resembled more the landless worker.[1] Although these poor peasants had diversified their occupations in order to supplement their incomes, a stunted urban industrial sector did not allow them the opportunity for a larger income in the city. The cities were unable to absorb job-hunting rural migrants; all land was under cultivation, so expanding frontiers were nonexistent. Peasants, therefore, had to remain in the village, unable to find additional work and thereby depressing rural wages.

These three segments—landlords, rich peasants, and poor peasants—made up the rural ruling class of Egypt after the Second World War. The aristocrats and their ^{c}ezbas maintained economic domination over the Egyptian countryside. In periods of expanded production, peasant families supplied extra labor (lowering wage levels) since they were unable to expand production themselves. In periods of constricted production, such labor returned to the family farm for its sustenance and reproduction. In these periods of decline, when labor was not needed on the ^{c}ezba nor needed in the job-scarce cities, families often mortgaged their crops and their land in order to survive. Over time, they finally lost free access to the means of production and any autonomous decision-making power over production, and joined the growing mass of landless.

This mass was not a small group of workers. Although its size in the 1940s is still difficult to estimate, Abdel Fadil (1975: 44) arrived at a most careful calculation of 44% of all rural families. This class differed internally according to their degree of proletarianization. Those who were (strictly) tenants and sharecroppers had the most secure access to land through customary ties to the landlord. There were also day laborers who were more or less permanently employed as field workers, livestock tenders, and machine operators. At the lowest rung were the casual laborers and migrant labor gang workers (*tarahils*) representing the most oppressed group in the rural division of labor. As a class, the landless had the least to lose by actively opposing the system but were the least capable of going beyond the occasional theft or estate take-over, for they lacked any real organizational base of their own (Abdel Fadil, 1975: 43-48; Hussein, 1973: 41).

THE RURAL TRANSFORMATION OF SOCIAL RELATIONS OF PRODUCTION

Samir Amin has suggested that while the Middle East in general exhibited a mercantile mode of production, such that agriculture was relatively unimportant compared to the urban merchant-nomad coalition, Egypt proved to be an exception. Egypt followed what Amin called a tributary mode of production which differed only slightly from the feudalism practiced in Europe. While the latter centralized political control but diffused economic power, Egypt centralized both. Like manorial feudalism, surplus production was coercively appropriated from peasant producers in the form of labor and/or rent, but more like its Chinese counterpart, the means of appropriation were independent of the contributions made by subordinate vassels. That is, Egypt relied on an external imperial power for state control of labor and the extraction of surplus rather than on an internally generated army (Amin, 1978: 18-20).

Egypt, then, represented a type of feudalism similar to the Asiatic mode of production. Yet in the eighteenth century, Ottoman weakness had permitted Mamluk Egypt a semblance of independence from Constantinople, with a concomitant reduction in the characteristically strong central authority. Accordingly, the fedualism of Egypt began more and more to appear as European feudalism, with Mamluk tax-farmers transformed, de facto, but not de jure, into private landlords (Richards, 1977: 10-14, 17-22).

With the rise of Muhammad Ali in the early nineteenth century, the relations of agricultural production were greatly altered. Egypt once again experienced a strong centralized state authority. Tax-farming was abolished, transformed into private ownership with tax collection a function of the village headman. Yet this "new" feudalism found in Egypt in the nineteenth and twentieth centuries was increasingly tied into the capitalistic production of raw cotton for textile mills in Manchester. Immanuel Wallerstein (1974: 91) noted that a "second serfdom" appeared in Europe in the sixteenth century, characterized by a strong central state, market production, and large latifundia. Similarly, the reappearance of a strong central state system accompanied by the commodity production of cotton on large ᶜezbas established a capitalistic feudalism in Egypt. But the difference in nineteenth-century Egypt was that this renewed feudalism operated under the domination of an already developed European industrial capitalism which subsequently warped Egypt's own economic development. The disintegration of a relatively autonomous Egyptian economy and its integration into the world-system, dating from the time of Muhammad Ali, organized economic activities in directions which reinforced the country's dependent status. The interests of European capital were best served by preserving Egypt's role in supplying raw materials while reducing domestic competition with imports (Hussein, 1973: 16-18).

Cotton production is extremely labor-intensive and, in Egypt in the 1940s, aristocratic landlords continued to rely on a large labor force. Workers from the interstitial small farms rented or sharecropped the divided ᶜezba. Additional labor was extracted, when needed, through unpaid corvée labor and debt peonage. Mechanization here was only slight. The encapsultion of this peripheral mode of production permitted the rural community to assume the cost of labor reproduction and shifted the risk of economic failure back onto the landlord.[2] Profits accruing to the landlord were not plowed back into production nor invested in nonagricultural, productive enterprises; rather, they went into luxury goods, urban real estate, quick return urban enterprises and/or foreign banks. Cotton merchants in Alexandria and England, in turn, benefited from lower finance and production costs by buying cheap and then skimming off as much as 50% from the subsequent sale of cotton.

As long as British cotton merchants monopolized Egyptian agriculture, such low capitalization went unchallenged. After the Second World War, however, with the American demand for cotton—especially during the Korean War—the ante for cotton production received a boost. Foreign competitors could increase their financing of Egyptian farmers, permitting the latter to pay daily wages instead of annual shares and to invest in new technology. Commodity markets could now be expanded into the countryside to take advantage of new rural economic activity. An outcome of this increased capitalization was the agricultural entrepreneur, geared toward market production and technological investment. But his ability to expand was limited. Attempts to legislate agrarian reforms were repeatedly frustrated in parliament by a recalcitrant aristocracy.

Until the 1930s, these aristocrats dominated the Egyptian countryside, controlling the rich peasant ᶜumdas and notables (*ayyan*) below and the palace policy-makers above. In 1931, however, the palace began bringing rich peasants directly into parliament in order to counter the heavy influence of the landlords and their Wafd party. In the 1936 elections, the Wafd began to actively recruit rich peasants as well, and by 1942 competition between the palace and the Wafd for their support accelerated. The 1940s saw further splits in the heretofore unified ruling class, splits which cross-cut political party lines which then no longer corresponded to well-bounded sets of economic interests. The Wafd party was headed by a big landlord, but it contained merchants professionals and socialists as well. The Independent party of the palace included compradores and industrialists, the latter also belonging to the Saadist party. Landlords also controlled the Liberal-Constitutionalists. Other organizations—the Muslim Brotherhood; the Peasant Union; the Young Egyptians, and their successor, the Socialist party; the various Communist associations (the New Dawn, the National Movement, the Peoples' Vanguard, and the C.P.E. itself); and workers' syndicates—recruited among the less powerful but the more numerous: poor peasants, petty urban merchants and craftsmen, students and intellectuals, and urban and rural workers. The Second World War exacerbated these political differences even further (Abdel-Malek, 1962: 91; Binder, 1978: 124-133; al-Sa^{c}id, 1976: 145-152).

We find, therefore, on the eve of the revolution the relations of agricultural production in Egypt in transition, in a dialectical struggle between a disintegrating feudalism of large estates and a paralyzed capitalism of small entrepreneurial farmers (Hussein, 1973: 24).[3] The dualism found in the Egyptian ruling class was not one between a rural feudalism and an urban bourgeoisie for these two, in fact, were still somewhat in alliance, if not actually congruent. Rather, the dialogue or tension was between an entrenched aristocratic order which was blocking any expansion of rural production by controlling capital resources (banks) and land prices and rents on the one hand, and a peasantry unable to become farmers or expand into nonagricultural occupations of commerce and government on the other.

The response to this internal "blockade" of economic and political expansion was social unrest. In the 1940s, poor peasants and landless workers reacted to their increased pauperization with violent take-overs of huge estates and a rapid rise in rural crimes (Baer, 1969b). Even the rich peasants, usually at least supportive of a system which preserved their privileged position, though at times opposed to specific policies of a reactionary palace and aristocracy, were in an unbearable position because of sky-rocketing rents and usurious extortions. The Zionist defeat in 1947 and the continued British presence along the Suez Canal constantly reminded the country and especially the young officers of the Egyptian army, of the country's enduring disgrace. On July 23, 1952, the Free Officers, under the leadership of Gamal ^{c}Abd el-Nasser, took over state power in order to prevent further economic and political deterioration and to promote greater national development by freeing the nation from the chains of British imperialism and the intransigence of the landed aristocracy (Hussein, 1973: 89).

THE REVOLUTION AND CLASS STRUCTURE: ALLIANCE, OPPOSITION, AND DOMINATION

The ruling class in Egypt has never been completely monolithic, nor completely divided into separate, isolated camps. Instead, segments within the dominant class have allied themselves to dominate yet another, only to split apart in subsequent quarrels over the spoils and benefits of the previous united front. In periods when capital flows into the country, the ruling class solidifies, dominates the state apparatus, and controls capital resources and labor. Yet because of its dependent status, the Egyptian economy subsequently loses this capital plus more in the form of extracted profits and reduced revenues. As the volume of capital decreases, the loci of control are reduced to one of the class's internal segments, be it the aristocracy, the state apparatus, or the burgeoning capitalists.

We have seen that while the aristocracy dominated the palace—indeed, it *was* the palace—and the landowning peasants, its hegemony was shattered in the post-Second World War decline. Increasingly, the palace separated from the ruling class not only as the sole benefactor of economic activity but also as a pole of opposition for the remaining branches of the ruling class and the working class as well.[4] The defeat of 1947 and the guerilla activity along the canal in 1951 demonstrated its growing inability to even control the state's means of repression—the army and the police. Finally, it was the army—defenders of the national integrity and an extension of the rural peasantry—which gave the final blow to a faltering feudal aristocracy.

Immediately, the new regime implemented a land reform program designed to eliminate the political power of the big landlords, encourage rich peasants to intensify capitalist production and pacify the poor peasants by tying their political ambitions to the state bureaucratic machinery. The size of land holdings was limited to 300 feddans, with excess land either sold on the market or confiscated and distributed by the state. Rents were reduced 25 to 30%. Further land reform measures are listed in Table 6.2 (Saab, 1967: 45).

Landlords were greatly weakened by land confiscation and formal exclusion from administrative offices. Some, however, assumed the role of capitalist farmer, overcoming their former hesitation to invest and expand production. The major beneficiaries of the land reform program were the peasants. Rich peasants benefited almost exclusively from private land sales in the first year of the reform program but they especially profited from rent reductions and improved finance conditions. Poor peasants and some tenants and sharecroppers benefited directly from the allocation of confiscated land, though the small scale of government distribution (only 10% of the cultivated land was affected) prevented any real change in their class position (Hussein, 1973: 96-97).

TABLE 6.2 Land Reform Legislation

Year	Law	Rent	Ceilings Personal	Family	Mortgage
1952	Land reform program	–	200/head 50/son	–	30 years 3%
1953	Land sales prohibited	–	–	–	–
1953	Royal estates confiscated	–	–	–	–
1957	Religious endowments confiscated	–	–	–	–
1958	Family ceiling mortgage	–	–	300/family	40 years 1½%
1959	Total land rented and owned	------	300	------------	–
1961	Second land reform law	50 Max	100/head	300/family	40 years none
1962	Family ceilings	–	–	100/family	–
1962	Sequestration	–	–	–	–
1963	Foreign owned land	–	–	–	–
1964	Sequestration	–	–	–	–
1969	Third land reform law	–	50/head	100/family	–

Politically, the rich peasants continued to dominate the local state apparatus, but now their sons and those of the poor peasants began to fill the ranks of government bureaus and newly created universities in Cairo. The middle-class revolution took time; not all feudalists were removed immediately. They continued to play an important role in rural society for many reasons: their still large landholdings, their experience with authority, and their ideological influence. Aristocrats occassionally allied themselves with reactionary members of the peasantry who could legally hold administrative offices in order to impede the growth of an invigorated agricultural capitalism. Nevertheless, they were gradually on their way out as farmers from the peasantry came to dominate them through their control of the state machinery which confiscated and distributed agricultural land. Local notables, former estate managers, and ʿumdas formed local committees with authority from the High Committee of Agrarian Reform to draw up lists of eligible recipients, to distribute confiscated land and to lease out state land not yet ready for actual distribution (Hussein, 1973: 102; Saab, 1967: 30-32).

The immediate result, then, of the 1952 revolution and its first land reform program was the overthrow of intransigent feudal aristocrats and the succession of rich peasants to a position of class domination. Previously these peasants had controlled the local level of state administration but were unable to gain control of the state machinery which, at higher levels, had had greater influence over rural political activities. By eliminating the landlords' monopoly over this state administration, entrepreneurial peasants could embark on economic expansion unimpeded by the reactionary policies of the state toward matters of finance, credit, infrastructure, marketing, and trade. The influx of new capital into the countryside and the fervor of the revolution united the ruling class: reactionaries were throttled while others adapted to capitalistic practices; rich peasants won greater benefits and a new dominant position within the ruling class; and poor peasants, divided between increased agricultural opportunities and expanded channels of professional employment, became pacified supporters of the system. Even rural laborers initially benefited: wages and work conditions were legislated, tenure was secured, unions permitted, and rents and shares reduced. But these benefits were crippled by several factors: a continuing increase in the rural working population, the inability of new family farms to absorb this excess labor, and the still slow development of urban industry. And the larger number of job opportunities expected from the land reform program was not forthcoming (Radwan, 1977: 92). All this pointed to a much greater malaise which began to take place in the last third of the 1950s and which ultimately forced the state power to take greater direct control of rural economic and political activities.

FINANCING ECONOMIC DEVELOPMENT AND THE STATE

In eliminating the major impediments to capitalist agriculture, it was hoped that potentially larger profits would renew confidence in the rural economy and motivate farmers to expand production. Farmers could then directly invest these profits, or the government could tax the improved value of the land and invest these revenues—all to finance industrial development. But taxes, along with rents and land prices (all interconnected), had been lowered by the reform program to add incentives for expanding production; increased tax revenues would only have led to a reduction in production, land value, and revenues. At the same time, had production, profits, and taxes increased, this would have meant a greater exploitation of rural workers which could produce violent disruptions. On the other hand, private investments also remained limited. Bonds used to indemnify expropriated land were not directed into industrial investment as intended but continued to go into urban real estate or overseas. And subsequent changes in the reform program made these bonds practically worthless. Investable agricultural profits were not forthcoming. This was due, in part, to the continued dependency of mono-crop agriculture on the world market and the extortional profits of local cotton merchants. Egyptian agriculture did not have the ability to become the *deux ex machina* of economic development for which planners had hoped.

Financing came, instead, from American aid programs and, after the 1956 Bandung Conference, from the Soviets as well. Nasser's policy of neutrality and nonalignment and his manipulation of the Israeli-Arab conflict forced these international rivals to up the ante in gaining Egypt's support and access to its markets. This international maneuvering brought some rewards, temporarily relieving the Egyptian peasantry of its financial burden, but in its stead, strengthening Egypt's dependent status through financial and military relations with the West and the Eastern bloc (Hussein, 1973: chs. 3 and 4; Abdel-Malek, 1962: ch. 6).

Any changes in these international relations could threaten Nasser's ability to satisfy various class demands for national development and to stay in power. Therefore, he increasingly turned back to the peasantry for capital and investment funds, but despite absolute increases in production, these were not available. The only alternative was to increase direct bureaucratic control of rural political and economic activities. Although the rural bureaucracy continued to be dominated by members of the rich peasantry, the overall state machinery was becoming increasingly influenced by other branches of the ruling class, i.e., financial, industrial, and mercantile interests—and its own. The interests of the state apparatus and the middle-class farmers, heretofore congruent, began to diverge as the former increased its demands for the capital of the latter. In the late 1950s, the balance between peasant farmers and state bureaucrats, formerly tipped in favor of rural property owners, now began to go the other way.

The state soon created two major institutions—the agricultural cooperative association which replaced the cotton merchant; and the local branch of the single state political party, which replaced the role of landlord—to accumulate state capital and to increase direct state power over agricultural production, credit sources, and markets. These institutions increased the state's domination of private rural capital. The *coup de grace* came when leaders from the peasantry were set against each other in practically useless competition for local offices, dividing their limited authority with rival administrators, all of whom became ultimately controlled by the increasingly powerful state machine.[5]

Cooperative membership was required of all peasants who had received land through the agrarian reform program. After 1957, these cooperatives seriously began to assume production, credit, and marketing functions. Two years later, the state expanded the number of associations by incorporating older, private credit cooperatives into the system. The cooperative acted as a method of appropriating surplus capital not by acquiring the means of production directly but by fixing the purchase price of crops and the selling price of production inputs and making itself the sole marketing outlet. The cooperatives took the place of merchant, landlord, and moneylender: it provided fertilizers, seeds, and tools, lent money and foreclosed on mortgaged crops (*not* land); it processed agricultural commodities and set prices. Until 1960, cotton was the only crop marketed through cooperative channels. By 1965, the state had totally monopolized cotton marketing and had extended a partial monopoly over wheat, rice, and sugar cane.[6] By controlling interest rates, acreage, and terms of trade, the state administration extracted as much as 15-16% of gross agricultural income out of the countryside.[7] Profits previously going to cotton merchants now began going into state coffers.

Just as the cooperative represented the means of state capital accumulation, the single political party was the means for insuring state domination of political activities. Up to 1960, the village headman remained the exclusive connection between the central administration and local property owners and laborers. The political parties of the 1950s—the Liberation Rally and the National Union—were formed more to exclude political participants such as ex-landlords than to provide a means of state control. But the autonomy of the middle class headman and notables soon disappeared. Many of their functions were taken up by local representatives of the government ministries. Village councils were created to counter balance the ʿumda's heretofore solitary influence. Even the power of the cooperative was divided between the supervisor appointed by the Ministry of Agriculture and a governing board representing local members (though the former usually dominated). Overseeing this proliferation of political activity—activity full of sound and fury but signifying nothing—was the local branch of the Arab Socialist Union (A.S.U.), the more forceful and better organized successor of the previous political parties. The A.S.U. dictated, explicitly or otherwise, the choice of office candidates, appointees, village welfare policies, and budgetary matters.

The mass nationalizations ordered by Nasser in the summer of 1961 signaled the supremacy of the state bureaucratic machinery over the interests of middle-class farmers. The question had been: who substantially controlled the flow of capital in Egypt? Investment funds were needed, and neither foreign capital (bank, state, or corporate) nor local private capital was cooperating. Nationalization visibly wrested control of commercial and industrial enterprises from foreign hands. But behind these headlines, the state also increased its control over rural production and capital accumulation by strengthening the cooperative associations and creating the A.S.U.

However, bureaucratic subjugation of rural peasants could not completely ignore their demands for fear of upsetting the state machinery's fragile position of growing dominance. Some caveats were necessary: a second land reform further reduced land ownership ceilings to one hundred feddans and limited land rentals to fifty feddans. More land became available for confiscation and distribution, mostly to poor peasants. In addition, the expanding bureaucracy absorbed many of the rural peasants unable to remain in agriculture.[8] A process begun with Egypt's union with Syria, the sudden halt in bureaucratic expansion caused by the 1961 dissolution of the union could have undermined the regime's control had not new positions been created.[9] But despite the benefits of more land and more government posts, there was still grumbling heard that the state had merely replaced the aristocratic landlords of nine years earlier. Indeed, it had.

In the 1950s, the ruling class unified for the first time since the Second World War—in the countryside this meant an alliance between private capitalist farmers and the state bureaucratic apparatus. The dialectical tension between feudal landlords and entrepreneurial peasants had, for all intents and purposes, disappeared. But by 1961, a new duality had arisen: an antagonism between state and private capitalists. Both supported the system of alienated labor and extracted surplus value, yet both competed vigorously for this surplus and for capital coming from outside the country. In the 1960s, both were becoming scarce. The West, now experiencing a period of capital expansion, no longer needed to invest so heavily abroad in order to raise its rate of profit—domestic production there was now becoming increasingly adequate. Therefore, Egypt had to begin relying more on its own domestic producers, which meant in the face of a still infant industry, the agricultural sector. But by 1965, domestic production had begun to suffer. As both foreign and domestic capital sources dried up, the state entered a period of major crisis.

The split within the ruling class between middle-class propertyowners and the state administration, acknowledged by the 1961 nationalizations, soon became a virtual chasm. The state continued to disarm middle-class bureaucrats by depriving their office of any autonomous power and strengthening the control eminating out of Cairo. Rural office-holders were subject to transfers, reassignments, reappointments, and sometimes even reelections. The state removed any possibility of rich peasants using their position to further their own interests over those of the state. Similarly, in the cooperative and agrarian reform program, land and crop confiscations were increasingly used to insure compliance with administration regulations. Farmers not meeting their mandatory quotas were fined, crop rotation was enforced, and deviation could mean loosing rights to land. The repeated limitations on land ownership created an insecurity heightened further by possible accusations of feudal recidivism. All these measures helped increase the emnity between landowners and the state administration (Abdel Fatah, n.d.: 18).

The usurpation of power by the state caused members of the rural middle class to respond by circumventing state regulations and enrich themselves illegally through black market activities, corruption, and neglecting cooperative production and bureaucratic duties (Waterbury, 1978a: 1-2; 1978b: 210-211). Crops were sold to private merchants, production inputs were diverted from the cooperative to private farms, government machinery was leased to nonmembers—all the while, officials were carefully paid to overlook such violations and to dispense favors to those who could afford them. Cooperatives became increasingly paralyzed as supplies, commodities, and services were surreptitiously sold by peasant farmers.

Who had to make up for the differences lost by cooperative corruption? Poor peasants and landless workers were increasingly exploited by both the state and the farmer alike. While these two competing branches of the ruling class struggled to command the largest share of surplus capital, the rural worker bore the major brunt of this conflict. From 1965 on, real wages fell drastically in the face of an inflation caused by increasing shortages of crops, due to a decline in fertilizer use, shortages in consumption goods as subsidies and administered prices promoted hoarding and withholding, and shortages in available loans due to the banks' preference for middle-class customers. No matter who won the struggle between private and public capital, the worker suffered the consequences. Thus, increasing crisis meant greater capital needs, greater state penetration of rural farms and markets, greater corruption and mismanagement, and ultimately, greater exploitation of rural workers. What the state needed was either a solution or a palliative.

MILITARY DEFEAT AND THE ROAD TO THE OPEN DOOR

The Israeli attack of June 1967 gave Egypt both a diversion and a cure. The Six Day War underscored the complete corruption of the state's military service and the emptiness of its officials. Yet Nasser succeeded, by resigning, in disassociating himself from the debacle. The working masses refused to accept his resignation and its implicit victory for Israel and

Egypt's corrupt state apparatus. The massive outpouring of indignation and support, forcing Nasser to return to power, gave the masses a false sense of power. The national defeat turned exploitation and poverty into a national sacrifice and suffering for the Arab cause (Hussein, 1973: 251-269). Worker protest became momentarily silent.[10] More land was confiscated and redistributed in 1969 to appease the demand for economic growth. Since, however, agricultural production was no longer based on the family farm, but instead on cooperative estates and state farms, the program had the effect of merely redividing the cooperative's income among more members, thus lowering individual incomes. The "circus" of patriotism and the "bread" of cooperative membership became the palliative used by the state.

On the other hand, the solution did not center on ending the class struggle between capital and labor but focused instead on resolving the conflict between the capitalists in the private sector and those in the state apparatus. This was done in favor of private interests. The state bureaucracy had fallen in disgrace; the only hope for "national redemption" lay in a rejuvenated private enterprise. And its cooperation was especially necessary if goals of increased production and national development were to be achieved. But the solution meant more than just the decline of a vacuous bureaucracy and the rise of private capital. More important was the sudden influx of capital from the oil-rich Arab nations. Egypt had become a frontline nation: its military preparedness and economic viability were necessary for the Arab cause. New capital softened the squabbles and competitive scrambles between the two branches since their raison d'être had now disappeared.

Three years after the war, Nasser died and was replaced by his vice-president, Anwar el-Sadat. As much as the 1961 nationalizations signaled the rise of the state administration, the accession of Sadat to the seat of state power reflected the rise of private capital. Very shortly, the Russians were thrown out of Egypt, leftiest elements were eased out of the government, and overtures were made to the West for military, economic, and diplomatic assistance. The ruling class began to line up behind Sadat. Farmers and bureaucrats made an alliance in order to acquire this new capital from abroad, to invest it for a profitable return, and to manage a regimented labor force (Waterbury, 1978b: 3-12, 217-274).

The public sector in Egypt soon began to crumble as state economic planners changed their emphasis from the public to the private sector. Programs of land reclamation, initiated to relieve the crowded Nile valley of its underproductive landless, sold land to those who could afford it and thus became an additional stronghold of the middle class. Cooperatives started to be replaced by private credit banks which took over all their agricultural duties with perhaps the exception of supplying fertilizer.

Private capital began to flourish, particularly with those funds illegally transferred from the public sector. But what had been black market activity soon became recognized and encouraged by the government (Waterbury, 1978a: 8-9). Unlike the 1952 revolution which eliminated the landlord-farmer duality in favor of the middle class, Sadat's succession did not do away with the new public-private dichotomy that replaced it. But he did steer the country away from its previous socialist tendencies and domination by the state apparatus. Instead, Sadat and his administration have sought support in a revitalized private sector.

The transition from public to private has not been smooth, and the resultant "strategic drift" has further worked to the benefit of the private sector and an interstitial parasitic "class" (Waterbury, 1978a: 1). There has not been a full resumption of the laissez-faire capitalism found in Faruq's day, for the state's capital needs have still not been met by private investment and tax revenues. Further reliance on a crippled public sector is pointless. Reliance on international capital has, therefore, increased. As economic conditions in the West begin to deteriorate, capital has once again flowed out to regions where higher rates of surplus value may help forestall a decline in the rate of profit. This flow coincides with Egypt's critical need for more capital to finance its sagging economy.

Perhaps the most far-reaching economic policy in Egypt in the 1970s has been Sadat's Open Door Policy. It has been viewed as resolving several problems: cutting ties with the Eastern bloc and reopening official ties with the West, as well as attracting foreign capital through subsidized free trade zones and abundant reserves of labor. Public Law 43, legislated in 1974, officially opened the door: the Egyptian pound was floated, private foreign trade encouraged, ceilings on land ownership raised, corporate taxes reduced, and joint ventures/foreign investments permitted. All these measures allow an invigorated private capital to expand even further. Later legislation has not only favored the entry of foreign capital; it has also opened the door to domestic growth. In 1975, rents were raised and labor contract conversion from tenancy to sharecropping facilitated. Workers protesting unfair contracts no longer have access to special local courts but are now forced to go to unfamiliar district courts instead. This has all helped to reduce labor costs, permitting larger profits from which the administration has hoped to benefit.

However, investments have been made in commercial ventures rather than in industrial development, and despite increases in taxes and land values throughout the 1960s and 1970s, actual government revenues did not increase proportionately. Again, it was found that development capital was not available from the Egyptian countryside (Waterbury, 1978a: 5; 1978b: 209).

Sadat has found himself in the same bind Nasser did in the 1950s: how was the state to finance economic development? State capital accumulation was impossible and the domestic private sector uncooperative. The Door was open, however, for an alliance with Western capital and the oil-rich Gulf nations to make up the deficits of a sluggish domestic economy—an alliance which has yet only benefited a minute portion of the ruling class. For the countryside, agricultural corporations—agro-business—have expressed an interest in establishing agricultural factories—ranches, orchards, sugar plantations, and fish farms—in the free trade zones along the canal.

Yet little of the potential of the Open Door Policy has been realized; corporations have hesitated to invest in anything but quick-profit consumer goods. Thus, in order to keep barely solvent, capital needs have been met, in part, by loans from multilateral finance institutions such as the World Bank, but with such stringent fiscal and economic demands that riots break out, as they did in January 1977, when food subsidies were momentarily eliminated.

In the previous period of crisis in the West, capital flowed to peripheral formations like Egypt to shore up a falling rate of profit in the core. During the current period of Western economic malaise, capital has not willingly gone from the center to the periphery in the form of bank loans and corporate investments so much as in the form of royalties to oil producers. Egypt's wind-catcher has corralled these funds only by way of Saudi Arabia and Kuwait. A heavy reliance on foreign aid has also increased. Egypt's economic fate has become more firmly tied to foreign capital but, unlike Nasser, there has been little room for maneuvering, in part due to the recent U.S.-Soviet detente and economic problems in Russia. The recent treaty with Israel provoked a cut-off in Arab funding, threatening further to strengthen Egypt's dependency on the West. The United States has committed itself to replace these funds removed by these Arab nations. Any reduction in the volume of capital may well result in a fragmentation of the fragile coalition of economic interests supporting Sadat.

CONCLUSIONS

The end of the Second World War saw the Egyptian class system break into three antagonistic groups. Feudal landlords consistently blocked the entrepreneurial endeavors of a frustrated peasantry precariously balanced between profits and foreclosure. Poorer peasants and landless workers were unable to avoid the back-breaking exploitation pursued by ruthless profiteers. The throne became increasingly isolated since it alone manipulated the shrinking supply of capital. Everyone else became progressively worse. The army, the embodiment of middle-class values, finally swept away the inept aristocracy and placed the peasant in firm control of the Egyptian countryside. Decapitation of the class structure and its subsequent unification did not resolve the problem of capital formation, however. Other cures involved overtures to the West, increased rural oppression, state capitalism, or, without any progress toward economic development, an undermining and an overthrowing of Nasser himself. Interestingly enough, Nasser did not choose any of these solutions initially. Instead he decided to play East against West and maneuvered with suppleness between the two giants. But when this international rivalry began to burn out, Nasser had little choice but to nationalize foreign enterprises and strengthen the state's control over agricultural production and reproduction through its cooperative and party system.

But the strategy backfired—or at best it could be said it was ill-timed, for it soon coincided with a general decline in capital resources. Local production began to fail and foreign capital avoided socialist Egypt. Private domestic capital skillfully made its way through the crisis and failing economy by diversifying into an illegal black market and corrupting the bureaucracy. The Six Day War was the public sector's *coup de gracê*. When the ruling class finally stood up after this fall and shook the dust from its clothes, it found itself dressed in the vestments of private enterprise. The regime could do nothing but applaud the king's new clothes and perhaps, even, buy him another suit.

Nevertheless, support for a renewed private sector of capitalist agriculture has brought the regime few rewards. Instead, it has had to seek development and investment capital from Western banks and corporations and from its brother nations rich in oil revenues. This has secured domestic tranquility by relieving farmers of the pressure to squeeze the agricultural sector dry. But their support has been whittled away by a stagnant productivity and an inflation in consumer prices caused, in part, by the economic penetration of agro-businesses and an expansion in the domestic money supply in the form of loans, grants, and military aid. Sadat's future, and the future of the fragile alliance of various economic interests supporting him, seems to be increasingly in doubt.

What seems to be happening to the Egyptian class structure is a cyclical alternation between duality and unity. Coming out of the worldwide depression, the ruling class had been united behind the palace aristocracy. But after the Second World War, this unity dissolved into opposing branches representing feudal landlords and peasant farmers. The revolution united the ruling class once again by eliminating the landlords and forging an alliance between the state machinery and the farmers. With the capital contraction of the 1960s, this alliance fell apart into warring factions. Military defeat and subsequent aid reunited the ruling class, but instead of the state administration on top, it is private farmers who now dominate.

Thus, the internal dynamics of capitalist development produce cyclic changes in the class structure of Egypt. The ruling class is neither completely unified nor completely fragmented. It oscillates according to critical cycles of capital expansion and contraction in the core. Economic dependency reproduces and perpetuates this class system. Fissures and alliances further incorporate Egypt into the lower divisions of the world capitalist system. As long as these dependent relations continue, Egypt will likewise continue to find itself underdeveloped and dominated.

NOTES

1. Except for those who were merchants, administrators, and moneylenders who had acquired a few feddans through the market, tax confiscation, or mortgage foreclosure.

2. So-called peasant self-sufficiency obviated the immediate need for a commodity market and thus allowed low wages and the continuation of an inadequate infrastructure. Because of low technology, production was risky; the solution of improved technology was only just developing. It required the cooperation of financial institutions and the technology transferring agent—both were usually in foreign hands. Landlord risk-taking reduced the need to finance the agricultural sector and maintained the foreign monopoly over technology.

3. Feudalism here specifically means the capitalistic feudalism, the "second serfdom" mentioned above.

4. This process has recently taken place in Iran and Nicaragua.

5. On cooperatives, see Abdel Fadil (1975: ch. 5) and Saab (1967: 53-91, 102-156). On single parties, see Mayfield (1971: chs. 5-7), Binder (1978: 41-62), and Harik (1972: chs. 5 and 6).

6. Important for later structural changes and class alliances, private merchants continued operating, though Greek and Levantine merchants were being replaced by members of Egyptian peasant families.

7. This ignores the intrasectoral flow of capital whereby successful cooperatives subsidized failures.

8. The abrogation of the Islamic law of equal inheritance for those in the agrarian reform program may have left a large number of disinherited sons unable or unwilling to remain on their brothers' farms.

9. See Hussein (1973: chs. 4 and 5) for details of the rise of the "state bourgeoisie."

10. The silence was only temporary; failure by the state power to actually improve conditions provoked riots in November 1967 and February 1968.

REFERENCES

ABDEL FADIL, M. (1975) Development, Income Distribution and Social Change in Rural Egypt (1952-1970). London: Cambridge University Press.

ABDEL FATAH, H. (n.d.) al-Quriya al-Mu^{c}asira bein al-Islah wa al-Thawra, 1952-1970 (The Modern Village Between Reform and Revolution). Cairo: Dar al-Thaqafa al-Jedida.

ABDEL-MALEK, A. (1962) Egypt: Military Society. Paris: Editions du Seuil.
AL-SA^CID, R. (1976) Tarikh al-Munazhamat al-Yisar al-Misri, 1940-1950 (The History of Leftist Organizations in Egypt). Cairo: Dar al-Thaqafa al-Jedida.
AMIN, S. (1978) The Arab Nation. London: Zed Press.
AULAS, M.-C. (1978) "Egypt confronts peace." MERIP Reports (November): 3-11.
BAER, G. (1962) The History of Land Ownership in Egypt. London: Oxford University Press.
——— (1969a) "The village Shaykh 1800-1950," pp. 30-61 in G. Baer, Studies in the Social History of Modern Egypt. Chicago: University of Chicago Press.
——— (1969b) "Submissiveness and revolt of the Fellah," pp. 93-108 in G. Baer, Studies in the Social History of Modern Egypt. Chicago: University of Chicago Press.
BINDER, L. (1978) In a Moment of Enthusiasm. Chicago: University of Chicago Press.
HARIK, I. (1972) The Political Mobilization of Peasants. Bloomington: University of Indiana Press.
HUSSEIN, M. (1973) Class Conflict in Egypt: 1945-1970. New York: Monthly Review Press.
MAYFIELD, J. (1971) Rural Politics in Nasser's Egypt. Austin: University of Texas Press.
RADWAN, S. (1977) Agrarian Reform and Rural Poverty in Egypt, 1952-1975. London: Mediterranean Studies.
RICHARDS, A. H. (1977) "Primitive accumulation in Egypt, 1798-1882." Review 1 (Fall).
SAAB, G. (1967) The Egyptian Agrarian Reform, 1952-1962. London: Oxford University Press.
WALLERSTEIN, I. (1974) The Modern World-System. New York: Academic Press.
WATERBURY, J. (1978a) Egyptian Agriculture Adrift. Hanover, NH: AUFS Reports.
——— (1978b) Egypt. Bloomington: University of Indiana Press.

Chapter 7

AGRICULTURE AND SOCIAL ORGANIZATION: BRAZIL'S AGRESTE, 1845-1978

Jason W. Clay

Garanhuns is a *municipio* in the state of Pernambuco in northeastern Brazil. It is both a market and a political center located in the *Agreste*, a transitional ecological zone lying between the humid coastal *Zona da Mata* and the arid, interior zone, the *Sertão*. While settlement began in the Garanhuns region as early as the seventeenth century, substantial agricultural production for extralocal markets did not begin until the nineteenth century. Agricultural development in Garanhuns is particularly interesting because to use current terminology, Garanhuns is a peripheral area within a peripheral region within a peripheral country. Cash-crop production for most of the last century and a half has been based on free, nonwage-earning systems of labor, and the historical study of this area affords us an opportunity to examine the development of noncapitalist production systems which encompassed diverse labor systems, yet were integrated into national and world markets. Certainly, local systems of production have changed, becoming either more or less capitalistic over time, but the changes have been uneven and, until recently, reversible. These changes in production strategies which produced simultaneous changes in production organization resulted from external stimuli as well as local ones. However, the extent of changes caused or contributed to by a single influence cannot be understood except through an understanding of the relationship of various segments of the local population to the production process.

Until the last few decades, the production of various subsistence and cash crops in the region was based upon noncapitalist organizational principles, that is, the exchanges made to secure access to the factors of production were not normally monetized. Until the last generation, tenants, the landless living on someone else's land, were granted the right to plant a *roça* for their subsistence needs. As the number of landless grew and the bargaining position of tenants deteriorated, they had to turn over an increasing amount of their cash crops to the owner and/or work for the owner on other cash crops, such as coffee, cotton, sisal, or cattle, for free a certain number of days per week or at wages far below those paid to temporary day laborers. In most cases, the stubble of the tenant's crop went to the landowner for his cattle. In this way, the tenants had land use rights to produce their subsistence needs and the owners had their tenants' labor to use for cash-crop agriculture.

Landless, who were not tenants, were often given the opportunity to plant roças on someone else's land. In the nineteenth century, when labor was scarce, these landless were allowed to plant their subsistence crops and cotton with few requirements from the landowner. Often the stubble and the clearing of the dense brush were considered payment enough. Records of the period indicate that what payments were made often were collected in the form of corn, beans, or *fava* rather than cotton. As the number of landless in the region grew, it became more difficult for them to locate arrangements for land use as generous as those described above. Increasingly, these landless had to cultivate the cash crop of the owner within their own subsistence plots, or they had to clear new areas of forest which would then be used by the owner or would be kept cleared and used as pasture. As the urban demand for foodstuffs and the number of potential tenants grew, those landowners who were still willing to allow others to use their lands often insisted on a share of even the subsistence crops being grown or a cash rent payment.

Cattle, cotton, and coffee, in that order of introduction to the region, have been the primary cash crops produced for extralocal markets. The introduction of each crop required subtle alterations or adaptations of the local labor systems. Cattle require constant attention, especially when they are grazed on open-range pasture. Through the nineteenth century, the cowboys were usually tenants, and they received one of every four or five calves born to the herd they were attending. This situation was favorable to the cowboys, whose families were also allowed to plant their own subsistence roças on the rancher's lands. In this way many of the nineteenth-century cowboys were able to slowly build up a herd which could be used for starting their own ranch. Now, however, with meat and milk prices rising, with the introduction of more valuable, improved cattle varieties, with permanent fences, and with increasing numbers of laborers seeking employment, the cowboys are paid a straight salary. Few live on the farms, and fewer still are allowed a plot of land to grow their subsistence needs. In sum, with the passing of nonwage forms of labor payment, the standard of living of cowboys has slowly deteriorated.

Cotton has been a cash crop in the interior of Pernambuco for more than 150 years. Initially, it was interplanted with other subsistence crops in roças in the manner described above. Only when the U.S. Civil War led to worldwide shortages of cotton and the price rose by 500% in five years (Denslow 1974: 134) did the crop come to be cultivated by itself. Often the landowners had their slaves grow cotton interplanted with other crops; or in the case of smaller landowners, they had their families plant it in this manner. With landless laborers so scarce, it was difficult for the landowners to demand the increasingly valuable cotton crop of the potential planters. Instead, landowners developed a system whereby they were sold the crop at the end of the season by those planting roças on their lands. The landowners used their slaves to gin the cotton during the off-agricultural season (January and February) adding more value to the cotton and utilizing their slaves more efficiently. After the end of the U.S. Civil War, when the price of cotton fell drastically, a system of sharecropping cotton developed. Laborers were required to give a portion of the crop or a fixed amount to the owner as a part of their verbal contract to use the land. This system appears to have resulted from the large number of unpaid debts arising from the drastic reversal of cotton prices shortly after the close of the U.S. Civil War.

Today, cotton is not produced on any of the large farms in the municipio; it is only grown by the *minifundistas*. The reason is that, although it has a very low price and thus yields a low return for their labor, it gives them some money just before the time to plant other crops. They use this income to purchase seeds or needed days of labor at planting time. Further, cotton uses their labor when they have very little else to do and fewer off-farm employment opportunities. It appears, though, that many of these minifundistas have abandoned the production of cotton in favor of working as day laborers on the large cattle ranches during the off-season. Although off-season wages are lower than those for the rest of the year (due to the numbers of people seeking employment) and the number of days labor is small, they can still make more money than they could from cotton cultivation due to the variability of the cotton harvest and the uncertainty of cotton prices.

The increased price of cotton in Brazil from 1860-1867 and its decline for the next fifteen years does not give us any indication of how this altered local strategies for producing cotton. How would the use of land, labor, and capital have been changed during the periods of increasing or decreasing cotton values? Could we have predicted that a system of fixed rent in kind and sharecropping would contribute to a 500% increase in local production of cotton within seven years, or that this system of production would contribute to debt peonage relationships once the price of cotton began to decline? How would we know that this labor system based on debt peonage would evolve into one of tenant labor, where workers would donate a number of days labor each week to the landowner in return for the right to use a plot of land for subsistence production? This system of tenancy eventually allowed for the planting of large areas of the municipio in coffee, without the expenditure of scarce capital by the landowners. It is clear, then, that without a more detailed understanding of local conditions and the historical use of land, labor, and capital, we will not begin to be able to understand local response to extralocal influences.

Coffee production became common in this area toward the end of the nineteenth century. The production of coffee appears to have depended upon the use of tenant laborers and piece workers. The larger farmers did not allow their tenants to interplant subsistence crops with coffee once it was producing, although small landowners frequently did this on their own farms particularly when the price of coffee was low.

It was on the larger coffee farms that the system of giving tenants a subsistence plot and then requiring either free labor or reduced wage rates from them became most developed in the Garanhuns region. These tenants had to help weed the coffee, take care of the new plantings, spread the husks around the coffee bushes (used here as a form of fertilizer) and often pick the coffee as well. The tenants, however, could not harvest the entire crop by themselves. From the earliest days, the landowners liked to use piece-work arrangements for these tasks. In this way they could set the wage rates according to the price of the final product.

Subsistence and cash-crop production in Garanhuns have been symbiotically related from the outset. The landless, would-be producers, depended upon landowners for access to the lands needed for subsistence production. Likewise, cash-crop cultivation depended upon manual laborers. For each successful cash-crop farmer, there had to be a number of small farmers or landless available to provide cheap or nonwage labor. The ability to keep large farms intact did not depend only upon the prices of the commodity being produced but also upon the number of laborers that could be used on the farm and the specific relationships with them that to varying degrees cut into the profits of the landowner. The cost of labor was rarely calculated in terms of money alone. But, the reason it was not dependent upon cash payments was because of the particular symbiotic relationships that had developed between landowner and landuser during the cotton era and had been reinforced during periods of economic recession as well as periods of expanding markets. This symbiotic relationship did not develop solely because there were potential landusers in need of subsistence and landowners in need of cheap labor. Its specific features also appear to have resulted from the complementarity of the agricultural cycle for subsistence production with that for cash-crop production. Further, through substitutions of land use for laborers, the landowners were able to reduce their production costs thus making them more competitive with other areas of the country or world.

The small landowners and landless using other people's lands were busiest during the periods of their subsistence production. Thus, peak labor needs fell mainly between April and the end of June. From July through September, they would have had some work with harvesting, but that would have been minimal. Certainly, then, by September, they would have had substantial time to "work out." The further from the harvest the year progressed, the more these individuals would have needed some kind of income to supplement poor harvest or future planting costs. This period coincided with the peak labor needs of many of the large landowners producing cattle or cash crops. Further, because this period represented an "off-season" for all subsistence agriculturalists, they were willing to work at wages which were less than half the rate offered during the planting and weeding periods of peak labor use in subsistence-crop production. In effect, then, the larger cash-crop producers were able to exploit the basic needs of the small farmers and landless in large part because of the staggered labor requirements of crops produced in the region.

If we take the crops individually, we can see how well the subsistence and cash-crop systems fit together. The major planting and weeding tasks associated with subsistence farming were from mid-March through May. In contrast, cotton was planted in August and weeded and collected through February and March. Coffee was weeded in September as well as in February or March and the major coffee harvest began in August and was completed in October. In addition to these agricultural crops, large-scale livestock production depended (and still depends) upon lower off-season agricultural wage rates to make it profitable within this region and competitive with produce from other regions. During the dry season, much labor was required to cut, transport, and chop *palma,* the cactus plant used for cattle rations. During the dry season, ranchers paid to have the brush cleared out of their pasture, wire fences constructed or repaired, and hedge-like fences trimmed or cut back. The construction of buildings, ponds, and corrals also was relegated to this period when reduced rainfall allowed the cement to set for houses and corrals and dried up creeks allowed for dam construction. Thus, ecological conditions encouraged farmers to construct improvements at the same time as the subsistence cycle allowed a large pool of potential laborers to compete for jobs which contributed to the lower, dry-season wage rate.

Beginning in the First World War, and accentuated in the 1920s and during the Second World War, the subsistence crops produced locally increased in value. These increasing values helped the small farmers who can now easily market their surplus production for prices that did not merely reflect local production conditions. With expanding production opportunities, these farmers needed less off-farm employment than before. Both of these conditions, the increasingly valuable subsistence crops and the decreasing number of small landowners seeking off-farm income, led to a basic change in the relationship between larger cash-crop producers and those individuals interested in land use in exchange for labor relationships. Large landowners were decreasingly willing to let valuable subsistence crops be grown on their lands without taking a share of them either in cash or kind. With this curtailing of the subsistence production system, the landless began to work for free for a given number of days each week in exchange for land-use opportunities.

Gradually, landowners began to use a system of temporary wage laborers in their attempt to capture the profits of the more valuable subsistence goods. Within the municipio, the number of permanent employees (who were usually tenants) decreased from 13,336 to 3,863 in the decade of the 1940s, while the number of temporary workers increased from 6,988 to 10,350 in the same decade. This shift to wage labor caused considerable conflict, leading to assassination, property destruction, and aborted cases of land takeovers, as ex-tenants realized their economic position was declining. Even where local conflict appears to have been minimal, the news of landowner-tenant clashes in neighboring municipios did much to hasten the removal of tenants. Of course, the increasing number of ex-tenants in local settlements forced wages down, and in many cases, laborers, finding that they could no longer support themselves or their families, were forced to migrate out of the region.

By the time of the Brazilian Revolution of 1964, urban-based politicians had passed a number of legislative measures designed to help the condition of rural tenants and laborers. These measures included such things as land reform bills, rural minimum wages, and indemnification for tenants when they were removed from farms. Although the military government quickly tabled all this legislation, the landowners did not know when or if they might ever be reactivated. Therefore, shortly after the Revolution of 1964, nearly all the remaining tenants were removed, and landowners were very reluctant to commit their lands to systems of agricultural production that would require large amounts of labor. Even the dependence on temporary laborers was drastically reduced as the larger landowners, aided by government programs designed to provide cheap food for urban residents, intensified the production of meat and milk. The majority of temporary laborers that were still used in the region were in the process of completing "one-shot" tasks such as planting pasture or building fences, corrals, and milking parlors.

Through government-subsidized credit programs, the landowners are attempting to reduce labor requirements even more. In the last decade, the number of tractors has increased substantially in the area. Grasses grown for dry season rations are replacing the more labor-intensive palma, previously the best source of fodder during the dry season. Machines are now used to chop the palma and fodder grasses where before they were cut by hand. One farmer has even installed electric milking machines.

The immediate effects of this switch to livestock production on most of the lands in the municipio are sweeping indeed. The landless can no longer find sufficient employment to remain in the region and many are leaving. Unfortunately, it has taken some longer to learn that there is no place for them in the present production system; and it is these individuals, in the regions switching to cattle ranching, that are contributing to the increasing death rates and rising infant mortality rates during the alleged Brazilian economic miracle of the late sixties and early seventies.

Local changes in production, however, are not limited to what is happening on the extensive cattle farms. The small farmers are affected as well. They cannot find land off their own farms to use for subsistence production; they cannot find sufficient off-farm employment; their lands are producing less and less each year due to overuse and a shortening of the fallow periods; and their standard of living is declining. Many of the small farmers look to urban areas for part-time jobs, or they have to sell their farms and migrate to regions where they hope to find employment. Either way, they are reducing further the chances of the region as a whole to adapt to future market changes in a successful manner, especially if the changes require substantial quantities of labor.

By 1978, the production system of Garanhuns appeared to have passed a point beyond which there was no return. In other periods, cash-crop production was directly related to the subsistence sector of the economy, and in this way cash-crop production was both possible and profitable. These old systems of production, although often oscillating between greater dependence upon subsistence or cash-crop production, always retained the essential features which allowed for production to shift emphasis quickly in response to ecological or market variations.

The key to maintaining this ability to shift production emphasis was that there was always a sufficient labor pool while at the same time there was a wide variety of heterogeneous production strategies. In large part, this labor pool was maintained through mutually necessary, if not always advantageous, relationships where landowners traded land use or part-time wages for labor from landless or near-landless groups. Even recently, there were always enough small landowners to provide for the labor requirements of the cash-crop farming operations. Now, however, with government policy and programs designed specifically to eliminate or ignore the small farmers, as they previously ignored the tenants, this form of part-time labor is also becoming eliminated.

CONCLUSIONS

The transition of labor forms in Garanhuns has been neither unilinear nor continuous. Major shifts in the relationship between landowner and landless have occurred and are related to a number of variables, the most important of which are commodity prices on local and extralocal markets, local production organization, ecological constraints and/or changes, population growth, and changes in national or international economic or political conditions. Historically, the ability of members of this system to adapt to the changing influences mentioned above has been directly related to the maintenance of a diversity of production strategies, or a heterogeneity of local strategies.

Heterogeneity within the production system allowed for the utilization of different ecological niches for new crops or crops with expanded market demand. Heterogeneity allowed for the maintenance of different systems of labor extraction that provided ready alternatives whenever changes occurred in the value of locally produced commodities. This is not to deny that the extralocal demand or sudden lack of it prompted most of the local changes in production, and particularly in the use of labor. However, knowing changing commodity values alone could not tell us how a particular production system would be adapted to the new conditions.

There are two major points arising from this research. First, as Frank has suggested, economic booms and recessions do not have the effects that one might assume. During periods of economic boom, individuals with restricted access to the factors of production continually saw their economic position deteriorating, while the larger landowners and merchants became the recipients of even larger profits. On the other hand, during periods of economic recession, individuals with few productive assets of their own were often able to gain access to those of others, particularly in the case of land. In this way, landowners were able to cut production costs and spread the risk of production on the laborers during periods of economic recession. Using these forms of substitution, the landowners could remain competitive producers for extralocal markets even in the face of declining commodity prices. It appears that these periods of recession, marked as they were by the intensification of exchange of landuse for free or reduced labor rates, were more favorable for the rural poor who did not have their own productive assets. For one thing, lower infant mortality rates seem to indicate a general improvement in living conditions. What Frank and others failed to point out, however, was that even during periods of economic recession, the local elites (landowners and/or merchants) were able to increase their monopolization of productive assets in the region, if not their absolute profits. This increased monopolization of productive assets eventually led to even greater profits during the next economic boom. Although the process is not terribly clear, it appears that the monopolization of productive assets (particularly land) by a few individuals, was what made the system of production based on land use in exchange for labor possible.

The second important finding indicated by my research is that, in this agricultural area, there was always a scarcity of at least one of the factors of production. In some cases the shortage existed for all local producers, while in other local instances, a small group monopolized access to one of the factors. In this production system, it was common for factor substitution to develop. These substitutions allowed individuals or groups to exchange factors of production which they held in excess of their ability to utilize them for factors which were more scarce. These types of nonmonetized means of access to the factors of production serve as adjustable mechanisms which change depending upon local conditions (supplies of land, labor, and capital) as well as upon extralocal ones (national laws, distance to markets, commodity values, off-farm employment opportunities, and investment opportunities in other areas of the nation). The exchange of the factors allows for the production of cash crops or even commercialized subsistence crops without the outlay of scarce capital. However, this type of exchange is most likely to develop in areas where there is an abundance of underused labor without adequate land to meet its subsistence needs, where most of the land is owned by a small percentage of the population, and where local capital reserves or sources of credit are not well developed. Obviously, these conditions are not universal, even in the peripheral areas of the world-economy, but that is precisely why critical evaluations of the development of different labor systems are necessary for a more thorough understanding of the world-system. If for no other reason, macroeconomic cycles and trends are not created in a vacuum. Cycles and trends represent at least in part the cumulative effect of microlevel influences from agricultural regions around the world. Without a basic understanding of the local-level influences on production organization and local responses to extralocal conditions, I doubt we will be able to comprehend the world-system.

Although "we are far from understanding how particular techniques of what some fondly call 'economic modernization' produce political consequences of specific kinds" (Mintz, 1976: 379), it seems to me that we will only begin to understand this process if we see moves to capitalism and wage labor as being "uneven, imperfect, and in part reversible" (Mintz 1976: 379). "Economic subsystems function alongside each other, even interpenetrate, and are in certain ways peculiarly interdependent, as well as conflictual" (Mintz 1976: 379). Within this context, then, it seems useful for our analysis to begin by defining "groups" in terms of how they gain access to the factors of production. Once we focus on these relationships, we can begin to understand how individual producers and larger systems of production and labor use of the region under study relate to the world-system.

REFERENCES

CLAY, J. W. (1973) "Agrarian change in the Agreste of Pernambuco." B.A. thesis, Harvard College.
––– (1979) "The articulation of non-capitalist agricultural production systems with capitalist exchange systems." Ph.D. dissertation, Cornell University.
DENSLOW, D. (1974) "Sugar production in northeast Brazil and Cuba, 1858-1908." Ph.D. dissertation, Yale University.
FRANK, A. G. (1967) Capitalism and Underdevelopment in Latin America. New York: Monthly Review Press.
GREENWOOD, D. (1979) "Contextualizing the factors of production: baseline data for the study of family farming." Mimeographed paper dated May 1979.
MINTZ, S. (1976) "On the concept of a Third World." Dialectical Anthropology 1: 377-382.
––– (1977) "The so-called world-system: local initiative and local response." Dialectical Anthropology 2: 235-270.

Chapter 8

CAPITALISM AND SOUTH AFRICAN AGRICULTURE, 1890-1920

Martin J. Murray

> I have only one grievance to ventilate as to land. My late father Nyabele before he died was desirous to be given land. Likewise I have nowhere to lay my head. There is no native chief with as many followers as myself in the Transvaal. My trouble and grievance is that I have no land or place to put my people.... My desire is that I should be allowed to have land where my own father lived.
>
> —Mahlangu (1916: 275)

> The Kaffir is like a horse. No horse in the wild state would want to come to the stable of his own accord. You must first catch him, and tame him, and break him in.
>
> —van Staden (1904: 365)

In the period roughly between the introduction of large-scale capitalist mining (diamonds and gold) operations in the closing decades of the nineteenth century and the early 1920s, truly dramatic changes took place within the arena of agricultural production and circulation of South Africa's countryside.[1] Specifically, the widespread existence at the end of the nineteenth century of noncapitalist forms of production in the countryside acted as a serious obstacle to capitalist expansion in agriculture. At least initially, embryonic capitalist farmers reluctantly incorporated older noncapitalist forms of production without immediately superseding them.

By the turn of the century, however, these capitalist farmers accelerated their class-based "employers' offensive" against European *rentier* landlords and African "squatters,"[2] demanding state aid in the elimination of both. State legislative action culminated in the 1913 Natives' Land Act, whereby African land ownership was restricted to so-called "Native Reserves" and the overwhelming proportion (87%) of the countryside was set aside for permanent white settler occupancy. Ultimately, the embryonic capitalist farmers were the direct beneficiaries of agricultural transformation and agricultural expansion. During this "phase of transition" (ca. 1890-1920), capitalist relations of exploitation gradually replaced noncapitalist ones. By the 1920s, capital and wage labor were consolidated as the hegemonic production relations around which all competing production relations were reduced to ancillary status (see Morris, 1976a, 1976b; Bundy, 1976 for detailed studies of these processes).

COMBINED AND UNEVEN CAPITALIST DEVELOPMENT

The development of capitalism in South African agriculture proceeded through different phases during the period 1890-1920. Indeed, these phases were discontinuous and self-contradictory, i.e., "that conditions created during one phase may come to present problems for a later phase of development (Phillips, 1977: 15). Put more precisely, capitalist expansion in South African agriculture was not a direct and inevitable process in which capitalist production relations undermined (and consequently eliminated) noncapitalist forms of production, thereby putting into motion the strictly capitalist accumulation of capital on an extended scale. Instead, capitalist agriculture evolved over an extended period, plagued by periodic crises and beset by internal contradictions.

The widespread "interconnectedness" between capitalist and noncapitalist forms of production in the countryside acted as a serious obstacle to capitalist accumulation in agriculture. Speaking descriptively, the (African) immediate producers ("sharecroppers," "squatters," and so forth) were able to cling tenaciously for quite some time to direct access to their means of subsistence and reproduction. As a consequence, they were not compelled by economic necessity to compete on the market in order to survive and reproduce. Thus, capitalist relations of production did not emerge at once and noncapitalist ones did not disappear at once. During this transitional conjuncture, hybrid forms of production predominated, combining features of both the old and the new. In short, an almost endless variety of forms of production characterized this transitional era where distinct relations of exploitation were, to use Lenin's (1972: 195) apt phrase, "actually interwoven in the most varied and fantastic form."

The development of capitalism in South African agriculture involved the formation of a home market (i.e., the development of commodity production and exchange on an extended scale). In Lenin's words,

> The separation of the direct producer from the means of production, i.e., his expropriation, signifying the transition from simple commodity production to capitalist production (and constituting the necessary condition for this transition), *creates* the home market [1972: 67-68].

Moreover, the process of this creation of the home market proceeded two distinct directions:

> On the one hand, the *means of production* from which the small producer is "freed" are converted into capital in the hands of their new owner, serve to produce commodities and, consequently, are themselves converted into commodities.... On the other hand, the *means of subsistence* of the small producer become the material elements of the variable capital, i.e., of the sum of money expended by the employer ... on hiring workers. Thus, these means of subsistence are now also converted into commodities, i.e., create a home market for articles of consumption [Lenin, 1972: 68].

Seen in strictly historical terms, embryonic capitalist farmers (albeit unevenly distributed throughout the rural districts) served as the active agents of capitalist penetration of the countryside. During the "phase of transition," these so-called "progressive" (European) farmers became increasingly dependent upon production for the market, and were thereby compelled by economic necessity to compete as petty capitals with other petty capitals and with larger capitals. Put in another way, South African embryonic capitalist farmers constituted "primitive," i.e., germinal, forms of capital (Sherry, 1976).

In South African agriculture, capitalist accumulation of capital presupposed two conditions: (1) the transformation of the instruments and materials of production into capital, and (2) the creation of a rural proletariat. By the late nineteenth century, the African people in the main were "expropriated" from their ancestral lands. Nevertheless, they were able to retain for a considerable length of time effective possession of the means of production, exchanging the payment of rent or the supply of "labor services" for the right to reside on the farmers' land, to cultivate crops both for market sale and household consumption, and to graze stock. These "squatting" arrangements represented a serious obstacle to capitalist expansion.

The particular path that capitalist development in South African agriculture took can only be described as a "transformation from above," whereby both large and small landed estates in the countryside were metamorphised into capitalist agricultural enterprises. As the principal agency of capitalist penetration of the countryside, embryonic capitalist farmers amassed means of production, hiring wage laborers to cultivate their lands with their implements. Put in a nutshell, the class struggle between the two principal classes in the countryside—farmers and direct producers—involved the transformation of the former from rentier landlords to enterprising capitalists and of the latter from rent-paying tenants to wage laborers and/or labor-tenants (Morris, 1976b: 3-5).

By the 1920s, the conjoined impact of social differentiation in the countryside and the state enforcement of antisquatter legislation undermined the "relatively independent" economic position of African petty commodity producers and thoroughly disrupted "squatting" in the countryside, thereby accelerating the supply of "expropriated" (i.e., divorced from the means of production) farm laborers for white landowners. Specifically, the labor-tenancy system evolved as the principal mechanism through which capitalist farmers appropriated surplus labor. The essential features of the labor-tenancy system can be summarized as follows: "the giving of services for a certain period in the year to the farmer by the Native and/or his family in return for the right to reside on the farmer's land, to cultivate a portion of the land, and to graze his stock on the farm" (Union of South Africa, 1932: 51). With the emergence of the labor-tenancy system, African direct producers were separated from effective possession of both the materials and instruments of production, and therefore from the means of their own reproduction. Put simply, labor-tenancy as a production relation represented a "primitive" or "transitional" form of wage labor (Morris, 1976a: 298-302). Capitalist farmers successfully assembled means of production and combined them with the concrete labor of their labor-tenants. Hence, to put it another way, capitalist farmers took direct command over the labor process, organizing and supervising the expenditure of labor time, with the expressed aim of appropriating surplus labor indirectly through the production of agricultural commodities for sale on the market.

In somewhat broader terms, the combined and uneven capitalist development in the African subcontinent as a whole determined the form of the structural contradictions between town and country. In Morris's words,

> Agriculture—no matter how fast it developed internally—could not do anything else but lag behind; and as secondary industry emerged from its own tortuous birth pangs in the 20th century, the whole process of uneven development was immensely exacerbated [1976a: 313].

Despite the remarkable development of capitalist agriculture in the first two decades of the twentieth century, agriculture lagged far behind mining and manufacturing. This uneven development had profound consequences for the class struggle in the countryside. The relative weakness of capitalist agriculture meant that capitalist farmers were forced to rely quite heavily on the state administration for a wide variety of services.

AGRARIAN CLASS RELATIONS AND THE TRANSFORMATION OF AGRICULTURE "FROM ABOVE"

At a descriptive level, the impulse for capitalist development in agriculture can be located in the accelerated demand for foodstuffs in the rapidly "urbanizing" areas. The development of capitalist accumulation processes (first in mining at the end of the nineteenth century, and later in manufacturing) in the first few decades of the twentieth century created new markets for agricultural commodities. Nevertheless, the spread and deepening of commercial networks between town and countryside alone provide an insufficient explanation of the origins (and eventual dominance) of capitalist social-production relations in agriculture.

The particular path that capitalist development took in the South African countryside (i.e., the so-called "Prussian path," or "transformation from above") cannot be understood without the analysis of the dynamics of class struggle between the principal agrarian social classes and their allies. The widespread existence of noncapitalist relations of exploitation (i.e., *rentier* landlords directly appropriating surplus labor in the form of rent from "squatter" tenants) acted as a serious class barrier to expanded accumulation via innovation in agriculture. Stimulated by competition engendered by the growth of urban markets, embryonic capitalist farmers unleased an "employers' offensive"—directly aided by the political support of the state administration through the enforcement of a wholesale battery of antisquatter laws—against the dominance of noncapitalist forms of production in the countryside. The transformation of agrarian class relations in agriculture was carried out from above. On the one hand, capitalist farmers literally "encircled" rentier landlords, isolating them, and thereby reducing their economic and political significance to ancillary status. On the other hand, the subordinated direct producers in the countryside were gradually converted into agricultural laborers from rent-paying "squatter" tenants.

At the most fundamental level, this transformation of capitalist agriculture "from above" coincided with the firm establishment of capitalist command over the labor process. Put in another way, the strictly capitalist labor process was the specific site of the production process of capital. Speaking historically, the dominance of capitalist production relations in the countryside in the aftermath of the 1913 Natives' Land Act did not result in headlong productivity increases via innovation in agriculture but instead led to an intensification of toil (i.e., in Marxist terminology, the production of absolute surplus value). In short, the labor process remained only formally subordinated to capital (Brighton Labour Process Group, 1977). To be sure, capitalist farmers engaged in crop rotation and diversification, introduced irrigation and drainage schemes for their fields, made improved seed selections as a means of expanding yields per acre, and so forth. On the whole, however, capitalist farmers in the main expanded outputs through "more efficient" social division and cooperation of labor and more stringent supervision of the expenditure of labor time.

The labor-tenant system encouraged capitalist farmers to rely quite extensively on recomposing the organization of labor time (instead of introducing technical changes in the labor process) as a means of expanding total output. Wage levels for farm laborers remained notoriously low. With the labor-tenancy system, capitalist farmers provided their labor-tenants with "wages" (whether in cash or kind) and with certain privileges (i.e., grazing, cultivation, and residential "rights") in exchange for capitalist command over the expenditure of concrete labor in a determinate labor process. In effect, labor-tenant households received a "guaranteed subsistence" in return for providing "labor services," the timing and duration of which were both determined in the class struggle between capitalist farmers and the direct producers.

Put bluntly, capitalist farmers were confronted with substantial price fluctuations for agricultural commodities from year to year, were plagued with persistent "labor shortage" crises, and could expect low returns for relatively high scale of operations.[3] Under this "extensive regime" of accumulation,[4] capitalist farmers came to depend upon the persistence of a noncapitalist *mileu* (i.e., the ancillary "rights" offered to labor-tenant households) as a means of subsidizing the very low wages and the long hours. Specifically, the reproduction of the labor-tenant household depended upon a combination of the "wage package" and "subsistence rights." For example, Lenin (1972: 203) describes a similar arrangement in the Russian countryside in his analysis of the "allotment" system:

> Since labour-service can only be undertaken by a local peasant, and one who must be "provided with an allotment," the fact of the tremendous drop in pay clearly indicates the importance of the allotment as wages in kind. The allotment, in such cases, continues to this day to serve as a means of guaranteeing the landowner a supply of cheap labour.

From the point of view of capital, the labor-tenancy system enabled capitalist farmers to remunerate the expenditure of labor time with a "wage package" that was actually below the social cost of reproduction of the labor-tenant household.

The payment of "wages" actually served as an added inducement to draw the African direct producers to work in a situation where outright physical coercion, or the threat of eviction (and sometimes both) were no longer sufficient mechanisms to accomplish their desired ends. For example, Edwin Peniston, a retired farmer, Estcourt District, reported that "[Africans] are not allowed on that farm, unless they work, and the amount of wages that a man will pay to a native is absolutely nil. The worst labour is the labour that you pay nothing for. You may work them for three months in a year for nothing but you will never get a man to work for nothing; if he gets nothing he will do nothing for it" (Union of South Africa, 1916: 441).[5] Moreover, the labor-tenant system coincided with a specific economic relation of discrimination and subordination, i.e., relations of personal dependence.

In conclusion, the development of capitalism in South African agriculture presupposed the disintegration of "independent" simple commodity production in the rural districts. To be sure, capitalism penetrated into agricultural production particularly slowly and in extremely varied forms. Nevertheless, it is not sufficient to possess, as Lenin (1972: 178) stressed, "too stereotyped an understanding of the theoretical proposition that capitalism requires the free, landless worker." By abstracting from the determinate processes out of the complexity of South African social-economic relations, it becomes evident that the formation of capitalist relations of production proceeded at a relatively brisk pace between 1890 and 1920. By the 1920s, embryonic capitalist farmers had successfully subordinated the direct producers to the logic of capitalist accumulation. Africans recognized quite clearly the implications of "expropriation" from the means of production: "Today the land is not ours, it is the Government's.... We do not consider that by paying taxes we are buying the country; we are just enriching the government." The Africans, Hoye and Nfuzewa, summarized the deteriorating plight of the indigenous population: "All the land now is owned by Europeans The whole country is taken up with farms. We are living on the edge of cliffs" (Union of South Africa, 1916: 489-490). This remarkably appropriate imagery captures the essential nature of the development of capitalism in the countryside.

NOTES

1. This article represents tentative theoretical conclusions drawn from an historical analysis of the gradual emergence of capital/wage labor production relations in agriculture in South Africa. Data have been excluded for reasons of brevity.

2. "As vacant or subjugated land was taken up by the European immigrants, dispossessed or fugitive natives or remnants of scattered tribes remained or penetrated for protection into the areas of European occupation, and were allowed to settle upon their farms, generally on a tenure of service. These natives are usually called 'squatters'. There is not statutory definition of this word, which is or has been made use of in many different connotations. Whether a native lives on an occupied or unoccupied farm, whether he pays rent or gives his own service or that of his family, whether or not wages are paid, whether the service is casual labour at call or seasonal or for specified periods, whether he cultivates for a share of produce—in all these cases he is called a squatter. The term therefore covers undefined lease-hold, metayage, labour tenancy, part-time service and, in fine, every condition of settlement except fixed leasehold and full-time wage service" (Herbst, n.d.: 6; cited in Johnstone, 1976: 22).

3. "While agriculture was making such great strides elsewhere, here it moved so slowly as to appear almost stationary.... [W]ithout wishing to be unjust to the farmers or to reflect upon the natural resources of the subcontinent, it may be safely asserted that there are few parts of the world occupied by Europeans... in which farmers are so exposed to so many risks and difficulties as South Africa, or where judged by the standards attained elsewhere, agriculture is in such a backward condition" (Director of the Transvaal Agriculture Department, in 1908; cited in Horwitz, 1967: 128).

4. This conceptualization can be attributed to Michel Aglieta.

5. This will also be referred to as the Beaumont Commission.

"As regards this Act, I would like to speak about the occupation by natives of European land. We want a certain number of natives to occupy that land for the sake of the labour. I do not think there is any inclination here to have natives living on land for the sake of getting rents out of them. I have had some experience of natives working in lieu of paying rent, and it is most unsatisfactory, and if it were possible I would like to have this Act amended giving us power to charge them rent and let them work it out. It seems to me that when the native under these circumstances is forced to work, he looks upon himself as a slave and expects to be driven to work, and one does not get satisfactory work out of them. The free labourer who gets payment is worth five times as much as these people who give their service in lieu of rent and, as I said, they seem to regard themselves as slaves and unless one has the inclination and the time to be a slave-driver no work is gotten out of them" (Beaumont Commission, p. 487).

REFERENCES

Brighton Labour Process Group (1977) "The capitalist labour process." Capital and Class 1 (Spring): 3-42.
BUNDY, C. (1976) "African peasants and economic change in South Africa, 1870-1913, with particular reference to the Cape." Ph.D. dissertation, University of London.
HERBST, J. F. (n.d.) "Memorandum on native labour in South Africa." Herbst Archives, Jagger Library, University of Cape Town.
HORWITZ, R. (1967) The Political Economy of South Africa. London: Weidenfeld & Nicholson.
JOHNSTONE, F. (1976) Class, Race and Gold. London: Routledge & Kegan Paul.
LENIN, V. I. (1972) The Development of Capitalism in Russia. Moscow: Progress.

MAHLANGU, F. (1916) Statement by the Chief of the Amandebele tribe, Pretoria District, in Report of the Natives Land Commission, Vol. II. Cape Town: Government Printers.

MORRIS, M. L. (1976a) "The development of capitalism in South African agriculture: class struggle in the countryside." Economy & Society 5, 3: 292-343.

――― (1976b) "Apartheid, agriculture, and the state: the farm labour question." Prepared for the Farm Labour Conference, South African Labour Development Research Union, University of Cape Town, Cape Town, South Africa, September.

PHILLIPS, A. (1977) "The concept of 'development.' " Review of African Political Economy 8 (January-April).

SHERRY, R. (1976) "Independent commodity production versus petty bourgeois production." Monthly Review 28 (May): 52-60.

Union of South Africa (1916) Natives' Land Commission. Cape Town: Government Printers.

――― (1932) Report of the Native Economic Commission, 1930-1932. Pretoria: Government Printers.

VAN STADEN, J. J. (1904) Testimony in Transvaal Labour Commission, 1904: Minutes of Proceedings and Evidence. London: Darling.

SECTION B
SOCIAL MOVEMENTS AND
THE POLITICS OF THE
CAPITALIST WORLD-ECONOMY

Chapter 9

THE FUTURE OF THE WORLD-ECONOMY

Immanuel Wallerstein

We are fond of temporal contrasts (the future and the past, the new and the old)—as well as temporal disjunctures—(the present, the crisis, the transition). But time is a social reality, not a physical one. And our visions of time (or rather of space-time) both reflect the social system of which they are a part, and in a very basic way are constitutive of those systems.

We cannot discuss what we think to be the future of the modern world-system unless we come to some agreement about which past it is to which we are referring. For me, the answer has become increasingly clear. The modern world is a capitalist world-economy, and this capitalist world-economy came into existence in Europe somewhere between 1450 and 1550 as a mode of resolving the "crisis of feudalism" that had shaken this same Europe in the period 1300-1450.

It came into existence as a mode of repressing the increasingly successful ability that the European work-force had demonstrated, during the period of crisis, to withhold surplus from the seigniorial and urban patriarchal strata who had appropriated it under the feudal system. From this perspective, the capitalist system that replaced the feudal system proved marvelously adept. The period from 1450 to 1600 registered a dramatic fall in the real income of Europe's direct producers and, with the constant widening of the geographic scope of the world-economy, this process of polarization (and therefore, in the old-fashioned phrase, of absolute immiserization) has never ceased to expand since. This can be empirically demonstrated, *provided* one measures the polarization in terms of the world-economy as a whole and not in terms of particular states.

In order to appreciate the real changes which are occurring today and which may occur in the future, we must assess what are the structural mechanisms by which the system has up to now reproduced itself, and what are the structural contradictions by which it has up to now undermined itself. I shall however do this somewhat briefly, as I wish to concentrate on the organizational responses of the oppressed strata, the politics of the antisystemic movements that have grown up in the course of the historical development of the capitalist world-economy. For it is these movements which themselves represent a principal nexus of both the undermining and the reproduction of the system.

All systems are both structure and change, have both cycles and trends. Intelligent analysis must always be wary of emphasizing the one at the expense of the other—of seeing only repetitive patterns, of discovering always what is "new." For much of the "new" has always been there, and the repetitions, such as they are, are spiral in character.

The basic economic mechanisms of the capitalist world-economy derive from the fact that the absence of an overarching political structure renders it likely that those producers who seek to operate on the imperative of ceaseless accumulation of capital will drive from competition, over the long run, those who would operate economic enterprises on any other normative principle. This means that producers/entrepreneurs tend to make their production and investment decisions in terms of what will optimize the medium-run likelihood of individual profit.

The basic contradiction of the capitalist system is found in the disjuncture of what determines supply and what determines demand. World production decisions are made on an individual basis. The sum of the activities of the individual producers/entrepreneurs constantly increases world production, which means that continued profitability for all is necessarily a function of an *expanding* world demand. However, expanding world demand is not a function of the decisions of the individual producers/entrepreneurs. If anything, the sum of their individual decisions, insofar as they press individually to reduce costs of their factors of production (and hence to reduce labor costs), serves actually to diminish world demand. World demand is fundamentally determined by a set of preexisting political compromises within the various states that are part of the world-economy, and which more or less fix for medium-run periods (circa fifty years) the modal distribution of income to various participants in the circuit of capital. This phenomenon often is discussed under such names as the existence of different "historic levels of wages." Wage-levels are indeed based on historic factors, but they are far from unchanging on that account.

An economic system in which world supply expands more or less continuously but world demand remains relatively fixed for medium periods of time is bound to create a cyclical pattern of production. Empirically the capitalist world-economy has in fact known such cycles of expansion and contraction since its beginning (that is, for at least 500 years). The most important of these cycles seems to be the expansion-stagnation cycle of 40-55 years that is often called the Kondratieff cycle.

In the stagnation phase of the cycle, precipitated by the excess of world production over world demand, individual entrepreneurs seek to maintain their own relative share of profit (or even expand it) either by expanding production, or by reducing costs (through reducing wages or through technological advance that increases productivity), or by reducing competition, or by some combination of these three methods. One of the many ways of reducing costs is to shift the locus of production to lower wage-zones (from city to country, or from core to peripheral zone both within states and within the world as a whole). Along with this goes pressure to redirect global flows of labor ("outward" from core toward periphery, rather than "inward" from periphery toward core, as occurs in expansion phases).

While individual entrepreneurs and individual goegraphic areas may benefit precisely because of stagnation, globally the effect is perceived as a squeeze, one felt on the one hand by weaker entrepreneurs (who face bankruptcy amidst the concentration of capital), and on the other hand by those segments of the world labor force previously steadily employed as wage workers. This latter group is unevenly distributed worldwide. Wherever wage workers are found in sufficient numbers, acute class struggles become the visible outgrowth of the stagnation phase. Wherever segments of the petty bourgeoisie are dispossessed because of the effects of stagnation, they join in the acute social conflict.

Over the period of this stagnation phase, the acute class struggles in the various states usually lead to a reopening of the previous historic compromises that had resulted in the existing distributions of appropriated surplus. In addition, semiperipheral zones are able to achieve either higher prices for their goods or a higher proportion of the world market, and thus retain larger segments of world surplus.

There results a redistribution of surplus—more to the bourgeoisie of semiperipheral zones, and more to parts of the labor force of core areas—which effectively expands world monetary demand enough to revive the inherent expansionist tendencies of the capitalist world-economy.

However, as a result of this redistribution of surplus, the world bourgeoisie, and particularly that segment located in the old core areas, is faced with a diminution of its share of world surplus, unless it takes two kinds of crucial countermeasures: technological advances which lead to temporary (but significant) superprofits deriving from temporary monopolies; and expansion of the outer boundaries of the world-economy to incorporate new zones of low-cost, not fully proletarianized, workers.

In this cyclical mechanism, we can see the pressures that lead to the creation and reinforcement of the four basic institutions of the capitalist world-economy: the states; classes; ethno/national status-groups; households. We shall briefly indicate the function of each.

It is by reinforcing and utilizing the state machineries of the states in which they are domiciled that entrepreneurs/producers can best increase their ability to profit, given the vagaries of the market, especially during the stagnation phase, both vis-à-vis other entrepreneurs and vis-à-vis the working classes. The consequent pressure to strengthen the efficacy of state machineries is not countered by working-class pressure in an opposite direction. Far from being antistate per se, the working classes of a given state in their struggle with the bourgeoisie of that state equally seek to strengthen the particular state machinery (whether their tactics are reformist or revolutionary), however much they are politically opposed to the domination of the existing regime by bourgeois elements. Hence, over time, and particularly in periods of stagnation, state machineries, in *all* parts of the world have in fact been systematically articulated and strengthened. This does not mean, however, that the initial difference between the greater state strength of core areas and the lesser state strength of peripheral zones has been diminished. Quite the contrary, despite the fact that all states have grown stronger in relation to internal forces, and there has been an overall trend to the ever-clearer institutionalization of a well-defined interstate system (which has reached its ideological culmination in the formation of the United Nations based on the formal insistence on sovereign equality), there has nonetheless also been an ever-increasing polarization of the strength of states.

The states are not the only institutions thus created by the operations of the world-economy. Classes are also created. Indeed, Marx's original insight that the operation of the capitalist system created two clear and polarized classes is in fact affirmed and not disconfirmed by the evidence. Whereas, originally, the multiplicity of social arrangements meant that the vast majority of households were in part of their activities the appropriated, and in another part the appropriators, hence both "proletarian" and "bourgeois," the slow but steady commodification of the work-force as well as of the managerial sectors has in fact diminished the "social veil" that blurred class structure. Most households today fall clearly into either a category which is receiving in *all* segments of its total income less than the social product it is creating (and hence is objectively proletarian) or into a category which is receiving a part of the global surplus product in all segments of its total income (and hence is objectively bourgeois).

What is important for our purposes is to note two things. This objective clarification, or lifting of the social veil, is in fact the product of the periodic stagnation phases and the consequent pressures on both entrepreneurs and workers. And the needs of both groups, especially insofar as they have wanted to manipulate state structures, have led to increasing class consciousness at both the state and the world level, initially historically of the bourgeoisie and then later of the proletariat.

The creation of classes is matched by the creation and recreation of the multitude of status groups (whether the lines are national, ethnic, racial, religious, or linguistic) as a mode by which sectors of the bourgeoisie and of the proletariat assert short-run interests amidst the cyclical rhythms of the world-economy. In the times of economic squeezes (the B-phases), groups seek extraeconomic legitimation for monopolistic hoarding of privileges (such as employment, education, etc.). In the times of expansion (the A-phases), upper- and middle-status groups seek to preclude the potential decline of market advantage by encrusting access to position through legislating cultural specifications of rights; or lower-status groups pursue class objectives in status-group garb in those situations in which working-class terminology has been preempted by middle-status groups. In all these instances, a renewed emphasis on status-group distinctions helps advance the interests of specific segments of the world-economy. When all is said and done, status-group formation, like state activity, serves as a mode of constraining and constricting both market and class forces in favor of some group or groups who would otherwise lose out in the medium run.

Finally, we should not ignore the fact that the capitalist world-economy has organized its bourgeoisie and its proletariat into income-pooling households of particular kinds. Despite the vaunted individualism of capitalist ideology, the members of classes and status groups are not individuals but these households. And these households too are creations of the world-economy in that the boundaries of the real economic units are the result of pressures upon kin and coresidential groups to expand and contract their boundaries in specific ways in order to produce the necessary labor-force at appropriate wage-levels in specific zones of the world-economy.

In particular, the so-called "extended family," which is often in fact not a purely kind group, is a created structure that optimizes the furnishing of part-life-time wage labor at below the minimum wage, by attaching such laborers to income pools fed by surplus value created by other members of the pool (or by themselves at other moments of time) to the benefit of the employer of the wage laborer. Conversely, the so-called "nuclear family," which may also be not a purely kin group, optimizes the creation of monetary demand, by reducing the proportion of consumption goods not obtained via the market. The contradictory pressures of the world economic forces create a cyclical pattern wherein household structures vary according to economic zone and to expansion-stagnation phases.

The periodic cyclical stagnations of the world-economy have been essentially resolved by a combination of three mechanisms. First, some producers have utilized advances in technology to create new and/or more efficiently produced commodities which would enable them to successfully challenge other producers who had previously dominated particular commodity markets. This provided new, so-called "dynamic" sectors of production. Secondly some segment of households which were previously "extended" and receiving only a small proportion of their life-time income from wage sources have found themselves dislocated, expropriated, or otherwise forced to become "proletarianized," that is, to become more fully dependent on the wage labor market for life-time household income. For those that survived the process of forced transition, this in fact has meant an increase in money income (if not at all necessarily an increase in real income). Thirdly, new direct producers have been incorporated into the world-economy, on its former "frontiers." These newly incorporated direct producers formed new pools of low-cost, part-time wage labor; they were of course also productive of new supplies of raw materials for world industrial production necessary for the new expansion phase of the world-economy.

Of the three mechanisms—technological change, proletarianization, incorporation—most writers refer to the first one as the most linear of all processes in the capitalist world-economy. In fact, the contrary is true, if one analyzes technology not as an autonomous process but in terms of its impact on the structure of the world-system as such. More than other mechanisms, the impact of technological change is the most cyclical and the least secular. Let me explain. What technological advance has accomplished above all is that it has regularly permitted one set of entrepreneurs to compete successfully with other entrepreneurs. This has had two consequences. The specific nature of the high-profit, high-wage commodities has repeatedly changed in favor of those in which the new technology has been invested. Particular commodities that were previously in this category have shifted downward in terms of overall profitability, and consequently in the attached wage structures. Secondly, the physical locus of the most "dynamic" sectors has also regularly changed—both within state boundaries and across state boundaries.

Hence, both the list of commodities involved in unequal exchange and the geographical location of core and peripheral economic processes have constantly shifted over time, without however transforming to any significant extent the world-wide structure of unequal exchange based on the axial division of labor. At first, wheat was exchanged against textiles; later textiles against steel; today steel against computers *and wheat.* Once Venice was a core zone and England semiperipheral; later Britain was core and the northern states of the United States semiperipheral; still later the United States was a core zone and Russia or Japan or many others semiperipheral; and tomorrow? In this way, technological advance has created a situation of constant geopolitical restructuring of the world-system, but has it *directly* undermined its viability? I suspect not.

It is rather in the two other cyclical processes—the reorganization of household structures and the incorporation of new zones into the world-economy—that I find the working-out of the essential contradictions of capitalism as a world-system, contradictions that are bringing about the contemporary systemic crisis in which we are living. Each time a segment of world household structures has been reorganized, the relative number of what we may call proletarianized households has grown as a proportion of the world labor force. Each time new zones have been incorporated into the ongoing production processes of the world-economy, the proportion of global land and population that is a real part of the operations of the capitalist world-economy has risen. But proportions inevitably have a limit. Their maximum is 100%. Ergo, these two mechanisms—proletarianization and incorporation—which serve to permit the regular renewal of expansion of the capitalist system also are its own undoing. Their success renders less likely their future utility as renewal mechanisms. This is one way to translate operationally the concept of the contradictions of capitalism as a system. These secular trends result from the basic contradiction of combining the anarchy of production with the social determination of demand.

The growing economic constraints produced by the secular trends precisely generate at the political level the rise of the antisystemic movements who are acting as the crucial social intermediary of global systemic change. These antisystemic movements have taken two generic forms since their emergence as important forces in the nineteenth century. These two forms are the social movement and the national movement.

While rural worker and urban poor discontent have been a constant of the system, and have periodically resulted in jacqueries and food riots, it was not until the relative concentration of proletarianized households in the core countries of the capitalist world-economy in the nineteenth century that the social movement emerged in the form of labor unions, socialist parties, and other kinds of workers' organizations. The social movement emphasized the growth of the polarity bourgeois/proletarian and called for a basic transformation of the system of inequality. *Ad interim,* however, the particular movements organized to obtain partial or total state power to advance the interests of the proletariat. The *Communist Manifesto,* for example, clearly exemplified this dual approach: on the one hand, the call for fundamental restructuring; on the other, the pursuit of *ad interim* objectives en route.

While the search of weaker states for greater strength has also been a constant of the system, it was not until the reorganization of the interstate system that followed on the Napoleonic wars and the subsequent Holy Alliance—with the increasing drive for culturo-linguistic as well as religious homogenization—that the peripheral and semiperipheral zones of Europe took up the banner of nationalism. The national movement emphasized the growth of the polarity core/periphery and called for a basic transformation of the system of inequality. *Ad interim,* however, the particular movements called for a somewhat stronger national entity (shifting from being an assimilated zone to being an autonomous zone, from a colony to an independent entity, from a weak state to a stronger state). 1848 was the Springtime of the Nations as well as the year of the *Communist Manifesto.*

Both the social movement and the national movement have had breathtaking careers since 1848. The social movement has spread from core to semiperiphery and periphery. Today there is hardly a corner of the earth that has not been touched by such movements. Conversely, the national movement, having swept the semiperipheral and peripheral zones of the world, has now reached the core, with the new explosion of political ethnicities in Western Europe and North America.

In the process of the social movement spreading from core to periphery and the national movement from periphery to core, the two movements have in fact rallied each other in two ways. First, they began their history in the nineteenth century as ideological rivals. But today, there is scarcely a social movement which is not nationalist, and there are few national movements which are not socialist. The confluence is not perfect, but it is great enough to argue that a social movement that is not nationalist and a national movement that is not socialist is suspect as a fraud to large segments of the world population. Secondly, and even more fundamentally, the two world movements have followed a similar trajectory. The initial ambiguity—the search for equality on the one hand via fundamental transformation and on the other hand via *ad interim* solutions—has revealed itself as being not an ideological option subject to the change of individual or even collective will but as being the result of a structural pressure of the world-system as such.

The capitalist world-economy is precisely a system in which the basic economic processes are located in a zone far larger than that of any political authority, and hence these processes are not *totally* responsive to the set of political decisions of any state—even to those of a hegemonic state; *a fortiori* to those of a state in the periphery. Yet, the mechanisms that are most easily manipulable are these same state structures of limited power, especially precisely for antisystemic movements. Hence both the social movement and the national movement almost necessarily have to seek medium-run gain via the control (or partial control) of a given state structure. Yet to achieve this control, they strengthen these state structures, which in turn reinforces the operations of the interstate system and thereby of capitalism as a world-system. The dilemma is not a minor one.

I should like to view this dilemma too as acting itself out historically in the form of a cycle and a trend. The cycle is very simple and has been widely observed, most often cynically. It is described in the following manner: The movements have emerged and asserted revolutionary objectives. They have succeeded and achieved power. Once in power, they have effectuated changes, which were however less fundamental than previously sought. Having compromised, they have thereupon been accused of "betrayal" or "revisionism." Finally, Thermidor has been imposed either by counterrevolution or by inner transformation of the movement. The adepts, such as survive, have been disillusioned, and for the next generation what had been revolutionary slogans became ideological and oppressive myths.

Is this simple cycle what has in fact historically happened? Only partially. It is true of course that the Social-Democrats of nineteenth-century Europe seemed to have followed such a path when they came to (partial) power in the early twentieth century. It is true that one could make a similar case for the various Communist parties, most prominently first that of the U.S.S.R., then that of China. And it is true that every anticolonial revolution has seemed to fit the pattern.

But are we telling the whole story? I think not. There has been first of all the impact of the initial mobilizations. Many particular movements were total failures, but those that succeeded did so because, over a period of time, they were able to create organizational structures of some kind that were able to mobilize their prospective audiences in three concentric circles of intensity: an inner circle of dedicated cadres, a middle circle of activists, an outer circle of sympathizers. The very process of creating these structures over time itself had major consequences for the political structure of the world-system, and first of all in terms of the political *rapport de forces* in the particular state in question.

For such movements to come to even partial power in given states represented a *conquest* of power, whose very achievement resulted not only in the specific reforms subsequently enacted but in shifts in collective mentality which were themselves continuing political facts. Nor are the "reforms" themselves to be lightly condemned. They may have seemed paltry next to the aspirations, but is this the appropriate measure? Should they not be seen rather as a mechanism, and a rather successful one, of slowing down the galloping polarization of the world-system as a whole, thereby preserving the material possibilities for anti-systemic activity? From this point of view, such "revolutions" have in fact been neither "false" nor without effect. But they have to be sure been "recuperated" in the sense that the achievement of state power has forced the movements sooner or later to conform to the norms of the interstate system and, more than they wished, to the law of value underlying the operations of the capitalist world-economy.

The fact is that, however radical the reforms that have been initiated by any such movement, these movements have discovered that no single state structure can enact a transformation either of the interstate system or of the world-economy, and there is no simple way in which the rest of the world can be wished away. A given state led by a given movement can attempt to "secede" from the politico-economic structures of the world-system. The Cambodia of Pol Pot has perhaps been the most dramatic example of such an attempt. But quite apart from whether this was at all a desirable tactic in terms of the results, it has become quite clear that it was not a feasible tactic, since the rest of the world-system was simply not prepared to let it happen—even for such a minor segment of the globe as Cambodia. Everywhere, the reality has been that the fact that a movement proclaims the unlinking of a state's productive processes from the integrated world-economy has never in fact accomplished the unlinking. It may have accomplished temporary withdrawal which, by strengthening internal production and political structures, enabled the state to improve its relative position in the world-economy. In this case, it has merely meant that, de facto, particular relative prices were imposed in fact on particular exchanges, such that—within the proclaiming state—some gained and some lost. But this is of course how the capitalist world-economy has always operated. Hence the logic of Mao Tse-tung's position on the continuing class struggle within states undergoing "socialist construction" is impeccable. The only issue is what to do about it.

Here we must return to the movements. The arrival at partial or total state power has meant always partial compromise. And in many cases, it has eventually meant total compromise, given movements having ceased altogether to be antisystemic movements. But we must view these movements historically. After the phase of mobilization came the phase of compromised power for an antisystemic movement. Compromised power was not at all the same as total abandonment of antisystemic objectives. It was this fact of a phase of compromised power that created the spiral effect, and turned what seemed to be a cyclical phenomenon into a secular trend of the world-system as a whole.

The achievement of power by given movements has had two important consequences beyond whatever reforms such movements were able to enact in particular states. These movements have, first of all, quite clearly served as inspiration and reinforcement for analogous neighboring movements, particularly at the very beginning of their phase of achieved power. One cannot imagine the political history of the twentieth century without taking into account this spread effect. Mobilization has bred mobilization, and the success of one has been the source of hope of the other. Secondly, the success of the one has created more political space for the other. Each time an antisystemic movement has come to partial or total power, it has altered the balance of power of the interstate system such that there has been more space for other antisystemic movements.

But if the coming to power of one movement gave both inspiration and space to others, should not the inevitable compromising in which movements in power engage have reduced both the inspiration and the space? Not at all, because the operations of the world-system are more complex than such a simple symmetry would suggest. The movements that have come later have not only been inspired; they have been instructed. They have learned that part of the world political struggle for them involves putting pressure on these movements in power, these movements who have compromised but whose internal strength depends in part on a maintenance of the continuity of ideology. The mobilizing movements have not hesitated to play upon this social reality and force these movements in power to "compromise" less than they would otherwise be inclined—extracting the space and even the inspiration they need from now reluctant partners.

Hence what seems like a simple upward-downward cycle of the political effect of antisystemic movements turns out on closer inspection to have been an upward-downward-upward thrust. If one cumulates such threefold thrusts across the world-economy and over time, one can quickly see that there would be, has been, a secular upward trend of the overall strength of antisystemic movements in the capitalist world-economy over the past 150 years, despite all the "recuperative" political mechanisms which exist within the system. This is why the prophets of doom are to be found not among antisystemic forces but rather among the defenders of the system. The importance of antisystemic movements is not in the reforms they achieve or in the regimes they establish. Many of these regimes are in fact parodies of their stated objectives. The importance of these movements is in terms of the changes they bring about in the world-system as a whole. They transform not primarily the economics but rather the politics of the capitalist world-economy. Joined with the more narrowly socioeconomic trends previously described, this secular increase of the strength of antisystemic movements undermines the viability of the world-system.

In the light of this analysis, let us look at the contemporary conjuncture. Worldwide, the downward turning point of the post-Second World War Kondratieff cycle was either 1967 or 1973. (It is hard to tell at such short historical distance.) If we take it at 1967, which for the moment seems to me the more plausible, we can see the accentuation of worldwide class struggle that occurred in the very early moments of this B-phase. The shakiness of world markets for the products of core countries (these products being essentially too numerous for world demand) was signaled by the end of the period where the U.S. dollar anchored the world monetary system. All over the world, in various forms, there came to be a squeeze on total social expenditure—reflected both in household spending patterns and in state and other collective "fiscal crises."

Social unrest was immediately visible. In China, there was an acute internal struggle known as the Cultural Revolution. In Czechoslovakia, a social movement within the Communist party led to the Dubček reforms, implying changes not only internally but in the whole relationship of eastern European states to the U.S.S.R. In the West, 1968-1969 was the high point of the antiauthoritarian uprisings by students and workers, which was combined in many countries with an intensification of the political demands of the ethno-nationalist movements within them, as well as a new "nationalism" in the social movement (e.g., Eurocommunism).

The weakening of the financial solvency and political stability of the core states meant that the United States could no longer offer efficacious opposition in Southeast Asia, or Portugal in Africa, to the persistent struggle of the nationalist movements in these areas. In 1973, the oil-producing states took advantage of the changed world economic situation to increase dramatically the price of their crucial product. The result of course was not only to reallocate distribution of world surplus, but to constrain world production. (It is for this reason that political opposition to OPEC in the core states has only been nominal.) In a number of peripheral areas, the world economic squeeze was felt in the form of acute famines, which cleared some rural zones of producers, forcing many of the survivors into a marginalized existence in urban areas. (This involves also a reduction in world agricultural production, to the benefit of the mechanized agrobusiness of certain core areas.)

This first outburst of political struggles in the current world stagnation seems to have been contained—reversal of the Cultural Revolution, the Soviet invasion of Czechoslovakia, the suppression of the various so-called radical movements in North America and Western Europe, the "socialist wars" in Southeast Asia, the pressures for "internal settlements" in southern Africa, the recycling of OPEC money. On the other hand, this B-phase is far from over. Relatively high unemployment rates, further fiscal crises, even perhaps an acute price crash are still to be expected throughout the 1980s.

One state in which further acute social unrest is likely is the United States which must go through a widespread income readjustment as a result of its relative decline vis-à-vis other core states. Acute class struggles that will center on the demands of Blacks and Spanish-speakers will probably result. This will be especially ture if the United States increases its support to white settler interests in southern Africa. We may perhaps see similar acute struggles within the U.S.S.R. The need to keep the lid on wages in order for Soviet products to compete in the world market may lead to migrations of Moslem/Asian populations to industrial zones and thus to accentuated de facto ethno-class stratification, which may in turn force class tensions there, as in the United States, to take on ethnic forms in the tight years ahead.

In the many semiperipheral zones in the world, the internal pressures created by the desire of each to profit from the conjuncture will lead many of them to have internal explosions. Wherever they occur, the explosion will of course eliminate that particular state from the race the semiperipheral states are conducting with each other, and in which there can only be one or two who gain substantially. Iran was the first such explosion, but explosions similar in effect if not in form are not to be ruled out in such diverse zones as China, India, South Africa, Brazil.

Finally, we are witnessing a major reshuffling in the interstate system. The reconciliation of China with the United States, and even more significantly with Japan, may be matched in the years to come by equally spectacular revisions of alliances. For example, I would not rule out a German-Soviet entente.

Finally, I expect the world-economy to take a marked upturn once again in the 1990s. The result of the turmoil and the realignments will in fact have been, as before, to increase world demand to a point high enough to stimulate a further expansion of world production. There will probably be significant cost-saving technological inventions, possibly centering on the provision of energy. There will be significant further "proletarianization," deriving on the one hand from the impact of the displacement of "traditional" industrial enterprises to semiperipheral areas and on the other hand from the reinforcement of wage-income-dependent household structures in the core. This further change in core household structures will be effectuated by a vast increase in the tertiary sector, the continuing entry of women into the full-time wage-labor force, and the redefinition of social roles sought by the various antisexist and antiracist movements. We shall probably enter the year 2000 to the renewed hosannas of the rosy-eyed optimists of capitalist apologetics. This will be particularly true if we survive the critical 1980s without any serious interstate war.

And yet underneath, both the structural contradictions of capitalism and the antisystemic movements it has bred in such force will continue to eat away at the entrails of the system. The details are impossible to predict, but the broad pattern is clear. We are living in the historic world transition from capitalism to socialism. It will undoubtedly take a good 100-150 years yet to complete it, and of course the outcome is not inevitable. The system may yet see several periods of remission. There may come again moments where capitalism will seem to be in bloom. But in a comparison of life-cycles of social systems, the modern world-system can be seen to be in a late phase. What will replace it will surely not be utopia. But with the end of this peculiar moral aberration that capitalism has represented, a system in which the benefits for some have been matched by a greater exploitation for the many than in all the prior social systems, the slow construction of a relatively free and relatively egalitarian world may at last begin. This it seems to me, and only this, is likely to permit each individual and the species to realize their potential.

Chapter 10

MAOIST CONCEPTUALI-ZATIONS OF THE CAPITALIST WORLD-SYSTEM

Edward Friedman

One of the less emphasized strengths of a world-systems approach to national societies is its critical comprehension of the limited possibilities of ruling groups transforming their societies into ones of socialist relations (Wallerstein, 1974a; Wallerstein, 1974b: 348, 351). One limit placed on the part by the whole, on nation-states by a capitalist world-market is the impossibility of building socialism. The imperatives of the world-market force state power-holders to act in a capitalist manner, that is, to organize their society for competition in world exchange.

The costs of not doing so are prohibitive. The nation falls behind in military technology and becomes vulnerable to its enemies or the consumption demands of its working people to stay abreast of their peers elsewhere are denied and suppressed or people are more deeply exploited to extract less competitive products which are dumped on the international market to earn the means to purchase desparately needed products or all three. That is, the tendency of change which increases the high technology component of military security, communications, and transportation, which increases the need for everything from primary products to advanced research also increases the inevitability of risky involvement in the capitalist world-market.

The likely consequence of ruling groups in "socialist" societies not responding to and involving themselves with world capitalist imperatives is that they become perceived at home as traitors and exploiters. That is, they create situations leading to their own discrediting, downfall, and replacement by patriotic groups more responsive to national needs and

---

AUTHOR'S NOTE: My thanks to Bruce Cumings, Vivienne Shue, and Mark Selden for their separate critiques of a preliminary draft toward this chapter.

popular demands and therefore to capitalist imperatives; or these discredited rulers become ruthlessly repressive of elite competitors and popular forces in order to hold on to power, in which case there is no prospect of working people moving much closer toward determining their own destiny, no prospect at all of socialism. Socialism is impossible in a statist era where national scarcities are delimited by an ever-deepening world capitalist market.

This is not to suggest that there is no difference between contemporary nations which style themselves socialist and those today imitating earlier capitalist nations. The difference actually is stark. The supposedly socialist state during the industrialization process includes more of its population in the notion of people. This more democratic experience of the citizenry tends usually to preclude denying such people basic human needs—jobs, food, medicine, education, etc. A greater part of production meets a higher definition of socially legitimate needs. To that extent, the laborer is not defined as a commodity. To that extent, there is a noncapitalist element in poor socialist societies as in many industrialized welfare states, nations of much greater wealth. The difference on the average adds over a decade to the life expectancy of the ordinary Chinese citizen. The difference obviously is real and substantial. Surely this difference is palpable and most significant. If one compares China with other large, poor, densely populated Third-World capitalist countries, one must notice the life-enhancing consequence of the socialist commitment.

Yet the difference does not make for socialism.[1] It does, however, permit us better to understand why socialist-oriented power-holders can have good conscience, can believe themselves true to their ideals of human liberation even while most outsiders notice that socialism is not being built. It is not very helpful to approach this failure to build socialism in terms of languages of betrayal or decay. There is a delimiting world structure that must be explored and some day, perhaps, exploded.

Betrayal and decay are natural languages of explanation, however, for progressive anti-imperialists in the imperialist world. We identify with the victims of imperialism. We struggle against the monster in whose belly we reside. We defend and romanticize the victims. We claim their cause as our own. That strikes me as the least human beings can do for each other.

We also publicly propagate our illusions about imperialism's victims. At first we ignore or apologize for the fact that the anti-imperialists in power turn out to be nationalists struggling against and necessarily compromising with the politicized world-market to survive and prosper.[2] Eventually most such good outside analysts lose their blinders and notice that the revolutionary state is also a national capitalist state. When we finally give up our illusions, we too often say "they" have betrayed us. The culprit actually is a too narrow and out-moded form of analysis which will not comprehend the cut-throat and constricted consequences for Third-World anti-imperialist patriots of the politicized world-market. One most interesting feature of the consciousness of the leaders of the Chinese revolution is that from early on they transcended merely parochial national analysis and committed themselves to a broad mode of anti-imperialist comprehension which gave priority to the world level, to their national destiny as limited by world forces.

I. FIRST IMPRESSIONS OF THE MODERN WORLD-SYSTEM: IMPERIALISM

For China's anti-imperialist revolutionaries, the modern epoch begins with the Opium War of 1840-1842. Britain, in the name of civilization and commerce, compelled China to open its doors to importing the drug. America's John Quincy Adams denounced China for barring opium imports, for opposing the universal enjoinder for commercial intercourse, for subverting basic human rights.

> China, not being a Christian nation, its inhabitants do not consider themselves bound by the Christian precept to love their neighbor as themselves.... This is a churlish and unsocial system.... The fundamental principle of the Chinese empire is anti-commercial.... It admits no obligation to hold commercial intercourse with others.... It is time that this enormous outrage upon the rights of human nature, and upon the first principle of the rights of nations, should cease [Julien, 1971: 223].[3]

Thus, China was made "part of the capitalist world market" in such a disgusting and hypocritical manner that it made manifest the thieving reality behind "the much-vaunted 'Western civilization' of the imperialist robbers" (Compilation Group, 1976: 112, 75).[4] Silver flowed out and the burden of currency was too often transferred to those Chinese least able to defend themselves. Textile handicrafts were injured, thereby causing certain rural dwellers to lose one of their cushions against bad times. Hunger would more likely be famine; barely surviving became uprooting. An international trade grew in Chinese coolie labor.

In the late nineteenth century, tea producers for export in China's southern coastal province of Fuchien lost out when Britain established tea plantations in Ceylon. Fuchien instead began to export poor males to the Philippines where Fuchienese had for centuries been trading and at times earning good silver profits as intermediaries in international trade. Poor Fuchienese villagers now became dependent on monetary remittances from the Philippines. The villagers therefore regularly renewed the supply of hard currency-earning young males and young brides to keep them content and in place. As with vulnerable Chinese coolies scapegoated in Colorado or Mexico, the Chinese migrants in the Philippines were continually potential or real victims of discrimination, deportation, or pogrom. A capitalist world-market and a weak Chinese state combined to turn millions of Chinese into defenseless, international commodities. At home tens of millions starved to death.

The 1900 Boxer rebellion in China against alleged foreign and Christian origins of flood, famine, debt, etc. was crushed by foreign armed forces. Kaiser Wilhelm is said to have told the German troops setting out to put down the nativistic Chinese struggle, "Give no quarter, take no prisoners, kill him when he falls into your hands" so that as with the Huns under Atilla, the German name will "resound through Chinese history a thousand years from now."

The victorious foreign forces imposed a huge indemnity on China, took closer control of its tariffs and taxes and left China further exposed to the vicissitudes of the world-market. China's first great Communist-led peasant revolution in the Hai-feng and Lu-feng area was then catalyzed by the same changes in the world sugar market which helped prod the Zapata rebellion in Mexico (Marks, 1977).

In Mao Tse-tung's home province of Hunan, fortunes in agriculture as well as antimony for arms and armament rose and fell with the First World War (McDonald, 1978). Mao's home area was a large rice-milling center. Foreign ships had to be permitted up the Yangtze River to take rice away from Hunan for export sale to the highest bidder (Rawski, 1972: 131). China had lost control of its customs, tariffs, and trade. Peasants would rebel against imposed rice exports as famine-inducing. Mao's father had been a rice merchant.

Wherever one looks, the same combination appears; whether it is cotton or tobacco (Gittings, 1974), cement (Friedman, 1968), or indigo (Sheel, forthcoming), a politicized, thieving, murderous world-system did in weak Chinese governments and defenseless Chinese people. China's revolutionary nationalists did not need Lenin to show them how the world was run by robbers. They knew only too well.

II. NATIONAL INDEPENDENCE AS A PROJECT FOR THE WORLD-SYSTEM

Even before the Bolshevik Revolution won power in Russia, before the new Russian government surrendered Czarist Russia's unequal treaty rights in China and gained a sympathetic hearing for the idea that the Europeans' First World War was a war among thieves for control of colonial possessions, China's left nationalist close to Sun Yat-sen such as Chu Chih-hsin and Liao Chung-k'ai already understood all that only too well. Germany was afraid that its European opponents would strengthen themselves by grabbing Germany's possessions and territories in China. Preferring to see a weak China strengthened, Germany offered its territories to a neutral China. Consequently, Chinese independence conflicted with the Allies' cause which, in China, was the cause of more Japanese expansion. Japan's European ally, the dominant European parliamentary democracy, Great Britain, had also long been the dominant imperialist power in China. Progress in the West was theft in China.

China was not a European colony. It was a pawn and a prize in a continuing imperialist power struggle. History and geopolitics combined to make the cause of Chinese independence require a tactical alliance with one or another reactionary imperialist nation. To overcome an immediate and murderous evil, one had to join with another.

China's nationalists did not like such tactics. They wanted real independence. They responded to Woodrow Wilson's call for genuine independence for weak and small nations. Mao concluded that big nationism was imperialism, that *ta kuo chu-i* was *ti-kuo chu-i* (Mao, 1976). The worst, most reactionary empires seemed to be breaking up, the Ottoman Empire, the Manchu dynasty, Czarist Russia, and Austria-Hungary. The progressive future of humankind seemed to lie with the small and the weak.

Mao would never abandon this notion of the superiority of many centers, much room for local initiative. Stagnation resulted when bureaucratic empires controlled people's destiny. Explaining what world-systems theory sees as the difference between world-empires and dynamic world-economies, Mao spelled this view out again forty years later.

> One good thing about Europe is that all its countries are independent, that each promotes its own purposes such that the economy of Europe develops comparatively quickly. Our country, since the Ch'in [Dynasty, 221 B.C.] took the form of a big nation [*ta kuo*]. The whole nation generally preserved its unified form over a very long period. One of the weak points of this was bureaucratism; the control was suffocating. Regions could not independently develop. Everybody hemmed and hawed. The economy developed very slowly. Now... we want... a relative unity which is also a relative independence [Mao, 1967: 226-227].[5]

But China's relative independence was betrayed at Versailles. The small and weak nations whose cause was ethically and ultimately appealing were abandoned to the will of the big nations. The words of Woodrow Wilson were incapable of checking Japan's further expansion into China. Independence for China, the number one issue for all Chinese patriots, therefore could not possibly be conceived of as a natural fruit of the liberal political tree, of the established, civilized powers. Civilization was run by crooks. The point then was, as Mao's mentor and a founder of China's Communist Party, Li Ta-chao, put it, to end a world-system where robbers could rob. Nothing less than a change at the world-system level could assure China genuine independence.

> Alas, the present world is a robber's world.... The reason why Japan can overrun the world with aggression wholly is because the present world still is a robber's world. It is not only those [Japanese] who have seized Shantung [province] who are our enemies. All thieving groups and activities in this robber's world ... are our enemies. If we as a nation lack the determination, if we lack the spirit for world reform to overthrow this robber's world, if we only kill some people ... we still won't achieve anything. We take an oath ... to reconstruct the robber's world [Li, 1962: 214].

It was no great difficulty for Li and other Chinese nationalists to rename the "large strong robber nations" as imperialists, "the world capitalist class," and to experience themselves, "the weak and small nations" as part of the world proletariat who had a double mission, to win their own national independence and secure it by overthrowing world imperialism (Chang, 1978: 95-96). What was special was the statist reconception of this task. But if the world level had priority and if states were the major actors and if patriotism and national independence were the major driving forces of the world proletariat, then nationalism was not a betrayal of socialism. Instead, the world proletariat, that is, the weak and small nations, the colonial and semicolonial peoples, in asserting their interest in national justice for themselves became the force for a just world. Surely the robbers wouldn't do it for them.

III. THE CATEGORIES OF GOOD CONSCIENCE IN SURVIVING IN THE WORLD-SYSTEM

The Bolshevik revolution in power, the Soviet state, would not easily appear as an obvious savior of the world proletariat from this Chinese statist reconceptualization of world classes. Lenin himself distinguished the Bolshevik revolution from anti-imperialist struggles. For Lenin, Czarist Russia was an imperialist state, but the weakest of imperialist states, the weakest link in the chain of imperialism.

Because Russian imperialism was relatively ineffectual, it could not win, according to Leninism, the superprofits needed to buy off a labor aristocracy, or to create a strong national bourgeoisie as bulwarks to counter revolution. Proletarian socialist revolutions were therefore possible, Marx to the contrary notwithstanding, in other than the most advanced capitalist states.

But what was the relevance of this theory for enslaved colonial peoples? Chinese nationalists did not notice that the Bolshevik revolution particularly weakened Japanese imperialism or made it less rapacious in China. In fact, Japan's rulers took the Bolshevik revolution as a pretext not only to intervene in Siberia but also to strengthen Japan's grip on northeastern China.

The new rulers in the Soviet Union found the major international threat coming from Europe to their west. China's anti-imperialist revolutionaries, on the other hand, were compelled to concern themselves first and foremost with the Japanese invaders. That life and death concern dictated temporary and tactical alliance with Japan's imperialist competitors in the West who also just happened to be the Soviet Union's worst enemies. Despite—yet because of—the passionate desire for true independence, weak, endangered Chinese anti-imperialists had to make compromises as principles. Mao's frequent subsequent dicta in that regard were a quintessential summation of prior lessons of survival. To stand alone was to surrender to a firing squad.

> Tactically . . . we must compromise. On Korea's 38th parallel, didn't we propose compromises with the Americans? In Vietnam, didn't we compromise with the French? In the various tactical stages, we must be good at carrying on struggles and at the same time good in making compromises [Mao, 1967: 135].

Chinese communists in 1928 argued for the correctness of their primary opposition to Japanese imperialism, for compromises with opponents of Japan to check murderous Japanese aggression. Power-holders in Moscow perceived the Chinese imperative as a Marxist-Leninist heresy. The Chinese Communist comrades were reprimanded. Clearly, the theory of socialist strategy was infused, if not poisoned, by normal conflicting statist interests of self-defense, security, and balance of power in response to real threatening, neighboring robbers in a statist robbers' world. National egoism had to distort national analysis of world class relations in the direction of national self-interest.

Yet the ethical intent was deep and genuine. From China's non-Communist progressive anti-imperialists in Shanghai's 1920s *Kuo-min jih pao* on out to the left wing of the C.C.P., Chinese sincerely imagined their cause as the cause of liberating oppressed humanity in all of colonial Asia and Africa. There was no difficulty in analytically linking this identification with the weak and small nations who were the victims of imperialism with the theory of Leninist Marxism. Li Ta-chao had already shown that Marx's comment that China's nineteenth-century T'ai-p'ing revolution— and the same holds true for a comment of Marx's on Ireland—could have sparked a revolution in Britain indicated that Chinese Marxist anti-imperialists could legitimately and logically believe that their struggle had global significance. It was an ultimate ethical cause. There was nothing peripheral or parochial in fighting for national freedom. Rather it was part of the socialist revolution.

> [The] Chinese revolution will throw the spark into the overloaded mine of the present industrial system and cause the explosion of the long-prepared general crisis, which, spreading abroad, will be closely followed by political revolutions on the Continent [Marx and Engels, 1972: 24].

This theory, in Chinese nationalistic guise, although worded in language similar to Lenin's was actually very different. In one pithy formulation by Li Li-san, the notion of the weakest link in imperialism is given a content opposite to Lenin's but in complete harmony with a broad anti-imperialist spectrum in China. Lenin, who never conceived of himself as other than advanced, used the idea of Russia as the weakest link in imperialism to mean that Russia's advanced proletariat was the least corrupted in the capitalist world. But Chinese used it to refer to backward, anti-imperialist China as an exploited nation, a proletarian people. The national revolution was integrally the socialist revolution.

> China is the weakest link in the ruling chain of world imperialism, it is the place where the volcano of the world revolution is most likely to erupt. Therefore, with the present aggravation of the global revolutionary crisis, the Chinese revolution may possibly break out first, setting off the world revolution and the final decisive class war of the world [Schram, 1966: 148].

It was normal for Chinese revolutionaries to find universal significance in their struggles. We all, after all, tend to value our own experience. Those with other experiences and conclusions, we too readily find stupid, obstructionist, and worse. Mao, as other patriotic Chinese revolutionaries, promised broader realms of human liberation as a consequence of China's victorious cause. Mao told Edgar Snow on July 23, 1936:

> The Chinese revolution is a key factor in the world situation, and its victory is heartily anticipated by the people of every country, especially by the toiling masses of the colonial countries. When the Chinese revolution comes into full power, the masses of many colonial countries will follow the example of China and win a similar victory of their own [Schram, 1969: 374].

Mao, on June 24, 1937 wrote to American Communist Party leader, Earl Browder, that "when we obtain victory, this victory can give very great assistance to the American people's struggle for liberation" (Mao, 1975, V: 231). These general celebrations of the yet richer fruits of the Chinese revolutionary tree led to an analysis of the soil from which it had sprung. History and geopolitics became Marxist theory, a theory—whatever its limits—surely far superior in its predictive expectations than that which just waited for the glorious revolution of the proletariat in advanced industrial societies.

The leading theoretician of the Chinese Communist Party, Liu Shao-ch'i, told Anna Louise Strong in mid-1946 that

> Mao Tse-tung's great accomplishment has been to change Marxism from a European to an Asian form.... He is the first that has succeeded in doing so....
>
> China is a semifeudal, semicolonial country in which vast numbers of people live at the edge of starvation, tilling small bits of soil.... In attempting the transition to a more industrialized economy, China faces... the pressures... of advanced industrial lands.... There are similar conditions in other lands of southeast Asia. The course chosen by China will influence them all [Dittmer, 1974: 25].

Ultra-left ideologue Ch'en Po-ta, except for his extreme chauvinism, was indistinguishable from Liu Shao-ch'i on this almost Helgelian understanding of China's role in world history. Ch'en argued that

> since the end of the 19th century, China was the focal point of the many contradictions in the East.... [O]nly the victory of the Chinese people's revolution could ... break the fetters of imperialism in the East....
>
> [T]he Chinese revolution is, above all, a revolution against imperialism....
>
> Obviously, it requires great theoretical courage on Comrade Mao Tse-tung's part to apply the general guiding principles of Marxism-Leninism to Oriental countries because here the conditions are very different from those in European capitalist states. The theory of Mao Tse-tung is a devlopment of Marxism-Leninism in the East.... For the entire world struggle as a whole, it is of universal significance [Ch'en Po-ta, 1953: 5, 8, 14, 84-86].

These are not isolated declarations but the general thrust, a shared heritage, ranging from China's Marxist idealists such as Lin Piao to its Marxist materialists such as Peng Chen.

Thus, much as in China, it has become possible for the people of all, or at least some, of the colonial countries in the East to maintain big and small revolutionary base areas and revolutionary regimes over a long period of time, and to carry on long-term, revolutionary wars, in which to surround the cities from the country-side, and then gradually to advance to take the cities and win nationwide victory [Mao, 1965: 71].

But certain decisive world features are obscured by the claims. They were not, however, ignored by ruling groups in the Soviet Union. For them, everything had to be subordinated to their battle with enemies to the west. In 1941, worried about attacks on the U.S.S.R., experienced as the socialist motherland, an international factor of unique and immense importance, the Soviets asked Mao's guerillas "that the struggle against Japan be intensified so as to prevent it [Japan] from striking at the Soviet Union from the rear." "Mao Tse-tung in effect refused the Commintern's direct request" (Kommunist, 1968), its invitation to suicide for China's revolutionary forces. What was openly revealed was that life insurance for the more powerful could mean death for the less powerful.

As the Second World War ended, the Soviet Union feared a nuclear attack from the United States. Mao's group believed, on the other hand, that talk of a Third World War, of a direct America-Russia clash, was camouflage for America's attempt to win influence in former colonies of Europe and Japan, that what was at stake behind the sounds raging from Washington was a furious effort to move into a vast intermediate zone between the two military giants. Mao ignored Stalin's advice that China's Red armies should not fight for victory. Stalin apparently feared that such a Chinese struggle might give Washington a pretext to hit Moscow with atomic bombs.

Mao by this time was projecting a generalized view of politics. The world was shaped like an egg. At one end were the ethical forces, China and its friends. At the other end were the worst enemies of humankind, the direct threats to China. In-between, as with the various patriotic elements in China, was a vast zone. Politics was the struggle to win over that great middle. Stalin, in contrast, saw politics as a struggle between two polar forces where, as with Russia's national bourgeoisie, the middle was inherently weak and corrupt.

The answer to the Chinese question, how does one survive in a robber's world was political. One made tactical deals to check a hegemonic force which could directly threaten one. That is much of what interwar diplomacy had been all about. The wisdom of the answer and the tactics could not seem enlightened self-interest to causes slighted or sacrificed in the political compromises and alliances.

Too much postwar historiography ignores the inevitably and inherently dubious political pragmatique. The tactical, time-buying Hitler-Stalin pact—perhaps because Stalin did not make use of the time won (more likely because he twisted the tactic into a principle of a projected epoch where socialists were said to be worse than fascists)—is incorrectly seen as uniquely immoral. In treating the Second World War as an obvious global combat pitting light against darkness, one forgets the nationalists as in India who wouldn't join the war on the antifascist side unless and until Britain first abandoned its imperialist position in India. One forgets the leftists in China who denounced Mao for his tactical alliance against Japan with Chiang Kai-shek, who ran a murderous, fascist landlord-usurer government. But that pragmatique of compromise tactics had become Mao's political principle. He knew that in the 1930s and 1940s his forces had survived only by utilizing anti-imperialist conflicts (Gittings, 1974). Victims had to embrace some thieving others in order to corral the major enemy, the biggest robber of all.

The 1950 military and economic alliance with Stalin is best seen in similar categories. Surely the Soviet Union won militarily and then plundered an empire in Eastern Europe. To befriend and be a friend of Stalin, Mao had to denounce Tito in 1948 and apologize for Soviet rule over the nations of Eastern Europe. Mao even went to the point of urging Khrushchev to crush the Hungarian rebels.

Most progressive Western historians of Chinese foreign policy do not describe these murderous compromises and bloody betrayals of 1950-1958 in their proper shade of red. The reason is not hard to find. In the West, that the Cold War was used to rationalize repression at home and American expansion and intervention in free elections in Italy, in coups in Guatemala, Iran, and Laos, in the attempted subversion of the governments of Cuba and Indonesia, and so much more which is reactionary is also well-known and well-established. These reactionary deeds were legitimated as opposition to Soviet Communist totalitarian enslavement as had already occurred in Eastern Europe. With the cause of liberty in Eastern Europe so tainted by its political usage in the expansionist United States, with progressive historians fixated on showing that Stalin wasn't merely an aggressor in Eastern Europe, there was little interest in closely examining China's compromises with Soviet tyranny in those areas.

In sum then, progressive Western preoccupations called attention away from the continuity in necessary horrible international compromises in the 1930s, the 1940s, and the 1950s. Add on to that the horrendous misreading of the Peking-Hanoi relation in the 1960s (Friedman, 1979), and we find that a particular misreading of a supposed Chinese betrayal in the 1970s, of a nonexistent sudden Chinese switch is an ordinary instance in which Western progressives' loss of illusions leads us misleadingly to call them, the Chinese, traitors. More important for the purposes of this chapter, that peculiar theory of a sudden Chinese betrayal permits people ridiculously to accept the notion of a Moscow-Peking split based on Khrushchev-Mao, bad-good ideological categories and a slighting of all the decision elements of a continuing Chinese struggle for relative independence and equitable development in a politicized world-market skewed against China. Rationalization replaces reality.

IV. WORLD-MARKET VERSUS SOCIALIST CAMP

Throughout all the compromises with the U.S.S.R., China's ruling groups could honestly experience themselves as true to their original ethical commitment of liberating the world's proletariat, the small and weak states, the colonial and semicolonial peoples. Upon China's liberation, Liu Shao-ch'i, doubting that the American proletariat would revolt and save the world, declared that in fact "the victories gained by the national independence and liberation movements of the oppressed nations in the colonies and semi-colonies, and every blow delivered to imperialism constitute the best and most direct help to the proletariat and the peoples in imperialist countries." Hence even in their own anticapitalist terms, let alone China's anti-imperialist conceptualization, Moscow's rulers were urged to

> give more support to the national independence and liberation movements in colonial and semicolonial countries, and take further steps in building up a united front with them in opposition to imperialism [Liu, 1969: 141-142].

But rulers in Moscow found that their fear of enemies to the west conflicted with any large steps on to the raging anti-imperialist battlefields. In the 1950s and into the 1960s with Algeria, Vietnam, and Laos the major wars of national liberation, whereas China gave great aid, the U.S.S.R. worried more about keeping France strong enough to balance a resurgent (and potentially revanchist) West Germany in Europe. Geopolitics, history, and the international strategy of the two major military powers permitted China to seem the more anti-imperialist party. The decisive global geopolitical and world-market forces which shaped very limited state options were not controlled either by Moscow or Peking.

Chinese ethics could seem a dangerous embarrassment to the Soviet Union. Indeed Moscow would eventually portray Peking to Washington as a capitol whose rulers sparked wars anywhere and threatened world peace everywhere. But rulers in China were well aware of their compromises in Korea, Vietnam, and Eastern Europe, and knew how much their policy had differentiated strategic and market dimensions, that it had never been a matter of fomenting global wars of liberation (Van Ness, 1970). American C.I.A. chief Allen Dulles ridiculed the idea of China, in comparison to the U.S.S.R., as a subversive menace since the Chinese "have had neither the time nor the resources to develop a technique of subversion" (Dulles, 1965: 208). China's leaders reminded Moscow that "In our foreign affairs over the past fourteen years, we have adopted different policies towards different types of countries and varied our policies according to the different conditions in the countries of the same type" [Jen-min jih pao]. China's Foreign Minister Ch'en Yi made the point most precisely. He explained that

> the Western press [is engaged] in linking any struggle for freedom and independence in the world with China, alleging that it is instigated by China which supplies arms and trains cadres. By doing so, they give China the honor of supporting all struggles of freedom, independence and liberation. But China has neither the ability nor the qualifications yet to accept such honor [Peking Review, 1965].

From the outset Mao had to twist and squirm to find the security conditions and economic wherewithal to raise living conditions in China. As the Second World War ended, Mao informed the U.S. State Department,

> China's greatest post-war need is economic development. She lacks the capitalistic foundation necessary to carry this out alone. Her own living standards are so low that they cannot be further depressed to provide the needed capital.
> America and China complement each other economically: they will not compete. China does not have the requirements of a heavy industry of major size. She cannot hope to meet the United States in its highly specialized manufactures. She [the U.S.A.] also needs an outlet for capital investment.
> China needs to build up light industries to supply her own market and raise the living standards of her own people. Eventually she can supply these goods to other countries in the Far East. To help pay for this foreign trade and investment, she has raw materials and agricultural products. America is not only the most suitable country to assist this economic development of China: she is also the only country fully able to participate. For all these reasons, there must not be and cannot be any conflict, estrangement or misunderstanding between the Chinese people and America. . . . Neither the peasant nor the Chinese people as a whole are ready for socialism. They will not be ready for a long time to come. It will be necessary to go through a long period of private enterprise, democratically

regulated. To talk of immediate socialism is "counterrevolutionary" because it is impractical and attempts to carry it out would be self-defeating.

The U.S. Treasury Department sent someone to Mao's headquarters to verify his position and found that

> Mao asked whether there was any chance for American support of the Chinese Communists.... The Communists wished to risk no conflict with the United States.... *The Communists do not expect Russian help* ... Mao thus indicated that the Chinese Communists *would prefer* to have an American rather than a Russian orientation. Cooperation between America and the Chinese Communists would be beneficial and satisfactory to all concerned. Mao said that... they supported the industrialization of China by free enterprise with the aid of foreign capital [Friedman, 1975: 4].

This experienced need for beneficial economic ties to the United States and the world it dominated was not a mere civil war tactic. Even in 1949, on the verge of power, Mao's group renewed such overtures to the United States for economic exchanges. In addition, the Chinese tried to expand economic relations with Japan. Only after Britain committed its troops to Korea did China start massive nationalization of British enterprise in China. The American-imposed embargo and blockade begun in March 1948 against Communist-held areas of China expanded and intensified during the Korean War. It was very costly to China. The Chinese did not have to wait for an accounting report to know in advance that economic dependence on the Soviet bloc would prove quite expensive.

During the revolutionary civil war period, left Chinese policies against rural merchants intended to check exploitative capitalism actually ended up hurting local villagers. The policy had to be called off. The revolutionary side eventually found it in the popular interest to facilitate the vitality of rural markets. Local livelihood depended on it. In addition, the enemies of the revolutionary side tried to blockade and embargo the revolutionary base area. Mao involved himself with questions of kerosene, salt, and medicine. Survival and success required learning to counter and defeat embargoes and blockades. Mao concluded, "There is nothing in the world that does not become a matter of exchange.... [W]hat we want is that it be done equitably" (Mao, 1967: 42). In sum, a host of extended and rather intense life and death experiences taught the Mao group the wisdom of benefiting from expanded exchange relations.

Moreover, China suffered all the dependent difficulties of most any other nation whose lop-sided development reflected the history of the expansion of the world capitalist system. Industry was concentrated in the northeast and the eastern coastal city of Shanghai. Transportation and other trade infrastructure conveniently ran to Japan and Britain. Overland routes to the U.S.S.R. and, more importantly, links among economically complementary Chinese regions, having been slighted, were inconvenient and expensive. A shipping line with Poland was quickly established after liberation. Virtually no Chinese commercial fleet existed on the sea or in the air since Chiang's forces destroyed or stole what there was. The rebuilding of that commercial fleet, a task personally overseen by Prime Minister Chou En-lai, was one of China's great gains in trying to reduce the overhead costs of international commerce.

Given the Chinese government's commitment to develop by means other than reducing consumption of its own people, and given the difficulty of accumulating new capital for new investment, these embargo costs, which raised transportation prices from nine to twenty-seven times, were cruelly burdensome. It was therefore inevitable that Peking seek to take advantage of its well-rutted economic and transport relations with Japan, Western Europe, and the United States.

In addition, Stalin's first response to China's overtures was of an ordinary imperialist kind, 50-50 joint stock deals similar to the United States in Saudia Arabia, machinery but not turn-key plants. China also had to accept quality and prices dictated one-sidedly by the Soviets. Stalin did better in 1952 and Khrushchev in 1954 was positively decent in giving China what it wanted. But by 1956 the pressures on Khrushchev to take care of Soviet consumers, to compensate for Stalin's plunder of Eastern Europe and to compete with the United States in the Third World, first in India, made China a much lesser economic priority for Khrushchev. Even before the failure of the Great Leap, Krushchev saw China as an endless rathole to which he wanted to reduce, if not extract, the U.S.S.R.'s economic commitment. By 1957 no more aid was given to China, and China had to pay back to the U.S.S.R. more than was coming in. It was more necessary than ever for China to seek other sources.

With the 1954 and 1957 Western European breaks with the extreme COCOM embargo against trade with Communist-controlled areas, China had new possibilities. With the bad experience of Stalin's imperialist ways of dealing with China followed by Khrushchev's using or discarding vital Chinese interests as suited Khrushchev's prior European and domestic needs, Mao by the mid 1950s desparately sought alternatives to continuing exploitative dependence on the U.S.S.R.

Oddly, Khrushchev returned in 1958 with various economic overtures to China, including a very decent trade and technical agreement. But by that time it was too late. For Mao, the Soviet Union was just another big thief in that robber's world. China's goal had to be to keep itself from being robbed. That perception led to some fundamental rethinking of the political world-market.

V. THE SOCIALIST WORLD-MARKET: PART OF OR ALTERNATIVE TO THE WORLD-SYSTEM?

By the second half of 1955 Mao committed China to break out from the Soviet pattern of state investment. Relatively more had to be done for agriculture and light industry. More of heavy industry's goods had to go to serve agriculture and light industry.

Most outside observers agree that the switch was wise and necessary, if anything, overdue and underdone. But the Soviet Russian government opposed it. Ruling groups in Moscow argued that the only way to build socialism was their way. They contended that should China choose to ignore Soviet advice, that would mean China would waste Soviet aid. Since there was no point in keeping technicians, advisers, and the like in China if Peking were going to contradict their wisdom and fritter away their scarce resources—which were much in demand elsewhere—Moscow asked Peking in 1956 (and again in 1958) if Peking would like Moscow to recall its people since China didn't want what these people had to offer. This was more than a veiled threat meant to keep China in line. The Mao group feared a direct conflict growing between the imperatives of independence and the consequences of subordination within the Soviet bloc.

Mao also saw the issue in terms of his general philosophical presuppositions. Big centralized states were imperialist states. He declared,

> it is far better to have the initiative come from both the central and the local authorities than from one source alone. We must not follow the example of the Soviet Union in concentrating everything in the hands of the central authorities, shackling the local authorities and denying them the right to independent action [Mao, 1977: 292].

In addition, whereas China was still a poor, underdeveloped country, the Soviet Russian state wasn't.

> The Soviet Union differs from our country in that, firstly, tsarist Russia was an imperialist power and, secondly, it had the October Revolution. As a result, many people in the Soviet Union are conceited and very arrogant [Mao, 1977: 306].

By January 1957, while he was still remaining quiet on a great deal, Mao made explicit his conclusion that rulers in Moscow "blinded by their material gains" were pushing "great nation chauvinism" and abandoning "revolutionary principles." In a blast against Stalin for concentrating all power and brutally suppressing all contradictory tendencies, Mao did everything but explicitly say the words that the big Russian state was an imperialist one. Mao did say that the rulers in the Kremlin certainly weren't Marxist; and they certainly did crush the popular, nationalistic Hungarian rebellion (Mao, 1977: 365, 376-378).

Within this framework and the well-known preferences of Mao, it is now possible to add one more large factor leading Mao to conclude that the Soviet Union was an imperialist state and that China still had to struggle for its national independence. What will further concern us is how the political requirements of that struggle induce not only silence and fabrication but the need to believe in one's own concoctions to have room for maneuver, including ideational space in which to survive. The dominant ethical principle, the viability of the national whole, one's own people, naturally leads on to ethnocentric thinking and acting necessarily rationalized in somewhat less principled ways. Ethics and ego harmonize and conflict in the same eternal moment.

In general, Mao found Khrushchev unreliable in international affairs. Mao believed Khrushchev mishandled de-Stalinization and thereby internationally discredited the Marxist cause. Mao believed that Khrushchev had botched the Hungarian incident. Mao concluded that Khrushchev had bungled opposition to the British-French-Israeli attack on Nasser's Egypt. Mao consequently would seek further independence from the Soviet Union. It was inconceivable to Mao that China's security and prosperity should rest on the shoulders of this Khrushchev who Mao saw as a spluttering clown.

Moscow meanwhile responded fearfully in 1955-1956 to the formation of Europe's Common Market. Rulers in the Kremlin worried—needlessly, as it turned out—that the Soviet bloc would be excluded from enhanced trade with the E.E.C. Hence Moscow committed itself to giving life to the hitherto largely empty form of its regional economic community, the Community for Mutual Economic Assistance.

North Korea was pressured at that time by Brezhnev to join the C.M.E.A. Kim Il-song refused. He led Pyongyang toward more independent industrialization and closer alliance to China, which, in pointed contrast to Soviet policy in Eastern Europe, pulled its Chinese troops out of North Korea.

China in addition made clear that it stood on the side of nations controlling not only their political and military destinies, but also their own economic lifelines. Poor nations should not be subordinated to a permanent international division of labor premised on continuing polar categories of advanced and backward, industrialized and agrarian. The "resurgent" C.M.E.A. in May 1956 established sectional standing commissions with headquarters in the responsible region, coal in Warsaw, oil and gas in Bucharest, nonferrous metallurgy in Budapest, chemicals in East Berlin, machine building in Prague, agriculture in Sofia, and in Moscow electricity, ferrous metallurgy, foreign trade, and soon thereafter general economic questions (Korbonski, 1966: 362, 366). The nerve center, the control, was Moscow.

The Soviet Union in 1956 also invited China, as it did Korea to join the C.M.E.A., according to China's Deputy Prime Minister Keng Piao (Keng, 1978). China declined the invitation. Instead, it merely sent observers.

According to Keng, the Soviet Union asked China to play its role in a coordinated C.M.E.A. by developing its agriculture, not its industry. China could then efficiently supply food grains to the Soviet Union and Eastern Europe while the industrialized European nations of the C.M.E.A., including the U.S.S.R., supplied machines to China. All parties would supposedly benefit from the international division of labor.

Such a relationship was totally unacceptable to China's nationalistic rulers. To them, to remain an agrarian nation, a food supplier, was to remain backward. Playing China's prescribed role in the Soviet script was to accept a permanent, bit part as a subordinate actor in a Soviet drama, the Soviet empire. China's revolution was intended to win China's people an equal place in the family of nations. Hence, the Soviet offers—Keng called them demands—and other subsequent unacceptable ones, Keng said, soured the relations between Peking and Moscow.

Actually, it is more likely that the unacceptable Soviet offers were interpreted within a relationship already going sour, as revealed by the end to Soviet aid, the Chinese debt position, the Soviet opposition to China's relative stress on light industry, and the Soviet threat to pull out technicians. In any case, China's anti-imperialist revolutionaries had not fought against one kind of foreign domination just to blithely welcome another kind of subordinate status. China would not open its door wide to just another robber. For Mao and many other Chinese patriots, the Soviet Union which did not offer China long-term trade deals to facilitate the realization of China's state plans, which was in the process of providing more steel to India than China, which insisted on particular deals in harmony with Moscow's notion of the proper role of heavy industry, centralized bureaucratic controls, and a special, overall role of generalship for the U.S.S.R., all legitimated by the superiority of an international division of labor, this Soviet Union had to seem anything but socialist. That conclusion is strengthened by the few external clues we have of a leadership debate at this time on the issue of whether there was or could be a socialist world-market.

VI: IS THERE A SOCIALIST WORLD-MARKET?

Between 1956 and 1958 there was a debate in China on the question of whether there was one capitalist world-market or whether there was now a rising socialist world-market challenging a crumbling capitalist world-market. With peace in Korea and in Indochina and with Austria united and independent, the worst Cold War (hot war) forces seemed to be abating. China was beginning negotiations with the United States in Geneva looking toward a solution of the Taiwan issue and normal U.S.-P.R.C. relations. China was looking for big, long-term deals with Japan, coal and iron ore for steel and agricultural machinery. China with the Bandung conference was reaching out to the Third World. This Mao-Chou united front approach to China's foreign policy,[6] maximizing its independent room for maneuver, its opportunities for trade and development, clashed with the Soviet comprehension of the world which legitimated Moscow's attempt to expand the C.M.E.A. to include China.

What could have been a most revealing political dialogue on the nature of the world-market was necessarily blurred by unstated statist assumptions and yet narrower ruling group interests. The pretense was theory; the practice was ideology. The "extremely important theoretical question" was said to be "whether or not the world [capitalist] market had collapsed." The united front position on that question was a resounding "no" (Ch'en Pi-wu, 1957).

Euphemistically, it was said that one had to explain the nature of relations "within the socialist camp founded by the Soviet Union" and "broad economic exchanges with nations with different systems." Actually, the muted theoretical exercise covered the bones of the structural political problem, explaining why China would not join the Soviet Union's economic bloc, the Community for Mutual Economic Assistance. The united front essay in *Kuang-ming jih pao (KMJP)*[7] argued against the notion of a naturally growing socialist world-market.

While Stalin in 1952 had found two markets, one of socialism and one of imperialism, *KMJP* argued against generalizing from the date of 1952. *KMJP* claimed that 1952 was a unique moment created by unusually "wild" American policies in a "comparatively tense" international situation, the unmentioned international red scare at the height of the Korean War. The United States irrationally overreached itself and with the Truman Doctrine, the Marshall Plan, blockade and embargo created a world where, in comparison to 1937, Britain's and France's trade with countries now called socialist was down, respectively, five-sixths and three-quarters. It was these wasteful, politically imposed, self-defeating U.S. policies which hastened the development of economic relations among self-styled socialist countries. The two markets, *KMJP* concluded, were the product not of two systems but of "the historical conditions of that period." The distortion would disappear as international relations normalized. With international tensions diminishing by the mid-1950s, ordinary world-market forces would also emerge.

KMJP's presupposition was that the world-market is not a creation of production forces of national character. The Soviet Union could not create a world-market. In fact, the world-market emerged at a time "when the socially produced division of labor transcended the scope of a state and assumed the character of an international division of labor." It was the result of capitalism as a world-system.

Consequently, American policies intended to isolate socialist states had to fail. Despite the U.S. and COCOM embargoes, the tendency of the last years of growing East-West trade was unstoppable. Except in peculiar and delineated periods, an ever-widening scope for international trade was an inescapable fact of life as capital accumulated and expanded. The laws of world capital compelled this. It was, *KMJP* explained, a "natural reflection of objective economic imperatives" under "present production conditions." These "unavoidable" market tendencies were "incompatible" with the notion of "two world markets." Trade among "socialist countries" could only be "a newly constituted part within the scope of the world market."[8]

In harmony with Marx, *KMJP* stated that true socialist trade, a genuinely mutually beneficial commerce, would be characterized by its undermining of the world capitalist division of labor. In contrast, the trademark of world capitalist expansion was the development of industrialized and of agricultural countries, an international division of labor manifested in plunder and exploitation of the majority of backward countries by the few industrially advanced states.

The unstated point, the next step in the chain of logic, the hidden conclusion seems rather obvious. It was censored, as the Chinese, we now know, censored a great deal to obscure Mao's very critical view of the U.S.S.R. in the mid-1950s for being un-Marxist and unprincipled, arrogant and mighty. It was revealed only in the 1960s when the Peking-Moscow split was irreparable and public. Then the Chinese would frankly describe the Soviet international division of labor as ordinary imperialism. The U.S.S.R. "acts as a metropolitan state and regards other C.M.E.A. members as its economic dependencies" (Foreign Languages Press, 1976: 35).[9] Combining Marx on the existence of a capitalist world-market with Mao on the ethical desirability of maximum national independence added up to Peking's antagonistic contradiction with Moscow's preference for a Soviet-centered economic region labeled a socialist world-market.

KMJP not only stated but stressed one world element which Moscow still slighted, independence for the colonial and semicolonial world, the larger ethical element in China's nationalism. Socialist states, *KMJP* urged, should be helping the independent, nationalist states of Asia and Africa[10] toward escaping or limiting the consequences of the international capitalist division of labor. Chinese aid, where it wasn't strategic, was often premised on that promise, as with the offer of ship pilots to Nasser after Britain and France tried to sabotage Egypt's nationalized Suez canal, as with rice to Guinea and aid to Albania after France and Russia tried to block their independent courses. Chinese analyses of the Maoist variety almost invariably sought, after guaranteeing the means of China's survival, the means for the world's victims to join together to end or check the robber's world.

Trade among Third World countries, *KMJP* claimed, had increased by 58% between 1954 and 1955. To be sure, that trade was hindered by persisting influences of old colonial relationships, but, *KMJP* confidently predicted, the future would surely witness the rapid development of mutually beneficial trade between socialist nations and independent nationalist states. A true socialist objective for all socialist states was that of facilitating ever-more independence from the capitalist division of labor for Asia and Africa. Socialist states should partake in complex struggles toward that end. By so doing, the world which operated by capitalism's laws would shrink, and since the health of capital is it expansion, such shrinkage would "progressively deepen the general crisis of capitalism." The proper goal was maximizing independent initiative, not subordination to any (read the Soviet Union's C.M.E.A.) international division of labor.

This *KMJP* united front analysis implicitly explicating why China should not join the C.M.E.A. was soon publicly criticized (Wang and Liang, 1978). It was attacked in *Ching-chi yen-Chiu (CCYC)* as "extremely erroneous" and "capable of producing very bad influence in practical work." What the critique reflected was not a deeper comprehension of world-market forces but politics. America still had the power and the will to rebuff China's attempt at full entry into the world-market. China had no place to go but back into its own resources and back to the U.S.S.R. A least desired, American-imposed alternative which made the Chinese pay the high costs of being kept out of much of the world-market had to be rationalized.

CCYC claimed, in direct conflict with *KMJP,* that there was a socialist world-market and that the Soviet Union was its leading core. That Soviet socialist world-market would serve the independence needs of the peoples of the world. *CCYC* shrewdly criticized *KMJP* for describing a unitary capitalist world-market with a capitalist division of labor which by some magic was said also to have an ever-expanding socialist part operating by laws other than capital's. How could there be a true part of a whole which was not truly part of the whole?

Sadly, *CCYC* did not follow up on this shrewd insight. World-systems theory suggests that socialism can't be built while the national parts are defined by a capitalist totality, the division of labor which is the capitalist world-market. Had *KMJP* had the freedom to reply, it might have claimed that what it dubbed socialist states were states ruled by groups trying to move in a socialist direction and seeking alliances with like-minded ruling groups elsewhere, a united front of proletarian nations in the interest of action at the global level to transform and regulate what was still a capitalist world-market, an imperialist world.

But as *KMJP* could not reply, so *CCYC* could not follow up on its shrewd point. What mattered was discrediting a competing political position. "Revisionism" was said to be "the main dangerous enemy" (p. 82). That is, in an attempt to woo back Khrushchev, Tito's Yugoslavia was viciously made a scapegoat and denounced as an imperialist appendage of America. Between autumn 1957 and spring 1960, for two years and a half, China talked—its action belied its words[11]—as if it were trying to persuade Moscow to drop detente, Soviet consumers, Yugoslavia, and India for a unity of true Communists with China.

Actually Yugoslavia, as China, had been trying to maximize Third World independence. It tried to build unity and power for nonaligned nations. It backed S.U.N.F.E.D. It, as China—and in contrast to the U.S.S.R.—gave great aid to the Algerian liberation movement, the major active independence movement around 1958. *CCYC* described such Titoist efforts at maneuver and independence as impossible since the alternative to partnership in the socialist economic system was "belonging to the capitalist world market" (p. 78).

Whereas *KMJP* saw capitalism as a long-extant international system of production, monetary circulation, and trade (international division of labor) into which states building socialism entered, *CCYC* described the whole as the sum of its statist parts. States were said to be socialist because their domestic production system was supposedly socialist, that is, composed of nationalized industry and collectivized agriculture. A socialist world-market then is the market created by already socialist states.

CCYC, however, did not argue for China's entrance into the C.M.E.A. It agreed with *KMJP* that socialism meant, as Marx said, undermining the capitalist division of labor. Soviet foreign policy allegedly proved that the U.S.S.R. was a socialist state. Only a socialist state would provide a backward, agrarian country such as China with the means for China to industrialize and move from its poor place in the world division of labor. In contrast to *KMJP* which argued that maximizing normal trade with the advanced capitalist world weakened the most rabid, hard-line, Cold War anticommunist forces in that capitalist world, *CCYC* replied that while that was good politics, it was bad economics. And economics had priority, the economics of drawing closer to other socialist states in the interest of liberating China from world capitalism.

CCYC denounced the *KMJP* position as bourgeois democratic, claiming that it refused to sharply separate friends and enemies. For *CCYC*, there were two worlds and two markets, socialism and capitalism, with a clear division between them. Capitalism, *CYCC* continued, traded not only to survive and earn profits, but also to destroy socialism (p. 75).

In retrospect, the *CCYC* position seems utterly antithetical to Maoism. Mao always isolated the fewest and worst enemies and allied with the broad middle. Here everything is dichotomized and polarized instead of focusing on the center of what Mao described as a three-part, egg-shaped world (us, the center, the enemy die-hards) with attention fixed on the politics of winning the center. Mao also always looked to the benefits of broad commerce and certainly no longer took nationalization and collectivization as a sufficient definition of socialism.

The bad politics were reinforced by worse economics. *CCYC* insisted that the data proved that the socialist world-market was the force of the future. *CCYC* selected the years 1948 and 1954, the former being but the first year the American Cold War took global hold and the latter being the last year before the erosion of Cold War forces began to have a significant international economic impact, and "proved" that rapidly growing trade among socialist nations could be a defining trend of future relations (p. 72). The intensifying Cold War was taken as a natural trend for the future even while Moscow moved for detente in Washington.

By 1959-1960, the *CCYC* position had been exploded. Moscow not only tore up its agreements to provide China with advanced military technology, it also pulled out its technicians and advisers, reneged on contracts, destroyed blueprints, demanded repayment of debt and interest, bruited it around the grain surplus world that a hungry, mismanaged, bankrupt China was a bad risk, and made it as difficult as possible for an energy-starved China to receive petroleum.[12]

Nonetheless, despite the economic attack on China by the U.S.S.R., the categories of the major-backer people who preferred alliance with the U.S.S.R. remained China's domonint, public categories of comprehension into 1963. The Chinese press continued to talk about two world-systems.

This position—whatever the economic realities—had a very useful international strategic component. Any semblance of Moscow-Peking unity did in fact decrease the likelihood of American nuclear blackmail of China and diminished the prospect that an American-backed war on China's periphery (India, Laos, Chiang Kai-shek's attacks) would be permitted to spill over into China lest it trigger some joint Moscow-Peking response. The Soviet build-up of forces on China's borders in 1963 changed all that.

Still we cannot help but notice how the categories of comprehension for Chinese rulers—and surely not merely Chinese rulers—of the politicized world-market are necessarily given life by very political parentage. International military-diplomatic strategy and domestic political struggles are, for state power-holders, too crucial not to have a primary impact on these understandings of the world-market.

This is most apparent with the new life and the new twist given to the paper tiger approach. As with the other tendencies among China's ruling groups, the paper tiger people worried that the problems of urban industrialization might undermine the egalitarianism and cooperative promise of China's rural revolution. All groups worried, as they put it, that Nanking Road, a thoroughfare in cosmopolitan Shanghai, could subvert Yenan, the Red Army's cave headquarters in guerilla days. On the eve of liberating what would become his capital, Mao is said to have asked, "Will the tattered clothes change Peiping or will the latter change the former?" (Kinoshita, 1963: 17). Consequently all groups tried to create ways of preventing the development of an urban ruling stratum which would exploit the countryside.

Such paper tiger people, supposedly gathering around ultra-left leader Chang Ch'un-ch'iao [Kuan] identified the promise of the millenial moment of the 1958 Great Leap, the universalization of the guerilla supply system, to each according to his or her needs, with immediate policies in China.[13] Rather than noting how Great Leap policies brought China to the brink of mass starvation, which in fact occurred, they intensified their millennial commitment to the Yenan supply system and saw their opponents—and the international imperialists (the U.S.S.R. and the United States) who made conditions so impossible for the Great Leap—as capitalist-roaders, reactionaries, and counterrevolutionaries. Cities were bourgeois cultural and political bastions. Worrying that China's cities had been peacefully liberated and therefore never truly revolutionized, they took the moment of the Cultural Revolution to begin to purify urban China, leading to the urban traumas of the Cultural Revolution and the policies of no urban wage increases and sending down to the countryside for transformation some 18 million urban young people and an untold number of officials, scientists, musicians, etc.

The market, the foreign, and the city, in this perspective, were the antithesis of revolution. Indigenous methods and back-breaking labor to produce sufficient food to get by on was the essence of independence.[14] It is these people who from 1970-1976 opposed the standard Mao-Chou policies of rapprochment with the United States and re-entry into the world market as capitalistic.[15]

The abstract and universally valued Chinese historical lesson that Chinese independence required international policies in which China joined with other anti-imperialist forces to transform the robber's world was sufficiently imprecise to cover not only *KMJP* and *CCYC,* but also all three Chinese foreign policy perspectives, united front, paper tiger, and major backer. The most prominent proponent of the major-backer position, Minister of National Defense P'eng Teh-huai, legitimated long-term association with the U.S.S.R. in which China would be protected by the Soviet Union's nuclear umbrella in the terms accepted by all Chinese ruling groups. By relying on Moscow's nuclear shield, China could keep defense costs low and therefore have more to invest in its own economy, more with which to help its rural poor. China as a result would develop the bases for genuine independence in a more popular and faster manner which would guarantee that the peasant would not be the victim of industrialization.

China in the 1960s continued aid to Third World liberation struggles—Mozambique, Angola, Zimbabwe, Palestine—and stepped up its developmental aid to Third World countries. China remained true at the same time to its commitment to maximizing local sovereignty. It had no desire to coordinate a true, worldwide socialist movement. The Chinese rejected Albania's suggestion for such a new international. To itself Chinese national independence and universal liberation, egoism and ethicality continued to be reconciled. But, as with the 1941 conflict between Moscow and Peking over how to deal with Japan's armies on the Chinese side of the U.S.S.R.'s borders, state power-holders naturally put national security first. In 1964 China sent separate overtures to Moscow, Washington, and Tokyo, none of which came to anything (Friedman, 1971). While most outside observers in the immediate post-1965 period were mesmerized by China's support for Vietnám and Third World storm centers, what mattered most was invisible, not only Moscow-Peking-Hanoi tensions, but the policies of the core industrialized powers, their rejection or slighting of repeated Chinese overtures. Should the core powers' policies change, China would have the calm and security and commerce its ruling groups had long but fruitlessly sought to make Chinese society as proper a place to live as possible for China's one billion people.

VII: THE WORLD PROLETARIAT AND THE THIRD WORLD

From 1965 to 1968, as he launched China's Great Proletarian Cultural Revolution, Mao defined that internal Chinese event as the essence of international relations and world history. As Mao saw it, the future of world socialism pivoted on whether China, in contrast to the U.S.S.R., could avoid a restoration of capitalism. That was the axis. All else was turmoil.

China's Ambassadors were recalled—although Prime Minister Chou En-lai managed to carry out some business such as arranging for the building of the Tanzania-Zambia railroad—and the Soviet Union was made an enemy of extraordinary proportions, the example of all that was to be avoided and negated. Mao overruled Chou, Teng Hsiao-p'ing, and P'eng Chen and other Chinese leaders and would not permit a united front with the U.S.S.R. against the U.S. enemies of Vietnam's independence.

For Mao, the world was characterized by great division, great disorder, and great reorganization. The U.S. camp had come apart. Europe, Japan, Australia, and New Zealand were rising and struggling for more independence. The socialist camp had crumbled. Asia, Africa, and Latin America were rising. China's cause was akin to all those struggling for more independence. It was a struggle, Mao declared, between the forces seeking control over others and those trying to defeat the forces of control.

Mao noted that the Soviets could not be stopped from gaining control in Cuba because Cuba itself "produced neither petroleum nor weaponry" (Mao, 1969: 456). The hegemonic struggle between the United States and U.S.S.R. focused on controlling the industrialized and nonindustrialized nations between them (Mao, 1969: 514). First place in that "conflict between control and anti-control... belongs to the nations of East Europe." Rumania would like to break out from Soviet control but Rumania "itself cannot manufacture weaponry" (Mao, 1969: 578).[16] These Maoist premises of 1964 prefigured the unique significance Mao would find in the U.S.S.R.'s 1968 reconquest of Czechoslovakia.

The politicized global market in a world of states seeking more genuine national independence imposed weapons and military matters as a crucial economic and political matters. That statist focus of market questions in world-systems theory with its stress on hegemonic core powers must be broadened to include the struggle for military independence by nonhegemonic powers as a major politicized market dynamic since military matters, given the nature of states, tend ordinarily to be priority matters.

As any player of a market, independence meant diversifying risks. Given the special controls military powers could impose, this meant for China that special attention should be given to gaining advanced technology from industrialized nations who could not be a military threat. Besides, not only are "Soviet products heavy, awkward and overpriced but they hold back something." "It is better to do business with the French bourgeoisie who still have some business ethics" (Mao, 1969: 456). Or perhaps, this should be put in terms of world-systems theory as an expression of the superiority of involvement with a world-economy over a world-empire?

In any case, Mao had to concern himself with foreign exchange. "We can't recklessly spend money." Food production had to be rapidly raised "so that we will no longer import grain and will save foreign exchange in order to buy more [foreign] technological equipment, technological materials" (Mao, 1969: 499).

In 1968 a number of domestic and international changes gave a more solid form to these Maoist preferences for independent maneuver. The Soviet Union reconquered Czechoslovakia and declared that it had the right to do the same to any country Soviet rulers decided was leaving the "socialist commonwealth." The U.S. dollar crisis intensified, and America had to concede to European central bankers, and Washington had to move to the bargaining table with Hanoi. For Mao, Soviet control over nations was expanding and intensifying while American control over Western Europe and others was clearly on the wane.

China's ultra-left led by Lin Piao, on the other hand, favored high military expenditures and taking on both the American and Soviet camp. China's ultra-left, although describing itself as the truly Maoist, abandoned the political and strategic essence of Maoism which included isolating the worst enemy, a tactical united front of all others, and securing the material interests of one's base of support. Instead the ultra-leftists took on many enemies at once and slighted the economic needs of their own base. Mao preferred maneuver, low military costs, and a maximum effort at a breakthrough for economic deals with America, Europe, and Japan. This strategy based on a reading of global trends and forces was naturally egocentrically China-centered, promising greater security and less poverty, misery, and back-breaking labor for China's people. But it also was situated within the ethical self-conception of Chinese nationalism as part of the liberation of all the world's poor people. Third World votes in 1971 supporting Peking's membership in the United Nations were in some part a response to China's own preferred identification with the cause of such nations.

"China belongs to the Third World" was the 1972 response of the C.C.P.'s Central Committee newspaper to the search for a reconciliation of proletarian ethics and nationalist egoism, ideology and interest in the era after any hope of a socialist bloc had been punctured (Jen-min jih pao, 1972).[17] The intellectual staff of China's ruling group reconceived a world in which China as part of "the world proletariat" would unite and overthrow world imperialism.[18] This stance has put China on the Third World side of almost every international economic issue that can be conceived of as a Third World issue, from O.P.E.C. to the host of items on the New International Economic Order agenda. And yet the essential strategic concept as always had to start from nation-state categories and concerns.

In the usual Maoist terms, China's ruling groups from 1968 to 1978 now put in those forms the content of the imperative of a struggle against an expansional Soviet Union, whose troops in forward array on China's borders rehearsed for an invasion of China, whose military policies had become the most immediate threat to China's national independence. Now the tripartite, egg-shaped world was us (China), the major imperialist enemy (rising Soviet imperialism), and all others. Directly in Eastern Europe, China would support Czechoslovakian, Rumanian, Yugoslavian, and all other independence forces.[19] A peaceful solution for Taiwan and the mainland of the People's Republic of China was read large not only for its implications for North and South Korea but also for East and West Germany. A united German nation would weaken the Soviet empire. What in general was needed were national independence struggles similar to those of the thirteen colonies in 1776 and Latin American nations in the nineteenth century.

For the Third World, the medium and small countries, seen as the major progressive global force, opposed to big nations, the imperialism of the world (Chen, 1979: 145), what was needed was an advance from neocolonial economic relations to true independence. This struggle was thought through in terms of an analogy with the Soviet Union's scissors crisis of the 1920s. China and other backward, rural, nonindustrialized nations had to change the international price structure so that the rural nations of the world would no longer be exploited by the "natural" forces of the world-market.

Yet politics was always primary. Militarized imperialist states preferred the superprofits that came from a hegemonic preponderance permitting plunder. They fought to be top dog. They did not trust hidden economic laws. What was dubbed imperialism was described as more war than pure market because of its essential political quality in a lawless statist world.

More than most comprehensions of global forces, the Maoist notions about the world-system have facilitated, with nontrivial contradictions, a continuing global ethical concern for the world's worst off as well as Chinese independence and human development.

> Ours is a developing country. We must ... develop the socialist economic base and develop the forces of production, so as to build our country into a socialist state with modern industry, modern agriculture and modern science and culture [Yenan Books: July 28].

What must finally concern us is what is omitted by this world view of a world-system run by robbers where the proletarian nation of China should join with all others to arrest the biggest thief of all. However well this world view has suited the needs of revolutionary Chinese nationalists, it also functions as ideology. It renders the unpalatable invisible, as any decent ideology should. Perhaps we can see and magnify what is otherwise hidden by asking questions from the framework of world-systems theory.

CONCLUSION: IS THE WAY UP THE WAY OUT?

A full generation after liberation, the People's Republic of China still holds a peripheral position in the world economic system. In 1949 China's new ruling groups committed themselves to raising food production to become self-reliant, ending the import of luxury consumer items, reversing the dependent situation where China imported industrial, technological products and exported primary products (Friedman, 1970: 2). Egalitarian redistribution at home and the use of labor-intensive techniques may indeed make for a more decent society inside China with less *unnecessary* dependence on advanced industrial societies, but such domestic factors do not shape the political structure of the world-economy, do not end structured dependence for peripheral nations.

China still imports billions of dollars of food-stuffs. China's export of rice and import of wheat used to be described as a clever ploy of a government in control of its own destiny, winning foreign exchange by selling the item of higher exchange value and buying the one of lower exchange value while trying to persuade its people to eat more wheat products, less rice products. The harsher facts were that China had a weak, internal transportation system (Hunter, 1974) and a growing population. The Chinese government sought alternatives to costly investment in new transport infrastructure. It tried to use labor-intensive water control methods to raise wheat production in the grain deficient north (Vermeer, 1977). It tried to build up grain reserves to counter nature's distempers when the inevitable dread draughts and downpours struck and the rickety water control system proved fragile and inefficient. The fact was that China was trapped as a big grain importer to feed its northern cities. (And should its government ever try to meet the repressed demand for more meat and finer grain, yet more imports would be needed.) The teeth of the trap bit hard when in the early 1970s large Soviet grain purchases, bad weather, and American shortages sent the price of wheat sky-rocketing. As with most other Third World countries, the consequent O.P.E.C. price rise and higher cost of fertilizer when added to recession in the core countries who reduced imports from the periphery, created a food and financial crisis. To be sure China's stress on food, capacity for equally sharing sacrifice, and lack of an elite with huge luxury imports permitted China to weather a lesser crisis.

Nonetheless, the clever "ploy" of buying wheat and selling rice was revealed as empty patter covering dependence. Hunger stalked the land between 1974 and 1976 as did a foreign exchange crisis. The alternative to a most painful belt-tightening of the thin, poor populace, who had been falsely sold a line by the ultra-left on China's grain self-sufficiency and ever-better food situation, was riskier entrance into the world market.

> During the spring festival of 1977... our country was confronted with many problems: the reserve grain could last for only ten months, many warehouses were empty, and our foreign exchange was almost exhausted. At that point, we, in a gamble, still appropriated reserve rain and used up all our foreign exchange to buy sugar, to import edible oils and flour [Chang P'ing-hua, 1978: 102].

What would China sell to pay for the food? Only nations with special ties and needs—for example, Rumania and North Korea—bought much Chinese heavy industry. Textiles was China's biggest foreign exchange earner. But in the late 1970s nontariff barriers were high and strong against Chinese textiles in the United States and rising in Western Europe against all parties, from Bulgaria to the Ivory Coast. China could try to sell high-value raw materials, such as coal or petroleum, but the full development of those resources required expensive and sophisticated foreign technology and much time. China was caught in a standard dilemma for a peripheral country. It was not and could not be self-reliant. To try to rise, it had to sell primary products for high-technology goods. It had to deepen its world-market dependence or fall behind economically and militarily.

Its military independence was not even secure. It was naked to the Soviet Union, yet still preferred to make military modernization the lowest priority. Popular wants would come first, if China's ruling groups had their way; although as with the world-market, with defense too, more than one would like, often the state simply had to respond to unhappy external forces.

The point then is not that China has acted peculiarly badly, stupidly, or indecently, but that there is a global structure which has priority in structuring the possibilities of those on the periphery. Those who were persuaded that "Withdrawing From the World-System" was an answer to its problems deluded themselves.[20]

China doubled its percentage of world trade between 1949 and 1959. Had not the Great Leap depression followed, its rulers intended more such growth. Once recovery ensued, China returned to the world-market with renewed vigor but proud and publicly loud about its success in paying off its debts to the Soviet Union. That breast-beating distracted outsiders from China's natural search for the best credits it could get at the best rates it could find. I wrote in 1973:

> The simple truth is that even while China first bruited about her solvency in 1964-65, she was negotiating Export-Import Bank trade credits in Tokyo. It was Japan's financial dependence on the USA and Washington's firm hostility to China that kept Tokyo from giving Peking the credits that China wanted. U.S. spokespeople for so long misleadingly argued that America was not to blame for the

lack of credits available to China that now [1973] they too easily dismiss such as the prediction of Japan's Association for the Promotion of International Trade based on the normal Chinese desire for such credits that in a decade over three billion dollars worth of Japanese exports to China will be financed by such credits [Friedman, 1973: 5].

China still suffers from the consequence of the hegemonic U.S. anti-China policies of the 1950s and 1960s which permitted Japan, Taiwan, and South Korea growth through easy entrance into the U.S. market while China was excluded from that expansive moment, gaining entry only when barriers and quotas had already gone way up.

Because there is a politicized world-market, because China is but a peripheral state, its scissors analogy cannot be read large to the world level. Within China, the government can change costs and benefits, prices and investments to reduce the urban-rural gap; and for the poorest it can budget resources and mobilize societal energies to put a floor under them. None of these most decent policies is possible within a world-market structured historically and "naturally" to benefit core states.

If China chooses simply to earn foreign exchange by sales in Hong Kong, it also automatically accommodates British colonialism as well as facilitating investment needs of Japanese and American capital. If China tries to earn foreign exchange by exporting petroleum and coal, it does not merely eventually put a small crimp into O.P.E.C.; it relieves crises pressures in the core states. But if China does not try to take advantage of its opportunities, it condemns its people to more exploitation by that world-market, less liberation from misery, and back-breaking toil. Exclusion from the world-market, as shown by opposition to harmful embargoes from Cuba to Rhodesia-Zimbabwe, hurts the people affected. The world structure functions whatever Maoists may will.

If the system is a politicized, structured, world-market, then the Soviet Union must pay the economic costs of its political empire. In fact, some Eastern European nations may gain the price the Soviets pay for their political loyalty even while their world-market integration deepens. One does not want to prettify the price of the loss of national independence, but the preferred Chinese language of imperialism to describe Soviet-bloc relations may be most misleading in slighting the costs of empire.

In general, the Chinese focus on independent states may de-emphasize decisive dynamics of the historically developing world-market. The Chinese in the late 1970s investigated the rapid rise of South Korea, Taiwan, and Japan—export processing zones, construction workers to the Middle East, etc.—but slighted the decisive political factor that made it all possible. American ruling groups had long persuaded themselves that a structure of world peace required America and its industrial allies to open Asia and themselves to Japan.[21]

One of the things world-systems theory calls our attention to in investigating the rise of a more peripheral nation is the political impact of a core power on the more peripheral nation. Surely Britain's anti-Russian politics helped nurture the early twentieth-century rise of Japan, as post-Second World War U.S. politics did the same for Japan subsequently. Surely the sucess of O.P.E.C., while very directly and deeply related to a changing energy market at a particular historic moment, is not divorced from American desires to see Saudia Arabia or the Shah's Iran become a stabilizing force in the Middle East as U.S. might and wealth could no longer afford it.

China on its own cannot compete with core powers. The experienced failure of its aid policies should bring that message back loud and clear to China's leaders. An isolated Sukarno may welcome Chinese aid, but it is all wasted when post-Sukarno rulers turn to core nations. China gave great aid to Ethiopia's self-styled Marxist regime, but when the Ethiopians wanted modern, expensive, military equipment that a poor China lacked, Ethiopia freely turned to China's adversary, the U.S.S.R. Chinese aid to Albania— continued even after Albania's siding with the Lin Piao group, and not followed by Chinese control of Albania—won China nothing when Albania decided to play a different international game. The liberation movement in Mozambique took its major socialist aid from China, but in power felt it needed more of what the more developed Soviet bloc economies could offer. Guerilla movements in Thailand and Zimbabwe, noting how in Angola and elsewhere the Soviet-backed side could and would swiftly move modern material and men while all a poor China, a respector of self-reliance and sovereignty did—could do—was comparatively little for its friends, can't help but consider moving in a more pro-Soviet direction. Hanoi's turn against Peking is an extreme instance exposing all the contradictions of competition versus a core power, Moscow. China didn't act treacherously. Rather, China simply is a very limited, poor peripheral Third World nation despite its unique combination of atomic weapons, population, civilization, revolutionary history, and Security Council seat.

What sense then does it make for China to consider itself a proletarian nation out to change the world of robbers by uniting with all other proletarian nations and antihegemonic forces? The proletariat certainly did not make the revolution in China, or for that matter in Algeria, Angola, Mozambique, Cuba, Vietnam, or Cambodia. The urban, industrial proletariat had little to do with the fighting of these revolutionary wars.

Mao's rationalization tried to obscure the lumpen and petty-bourgeois social base of China's great revolution, expanding if not inventing notions of the rural proletariat, semiproletariat, and poor theoretically to pit almost all China's exploited, poor people, the people, against a handful of exploiters, the enemies of the people. It was brilliant and successful, but was it at one with Marx's notion of proletarian revolution? Marx wrote against those who "to make this phrase [the people] effective [found] it was necessary to describe the petty-bourgeois as proletarians" (Draper, 1978: 639).

Informed analysts differ on how to comprehend the Marx-Mao relation. Some see Mao as non-Marxist. Others see Mao as developing and applying Marx to new circumstances. I would suggest, rather, that as Fanon and others have pointed out, in rural Third World countries, in the early stages of industrialization, the industrial proletariat tends toward a relatively privileged position. It is an intermediary class, not the negation of the privileged ones.

But Mao's Marxism which seeks the broadest united front against the world's robbers, which seeks to unite the former colonial and semicolonial countries, the poor and weak, the small- and medium-sized nations may prove both liberating and shrewd. In contrast to the attempt of dominant powers to split the richer Third World from the others so that the Third World can't unite against core powers, the Maoist approach denounces the notion of a fourth world as an attempt by the industrialized world to split the world proletariat, defined in Mao's way described above.

This meant according to a Chinese Deputy Prime Minister (Keng Piao) that, not unexpectedly for a history of identification with the cause of the people against imperialism, that the antithesis of truly moving in a socialist direction was moving in a social imperialist direction. Three criteria distinguished the two paths. First, was the domestic policy socialist or fascist? That is, did it put the needs of the people first or did repressive and statist priorities such as a secret police, the military and bureaucratic corruption take the top spot on the national agenda? Second, was its international policy sincerely committed to aiding independent development or to controlling another nation's destiny? Arms, advisers, and aid should be offered sincerely, that is, to serve the needs of the recipient nation or not given at all. It shouldn't be offered with political strings leading to control, exploitation, annexation, expansion. Third was a similar item only with regard to liberation struggles. That is, did one foster true national independence or control in the interest of your outside state? In sum, the definition of the socialist path was informed by the needs and desires of Third World developing nations in a statist world of hegemonic conflict, of imperialist global combat. The Chinese were trying to be true to their original revolutionary anti-imperialist hereitage. The continuing ethical identification of China with independence and betterment for the exploited of the world is one important consequence of its redefinition of the proletariat out of its valued historical experience, its attempt to move toward Marx's humane world in conditions which Marx did not find most propitious for that movement.

As Mao calls our attention to the struggle for the broad middle, so world-systems theory invites us to look more closely at the intermediate level, the semiperiphery. Yet the Maoist notion of a struggle for the intermediary zones has been complicated by the notion of the industrial intermediate zone, Europe and Japan, as a Second World more in harmony with the nonindustrial intermediate zone, the Third World, because both share an interest in national independence from the two militarily hegemonic powers, the U.S.S.R. and the United States.

World-systems theory, while not gainsaying the importance of financial and military hegemony, does not put a Japan or West Germany, taken as core states, into such a decidedly second-rank position as does the Maoist reconceptualization. What we find here is the place where China's national egocentrism necessarily takes command. Whether the target enemy was Japan in 1915, the United States in 1951 or the U.S.S.R. in 1969, China's nationalistic ruling groups necessarily experience the world so that the major threat to China is comprehended as the world's biggest robber. All nationalistic ruling groups in a statist world of market and military share this perceptual and experiential tendency. In addition, China cannot escape the need to exploit its dependence, that is to move in the smooth grooves cut out by the historical development of Japan's and West Europe's imposed market on semicolonial China.

Looking at the momentary embodiment of such Chinese imperatives and reconceptualizations in mid-1979, Japan's relationship with the United States was described as combining dependence and struggle. With the neighboring superpower, the U.S.S.R., Japan would like to develop better economic relations but is hindered by the Soviet Union's "big nation [*ta kuo*] attitude." With the American decline into military parity with the U.S.S.R., with the American normalization of relations with China, Japan has supposedly abandoned the path of militarism (*chun shih ta kuo*) for one of normal economic exchanges in which Japan, no longer able to rely on or replace American military hegemony, must give ever better economic terms to the Third World to win access to the raw materials Japan so badly needs. This is said to be especially true in Southeast Asia where there is the additional threat to normal economic exchanges from Soviet military hegemony allied to Vietnam. Indeed in the entire Asia-Pacific region,

> like America with regard to Central and South America, and France and West Germany with regard to the nations of Africa, [Japan] is building a guaranteed base for raw materials, export markets and a yen currency circulation region [Shijie zhishi, 1979: 3].

But the Chinese distinction between bad, military intervention and ordinary, mutually beneficial economic deals is too broad. France has intervened militarily in Africa quite regularly over the last decade. The United States record in places such as the Dominican Republic and Chile is well known. It is difficult to believe that Germany's and Japan's economic power will not eventuate in a military component.

Prime Minister Chou En-lai in the summer of 1971 had no trouble in making that point. This

> lopsided development of Japan, what will issue from it? She needs to carry out an economic expansion abroad. Otherwise she cannot maintain her economy. And so, being in a capitalist system, following this economic expansion, there is bound to come with it military expansion. Isn't this so? [Committee, 1972: 358].

This conceptualization explained much of Japan's economic growth as the fruits of militarism. Japan wasn't a capitalist miracle or an imperialist monster. It was peculiarly militarist. This view, expounded early in the twentieth century by Thorstein Veblen and Joseph Schumpeter, has been given its greatest detail in English in the powerful and persuasive historical scholarship of John Dower. The world-famous economist, Simon Kuznets put it this way:

> The real question [regarding the 30-40% of Japan's budget put into Japan's military] is whether Japan would have ever gotten rid of restrictions of extraterritoriality on tariff autonomy and the like if it did not demonstrate in actual warfare the fact of its power to resist western pressure.... [A]t least in the nineteenth century, one way in which a nation demonstrated its maturity was to show that it was strong enough to resist aggression, and in fact, exercise aggression of its own [Kuznets, 1973: 30].

Prime Minister Chou saw Japan's post-Second World War development as in harmony with this earlier militarism which won Japan food, raw materials, markets, indemnities, land for settlers, cheap migrant labor, and government subsidies for advanced military-related technologies.

> There is one characteristic of their economy, that is, they made a fortune on wars fought by others, that is, [the Chinese civil war of 1946 to 1949,] the war of aggression against Korea and the war of aggression against Vietnam....
>
> Japan makes fortunes through these wars [Committee, 1972: 356-357].

There is no difficulty in understanding why this conceptualization of Japan's global role was slighted in the late 1970s. China worried about forward U.S.S.R. encirclement of Asia. It didn't need to alienate Japan, especially when China's modernization rested so heavily on its economic relations with Japan. In fact, China's trade with the Second World virtually quadrupled in the first half of the 1970s (Yahuda, 1978: 257).

But what caused the 1971-1972 magnified Chinese militant hostility to Japan when Mao's poet-scholar confident, Kuo Mo-jo, compared Japan to a frozen viper that a naive America was pressing to its warm breast? Chou En-lai then warned that "the U.S. has promoted the development of Japan toward miliarism by the indefinite prolongation of the Japan-U.S. security treaty" (Chou, 1971).

There seem to have been political reasons for the 1971-1972 campaign against Japanese militarism. Peking's ally in Pyongyang worried that Peking-Washington normalization would leave North Korea naked to a Japan securing its economic interests in Asia in the old way once the wide access to the American market was lost as U.S.-Japan economic competition intensified. China wanted to reassure its Korean ally. It surely didn't want Pyongyang turning toward Moscow. Also it wasn't clear what role Japan would play in Asia in the era of the Nixon doctrine, American military withdrawal from continental Asia. China wanted to stop the worst case from eventuating. Finally, the ultra-left of Chang Ch'un-ch'iao and Yao Wen-yuan may have had a political interest in stressing continuing American-launched military perfidy in Asia while Chou, the leader of their opposition, focused on the economic aspects which opened new vistas for China's rapid development.[22]

In both conceptualizations, the early 1970s one of a militarist Japan and the late 1970s one of Japan as an economic actor forced to make concessions, these are security, alliance, and power politics factors at work. These elements are so weighty in grinding the lenses of perception that actors in a statist world cannot afford the luxury of a disinterested conceptualization of the political economy of the world-system. Politics is in command.

So, as with the Chinese nationalistic preference for Germany in 1918 or an imperialistic United States and U.K. during the Second World War or the U.S.S.R. occupiers of Eastern Europe in 1950, the contemporary Chinese contradiction is just another ordinary consequence of the inevitable national egoism-global ethics contradiction this essay has detailed more than once which effects all nations. There is no one line except for Manicheans which allies all the forces of good against all the forces of evil. What world-systems theory calls our attention to is something else.

The difference between the Maoist conceptualization of the world and the comprehension of world-systems theory is large. In the Maoist views, deriving from the need to envision China's national revolution in Marxist categories, there are two worlds and two kinds of revolutions. There is the imperialist world and the victims of imperialism. China's revolution and politics is seen as in harmony with the latter and the need to negate the imperialism of the advanced world, first and foremost by taking advantage of the splits and contradictions in that world. It never develops its insights about a robber's world, one world-market, the Soviet Union as imperailist, etc. in terms of a world-level analysis. In contrast, world-systems theory sees one world, a market, a dynamic structure, a politicized economic system. The focus is on the process maintaining and continuing the whole. The changes that occur are not explosive negations but painful rearrangements.

What if, as suggested above, nations rise in the world-system only when a more core power's politics permits the rise? In that case, understanding that Japan in this era may have a politics which can permit the rise of China could well be the essence of wisdom and insight for a Chinese state, for the Chinese people. The Maoist conceptualization facilitates enlightened self-interest. It is not the purpose of this essay to inquire into that experienced political need in Japan—fear of international financial disorder and high tariffs, desire for energy and other raw material insurance, etc.—which may provide China with better economic deals from Japan. All we ask is whether the pragmatique of world-systems theory may somewhat illuminate what the contradiction in China's attempt to change the robber's world and yet rise within it obscures.

It is not that China's ruling groups are particularly evil or selfish or blind. In fact, I find the opposite is very much the case. But structured, unequal, and uneven development in the world-market confined by statist conflict is utterly and inescapably ruthless. To end one's victimization, one becomes complicitous with robbers. One tries, literally, to change places. What is amazing and humanly superior and beyond the reach of world-systems theory is the continuing, profound Chinese commitment to the cause of the world's exploited proletarian nations. What world-systems theory suggests, however, is that in a world dynamically structured as it is, the successful yet victimized proletarian states cannot fully comprehend or arrest the robber's world. Not yet. But if they do, it will take concerted political actions of states at the world-market level.

In sum, Hegelianism is a hypocrisy of the statist era. Whether it is Hegel identifying universal progress with the Prussian state, Marx with the British proletarian, Stalin with his Soviet ruling group or Mao with China's proletarian role in an international united front, there is too much weight put on the shoulders of one nation. A virtue of world-systems theory is its concern with core states, semiperipheral states, and peripheral states. This concern better explains why the politicized world-market system continues no matter what one state does. It explains why so little is achieved at the world level despite principled and mighty efforts at the state level. It leads to a reconceptualization of the prerequisites of liberation from imposed, inhuman imperatives—and an understanding of why the efforts of Maoist ruling groups and others necessarily fall far short of achieving their sincerely stated goal of ending the robber's world.

NOTES

1. There is no liberation from necessary labor time as a defining experience of life. With state control over travel, residence, and job assignments, there is nothing like a socialist liberation from the realm of necessity to that of freedom. In China, state power-holders proved incapable of finding sufficient urban jobs for young city dwellers except at a cost of such overhead capital and high investment that it threatened to take too much from the rural poor. This state has ripped some 20 million such young from home, family, neighbors, friends, and all that is familiar for life-time rural work assignments in often harsh frontier areas. For the populist and paternalistic state, a commodity-like calculation is being made. The workers sacrifice community or the peasants sacrifice equality. In either case, humanity cannot prevail, only a lesser evil.

2. Regis Debray wrote that "all the revolutionaries I have known personally were ardent patriots whose 'internationalism' was generally a national messianism, and that in Cuba and Vietnam being a revolutionary . . . means being a nationalist" (Debray, 1977: 39).

3. Immanuel Kant put it this way: Nature "unites nations by means of their mutual self-interest. For the spirit of commerce sooner or later takes hold of every people, and it cannot exist side by side with war. . . . Perpetual peace is guaranteed by no less authority than the great artist nature herself. The mechanical process of nature visibly exhibits the purposive plan of producing concord among men, even against their will and indeed by means of their very discord" (Kant, 1970: 114, 108).

4. The ideological apologetics of the First World, however, continue. As Carlos F. Diaz-Alejandro comments, "Fame and glory surely await the graduate student who shows that the Opium War led to a Chinese takeoff that was aborted by later attempts to restrict trade" (1978: 150). For a world-systems approach to the Opium War, see Basu (1979). For a critique of world-systems approaches to China, see McDonald (1979). Marx on the Opium War is so nicely straightforward: "[T]he illicit opium trade . . . feeds the British treasury at the expense of human life and morality" (Marx and Engels, 1972: 115).

5. This was not a new opinion which Mao had suddenly arrived at. As with the decision at the end of the 1930s to remake China's Communist Party in order to avoid the horrors of Stalinism (Cressy-Marcks, 1972: 46) so by 1942, noting that "If we centralized, that would destroy . . . enthusiasm," Mao opted for "a new model of the national economy," a Chinese model which maximized initiative from the people concerned, a model that "is neither the old Bismarckian model of national economy, nor the new Soviet model of national economy" (Selden, 1979: 714).

6. I detail this united front position and two other competing positions (Friedman, 1971a). What I analyzed in terms of social base and historical experience as united front, paper tiger and major military backer approaches to the world has more

recently and too abstractly been called moderate, radical, and military approaches (Winckler: 1979: 65).

7. *Kuang-ming jih pao (KMJP),* in the spring of 1957 was very much an organ of the united front approach associated with people such as Chou En-lai, Ch'en Yun, and Teng Hsiao-p'ing.

8. *KMJP* treated the point as obvious. The paper did not detail how shipping, insurance, finance, markets, technology, etc. had an international aspect which was more than national production. Marx in *Capital* volume I, had written that "modern industry ... makes science a productive force distinct from labor" (Santamaria and Manville, 1976: 93). The usual focus on such snippets from Marx is to see whether or not a noncapitalist technology is a useful category. But all we need see is how production forces are multiplied by scientific developments which, as with science itself, can not be a matter of single nation hegemony. Marx, discussing France of about 1848, commented that "French relations of production are conditioned by ... her position on the world market and the law thereof." A proletarian revolution therefore could not win in France. "Accomplishment begins only at the moment when ... the poletariat [revolution] is pushed to the van of the nation which dominates the world market" (Draper, 1978: 245). The world-systems approach which sees a number of core states explains why the lever of revolutionary change has no single fulcrum.

9. For a fuller analysis of the issue of Soviet economic imperialism, see Ray (1978). A 1975 Soviet defense of the C.M.E.A. argued that "division of labor between socialist states cannot be reduced to some countries developing their natural wealth with due regard for the needs of fraternal states" because with some products the producer nation is also permitted to become the processor and even manufacturer of end products. But in investment-accumulation, "member states are able to concentrate their efforts on creating and expanding a number of sectors for which they have favorable conditions" (Mikulsky: 86, TS). To the extent that this permits greater national independence of the U.S.S.R. for Eastern Europe, to that extent Chinese critiques of Soviet domination through the C.M.E.A. may perhaps be said to have been not without consequence.

10. Before the Cuban Revolution, Latin America was seen as the United States, impenetrable, fenced-off back-yard.

11. China's commitment by May 1958 to build nuclear weapons absolutely contradicted any tendency to woo the U.S.S.R.

12. The two usually unmentioned things the U.S.S.R. did do were to permit this hungry China not only to repay the debt in textiles rather than food but also to import some food from the U.S.S.R. It is true that China also exported food to the U.S.S.R. in this period and that piece of the trade is stressed by Chinese patriots out to discredit the U.S.S.R. for its clearly inhuman treatment of the Chinese people in China's moment of great need.

13. This Hong Kong journal writes with authority. It was said to be related to people in the Teng Hsiao-p'ing ruling group.

14. There are 1960 writings of Mao which could be used to legitimate this position. "Where food is concerned, reliance on other countries or other provinces is extraordinarily dangerous." "We must disperse the residents of big cities to the rural areas and construct numerous small cities for under the conditions of atomic war this would be comparatively beneficial" (Mao, 1967: 226-227). These sentences alone actually could be accommodated by all three tendencies in China, united front, paper tiger, and major military backer.

15. This essay in *Cheng ming* (Kuan, 1979) argues that as China's ultra-left took a leap into inhumanity by this interpretation, so Cambodia's Pol Pot regime took the

next great leap in this chain of preposterous logic. That is, corrupt cities must be purified. The metropolises of the world are the enemies of revolution. Hence the Pol Pot regime's war on Cambodia's cities was not merely a functional imperative of preventing starvation and stopping saboteurs.

16. Independence and one's own modern weaponry were inseparable for Mao. "If we are not to be bullied... we cannot do without the bomb" (Mao, 1977: 288). He noted that "Lumumba's Congo had launched a guerrilla war, but lacked any modern weaponry" (Mao, 1969: 456).

17. This was a special front page editorial. The public position reflects earlier commitments. Chou En-lai declared in December 1971, "We are resolutely on the side of the third world" (Chen, 1979: 133).

18. The most accessible English language guide to this reconceptualization is the collection of 1972 articles gathered by Yenan Books of Berkeley, California (2506 Haste St.) and titled "On Studying World History."

19. The post-1968 openness to Yugoslavia alienated Albania, which allied itself with Lin Piao and China's ultra-left. Not surprisingly, behind Albania's ultra-left phrases is the priority of statist thinking in a world where all is defined by relations to the major threat to one's independence seen in Albania as Yugoslavia. Thus, as in the 1950s and 1960s, indeed throughout the history of the Maoist movement, a world drawn from a Chinese nationalistic focal point did not harmonize with all other nationalisms. The notion that China changed its general approach to the world in the 1970s, however, is wrong. What changed was Moscow's and Washington's policies toward Peking. For more on Mao's views on the need to compromise with all imperialisms but the worst in terms of China's national plight, see his December 25, 1940 directive "On Policy." Mao concludes: "The Communist Party opposes all imperialism, but we make a distinction between Japanese imperialism which is now committing aggression against China and the imperialist powers which are not doing so now, between German and Italian imperialism which are allies of Japan and have recognized 'Manchukuo' and British and U.S. imperialism which are opposed to Japan, and between the Britain and the United States of yesterday which followed a Munich policy in the Far East and undermined China's resistance to Japan, and the Britain and the United States of today which have abandoned this policy and are now in favor of China's resistance. Our tactics are guided by one and the same principle: to make use of contradictions, win over the many, oppose the few, and crush our enemies one by one" (Chen, 1979: 70). This essay cannot take the space to provide the facts which give the lie to some 1970s distortions of Chinese foreign policy such as an alleged Chinese opposition to Chile's Marxist Allende and a supposed preference for Chile's fascist Pinochet. Actually, Allende, Chair of Chile's China Friendship Organization, received great aid from China. Peking, a copper importer (still trying to develop copper mines) cooperates with copper producers Zaire, Zambia, and Chile as Cuba, a sugar exporter, cooperates with Brazil's murderous rulers, who are also sugar exporters. The alternative to such cooperation is deep injury to one's own citizens from ruthless world-market forces.

20. For that position, see Kraus, 1979. For a toppling of that position, see Diaz-Alejandro, 1978.

21. The staying power of that U.S. ideology is impressive. It held even after Nixon's Japan shocks of 1971. "There is a story that when President Nixon was holding his pre-Peking mini-summits with British Prime Minister Edward Heath, President Pompidou of France, and Chancellor Willy Brandt of West Germany, he lectured on the need to help ensure that Japan retained its place in the liberal world order—and that Willy Brandt later asked his aides what on earth the President was talking about" (Wilson, 1973: 43).

22. The interplay between Yao, Chou, and Chang (Committee, 1972: 352-359) is instructive.

REFERENCES

BASU, D. K. (1979) "The peripheralization of China," pp. 171-187 in W. Goldfrank (ed.) The World System of Capitalism. Beverly Hills: Sage Publications.
CHANG HSIEN-WEN (1978) "Li Ta-chao t'ung-chih shih chieh-ting ti Ma-k'o-ssu chu-i-cho." Nan-ching ta-hsueh hsueh-pao 4: 94-99.
CHANG P'ING-HUA (1978) Speech. Issues and Studies 14.12 (December).
CHEN, K. C. (1979) China and the Three Worlds. White Plains, NY: M. E. Sharpe.
CH'EN PI-WU (1957) "A discussion with regard to the crumbling of a unified world market." Kuang-ming jih pao (May 22).
CH'EN PO-TA (1953) Mao Tse-tung on the Chinese Revolution. Peking: Foreign Languages Press.
CHOU EN-LAI (1971) "Official transcript of Reston's conversation with the Chinese premier in Peking." New York Times (August 10): 14.
Committee of Concerned Asian Scholars (1972) China: Inside the People's Republic. New York: Bantam.
Compilation Group for the "History of Modern China" Series (1976) The Opium War. Peking: Foreign Languages Press.
CRESSY-MARCKS, V. (1972) "Wo gen Mao Tse-tung t'an-hua." Tung-fang tsa-chih 7 (March): 45-48 (from Journey Into China, 1940).
DEBRAY, R. (1977) "Marxism and the national question." New Left Review (September-October): 25-41.
DIAZ-ALEJANDRO, D. F. (1978) "Delinking North and South: Unshackled or Unhinged?" pp. 85-162 in Rich and Poor Nations in the World Economy. New York: McGraw-Hill.
DITTMER, L. (1974) Liu Shao-ch'i and the Chinese Cultural Revolution. Berkeley: University of California Press.
DRAPER, H. (1978) Karl Marx's Theory of Revolution, Vol. II. New York: Monthly Review Press.
DULLES, A. (1965) The Craft of Intelligence. New York: Signet.
Foreign Languages Press (1976) Ugly Features of Soviet Social-Imperialism. Peking.
FRIEDMAN, E. (1968) "The center cannot hold: the failure of parliamentary democracy in China, 1911-1914." Political science dissertation, Harvard University.
--- (1970) "Political independence in China and the international political economy of imperialism." Centre of Asian Studies Working Paper. Hong Kong.
--- (1971a) "Superpowers and challengers: the United States and China." in S. Spiegel and K. Waltz (eds.) Conflict in World Politics. Cambridge: Winthrop.
--- (1971b) "Mao's long courtship bears late fruit." Washington Post (July 18).
--- (1973) "The succession to Mao and changing China's foreign policy." Department of State Conference, Washington.
--- (1975) "China's changing role in the world economy." Stanford Journal of International Studies (Spring): 1-14.
--- (1979) "How Vietnam made China its enemy number one. New China (Fall).
GITTINGS, J. (1974) The World and China, 1922-1972. London: Eyre Methuen.
HUNTER, H. (1974) Chinese and Soviet Transport for Agriculture. University Center for International Studies, University of Pittsburgh.

Jen-min jih pao (1963) "Polemic on the general line of the Communist movement." December 12.
——— (1972) Editorial. June 15: 1.
JULIEN, C. (1971) America's Empire. New York: Pantheon.
KANT, I. (1970) Kant's Political Writings. Hans Reiss, ed. Cambridge: Cambridge University Press.
KENG PIAO (1978) Interview with a US delegation of Civic and World Affairs Leaders. Peking, November 25.
KINOSHITA, J. (1963) "The World viewed from China." Sekai (September). Translated in Summary of Selected Japanese Magazines (November 12).
Kommunist (1968) No. 4 (April).
KORBONSKI, A. (1966) "COMECON," pp. 351-403 in International Political Communities. Garden City, NY: Anchor.
KRAUS, R. (1979) "Withdrawing from the world system," pp. 237-259 in W. Goldfrank (ed.) The World System of Capitalism. Beverly Hills: Sage Publications.
KUAN FENG-YUEH (1979) "The preposterous theories of Chang Ch'un-ch'iao and the Cambodian Communists." Cheng ming yueh-k'an No. 17 (March 1): 32-33.
KUZNETS, S. (1973) Oriental Economist (January): 30.
LI TA-CHAO (1962) Li Ta-chao hsuan-chi. Peking: People's Publishing House.
LIU SHAO-CH'I (1969) Collected works of Liu Shao-ch'i. Hong Kong: Union Research Institute.
MAO TSE-TUNG (1965) Selected Works of Mao Tse-tung, Vol. I. Peking: Foreign Languages Press.
——— (1967) Mao Tse-tung ssu-hsiang wan sui. Reprinted in Japan and Hong Kong.
——— (1969) Mao Tse-tung ssu-hsiang wan-sui. Hong Kong: Po wen Bosk Publishers.
——— (1975) Mao Tse-tung chi. Hong Kong.
——— (1976) "Mao Tse-tung and the Hunan self-government movement, 1920: an introduction with five translations." Angus McDonald, trans. China Quarterly (December): 750-777.
——— (1977) Selected Works of Mao Tse-tung. Vol. V. Peking: Foreign Languages Press.
MARKS, R. (1977) "On the social origins of peasant revolution in east Kwangtung." Ph.D. dissertation, University of Wisconsin.
MARX, K. and F. ENGELS (1972) On Colonialism. New York. International Publishers.
McDONALD, A. (1978) The Urban Origins of Rural Revolution. Berkeley: University of California Press.
——— (1979) "Wallerstein's world economy." Journal of Asian Studies 38, 3 (May): 535-540.
MIKULSKY, K. (1975) Lenin's Teaching on The World Economy and Its Relevance to Our Times. Moscow: Progress Publishers.
Peking Review (1965) September 10.
RAWSKI, E. S. (1972) Agricultural Change and The Peasant Economy of South China. Cambridge, MA: Harvard University Press.
RAY, D. M. (1978) "Chinese perceptions of social imperialism and economic dependency." Stanford Journal of International Studies (Spring): 36-82.
SANTAMARIA, U. and A. MANVILLE (1976) "Lenin and the problem of transition." Telos 27 (Spring): 79-96.
SCHRAM, S. (1966) Mao Tse-tung. Harmondsworth: Penguin.
——— (1969) The Political Thought of Mao Tse-tung. New York: Praeger.
SELDEN, M. (1979) The People's Republic of China: A Documentary History of Revolutionary Change. New York: Monthly Review Press.

SHEEL, K. (forthcoming) "A social history of the north Kiangsi base area." Ph.D. dissertation, University of Wisconsin.

Shijie zhishi (1979) "Japan's current foreign policy posture." No. 7.

VAN NESS, P. (1970) Revolution and Chinese Foreign Policy. Berkeley: University of California Press.

VERMEER, E. B. (1977) Water Conservancy and Irrigation in China. The Hague: Leiden University Press.

WALLERSTEIN, I. (1974a) "Dependence in an interdependent world." African Studies Review 17 (April): 1-26.

––– (1974b) The Modern World-System. New York: Academic Press.

WANG JUI-SHENG and LIANG SHIH-P'ENG (1978) "An essay in refutation of 'A Discussion with regard to the Crumbling of a Unified World Market'." Ching-chi yen-chiu 1: 70-82.

WILSON, D. (1973) "The EEC." Far Eastern Economic Review (January 15).

WINCKLER, E. A. (1979) "China's world-system: social theory and political practice in the 1970s," pp. 53-69 in W. L. Goldfrank (ed.) The World-System of Capitalism: Past and Present. Beverly Hills: Sage Publications.

YAHUDA, M. (1978) China's Role in World Affairs. London: Croom Helm.

Yenan Books [ed.] (1972) On Studying World History. Berkeley.

Chapter 11

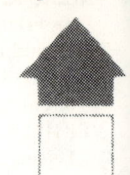

PROLETARIANIZATION AND CLASS ALLIANCES IN THE AMERICAS

Susanne Jonas
Marlene Dixon

Any serious examination of the current situation on this continent from the point of view of the workers' movements—that is, from the point of view of formulating strategies and class alliances for intervening in the current situation in order to change it—must start from a scientific understanding of what are the possibilities and the limitations in the conditions of struggle today. On the one hand, this is a time of international capitalist crisis, of the decline of U.S. imperialism, of intensified working-class struggle throughout the globe, not least in the United States and other core countries. On the other hand, one might say history and capitalist development have outstripped the political understanding and the organizational readiness of the working class—certainly in the United States. If we are to intervene in these circumstances to the benefit of the workers' movement and the destruction of capitalism, we must begin with an attempt to understand the global changes taking place in the capitalist world-economy.

From a Latin American perspective, the workers' movement has serious rethinking to do and serious defeats to account for:

> It's not possible today to cling to old formulas with the desire of defending the continuity of worn-out historical symbols; in reality, if we observe the historic course of Latin America in the last two decades, we can only arrive at one basic conclusion: from the

---

AUTHORS' NOTE: This chapter is based largely on the conceptual foundations laid out in Marlene Dixon's seminal "Abstract: The Degradation of Waged Labor and Class Formation on an International Scale," which appeared in *Synthesis*, Spring 1978, and it represents an effort to extend and apply the analysis in that abstract.

triumph of the Cuban Revolution until today, the struggle of the peoples of the region has brought only oppression and death. Therefore it is time to ... admit the misery of our situation and to set ourselves modestly to the task of rethinking everything about our region, beginning with the most basic points [Vusković and Martínez, 1977: 5].

In this spirit, we present in this chapter a series of preliminary general working hypotheses. These are by no means firm or fully researched conclusions or detailed case studies, but starting points of analysis which we hope to develop fully in coming years. (Even where we make direct assertions, these should be understood as hypotheses.) Further, in this chapter, we shall touch upon many themes which we cannot fully develop here, but which will serve to indicate our general directions and priorities for future research.

Specifically, we shall sketch the crisis in the capital accumulation process and the corresponding shifts in the international capitalist division of labor; as well as the penetration of capitalist relations of production deeper and deeper into the economies of the peripheral and semiperipheral countries. Taken together, these phenomena result in the formation of new sectors of the proletariat and the bourgeoisie. We shall see how the penetration of a particular form of relations of production results in the expansion of wage labor and the deskilling of the proletariat. Finally, we shall attempt to understand the consequences for revolutionary process and class alliances of these changes in the international division of labor and the processes of class formation. Our examples are taken from Latin America and the United States. However, some of the processes we trace here are characteristic of the entire capitalist world-system, including the countries currently undertaking socialist construction.

BASIC CONCEPTS

Let us begin with a few brief clarifications about basic concepts and terminology. Since we are dealing with the capitalist world-system, we must clarify our use of "capitalism." We take as the defining characteristic of capitalism neither the exploitation of free wage labor by capital (though such exploitation is the highest form of capitalist relations of production) nor the predominance of exchange on a market. Rather we understand capitalism as production solely for capital accumulation, based on the appropriation of surplus value from the direct producers, where the greater part of the surplus value is reinvested; the market *under capitalism* is organized so as to maximize capital accumulation. Capitalism is the only mode of production in which capital accumulation is maximized for its own sake (irrespective of human use value), which creates a pressure for constant expansion. Capitalism is a world-system whose dynamic is: expand or die. This urge for expansion explains why, as Paul Sweezy (1979: 3) put it, "there can never be a settling down of the system as a whole, never an equilibrium that is more than temporary and precarious."

We proceed from the premise that there exists a single division of labor in the world today, produced by this world process of capital accumulation. Capitalism is and has always been a world-system (though its global reach has only in the twentieth century been fully extended). As Bukharin (1973: 27) summarized it sixty years ago:

> By and large, the whole process of world economic life in modern times reduces itself to the production of surplus value and its distribution among the various groups and sub-groups of the bourgeoisie on the basis of an ever widening reproduction of the relations between two classes—the class of the world proletariat on the one hand and the world bourgeoisie on the other.

We view the basic division of labor in the world-economy in terms of the direction of capital accumulation. Those countries which are generally referred to as "core" are the recipients or beneficiaries of capital accumulation; moreover it is the capital accumulation process in these core countries that dominates and shapes the development of the system as a whole. "Peripheral" countries are those which generate but do not accumulate capital at an equal rate, and which are systematically disadvantaged with respect to the benefits of capital accumulation. "Semiperipheral" or intermediate countries are those in which both core and peripheral processes of capital accumulation take place. The terms core, periphery and semiperiphery are, as Immanuel Wallerstein (1979a: 293) put it, "simply phrases to locate one crucial part of the system of surplus appropriation by the bourgeoisie," ways of summarizing the basic processes and forms of class conflict in the capitalist world-economy.

It is within this framework that we understand unequal exchange as a series of mechanisms which reproduce the channeling of surplus from periphery to core—those "state operations [which] intervene to tilt the sharing among bourgeois toward those bourgeois located in the core states (Wallerstein, 1979a: 292). Thus, we view Latin America (which includes both peripheral and semiperipheral regions) as part of the division of labor by which capital accumulation occurs in the United States and other core countries.

THE CRISIS IN INTERNATIONAL CAPITALISM AND THE RESTRUCTURED INTERNATIONAL DIVISION OF LABOR

What is commonly known as the current crisis in international capitalism is a crisis in worldwide capital accumulation. This crisis is associated with (though it does not solely consist of) the relative decline of U.S. imperialism—the end of post-Second World War U.S. hegemony over the other core capitalist powers (for reasons which we shall not detail here). Particularly at times when there is no one hegemonic power, the world wide capital accumulation process does not proceed uniformly or smoothly. Thus, although it is only one aspect of the more general crisis, the U.S. decline cannot fail to affect the entire system profoundly.

The current general crisis of capital accumulation became evident toward the end of the 1960s, when the long postwar boom began to falter—that is, when the rate of profit in the major industrialized countries began to decline and profitable investment opportunities using existing technology began to shrink (Frank, 1977a). These tendencies gave rise to a full-fledged recession by 1973-1975—the most serious since the Great Depression of the 1930s. This crisis is structural, i.e., inherent in the very structure of postwar capitalism; it is the result of forces which have been at work for more than twenty-five years and is, in part, the outgrowth of the very measures devised to "save" world capitalism in the 1930s. It is a generalized crisis of overproduction, with insufficient demand worldwide as a result of the existing distribution of world income (Wallerstein, 1979b: 273).

In the traditional industrial or core countries, this crisis is manifested in growing unemployment, a greater number of bankruptcies and mergers, cutbacks in production and overcapacity, a declining rate of investment, and the combination of stagnation and inflation known as "stagflation" (Froebel et al., 1978a: 124; 1977: Sweezy, 1979: 8). In the periphery the principal manifestations are "declining real standards of living for the masses; astronomical rates of unemployment, often reaching 30 to 40 percent of the labor force; misery, malnutrition, and even starvation, with no let-up in sight or improvement in prospect" (Sweezy, 1979: 8).

In a period of general crisis of accumulation—in order to solve its problems—capital must make many adjustments and modifications. We shall refer to this process of adjustment as the restructuring of the international division of labor. Some authors refer to what is happening today as a "new international division of labor," while others question whether it is unprecedented, unique, or irreversible.[1] What is of primary significance is that it represents a restructuring or transformation of the previously existing post-Second World War international division of labor, and as such has profound consequences throughout the world.

A second clarification: Above we referred to a general international division of labor in the worldwide capital accumulation process—that is, core, periphery, and semiperiphery. We shall now use the term "international division of labor" more specifically, to refer to the production process—that is, the subdivision of the production processes into component parts which are carried out in different national settings.

This particular crisis of capital accumulation is bringing about a profound shift in the production process and in the international division of labor; and in a sense, this crisis marks the end of an era:

> A phase in the development of the capitalist world-economy has come to an end with the recession in 1975. . . . The preconditions for the expansion and accumulation of capital have experienced fundamental qualitative transformations, with the result that a new international division of labor is replacing the "classical" international division of labor that has existed up till now. This process has farreaching consequences for the living and working conditions of people all over the world [Froebel et al., 1978a: 123].

Without analyzing in detail here the causes and mechanisms of this transformation, which culminated in the recession of the 1970s, we may characterize it as follows: The classical division of labor could be best expressed in the image of town/country (industry/agriculture). As laid out by Marx,

> The foundation of all highly developed divisions of labor that are brought about by the exchange of commodities is the cleavage between town and country. We may say that the whole economic history of society is summarized in the development of this cleavage [see Bukharin, 1973: 21].

As further developed by Bukharin,

> The cleavage between "town and country" as well as the "development of this cleavage," formerly confined to one country only, are now being reproduced on a tremendously enlarged basis. Viewed from this standpoint, entire countries appear today as "towns," mainly the industrial countries, whereas entire agrarian territories appear to be "country." International division of labor coincides here with the division of labor between the two largest branches of social production as a whole, between industry and agriculture, thus appearing as the so-called "general division of labor" [1973: 21].

Specifically, this implied a "division of labor" between industrialized (core) countries producing capital and consumer goods, and underdeveloped (peripheral and semiperipheral) countries incorporated into the capitalist world-economy as suppliers of raw materials and agricultural goods.

If the classical division of labor is expressed in the town/country dichotomy, the emerging—by no means fully completed, by no means absolute (Froebel et al., 1978a: 131; 1977: 84; see also Trajtenberg, 1978:

21)—division of labor is between those processes which are heavily labor-intensive, which can be reduced to the most simple and Taylorized processes (which can be located in the periphery and semiperiphery as well as in core countries), and those which cannot be thus reduced, which are capital-intensive, which require more skill and training, and which hence cannot be conveniently relocated. Thus, the basic division of labor in the world-economy is increasingly not by product (*what* is produced) but by the degree of complexity of the production process.

This shift, whose contours have become clear since the late 1960s (though its roots are much older), has found its most evident and visible expression internationally in the relocation of industry. This tendency represents a breakdown in the classical scheme in which the industrialized "core" countries were assumed to provide the best conditions for capital accumulation in industry; it is an adaptation to the crisis (including declining profitability) of that scheme, and is designed to take advantage of an almost limitless worldwide reservoir of potential labor (including, as we shall see, in the socialist countries) (Froebel et al., 1978a: 126). We shall return to an examination of the specific character of the new proletarianization below.

A central aspect of the restructured international division of labor, which is based on utilizing the cheapest possible labor force, is industry producing for the world-market located in the peripheral and semiperipheral countries. Many of these world-market factories are runaway shops, i.e., plants (often subsidiaries of transnational corporations) which have closed down their operations in the United States or other core countries because of relatively high wages there and relocated in cheap labor areas. The ultimate extreme of runaway operations are the free trade zones—enclaves in which the local government offers special incentives so that the transnational corporations will locate there that part of their production which requires large amounts of cheap, unorganized labor.

Because these are the operations of transnational corporations which have developed the technology for opening up and shutting down plants with great facility, they remain in a given location only so long as the conditions for capital accumulation remain optimal, i.e., so long as labor remains sufficiently cheap and docile. "Capital which is attracted to one region today may leave again tomorrow only to return possibly again the day after" (Froebel et al., 1977: 87). The Mexican border boom/bust cycle is a perfect illustration of this phenomenon.

Industrial relocation in cheap labor havens (areas) is perhaps the most visible aspect of the tendency toward a restructured international division of labor (and with the most obvious consequences for class formation), but it is by no means the only aspect. The obverse side of the same process is the importation of low-wage workers from peripheral and semiperipheral areas into the core countries, expressed in the form of increasing immigration to the core. We shall examine some aspects of that process below.

Generally, for the core countries the restructured international division of labor means increasing specialization in supersophisticated high-technology industry; to the extent that they maintain more standard industries, they do so through rationalization schemes as a means of maintaining profitability, reducing the number and skill of employees through technology and reorganization of labor (Froebel et al., 1977: 87; 1978a: 124).

Meanwhile, in the periphery and semiperiphery, whole societies are taking on the character of cheap labor havens, in that they are oriented toward production for the capitalist world market and make no pretense of developing a domestic consumer market. This pattern is not limited to runaway industrial production; the same effects come from reorganization of the economy to revolve around new forms of export agriculture, extractive mining, etc. The key is that the producers in these countries are no longer the consumers of what they produce (in contrast to the import-substituting industrialization model) and are decreasingly consumers at all.

A dramatic and extreme example is Chile, which has been *de*-industrialized and whose economy has been destroyed since the 1973 coup, in order to make it serve the needs of transnational capital—with devastating effects for the Chilean working class. As Andre Gunder Frank has described it, "the Chilean model of a military corporativism [is] designed first and foremost vastly to increase the rate of super-exploitation by depressing the wage rate to a level where even the reproduction of the wage force becomes impossible" (Frank, 1974). This pattern, which is spreading in Latin America, has profound social implications that we shall examine below.

A further aspect of the restructured international division of labor is an increasing differentiation among and within countries of the "Third World." Specifically, some semiperipheral or intermediate countries (also sometimes referred to as "subimperialist") are able to take advantage of the capitalist crisis to advance their relative standing in the international hierarchy (e.g., Brazil, Iran).

In this regard, it is important to point out that the countries engaged in socialist construction—many of which are semiperipheral or have become semiperipheral in no small measure by virtue of their revolution—do not stand outside the international capitalist division of labor:

[T]he socialist countries occupy an intermediate position in the international division of labor, in this regard not unlike the most developed "sub-imperialist" underdeveloped countries like Brazil. They import advanced technology manufactures from the industrially developed capitalist countries, paying for them with raw materials and incurring a growing trade deficit. And they export less sophisticated manufactures to the underdeveloped countries, with whom the socialist countries run up a trade surplus, part of which they use to reduce their trade deficit with the imperialist countries, also not unlike the sub-imperialist capitalist countries [Frank, 1977b: 101].

One visible reflection in socialist countries of the shifts in the capitalist international division of labor is the system of contract processing, under which capitalist enterprises transmit intermediate products to factories under contract in these countries for further processing (Froebel et al., 1977: 86; see also Frank, 1977b). This and related aspects of socialist construction within a capitalist world-economy have far-reaching consequences for our hypotheses below.

PROLETARIANIZATION AND BOURGEOISIFICATION ON A WORLD SCALE

The changing capital accumulation process roughly outlined above implies corresponding alterations in the process of class formation worldwide. To clarify our conceptions: at the broadest level, we view the bourgeoisie as those who appropriate surplus value created by others and invest a portion of it to accumulate capital; and the proletariat as those who are forced to yield a portion of the value they create to others. The implication is that bourgeois does not refer simply to "free" entrepreneurs, nor proletarian simply to industrial wage laborers (Wallerstein, 1979a: 288-289).

We consider that those professionals and managers who form the "head" to the proletarian hands in the capitalist labor process constitute the lowest stratum of the bourgeoisie (petty-bourgeois), because they receive, above their subsistence, a fraction of the surplus value appropriated by the bourgeoisie from the proletariat. What demarcates them from the rest of the bourgeoisie is that, while they participate in and benefit from capital accumulation, they do not control to any significant extent the allocation (investment) of the surplus, and therefore do not make the controlling decisions in the accumulation process.

It is also important to clarify the dynamic nature of class formation. When a worker's income and rights expand to the point that he is living off the surplus value of others and organizes/commands/controls the labor process of others, he becomes petty-bourgeois. As we shall see, this is the genesis of a growing stratum in peripheral and semiperipheral countries, which we view as a stratum of the international bourgeoisie.

We shall now examine briefly how the shifting process of international capital accumulation is shaping certain strata within the two polar classes in particular ways, both in the periphery and semi-periphery and in the core.

PROLETARIANIZATION AND TAYLORIZATION IN THE PERIPHERY AND SEMIPERIPHERY

In referring to one aspect of the process of class formation as "proletarianization," we go beyond the broad definition of proletariat laid out above, as those (direct producers) who are forced to yield part of the surplus they create to others. We wish now to describe a more specific process—i.e., the formation of *waged* labor, the subordination of (often formerly rural) populations to the regimen of wage labor. Worldwide the percentage of wage-labor as a form of labor has been steadily increasing throughout the history of the capitalist world-economy; this is what is generally referred to as proletarianization (Wallerstein, 1979a: 291). Further we use the term to denote the *intensification* of capitalist relations so that all previous (noncapitalist) forms of class relations tend to be destroyed.

Within the framework of analysis developed here, "proletarianization" includes additionally the *Taylorization* which accompanies the process of accumulation today. Our analysis of the capitalist labor process is derived from Harry Braverman's analysis of detail division of labor in U.S. industrialization. The subdivision of the labor process was "predicated upon the separation of the wage laborer not only from control over his product but also from his skill, transferring complete control over his labor process to a subaltern stratum of technocrats and managers" (Dixon, 1978a: 50)—separation of head and hand. This separation has been accompanied by a relentless intensification of the hand-work.

> The development and refinement of technology and labor organization [has made] it possible to decompose complex production processes into elementary units so that even an unskilled labor force can easily and quickly be trained to perform [them].... In this way skilled labor receiving high wages can be replaced by unskilled or semi-skilled labor receiving lower wages [Froebel et al., 1978a: 128].

The penetration of capitalist relations of production into almost all areas of world-economy, with the consequence of deskilling and degrading wage labor, has occurred in two ways: first, as industrializing states have adopted the U.S. model of industrialization (or had it forced upon them by international capital) (Dixon, 1978a: 50-51); and secondly, as a result of the international nature of capital accumulation (i.e., the proletariat is often located in a different country than the bourgeoisie) and with the rise of a single world-market for labor which "for the first time effectively encompasses both the traditional industrial countries [and] the underdeveloped countries" (Froebel et al., 1978a: 130; see also Hopkins, 1977:

71). In short, the world's waged proletarian classes increasingly become the "hands" to the petty-bourgeois "heads" in the capitalist production process.

At the most general level, then, Taylorization on an international scale implies the separation, worldwide, of wage laborers from their skill, transferring control over the labor process to a petty-bourgeois stratum of technocrats and managers. Moreover, Taylorization signifies the subdivision of the manufacturing process so as to require only (and increasingly) unskilled, hence cheap, labor. In short, proletarianization today *means* principally the degradation of wage labor on an international scale. Proletarianization is thus an international—global—process. We shall come back to this point later. But for the moment, we can focus first on its occurrence in the periphery and semiperiphery, and then touch briefly on the implications for the core.

Let us take Latin America as somewhat typical of processes occurring in all parts of the periphery and semiperiphery today. (The difference between periphery and semiperiphery, between El Salvador and Mexico, for example, is not essential for our purposes here.) Capitalist penetration of the countryside in Latin America, bringing mechanized farming, and plantation economies (producing for export), has also meant increasing capitalist appropriation of the land. As the peasants are dispossessed of their land and deskilled on a massive scale, they are forced into urban areas as impoverished wage laborers. They are converted into an urban proletariat in highly Taylorized industries, or often are left without work, swelling the ranks of the industrial reserve army.

The deskilling process implies the cheapening or undervaluation of labor power. That Latin America stands as a cheap labor reserve for the United States is by no means a new development. What is new, however, is: (a) that the whole strategy to maximize capital accumulation is *based* primarily on the undervaluation of labor power (i.e., wages less than what is required to produce and reproduce labor power) in areas such as Latin America; and that, at this time of international capitalist contraction, this has become the principal determinant of foreign capital investment in Latin America (Trajtenberg, 1978: 10-11); and (b) that the overall social direction is not toward "development" (as was the case, at least in theory, with the import-substituting industrialization model of the 1930s-1960s), but toward pauperization—the spread not of development but of poverty and misery.

Let us look at the social implications for Latin America. Those who are employed as wage laborers of this restructured international division of labor are more intensively exploited—for even as their wages remain at 10-20% of those in the core countries, they are being forced to work longer hours and more rapidly, and to become more productive. In fact, studies have shown the productivity of assembly workers in low-wage countries to be equal to or higher than in the United States (Trajtenberg, 1978: 33-35). Their working conditions, meanwhile, are not dissimilar to those of the initial decades of the Industrial Revolution (Trajtenberg, 1978: 11). Moreover, Taylorization has brought about a proportionally higher percentage of women and children laborers (who can be employed more cheaply to do unskilled detail work)—especially younger women, who require minimum wages and whose youth enhances their productivity—until they go blind or get arthritis from the work at the age of twenty-five, at which point they are discarded and replacements easily found (Froebel et al., 1978: 139; also see Baird and McCaughan, n.d.: ch. 1).

At least—so say the latter-day apologists for the runaway shops and free zones in Latin America—these superexploited workers have a job, which means a step in the direction of resolving the grave problems of unemployment. But, beyond those relatively few individuals who (temporarily) have the jobs, for the population as a whole, the net effect is absolute pauperization and increased unemployment and starvation:

> This process does not have the potential to abolish unemployment and under-employment in the Third World; it has only the potential of absorbing a small part of the hundreds of millions of unemployed, and this for the lowest possible wages; in consequence, the majority of the unemployed mass falls into or even sinks beneath the position and condition of an industrial reserve army [Froebel et al., 1978b: 27].

Increasingly, entire populations in Latin America are being maintained at less than subsistence levels, as labor power of the employed is undervalued, and as the ranks of the permanently unemployed or underemployed—the "marginal" or "subproletarian" masses—are swelling. This is a reflection of the more general tendency toward "absolute pauperization of roughly two-thirds of the population in the periphery" world wide (Froebel et al., 1977: 76; Vusković and Martínez, 1977: 6-7). Nor is there any tendency toward improvement of this situation; on the contrary, if through organized political action wages or working conditions should improve in a particular country, that country loses its cheap labor advantage, and international capital moves on to more exploited climes.

The international recognition of the above situation is reflected in the United Nations' preoccupation with problems of unemployment and starvation. In the 1950s and 1960s, the United Nations focused on "terms of trade," which was a national formulation (one nation's bourgeoisie against another nation's bourgeoisie). Today the international issues of unemployment and starvation are stark *class* issues of the global proletariat vs. the global bourgeoisie.

ATTACK ON LABOR IN THE CORE

The above affects not just Latin America (or the entire "Third World"), but rather the entire capitalist world-system. Workers in core countries are today being forced to compete for jobs on the worldwide labor market and/or are being completely displaced by runaway shops in low-wage areas; hence, under-valuation of labor-power in Latin America leads to the cheapening of labor-power (lowering of wages) and/or to greatly increased structural unemployment in the United States and other core countries (Froebel et al., 1978a: 133, 136, 138).

These phenomena are part of the *general attack against labor* being waged by capital in the core—an attack against the traditionally higher living standards and greater political rights (as well as higher wage levels) of the U.S. working class. This attack is capital's response to its own crisis. Because of its profit squeeze, capital is no longer able to lay out a fraction of the surplus to maintain "peace" with the U.S. working class. Hence, *austerity capitalism* and the attack on labor, with the accompanying labor unrest. Manifestations of this general attack on labor include: speedup and layoffs, austerity measures and cutbacks in necessary public services, *engineered* unemployment (which was a deliberate policy of the Ford and Carter Administrations), and a frontal assault on the rights of labor to strike and organize (see the analysis in Rebel Worker News Journal, 1977).

Transnational corporations use their ability to relocate production in cheap-labor havens (and their ability to *threaten* to do so) to discipline U.S. workers, forcing them to accept real wage cuts, harsher working conditions, speedup, or infringements on their rights. In this sense, the pauperization of the proletariat is a tendency of the proletariat *worldwide*.

Workers in core countries are profoundly affected by another aspect of the shifting international division of labor: capital's importation of low-wage workers into the core countries (for our purposes, the United States). Without going into great detail here, we can see the general outlines. The same process of capitalist penetration which uproots small farmers from their land, drives them into the cities, and proletarianizes them in Latin America (for example in Mexico and Puerto Rico) simulataneously attracts portions of this new labor force to the United States (where they will be paid far below the going wage rates). As Braverman (1974: 384-385) describes the process:

> In Northern Europe and the U.S., the capitalist economies have increasingly made use of the masses of former agricultural labor in the colonies and neo-colonies. These masses are thrown off by the

> process of imperialist penetration itself, which has disrupted the traditional forms of labor and subsistence. They become available to capital.... As a result of this, the movement of labor has to some extent become internationalized, although still regulated in each country by government action.... In the U.S..... Puerto Rican, Mexican, and other Latin American workers ... have been added to the pool of lowest-paid labor which is made up chiefly of black workers.

Historically, the border has functioned as a mechanism for the absorption or expulsion of labor, regulated in part by the needs of the U.S. economy. Particularly in times of boom and expansion, immigration has been encouraged to meet the cheap labor needs of corporations in the United States, to use a portion of the vast industrial reserve army of Latin America as a low-waged sector of the U.S. proletariat.

From the 1940s through the end of the 1960s, during the expansion of U.S. and international capitalism, the border was usually an open door. (The exception was the late 1950s, a time of recession which gave rise to the "wetback operation" of massive deportations.) With the recession of the 1970s, the border is being reconstituted as barbed wire, and the U.S. ruling class has carried out wholesale roundups and deportations—even while continuing to use cheap immigrant labor to depress wage levels for the entire working class. Clearly, the bourgeoisie in the United States (as in other core countries) is worried about what to do with the unemployed masses on both sides of the border; and their response has created a political problem for the workers' movements on both sides of the border—to which we shall return below.

THE NEW PETTY-BOURGEOISIE IN THE PERIPHERY AND SEMIPERIPHERY

The same international process which intensifies and accelerates the formation of the proletariat—the "hands" of the capitalist labor process—brings to life simultaneously new sectors of the bourgeoisie—the "head" of the capitalist labor process. In particular, it spawns a "middle managerial" level, the repository of skill and knowledge once possessed by the working class. As such, it forms a new stratum of the petty bourgeoisie, owning a small store of the intangible means of production, which allows it to control, command, and organize the labor of the working class on behalf of capital, in return for a larger share of the surplus. This stratum includes both middle-level managers of private firms (transnational corporations) and government bureaucrats, technicians, professionals, and a number of others who perform functions of disciplining the working class. This is a stratum of the international bourgeoisie, in that its members live off the surplus created by others; the fact that they are salaried is beside the point. As stated above, they are, however, distinct from those bourgeois who actually *control* the accumulation process.

Like its parent/employer/patron, this stratum is international. At an early stage of penetration by transnational capital, the technical and managerial staffs are imported from the United States (often from the headquarters of the transnational corporation). These are followed by cadres of indigenous managers and professionals trained in the core countries, who bring with them the "culture" and "education" absorbed during training abroad—as well as a deep-seated loyalty to transnational capital. This indigenous stratum is very similar to the new petty-bourgeoisie in the core countries, in that it commands the technical, engineering, and managerial skills which have been separated from (or never imparted to) the mass of the working class. Given the simultaneous weakening (and gradual disappearance) of any "national bourgeoisie," oriented foward the domestic consumer market in Latin America, this new petty bourgeoisie, tied to international capital and the world market, is unlikely to present any nationalist/anti-imperialist challenge. This is truly a lower or subaltern stratum of the international bourgeoisie.

The growth and power of this stratum is especially marked in semi-peripheral countries such as Mexico (e.g., the huge P.R.I. bureaucracy). Even in peripheral countries and regions such as Central America, however, it is a rising force, equally beholden and subservient to transnational capital, equally committed to the subordination of the proletarian force it controls. (In Central America, the most obvious example of transnational capital's deliberate creation of this stratum is the Harvard-founded Central American Institute for Business Administration, which trains and literally produces managers for the subsidiaries of the transnational corporations, and bureaucrats to run the state apparatuses in accordance with the needs of those corporations.)

The state sector of this new petty-bourgeoisie takes on increasing importance as part of the process of class formation described above: for, particularly as the ranks of the reserve army of the unemployed are swelled, as the majority of the population lives under subhuman conditions, and as the gap between proletariat and bourgeoisie steadily widens, the need for a military-bureaucratic lid to contain potential explosion grows. It is for this reason that cheap labor havens in Latin America are typically ruled by right-wing regimes: for it requires a high degree of control and repression to maintain a climate "favorable" for foreign capital.

Finally, insofar as they participate in and are drawn into the global process of capital accumulation, and insofar as they have adopted many of the methods developed by the U.S. bourgeoisie for rapid industrialization (Dixon, 1978a), the countries undertaking socialist construction (especially the Soviet Union and Eastern Europe) are developing elements of capitalist relations of production. The adoption of the capitalist detail division of labor (i.e., Taylorization), together with the importation of Western capital and technology, tends toward the importation of (and consequently tends toward reproduction of) the corresponding forms of organization and relations of production (Frank, 1977b). To the extent that this is the case, it has engendered the formation of a stratum of state bureaucrat/managers who are functionally similar to (perform some of the functions of) the new petty-bourgeoisie in the United States and other core countries.

However, these state bureaucrat/managers differ vastly from their counterparts in the capitalist countries (both core and semiperipheral) insofar as their apparat is a workers' state. To mention only the most obvious difference, while the state bureaucracy does maintain a stable, disciplined, and relatively cheap labor force in the socialist countries, it also exists to provide for the basic necessities of life for the entire population, and to eradicate the very blights—starvation, massive unemployment, and increasing pauperization—that are currently being generated by capitalism.

THESES ON THE POLITICS OF THE WORKERS' MOVEMENTS

The international capitalist crisis and the shift in the international division of labor raise political issues of profound consequence to the workers' movements in Latin America and the United States. On the basis of our analysis above, and of the concrete experiences of the last thirty years, we shall suggest a number of political theses concerning the contemporary workers' movements on this continent.

Most broadly: the only reliable, strategic, long-lasting alliances open to the workers' movement in any particular country (including the United States) are *not* alliances with any supposedly "national"(ist) or progressive sector of the petty-bourgeoisie or bourgeoisie within their national context, but rather, alliances with other sectors of the workers' movements, across national borders. Let us break down this proposition into its two basic parts: (1) no strategic reliance on "united front" cross-class alliances, and (2) the necessity for transnational unity at the level of the workers' movements—and, as the most obvious corollary, the limitations and dangers of nationalism without class analysis. Once again, on occasion we shall overstate our case, in order to make it clear.

1. CLASS-BASED POLITICS: AGAINST SOCIAL DEMOCRACY

There are two kinds of politics in the modern world-system: the class struggle between bourgeois and proletarian, and the political struggles among different bourgeois [Wallerstein, 1979b: 272].

Historically, in a number of peripheral and semiperipheral countries, revolutionary movements have taken the form of anti-imperialist "united fronts" between the workers' movement and "progressive" sectors of the bourgeoisie or petty-bourgeoisie. It is our thesis that: (1) even in the past, those movements were not successful, or at least did not sustain their revolutionary (or even progressive) character, unless the workers' movement held clear hegemony within them; and (2) present-day international material reality and the strategic role of the new petty-bourgeoisie in the state, and in enforcing capitalist relations of production, make united front politics, as it is traditionally known, as a strategy even less viable. To be sure, tactical class alliances are required at this or that moment in the struggle against imperialism. However, given the intensity of proletarianization and class polarization, only a movement under the hegemony of proletarian forces (generally a party) will be capable of decisively challenging imperialism. In short, it is always a question of which class dominates and gives any alliance its class character. Generally speaking, the issue of class hegemony forms an ideological struggle within the workers' movement; thus it becomes a question of drawing lines of class analysis within that movement.

One is always tempted to qualify and water down such absolute-sounding statements as the above; however, in this case, many different kinds of experience over a period of nearly fifty years in Latin America all suggest essentially the same conclusion. The examples are so numerous that we may cite only one of the most recent and obvious, that is, the lesson of Chile.

Why, despite the real advances it made in the lives of the Chilean masses, did the Unidad Popular (Allende) government of 1970-1973 terminate in, and in a sense pave the way for, the fascist junta currently in power? Why was the U.P. government so vulnerable to the reactionary machinations of U.S. imperialism? Briefly, because the U.P. government did not use state power to establish the rule of the working class over the national and international bourgeoisie, but rather acted on the hope of "winning over" the middle class. Thus, with its negotiations and compromises with the bourgeois Christian Democratic Party, and by essentially giving them assurances that it would keep the working class in line, the Unidad Popular government left the Chilean bourgeoisie and U.S. imperialism the space they needed to regroup and launch the counterrevolution, and refused to move decisively against those forces. Since 1973, of course, the realities of the coup have forced a sharp debate over the issues of class alliances and state power within the Chilean workers' movement.

Throughout Latin America (most recently in Nicaragua), the experiences and lessons have been similar: never mistake intrabourgeois struggle (including simply "anti-imperialist" struggle) for class struggle. Historically, social-democratic movements in Latin America, in which the working class made cross-class alliances which it did not dominate, only served to put the bourgeoisie and petty-bourgeoisie in power (for example, see Bodenheimer, 1969, Bodenheimer 1970). And today, given the strategic role of the new petty-bourgeoisie in the state and in enforcing capitalist relations of production, any such alliance becomes even less thinkable for the workers' movement. The new petty-bourgeois may, as in Nicaragua, oppose a particular dictator or regime, but they hardly propose to alter the class character of state power.

Finally, we may add that the issues of the restructured international division of labor and relations of production—Taylorization, subdivision and intensification of the labor process, massive unemployment, and so on—are issues which pit the working class *directly* against the bourgeois masters and the petty-bourgeois task-masters. This polarization is manifested politically in the decomposition of cross-class forms of organization and ideology, as each class seeks the logical expression of its class interests (Vusković and Martínez, 1977: 11).

If social democracy and cross-class united front-type alliances have these consequences even in the countries under the imperialist yoke, then certainly in the United States and other core countries, where class issues are clearly the primary issues, and where labor process issues are increasingly prominent in the workers' movements, social democracy is not simply a distraction from the class struggle; it represents an attack on the workers' movement. Elsewhere we have made the case in full detail against social democracy and united front politics in the United States today (Dixon, 1976a, 1976b, 1976c, 1978b). Suffice it to say here that in the contemporary context, working-class alliances and "historic compromises" in the United States and Western Europe represent in reality collaboration with capital in the reorganization of the economy and labor process (including lower wages) as engineered by the bourgeoisie, and to its advantage (Frank, 1974).

2. "NO HAY FRONTERA": AGAINST SIMPLE NATIONALISM

Classes *an sich* are classes of the world-economy; but classes *für sich* organize themselves ... at the level of the territorial states. [This] accounts for the acute political difficulties of the world socialist movement [Wallerstein, 1977: 105].

Working-class politics today is organized at the national level and takes a national form. To deny or deplore this reality is useless. Objectively, the world's working classes are increasingly workers of the world; yet today there is no united world proletariat, and that unity will have to be built in the struggle. Nevertheless, given the material realities of the modern world-economy, if we fail to see *beyond* the limits of this or that nation-state, or to understand the underlying transnational structure of the world-economy, quite simply our movements will continue to spend themselves without advancing. At the very least, we must start from the comprehension that at one level, at least, nations are not the principal acting units of the modern world-economy (Hopkins, 1977: 70):

> The arena of modern social action and modern social change has been and continues to be the modern world-system. . . . What the states try to unify, the world-economy tears asunder [Hopkins and Wallerstein, 1977: 112-113].

How, then, do we view nationalism and nationalist movements? Nationalism, in and of itself, if divorced from class analysis, obfuscates the class contradictions within a given national context, as well as the world division of labor and relations between the world proletariat and world bourgeoisie. It is not, therefore, an ideology of the proletariat, but an expression of struggles among sectors of the bourgeoisie. National aspirations can and do take on a progressive character at particular moments, but if its projects are taken as the end or goal, they objectively frustrate the genuine long-term interests of the workers' struggles.

Let us look at the specific implications, at several different levels. First, for revolutionary movements, Central America illustrates the need for unity across national borders. The point becomes clear if we examine the operations of transnational capital. For a number of specific reasons (super-cheap and -abundant labor, etc.), in the early 1970s, the transnational corporations found El Salvador particularly appropriate for their runaway and free zone operations. With the consolidation and spread of a militant workers' and peasant movement in the late 1970s (whose tactics include kidnapping corporate executives), El Salvador has become less optimal for the operations of transnational capital. So what do the corporations do? They pack up and relocate in Costa Rica, a few hundred miles away. If and when the Salvadorean bourgeoisie and U.S. imperialism temporarily bring the movement in El Salvador under control, the corporations will no doubt come back. They are set up to operate that way.

Moreover, even if the revolutionary forces take state power in one country—as has just happened in Nicaragua—they could be faced with U.S.-trained armies invading from neighboring countries. With so transnational an enemy, the proletarian forces in Central America must find a way to organize transnationally—at the very least, to initiate a minimal level of coordination on common problems at the regional level (as the African movements have done). This process, which has in fact begun, is a small step toward the "continentalization" of the class struggle (Vusković and Martínez, 1977: 19).

Next, we come to the larger issue of Latin American nationalism, expressed in the form of simple anti-imperialism ("Go home, Yanqui"). Certainly, this is a form of class consciousness and of resistance to exploitation and oppression in Latin America. But if anything has become clear over the past twenty years, it is the limitations of purely anti-imperialist consciousness. In the beginning and in the end, the struggle against U.S. imperialism remains primary; but this struggle can only be successful if it goes beyond a simple anti-imperialist perspective and deals with the issues of class. As seen above, Chile is living testimony. Further, this includes an analysis of class at the global level. For although in one sense there are rich and poor (core and peripheral) countries, the underlying protagonists of struggle are two global classes which cut across national borders.

Thus, we return to a point made earlier. The major social-economic issues of the day—intensified exploitation, massive unemployment, and starvation—are issues of world classes, of the global proletariat against the global bourgeoisie. Objectively, as we have seen, the very process of capital accumulation is tending toward a leveling of the working classes of the capitalist world-economy (as expressed, for example, in the creation of one global labor market). On the one hand, this is a measure of the degree to which transnational capital has been able to carry out its attack against the living standards of the working class in the core countries. On the other hand, despite its very regressive nature, the new pattern of capital accumulation worldwide lays the objective basis for and creates the real possibility of unity and common interests between the Latin American peoples and the U.S. working class. This situation, as two Latin American analysts have noted,

> tends to produce an objective drawing together between the popular struggles of our continent and the workers' and popular movement of the [core capitalist] countries—a tendency which is being accentuated as a result of the current capitalist crisis [Vusković and Martínez, 1977: 19; see also Vusković, n.d.: 6-8].

IMMIGRATION AND UNDOCUMENTED WORKERS

For the workers' movement in the United States, the internationalist perspective is definitive. It is not only a question of proletarian internationalism, unity, and solidarity with the workers' movements of Latin America. The restructured international division of labor has made it an issue *within* the workers' movement of the United States. Specifically, we refer to increasing immigration from Latin America and the issue of undocumented workers ("illegal aliens"). There can be no question that the international bourgeoisie and the U.S. bourgeoisie see one working class between the United States and Mexico. From their perspective (and objectively), immigration represents the continuing construction of the U.S. proletariat, the incorporation of a new superlow-wage sector of the proletariat. For them, the border exists only to be manipulated for the purpose of maximizing capital accumulation.

At times of international capitalist contraction, as now, they are worried about what to do with the unemployed masses on both sides of the border. Hence, the statement by ex-CIA chief William Colby (1977) that the unstable U.S.-Mexican border represents the greatest threat to U.S. national security. This concern led the U.S. ruling class to launch an all-out attack on undocumented workers (the "Carter Plan," including fines for employers hiring them, massive deportations, heavy militarization of the border, etc.).

However, this is only one side of the picture. Even while the international capitalist crisis has given the U.S. ruling class reason to be concerned about undocumented workers increasing the pressure on an already serious unemployment situation, the capitalist continue to need and to profit from this supply of cheap (because "illegal") labor. It is for this reason that big capital did not in the end support the Carter immigration plan (Baird and McCaughan, n.d.: 164-165 ff.).

But there is another reason, more fundamental than maintaining access to an unrestricted supply of supercheap labor, for this response by the U.S. ruling class. The fundamental importance of immigrant labor is as a lever for depressing the wage levels and curbing the rights of the entire U.S. work force, in order to keep profits up. Immigration policy becomes an instrument of policy to counter the effects of the business cycle. Thus, to put the point more broadly, immigration policy "cannot be reduced simply to the manpower needs of the economy"; despite economic recession and increased unemployment, "the long term trend is continued growth in immigrant labor.... Immigration is not a conjunctural phenomenon ... but a structural tendency characteristic of the current phase of monopoly capitalism" (Castells, 1975).[2]

As such, immigration policy becomes the focus of contradictions for both bourgeoisie and proletariat. The bourgeoisie in the advanced industrial countries today is faced with the contradiction of how to meet its continuing need for cheap immigrant labor, while at the same time keeping the lid on social disruption. The key for them is to attempt: (a) to control the immigration flow (there are plans for a new, more controlled "guest worker" immigration program in the United States based on the European model) (Baird and McCaughan, n.d.: 165-166); and (b) to maintain undocumented workers illegal and afraid, hence vulnerable, unorganized, and docile.

This, in turn, poses the political problems or contradictions for the U.S. proletariat, both undocumented and documented. For what appears as simply an attack against undocumented workers is in fact part of an assault against the entire U.S. working class—part of the strategy of depressing wage levels and weakening the entire class by playing on divisions within it. By maintaining undocumented workers as a limitless reserve army to be absorbed into or expelled from the U.S. work force at the will of the bourgeoisie—that is, maintaining them economically at the disposal of capital because of their politically "illegal" status—the bourgeoisie can use them to depress wage levels of the entire U.S. work force (even at the same time it is expelling and deporting masses of them).

Thus, when the A.F.L.-C.I.O. leadership supported the Carter immigration plan on the chauvinist grounds of saving jobs for "American workers," it was acting against the interests of the U.S. working class as a whole. In effect, it was allowing the bourgeoisie to blame so-called "illegals" for the malaise imposed in fact by the capitalist class, and allowing the bourgeoisie to weaken the entire labor movement by treating immigrant workers as individual wage-earners, as if the labor movement did not exist (among other sources, see Cook, 1977; San Francisco Chronicle, 1977; AFL-CIO, 1977: 34; also see Castells, 1975: 51). In short, the bourgeoisie attempts to use racial/national (as well as sexual) divisions and national boundaries to divide one group of workers from another; their ability to do so is their most dangerous weapon against the working class as a whole. Conversely, the incipient struggles by undocumented workers in the United States, both to organize on their own behalf and to participate in broader struggles of the U.S. working class, are absolutely crucial and do represent a serious challenge to the ruling class.

In the end, both the wage levels and living standards, and the fundamental political rights, of the U.S. proletariat are undermined by any failure to view itself as a sector of an international proletariat. Not only immigration, but also runaway shops and industrial relocation generally, are issues which cut across national boundaries and reveal the material links of the U.S. proletariat with the proletariat of Latin America. From this perspective, it is clear that the political strategy of workers' movements on this continent must be based on understanding themselves as part of the international working class. While there is a material basis for increasing international proletarian unity in the long range, those same conditions have created short-range divisions within the U.S. proletariat and between the proletariats of different nations. This contradictory situation poses the political problems which must be addressed and resolved by any serious proletarian organization—in the United States, in Latin America, and throughout the world.

IMPLICATIONS FOR SOCIALIST CONSTRUCTION

Finally, we touch very briefly on the implications of the above for the countries engaging in socialist construction. The issue of class alliances and hegemony within them takes, to be sure, a different form in the workers' states, but that issue is not liquidated or automatically resolved by the existence of those states. During the period of socialist construction, the issues are totally redefined by the reality of a proletarian party in power and in control of the state apparatus. This is the fundamental difference between Chile under the Unidad Popular and Cuba today. For our continent, Cuba represents the first resolution of internal class struggle in the course of anti-imperialist struggle in Latin America in favor of the proletariat, and it reconfirms that proletarian hegemony is a necessary condition for any definitive challenge to or victory over imperialism. Nevertheless, even here, there are limits and constraints imposed by the fact that the Cuban Revolution (a revolution of national liberation) occurred within the capitalist world-economy, ninety miles from the leading core country. No one is more aware of these limitations than the Cuban government itself; hence its profound and thoroughgoing internationalism, most especially in Africa today.

Since we do not have an opportunity here to go into detail, we shall touch only briefly on the issues discussed above, in their manifestations for socialist construction in the world today:

(1) Class alliances and class struggle: We have seen above that the socialist countries by no means stand "outside" the global process of capital accumulation or the international capitalist division of labor—to the point that some of these countries house forms of runaway shops. Moreover, a number of them, beginning with the Soviet Union, have adopted the "American Plan" (Taylorization) for rapid industrialization, which brings with it the tendency to create capitalist relations of production. The contradiction is that they did so in order to survive and to compete with the established capitalist powers and imperialism. This reality poses the issue of control over the labor process, which arises as a proletarian demand "wherever an industrial proletariat formed by the 'American Plan' arises within the world-economy" (Dixon, 1978a: 52). Moreover, it feeds the growth of a stratum of state bureaucrat/managers functionally similar to the new petty-bourgeoisie, which enjoys relative privilege, and which acquires its own stake and vested interest in prolonging the necessary transition state of the dictatorship of the proletariat.

This is, no doubt, the course of the camp of the "capitalist roaders." Clearly then, the period of transition to socialism or socialist construction *is* a period of continuing class struggle. The nature of that struggle is decisively shaped by the fact of a proletarian party in power—and this is the source of the countervailing tendency or camp, i.e., the camp of the "socialist roaders," who are carrying forward the transition toward its historical objectives.

(2) Socialism in one country and proletarian internationalism: Nationalism in the socialist countries expresses itself as the doctrine of socialism in one country. Without attempting here to evaluate the long historical experience of socialism in one country, especially in the Soviet Union, we can state briefly that we view this too as a response *to the necessities* of constructing socialism within the capitalist world-system.

This necessity does, however, raise questions about what are the limitations on proletarian internationalism. At least such questions will ground us in material reality and prevent us from falling into idealistic expectations about proletarian internationalism. Proletarian internationalism is possible—but largely to the extent that it coincides with the necessities of national development. Therefore, it is from a country like Cuba, whose "national development" requires internationalism, that we have seen some of the clearest examples of proletarian internationalism (especially in Africa today). In these examples, we see the seed, the potential, for a broader socialist internationalism.

There is another respect too in which the "national development" of the socialist countries is not simply a matter of their national development. As Wallerstein (1979a: 293) put it,

> These various national thrusts to a change in structural position ... do affect, indeed over the long run do in fact transform the world-system. But they do so via the intervening variable of their impact on world-wide class consciousness of the proletariat.

In short, we do not share the pessimism of a number of analysts of socialist construction regarding the limitations of that construction in a capitalist world-system. True, the limits are very real. But even as they limit the possibilities within the particular country, on an international scale they are part of the process of the transition from capitalism to socialism—a process which has already begun—and they move that transition forward.

Moreover, the very contradictory dynamics of capitalist accumulation push forward the world transition. The new pattern of capital accumulation contains a very profound contradiction: to the extent that it is based on cheapening labor worldwide, it is bound to be plagued by overproduction and underconsumption crises. A basic contradiction of capitalism as a system is becoming less a periodic cyclical recurrence, and increasingly a permanent feature, thus creating a permanent crisis of sorts.

Finally, there is another area of contradiction, exemplified most clearly in recent times by the revolution in Iran. This revolution is the product of capitalist-style "modernization" and "development" in the semiperiphery. Recent events in Iran—and in Nicaragua—also make clear the error in viewing the system of capital accumulation and the capitalist international division of labor as a closed system controlled by the international bourgeoisie. Far from it: what happens in Iran, in El Salvador and Nicaragua, in Southern Africa, in Italy, in the United States really is the outcome of a struggle between two classes, *not* the outcome of what one class (the bourgeoisie) decides to impose on the other (the proletariat). For the workers' movement, the question is not whether to intervene in history, but how and where to intervene, and what are the weak points of the class enemy.

NOTES

1. The former view is laid out by Froebel et al., the latter by André Gunder Frank. See Frank's book review in *Synthesis,* III, 1 (Fall 1979).
2. The above analysis of immigration relies heavily on Castells' work.

REFERENCES

AFL-CIO (1977) Statements and Reports Adopted by the Executive Council, Bar Harbour, Florida, February 21-28.
BAIRD, P. and E. McCAUGHAN (n.d.) "Beyond the border." (unpublished)
BRAVERMAN, H. (1974) Labor and Monopoly Capital. New York: Monthly Review Press.
BODENHEIMER, S. J. (1969) "The bankruptcy of the social democratic movement in Latin America." New Politics (Winter).
--- (1970) "The social democratic ideology in Latin America: the case of Costa Rica's Partido Liberación Nacional." Caribbean Studies (October).
BUKHARIN, N. (1973) Imperialism and World Economy. New York: Monthly Review Press.
CASTELLS, M. (1975) "Immigrant workers and class struggles in advanced capitalism: the Western European experience." Politics and Society 5, 1: 36-44.
COLBY, W. (1977) U.S. Congressional conference on National Security, May 11-12, 1977.
COOK, A. (1977) "How illegal aliens pay as they go." New West (May 23).
DIXON, M. (1976a) "Proletarian vs. petty bourgeois socialism." Synthesis 1 (Summer).
--- (1976b) "The American petty bourgeoisie and socialism." Synthesis 1 (Fall).
--- (1976c) "In defense of Leninism: against social democracy." Synthesis 1 (Summer).
--- (1978a) "Abstract: the degradation of waged labor and class formation on an international scale." Synthesis 2 (Spring).
--- (1978b) "What's in a name?" Synthesis 2 (Spring).
FRANK, A. G. (1974) "World crisis, class struggle, and 1984." Delivered at the Eighth Congress of the International Sociological Association.
--- (1977a) "World crisis and underdevelopment." Contemporary Crisis 1.

––– (1977b) "Long live trans-ideological enterprise! The socialist economies in the capitalist international division of labor." Review 1 (Summer).

FROEBEL, F., J. HEINRICHS, and O. KREYE (1977) "The tendency toward a new international division of labor." Review 1 (Summer).

––– (1978a) "The new international division of labor." Social Science Information 17, 7.

––– (1978b) "Export-oriented industrialization of underdeveloped countries." Monthly Review (November).

HOPKINS, T. (1977) "Notes on class analysis and world-system." Review 1 (Summer).

––– and I. WALLERSTEIN (1977) "Patterns of development of the modern world-system." Review 1 (Fall).

Rebel Worker News Journal (1977) Volume 1 (May).

San Francisco Chronicle (1977) September 11.

SWEEZY, P. (1979) "On the new global disaster." Monthly Review (April).

TRAJTENBERG, R. (1978) "Transnacionales y Fuerza de Trabajo en la Periferia." Estudios ILET DEE/E/2, Mexico.

VUSKOVIC, P. (n.d.) "La Lucha del Tercer Mundo y la Aportación Latinoamericana." (unpublished)

––– and J. MARTINEZ (1977) "Once Proposiciones sobre la Situación de América Latina." Estudios Politicos 2 (October-December).

WALLERSTEIN, I. (1977) "How do we know class struggle when we see it?" Insurgent Sociologist 7 (Spring).

––– (1979a) "Class conflict in the capitalist world-economy," in The Capitalist World-Economy. Cambridge: Cambridge University Press.

––– (1979b) "World networks and the politics of world-economy," in A. H. Hawley (ed.) Societal Growth: Processes and Implications. New York: Free Press.

Chapter 12

CELTIC NATIONALISM IN BRITAIN: POLITICAL AND STRUCTURAL BASES

Charles C. Ragin

INTRODUCTION: NATIONAL AND SUBNATIONAL IDENTITIES

Social scientists have yet to provide a satisfactory account of subnationalisms such as ethnic separatism. The reason for this, I believe, is that because many, if not most, subnationalisms are ethnically based, social scientists have tried to use models of ethnic mobilization to explain ethnic subnationalism. Even those cases in which ethnicity is a very minor factor (e.g., Scotland) have been forced into the ethnic mobilization mold (e.g., by Hechter, 1975). I argue below that theories of nationalism do a better job of explaining ethnic subnationalism than theories of ethnic mobilization. I suggest further that many "ethno-nationalisms" are not nationalisms at all; they are examples of ethnic mobilization and are relevant to theories of ethnic mobilization, not to theories of nationalism.[1] I then develop a theory of subnationalism based on existing theories of nationalism and apply this theory to the Celtic subnationalisms in Britain.

Following Weber (1946), I argue that national identities are both politically and historically defined. They are politically defined in the sense that national identities link individuals (citizens) to national governments and thereby sanction the omnivorous activities of these governments. Indeed, the existence of a national identity can be seen as one of the essential features of a nation-state conceived ideal-typically.[2] It follows from this conceptualization of national identity that to change some essential, formal trait of a nation-state (e.g., from a fascistic to a democratic or from a unitary to a federal form of government) is also to alter the character of the national identity which links the territorially defined population to the nation-state. To impose a centralized, unitary government in Canada, for example, would surely alter the meaning of

Canadian national identity. This is not a causal argument; the point is simply that the way in which a national government is constituted and the formal structures of its governing imply a definition of what is and what is not national.

National identities are also historically defined. To claim a national identity, or for that matter an ethnic or cultural identity, is to claim a collective history. Obviously, for a particular event or set of events to effect an identity, these events must be broad in scope; that is, they must be large-scale historical events. The greater the reach of a particular set of events, the larger the collective identity the events define. The number of collective histories is infinite, as is the number of collective identities. Sometimes the different collectivities within a national entity share only a small portion of their respective histories, and it is this shared portion which constitutes a national collective history and contributes to a national collective identity. In other nation-states the sense of collective history may be much stronger, particularly if, for example, the collective history is one of frequent conflict with powerful neighbors.[3]

The same can be said of subnational identities, that they are politically and historically defined, with perhaps even greater force. The definition of a national identity in a modern nation-state is a definition of potential subnational identities, for the national identity also defines what is not national. Thus, the content of an existing national identity is responsible, in this sense, for existing subnational identities. In addition to variations in content, however, a national identity also may be more or less specific, and it may vary in intensity independently of variations in specificity or content. All such variations may affect the viability of a potential subnational identity.

The historically determined nature of large-scale identities is also relevant to subnational identities, for it is unlikely that the population contained within the territorial boundaries of a given political entity will possess a single collective history. Indeed, virtually every modern nation confronts historically induced cultural and ethnic heterogeneity. To the extent that existing, heterogeneous collective identities are independent of or at odds with each other, subnational identities are likely to coalesce. Territorially based identities are particularly favored because of the differences in territorial collective histories that are induced by variations in terrain, ecology, and adjacent collectivities.

NATIONALISM AND SUBNATIONALISM: CONTEXTUAL DIFFERENCES

While national and subnational identities are similar in that both are large-scale, collective identities that are politically and historically defined, it is necessary to distinguish between nationalism and subnationalism historically and formally. While nationalism is a persistent force in the modern world, the heyday of nationalist mobilization has passed (Smith, 1971). As an emergent world force, nationalism was associated with the creation of modern nation-states, first in the West and, more recently, in the Third World. Most modern states were created out of fragments of world or colonial empires; most, if not all, such empires have disintegrated. Nationalists, for the most part, therefore, confronted empires; subnationalists, however, confront modern nations and modern nationalisms. The problem for the subnationalist is not only to engender feelings of nationhood, but also to counter existing nations and national identities.

Conceived ideal-typically, nationalist mobilization involves the collective movement of at least part of a territorially defined population in possession of at least one common status attribute (e.g., a distinctive culture) toward the self-government of their area of residence. While many, if not most, nationalist movements conform to the ideal-typic conditions specified in the above formulation, most contemporary subnationalisms approximate these conditions less perfectly because of the difference in historical context mentioned above.

With respect to the requirement of common status identification, the experiences of subnationalist movements vary considerably. Though many contemporary subnationalist movements are ethnically based, ethnicity is not always a factor. Other status identities, such as an historically relevant, territorially based identity, often supply the necessary status distinction. It is difficult to establish in many cases that a common status identification existed prior to the formation of the subnationalist movement. One of the goals of every subnationalist movement is to heighten awareness of a particular status identification by creating cultural and ethnic distinctions where none may have existed before (Wallerstein, 1979: 186).

The collective goal of self-government is also problematic when applied to subnationalisms. Often this goal serves the subnationalist movement in much the same way that the vision of the socialist society serves working-class political movements—as a distant objective that is brushed aside when the opportunity for short-run practical gain arises. Thus, subnationalists may claim separation as their goal but then rejoice when a national government shows favoritism toward their constituency, even when this favoritism binds the subnational collectivity more firmly to the national government.

Of the three formal features of nationalist movements outlined above, territoriality is the most problematic. Rarely do all of the potential members of a subnationalist movement (i.e., those who might claim the subnational identity) reside in the prospective national territory. More importantly, it is rare that the present occupants of that territory uniformly would or could claim or accept the subnational identity. Thus, there are cases of territoriality without a widely accepted subnational identity, and, at the other extreme, there are cases of a well-defined subnational identity without a well-defined prospective national territory.

In many respects the territorial dimension is the most important of the three formal features discussed above. The importance of territoriality is apparent when the two hypothetical extremes of what might be called degree of territorial integrity of the subnational population are considered. At one extreme is territorial exclusivity; the subnational population occupies a separate territory. At the other extreme is territorial coincidence; the subnational population is dispersed throughout the larger national territory.

In a situation of territorial coincidence, the differences between the subnational population and the national population are likely to be described as ethnic or cultural differences since such markers are necessary for a subnational identity to persist. The conflict between the subnational population and the national population is also likely to be seen as ethnic, given the likelihood of individual-level conflict over scarce roles and resources. Given inequality between the two populations, those who claim the subnational identity are likely to favor the establishment of formal rules insuring an equitable allocation of scarce goods. Separatism, however, would not be much of an issue given the scale of the disruption that the separation of the two populations would entail. Furthermore, in situations of territorial coincidence a cultural division of labor is likely such that class cleavages overlay the ethnic cleavage. Once a cultural division of labor is disrupted, the pressure for particularistic rules insuring an equitable distribution of goods should increase (Nielsen, 1979).

In a situation of territorial exclusivity, however, the conflict between a national and a subnational population is much more likely to be defined as a national, as opposed to ethnic or cultural, conflict, and the conflict is much more likely to be seen as one involving the divergent interests of different territorially defined populations.[4] In a situation of territorial exclusivity it is much easier to point to qualitative disparities between the two populations (e.g., the absence of a university in the subnational area), and these qualitative inequities magnify the salience of quantitative inequities. Given qualitative and quantitative inequities and the political power differential associated with such inequities, the subnational population is more likely to favor separation from the national population than some show of particularism on the part of that government. While a particularistic allocation of national resources might satisfy subnationalists in the short run, in the long run such policies should increase the tension between the national and subnational populations, for members of the national population may feel that they are being forced to sacrifice for the subnational population.

TOWARD A THEORY OF SUBNATIONALISM

Most of the theories that have been used to analyze ethnic subnationalism are not theories of nationalism; they are theories of ethnic mobilization. What distinguishes these as theories of ethnic mobilization is their failure to consider territoriality. In the terminology developed above, these theories are relevant only to situations of territorial coincidence, for no allowance is made for the possibility of territorial dismemberment. These theories of ethnic mobilization include the developmental perspective, the reactive ethnicity perspective, and the ethnic competition perspective.

In the developmental perspective ethnicity is viewed as a primordial sentiment (Geertz, 1963) which should wither away in societies that experience significant structural differentiation (Parsons, 1975). In a modern setting, therefore, ethnic mobilization is seen as aberrant. This view of ethnic mobilization has been applied to the analysis of political cleavages by Lipset and Rokkan (1967: 1-64). They argue that political cleavages that are culturally based should be superseded by functional cleavages which reflect economic interests. This predominance of functional cleavages is seen as a consequence of social structural modernization, in general, and the Industrial Revolution, in particular (Alford, 1963).

In contrast with the developmental perspective which argues that social-structural modernization erodes ethnic affinity, the reactive ethnicity perspective argues that a particularistic allocation of roles and resources may preserve ethnic affinity in modern societies since a particularistic allocation can occur at any level of social structural differentiation (Gellner, 1969). This "cultural division of labor" (Hechter, 1975) can exist in an industrial society such that high status positions are reserved for members of the culturally dominant population, and members of the culturally subordinant population are relegated to low-status positions. Class mobilization does exist as an alternative to ethnic mobilization in societies with a cultural division of labor. However, should national working-class organization fail to meet the needs of the culturally subordinant lower strata, ethnic mobilization is likely (Hechter, 1975: 309).

The ethnic competition perspective argues that social-structural modernization affects ethnicity in two, apparently contradictory ways: (1) Modernization reduces ethnic diversity by eroding small-scale, ecologically bound identities. (2) Modernization increases the importance of large-scale ethnic identities by altering the conditions of competition in large systems (Hannan, 1979). Specifically, because the size of the most powerful competitor (e.g., the core in a nation-state) increases with modernization, organized resistance to the core will succeed only when such resistance is organized around large-scale identities. Competition is a key consideration in this perspective, for it is assumed that large-scale ethnic identities will be mobilized when ethnic groups are forced to compete for the same rewards and resources.

Again, these three perspectives address only questions related to ethnic mobilization. They do not address nationalism or subnationalism, nor do they address the question of territoriality. Above, I suggested two hypothetical extremes of territoriality, exclusivity and coincidence. These two extremes can be conceived as ideal-types, for both are exaggerations; that is, they are analytically useful utopias. Theories of ethnic mobilization are not relevant to situations approximating territorial exclusivity because: (1) questions of equality involve important qualitative considerations in addition to the quantitative considerations involved in cases of territorial coincidence; (2) the possibility of secession exists; (3) nationalist sentiments, which are distinct from ethnic and cultural sentiments, are likely to be a factor; and (4) the possibility that class conflict within the subnational population will impede subnational mobilization is present.[5]

Of these four considerations, the last one is a key consideration. The other three more or less define what distinguishes subnationalist mobilization from ethnic mobilization. The fourth is relevant to questions concerning the conditions which are conducive to subnationalist mobilization. This consideration provides a basis for the alternative perspective on subnationalism I develop below.

Few social scientists have addressed the fourth consideration above concerning the relationship between class and nationalist or subnationalist mobilization. The most notable exceptions are Nairn (1977) and Wallerstein (1974: 353). Nairn in his analysis of the twilight of the British state presents a rudimentary theory of nationalism relevant to subnationalism. In a nutshell, he argues that nationalism is always a joint product of external pressure and an internal *balance* of class forces. External pressure is broadly conceived in Nairn's framework to take into account a variety of exogenetic forces. Primary among these, however, Nairn argues, are processes associated with the world capitalist economy. He states that nationalism as a social movement "typically ... has arisen in societies confronting a dilemma of uneven development—'backwardness' or colonization—where conscious middle class elites have sought massive mobilization to right the balance" (1977: 25). Wallerstein (1974: 353), essentially in agreement with Nairn on the structural origins of the nationalist impulse, argues that the local dominant strata of an exploited area attempt to avert internal class conflict by creating local solidarity against external exploiters. Often, according to Wallerstein, the creation of internal solidarity involves establishing distinctive cultural "traditions" where none may have existed before. While the potential for class conflict is the major factor which may provoke the mobilization of solidarity against the outside by local dominant strata, this potential for class conflict cannot be a realized potential (Nairn, 1977: 27). Otherwise, the probability of successful cross-class mobilization is greatly diminished.

Applied to subnationalism in countries that approximate the model of territorial exclusivity, this perspective predicts that the dominant strata of the subnational population will side with national dominant strata during periods of class conflict. If class conflicts subside for an extended period, however, and appear to be more or less dormant, subnationalism may become attractive to the local dominant strata of the subnational area. For the subnational alternative to become attractive, however, this decline in overt class conflict must coincide temporally with external pressures of the sort suggested by Nairn and Wallerstein. The range of pressures which may contribute to the viability of a subnational appeal is great. They include changes which are intranational in scope, though exogenetic to the subnational area, as well as changes international in scope which may or may not be mediated through the nation-state. While many of these external pressures no doubt originate in the world capitalist system and are economic in nature, to political actors they may appear to be intranational and politically based. In any event, these external pressures must be such that they contribute to the belief that national and subnational interests are divergent.

Below, I apply this rough outline of a perspective to Celtic subnationalism in Britain. This application involves primarily the presentation of various statistical data relevant to (1) the preconditions for subnational mobilization specified above and (2) the contemporary class and political bases of Celtic nationalism in Britain. First I show that there has been a decline in the intensity of the expression of class conflict in the political arena in Britain. This establishes that a favorable class climate for subnationalist mobilization exists in Celtic Britain. Second, I illustrate an intranational process of neo-peripheralization which constitutes an external pressure of the sort described by Nairn and Wallerstein. Thirdly, I present contemporary survey data concerning the relationship between class mobilization and subnationalist mobilization. These data show that most gains for Celtic nationalist parties have occurred at the expense of the Conservative Party and that Celtic subnationalism has yet to disrupt Labour support or working-class support for Labour in Celtic Britain.

CELTIC NATIONALISM IN BRITAIN

Britain is a multinational state (Rose, 1974). The great majority of people in Wales think of themselves as Welsh first and British second; the parallel thing is true of the residents of Scotland. The English, on the other hand, acknowledge that the Welsh and the Scots are British, but reserve the label English for those specifically of English descent. Both Scotland and Wales were at one time independent of England. Wales was joined to England via dynastic inheritance. The union was not achieved without considerable resistance, however, before and after the union. Agrarian revolts were common in Wales throughout the Middle Ages, continuing into the nineteenth century. Scotland has a longer history of political independence from England. Scotland existed as a partially independent kingdom until 1707, being joined gradually to England from 1603. Though Scotland existed as a separate entity throughout most of the period prior to the union, it was a weakly integrated area with periphery problems of its own. Rebellion in the Highlands was not finally quelled until 1745, after the Union of 1707.

There have been flurries of nationalism in Wales and Scotland for over a century. These flurries subsided after the First World War following the extension of the franchise to all adult males and the subsequent mobilization of the working class in Britain by the Labour Party.[6] (Before 1918, the majority of English and Celtic workers were not permitted to vote.) Prior to this period most Celtic nationalist sentiment was expressed through the Liberal Party, mostly in the form of an appeal for "home-rule all round," sparked primarily by Irish nationalism. With the decline of the Liberal Party, however, political expressions of Celtic nationalism also declined.

The contemporary Celtic nationalist movements are not newcomers to the political scene. The Plaid Cymru (Party of Wales) was formed in 1926; the Scottish Nationalist Party in 1934. However, these parties gained only minimal and scattered electoral support until the 1960s. The greatest surge in support for the nationalist parties occurred between 1964 and 1970. (Support for the Scottish Nationalist Party continued to grow in the 1970s following the discovery of North Sea oil.)

Why this resurgence of Celtic nationalism in the 1960s? The rudimentary theory of subnationalism developed above suggests that this resurgence of Celtic nationalism is due to a conjunction of two trends, a decline in the salience of class in the British polity as a whole and the rise of exogenetic pressures which have increased the attractiveness of the subnational alternative. Further, this perspective argues that since Celtic subnationalism has dominant strata origins, Celtic nationalist political gains must occur primarily at the expense of the Conservative Party and dominant strata support for the Conservative Party. We turn now to an examination of these issues.

THE DECLINE OF CLASS

Britain has experienced in common with other Western countries a decline in overt political manifestations of class conflict. Lipset and Rokkan, (1967: 50), for example, have argued that the British experience fits the class-integrated polity model very closely: "the most unified and most 'domesticable' working class movements emerged in Protestant-dominated countries with the smoothest histories of nation building: Britain, Denmark, Sweden." Though historically class antagonisms have been more intense in Celtic Britain than in England, especially during the interwar period, such antagonisms have decline in both areas since the Second World War.

In Britain, the decline of class antagonisms has been reflected, in part, in a weakening of the relationship between class and party support (Alford, 1963; Butler and Stokes, 1969). More significant and more indicative of the nature of this decline is the fact that support for the Communist Party has dwindled. In Table 12.1, I show the volume of support for the Communist Party in England and in Scotland and Wales (combined) over time. I report the total vote for the Communist Party, the number of Communist Party candidates, the average Communist poll, and the ratio of the average Communist poll in Celtic Britain to that of England. Data are presented from 1931, the election which inaugurates Labour-Conservative dominance in Britain, to 1974. These data show a steady decline in the average poll of Communist candidates in both Celtic Britain and England, especially since the 1945 to 1950 period, when the Labour Party first won a majority of seats in Parliament and formed a government on its own. Of special relevance is the last column in Table 12.1, which shows the ratio of the average Communist poll in Scotland and Wales to the average Communist poll in England. These figures show that while Communist Party candidates have generally fared better in Scotland and Wales than in England, the magnitude of the difference has decreased: Communist candidates at one time received about twice as many votes in Celtic constituencies; since the 1960s they have fared only slightly better than Communist candidates in English constituencies. Overall, these data show that class imagery has waned in Britain as a whole and that its appeal has decreased most where it was once strongest, in Scotland and Wales.

THE NEO-PERIPHERALIZATION OF CELTIC BRITAIN

The second joint precondition specified in the tentative theory of subnationalism presented above is external pressure. A decline in the intensity of class conflict (i.e., the submersion of class antagonisms) in and of itself is not sufficient to encourage subnationalist mobilization; some

TABLE 12.1 Communist Party Support in England and in Celtic Britain, 1931–1974

	England			Scotland and Wales			
Election Year	Number of Votes	Number of Candidates	Average Poll	Number of Votes	Number of Candidates	Average Poll	Ratio Average Poll
1931	21,452	15	1,430	53,372	11	4,852	3.39
1935	0	0	0	27,117	2	13,558	*
1945	53,754	15	3,584	49,026	6	8,171	2.28
1950	55,158	80	689	36,607	20	1,831	2.65
1951	7,745	5	1,549	13,895	5	2,779	1.79
1955	15,405	11	1,400	17,739	6	2,956	2.11
1959	12,204	10	1,220	18,692	8	2,336	1.91
1964	24,824	22	1,128	21,618	14	1,544	1.37
1966	33,093	34	973	28,999	23	1,261	1.30
1970	20,103	35	574	17,867	23	776	1.35
1974F	13,324	23	579	19,418	26	747	1.29

* Ratio cannot be computed.

external pressure must make the subnationalist alternative attractive to the subnational population.

In many respects, external pressure has been virtually a constant feature of Celtic life. Both Scotland and Wales in the 1800s became dependent, heavy industrial appendages of the core English economy (Hechter, 1975). In part, this pattern of dependent industrial development accounts for the greater role of working-class mobilization and action in Celtic Britain. Support for both the Labour Party and the Communist Party is greater in Scotland and Wales, and industrial class conflict has been more pronounced (Pelling, 1958, 1968). Indeed, if not for the strong class-based support the Labour Party receives in Celtic Britain, Great Britain would have known few, if any, Labour governments (Kinnear, 1968).

Since the Second World War, however, the place of Scotland and Wales in the British national economy has changed. Heavy industries and extractive industries have declined in importance throughout Britain, most markedly in Wales and Scotland where they were once strongest. Many nationwide industries have attempted to modernize and have closed down outdated plants. Outdated plants are, of course, located in the older industrial areas, mostly in Scotland, Wales, and the northern half of England. Thus, Celtic Britain (in common with the older industrial areas of England) has experienced a fundamental alteration in industrial and occupational composition.

If this change in industrial and occupational composition meant only that Scotland and Wales have been modernized at the same pace as the South of England and put on an equal footing, this would hardly constitute an external pressure sufficient to provoke subnational mobilization. However, the void left by the departure of traditional heavy industries has not been filled in the same manner throughout Britain. While it is true that the tertiary sector has expanded in Celtic Britain, as it has in England, this expansion has not involved an increase in the proportion of middle-class occupations. In England, particularly in the South of England, the expansion of the tertiary has involved an expansion of technical, administrative, and professional employment. In Wales and Scotland, however, the expansion of the tertiary has involved mostly an expansion of middle- and lower-level service occupations.

I illustrate these changes in industrial composition with occupational data in Table 12.2. I report in this table the magnitude of the differences between Scotland and Wales (combined) and England on two measures, the proportion of the adult, male labor force employed in heavy industries (including extractive industries) and the proportion of the adult, male labor force employed in middle-class occupations (professional, technical, administrative, and commercial, excluding clerical and sales). In this table positive scores indicate the degree of overrepresentation of an occupation

TABLE 12.2 Differences Between England and Celtic Britain in Occupational Composition, 1881–1971

Year	Proportion Employed in Heavy Industries*	Proportion Employed in Middle-Class Occupations*
1881	.067	(−.002)
1891	.074	(−.000)
1901	.136	(−.008)
1911	.136	(−.030)
1921	.115	(−.021)
1931	.092	−.027
1951	.059	−.045
1961	(.046)	−.046
1971	(.041)	−.048

*The scores in this column indicate the magnitude of the differences between England and Celtic Britain, net of differences in urbanization. Differences in occupational composition which are not statistically significant are reported in parentheses.

in Celtic Britain; negative scores indicate the degree of underrepresentation. I have removed with regression techniques the differences between Celtic Britain and England in occupational composition due to differential urbanization. The figures reported in Table 12.2 are based on decennial census data, 1881 to 1971.

The figures reported in Table 12.2 show that: (1) employment in heavy industries in Celtic Britain has only recently declined to the English level (since the Second World War); and (2) employment in middle-class occupations has declined in Celtic Britain, relative to England, since the interwar period. Overall, these patterns support the argument that while the heavy industrial sector no longer dominates the economy of Celtic Britain, its decline does not represent a convergence of Scotland and Wales with England in terms of occupational composition. Indeed, the present Celtic deficiency in percentage employed in middle-class occupations is relatively recent in origin and appears to be growing.

The external pressure on Celtic Britain, therefore, can be viewed as a structural pressure in the sense that it originates in the cross-regional economic bonds which link Celtic Britain to England. Specifically, these bonds induce distortions in the Celtic economies making them complementary to the English economy. Britain's decline in international status is reflected in the two patterns illustrated above, for the decline of heavy industry (much of which at one time was export oriented) and the stunted growth of middle-class occupations are national British patterns which have been amplified in Celtic areas.[7]

SUBNATIONALISM AND CLASS POLITICS

Social scientists usually argue that subnationalist mobilization implies a denial of class interests on the part of members of the subnational population. This argument is based on the belief that class interests are particular interests and that they oppose national interests which are general interests. The tentative theory of subnationalism outlined above, however, argues that subnationalist mobilization is likely to be the child of "conscious middle class elites" (Nairn's term) or "local dominant strata" (Wallerstein's term). This framework thus suggests that subnationalism is consistent with the class interests of the upper strata of the subnational population vis-à-vis both the subnational lower strata and external, national and international actors and processes and that the progress of subnationalist mobilization will depend on the successful submergence of class antagonisms.

According to this reasoning, to support one of the parties sympathetic to Celtic interests is to support a Celtic alternative to the national Conservative Party. In Scotland and Wales to vote for any one of the third parties, the Plaid Cymru in Wales, the Scottish Nationalist Party in Scotland, or the Liberal Party in either Wales or Scotland, is to support a party sympathetic to Celtic interests. (Voting Liberal in Celtic Britain is qualitatively different from voting Liberal in England, for the Liberal Party advocates greater autonomy for Scotland and Wales and thus fashions itself as a less strident subnationalist party for both Scotland and Wales. In England it provides no such alternative to the thoroughly English and national Conservative Party.) The perspective developed above thus argues that Celtic nationalist gains must occur at the expense of the Conservative Party and Celtic middle-class support for the Conservative Party.

One way to address this relationship between subnationalist mobilization and class mobilization is to examine differences between Celtic Britain and England in aggregate patterns of party support. Specifically, if it is true that the effect of Celtic nationalism has been to weaken the position of the Conservative Party and to decrease the Conservative Party's class support, then a comparison of Celtic Britain with England should show: (1) greater support for the third parties (i.e., the Celtic nationalist parties and the Liberal Party) and less support for the Conservative Party in Celtic Britain than in England, and (2) a lower proportion of the middle class supporting the Conservative Party in Celtic Britain than in England. Additionally, to the extent that Celtic nationalist mobilization has not disrupted the historical position of the Labour Party in Celtic Britain, one would expect greater support for the Labour Party and a larger proportion of the working class supporting Labour in Celtic Britain than in England.

TABLE 12.3 Party Support and Degree of Class Support for the Labour Party and the Conservative Party in England, Scotland, and Wales, 1966–1970

Measure	England	Scotland	Wales
Proportion supporting Conservative Party	.529	.362	.342
Proportion supporting Labour Party	.362	.405	.503
Proportion supporting third parties	.109	.233	.155
Proportion supporting Celtic nationalist parties	–	.170	.049
Proportion of middle class supporting Conservative Party	.690	.551	.512
Proportion of working class supporting Labour Party	.452	.480	.592

Data relevant to these arguments are presented in Table 12.3. These data are based on an aggregation of a series of National Opinion Poll surveys conducted in 200 British constituencies (170 English constituencies, 19 Scottish constituencies, and 11 Welsh constituencies) between 1966 and 1970.[8] The data are constituency-level, but they are based on aggregations of individual-level responses. The number of respondents per constituency varies from about 200 to about 500. I computed the following measures with these data:

(1) Class-support measures
  (a) Percentage of the working class supporting the Labour Party
  (b) Percentage of the middle class supporting the Conservative Party

(2) Aggregate levels of party support
  (a) Percentage of eligible voters supporting the Labour Party
  (b) Percentage of eligible voters supporting the Conservative Party
  (c) Percentage of eligible voters supporting the third parties
  (d) Percentage of eligible voters supporting nationalist parties (Scotland and Wales only)

The figures reported in Table 12.3 confirm the aggregate patterns predicted above. Labour support, third-party support and working-class support for the Labour Party are greater in Celtic Britain than in England, while Conservative support and middle-class support for the Conservative Party are less. These data support the contention that the Celtic nationalist parties provide local alternatives to the British national Conservative Party and have not yet dented Labour support or working-class support for the

Labour Party. While it is true that these comparisons of England and Celtic Britain are static comparisons, they illustrate dramatically the obstacles faced by the Celtic nationalists, for Celtic Britain remains solidly in the Labour camp. These findings support the rudimentary theory of subnationalism advanced above. This theory argues that the local dominant strata of a subnational area are faced with a choice between alignment with national conservative forces and subnationalism. In the late 1960s, at least, it is clear that subnationalism in Celtic Britain was fueled by defections from national conservative forces.

DISCUSSION

In this paper I have presented a rudimentary theory of subnationalism based on existing theories of nationalism. This theory emphasizes territoriality, the existence of class cleavages within a territorially based subnational population, and the choice between alignment with national conservative forces and subnationalism faced by the dominant strata of the subnational population. Further, I have argued that the subnational alternative becomes a viable alternative only given a submergence of class cleavages within the subnational population and the existence of some external pressure which increases the attractiveness of the subnationalist alternative. I then applied this perspective to the Celtic nationalism in Britain.

The results of the British general election of 1979 support the interpretation of Celtic nationalisms I have advanced. In this election the Celtic nationalists fared very poorly. I argue that their poor showing is due to the strongly anti-Labour and antisocialist stance taken by the Conservatives during the election. This position drove voters, Celtic and English, away from third parties and back to the two main (British national) class parties. Paradoxically, this turn of events suggests that the Conservatives can best combat the Celtic nationalists by maintaining strong class imagery, even though this imagery increases Labour's support in Celtic Britain. In England, the Conservative Party can use class and (English) national appeals to gain support. In Celtic Britain, however, the Conservatives can only use class imagery to boost their support, for the Conservative Party has no claim to the title national party in either Scotland or Wales.[9] Should the salience of class imagery again subside, the Celtic nationalists should again win the support of large number of Celtic voters.

NOTES

1. Wallerstein (1979) uses the term "ethno-nationalisms" to cover two very different kinds of action. The first kind, which he argues is more or less core-specific,

results from a cultural division of labor in the cities. The second kind, which he argues is more or less periphery-specific, results from the political subordination of a culturally distinct, territorially specific group. I argue that (1) these are very different phenomena and require very different theories, and (2) it is a mistake to see the former as core-specific and the latter as periphery-specific. (Wallerstein [1979: 188] acknowledges this latter difficulty.)

2. I use the term nation-state timidly, realizing the ambiguities often associated with it. An ideal-typic methodological strategy, however, allows a heuristic approach to the use of concepts that are only approximated by empirical configurations.

3. Weber's (1946: 171-179) writings on the nation largely have been ignored by social scientists. This is unfortunate, for they clarify issues concerning the variability of national identities.

4. Ecologically based economic differences and conflicting orientations toward the world economy can induce such divergent interests. Consider, for example, the U.S. South, especially prior to the Civil War.

5. In situations of territorial coincidence the overall dominance of the upper strata of the dominant, national population will be apparent to the subordinate strata of the subnational population. This reduces the likelihood that the upper strata of the subnational population will be viewed as possible class enemies by the lower strata of the subnational population.

6. This historical pattern is consistent with the perspective I have advanced in this paper.

7. Myrdal (1970) argues that a decline in international economic status can induce backwash effects such that the peripheral areas and sectors of the declining national economy must bear the brunt of this decline.

8. Note that these surveys were conducted during the period which saw the greatest growth in Celtic nationalist support.

9. National conservative parties in general attempt to maintain a class image and at the same time maintain the impression that they stand for the good of the whole nation and not for the good of any particular class of citizens (e.g., workers). This claim to represent national interests often falls on deaf ears if sizeable subnational populations exist (as in Britain).

REFERENCES

ALFORD, R. (1963) Party and Society: The Anglo-American Democracies. Chicago: Rand McNally.
BUTLER, D. and D. STOKES (1969) Political Change in Britain. New York: Saint Martin's.
GEERTZ, C. (1963) "The integrative revolution: primordial sentiments, and civic politics in the new states," pp. 105-157 in C. Geertz (ed.) Old Socieities and New States. New York: Free Press.
GELLNER, E. (1969) Thought and Change. Chicago: University of Chicago Press.
HANNAN, M. (1979) "The dynamics of ethnic boundaries in modern states," in M. Hannan and J. Meyer (eds.) National Development and the World System. Chicago: University of Chicago Press.
HECHTER, M. (1975) Internal colonialism: the Celtic fringe in British national development, 1536-1966. London: Routledge & Kegan Paul.
KINNEAR, M. (1968) The British Voter. New York: Cornell University Press.

LIPSET, S. M. and S. ROKKAN (1967) Party Systems and Voter Alignments. New York: Free Press.

MYRDAL, G. (1970) The Challenge of World Poverty. New York: Pantheon.

NAIRN, T. (1977) "The twilight of the British state." New Left Review 101-102: 3-61.

NIELSEN, F. (1979) "The Flemish movement in Belgium after World War II: a dynamic analysis." Unpublished paper, Department of Sociology, University of Chicago.

PARSONS, T. (1975) "Some theoretical considerations on the nature and trends of change in ethnicity," pp. 56-71 in N. Glazer and D. Moynihan (eds.) Ethnicity: Theory and Experience. Cambridge: Harvard University Press.

PELLING, H. (1958) The British Communist Party. London: Black.

--- (1968) Popular politics and society in late Victorian England. New York: Saint Martin's.

ROSE, R. (1974) Politics in England. Boston: Little, Brown.

SMITH, A. (1971) Theories of Nationalism. New York: Harper & Row.

WALLERSTEIN, I. (1974) The Modern World-System. New York: Academic Press.

--- (1979) The Capitalist World-Economy. New York: Cambridge University Press.

WEBER, M. (1946) From Max Weber: Essays in sociology. New York: Oxford University Press.

Chapter 13

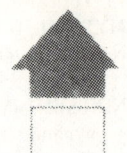

STATE-BUILDING AND ETHNIC STRUCTURES: DEPENDENCE ON INTERNATIONAL CAPITALIST PENETRATION

Cynthia H. Enloe

INTRODUCTION: THE ANALYTICAL USES OF ETHNICITY

To understand how the world-system becomes a system we need to pinpoint those critical vehicles through which contemporary states are integrated into the international political economy. We need also to grasp state elites' motivations for utilizing a particular vehicle. The following discussion also suggests under what conditions one such vehicle for international integration can provide a basis for resisting (only occasionally successfully) such state-fostered penetration. The vehicle examined here is ethnic communalism. Ethnicity is a distinctive form of collective action and ideology that is often dismissed by observers as either analytically obsolete or deceptive—i.e., in the 1970s ethnicity is presumably no longer a useful explanatory concept or, perhaps more dangerous, a concept that when employed only diverts observers from dynamic realities fueling state expansion and world-system integration.

The argument pursued here is that the relationship between a given state structure and the interethnic structure on which it is based is a key determinant of both quality and depth of international penetration in a particular country. The level of state-building (institutionalization, organizational differentiation, spatial scope, and degree of centralization) and the level of interethnic differentiation and ethnic politicization vary. State-building and ethnic differentiation and politicization are, in other words, historical phenomena. Both the state and any given ethnic group must be seen as dynamic, as historical. Just *when* the content and autonomy of state and ethnic group(s) and the relationship between them are such that they foster integration into the world-system (thus expanding the latter's scope) is the question we are addressing here.[1]

In the latter half of the 1970s some countries in which the levels of state-building and ethnic politicization are such that they encourage international capitalist penetration are: the United Kingdom, Canada, Peru, Trinidad, Sudan, Soviet Union, Philippines, Liberia, South Africa, Kenya, Brazil, Zaire, Indonesia, Lebanon, Burma. Among those in which the patterns are either less clear or more fluid, but whose position in the international capitalist system nonetheless may be clarified by taking explicit account of this state structure-ethnic structure relationship are: France, Spain, Algeria, Nigeria, Vietnam, Iran, Mexico, Saudi Arabia, the United States.

Most state structures develop (are elaborated, centralized, legitimized, expanded) when statist strategists attend not only to the variety of ethnic groups in the territory of would-be jurisdiction, but to the relationships within and between those ethnic groups. The resultant ethnic structure on which a developed state rests is most starkly revealed in state military and police security formulas (Enloe, 1980, 1979b). Some groups are treated by state-builders as dispensable (literally), some as marginally useful and unthreatening; other groups are deemed valuable but only for unskilled labor and cannon fodder; still others are seen by state builders to possess resources needed by the expanding state but are not considered sufficiently loyal or assimilated to be fully trusted; finally, one or two ethnic groups are conceived of by expansive but insecure state-builders not only as intrinsically identified with the state ideologically but as strategically important to the maintenance of state-defined order. Such a pattern of ethnic group relationships to the central state, of course, can change over time: trust, utility, and loyalty—these are slippery attributes in most state systems.[2]

The entire structure of interethnic relations—to the state and to each other—is the most useful reference point for comprehending state-ethnic dynamics and their implications for international economic penetration. It is not enough, for instance, to determine whether the internal colonial model best captures the relationship between the French Canadians and the Canadian state, or between Bretons and the French state. To comprehend the foundations of the Canadian state at any particular time one must examine the relationships of dependence, alliance, dominance, and isolation between French, English, Indians, Eskimos, Ukrainians, West Indians in Canada and how those relationships consolidate or undermine the power of the Canadian state.[3] Likewise, the strategies by which the French state (Bourbon, Jacobin, and Gaullist) has been developed are revealed by looking not just at the internal colonization of the Bretons, but at the particular patterns of marginalization, absorption, and domination that relate Parisian French, Corsicans, Basques, Alsatians, Occitainians, and, now, Algerians, Italians, and Turks to the French state.[4] No ethnic group's "ethnicity"—the content of its shared beliefs and values—will be stagnant; it too must be sensitively monitored. In this sense, ethnography still has much to offer to students of the world-system's expansion or contraction.

The tendency for a state to increase its structural autonomy is constrained by its persisting dependence upon a hierarchical class structure, with the dominant class having particular access to, and stake in the state as currently structured and legitimized. In addition, states in a great many countries are inhibited in their autonomist tendencies by reliance on a particular interethnic structure, with one ethnic group (especially its own upper class) enjoying special access to, and stake in the state as then organized and state elites drawing operational and ideological sustenance from that special relationship.

Ethnicity-state relationships, like *class-state* relationships, limit the autonomy of most states. What is more, those two sets of relationships—structurally interactive but analytically distinctive—can provide important incentives for state elites to actively encourage the penetration of international capital for the sake of sustaining the state in a form that insures that a given ethnic group, class, or "eth-class" keeps its privileged position in the state structure.

Which ethnic groups are most likely to encourage state policies that open up the country to foreign investments and extraction? They seem to be those ethnic groups which (1) are themselves internally stratified by class, (2) see themselves challenged by other groups but are dependent for capital and technology on the state since they cannot accumulate those resources within their own community, (3) have achieved control of the apparatus of a state which, at the time of initial control, still has insufficient resources for rapid economic growth, (4) control states that embrace within their established jurisdictions labor or natural resources economically attractive to foreign capital.

I explore these queries and theses below through, principally, a report on international capital's role in slave-ethnicity relationships in Malaysia, with an addendum on analogous patterns in Indonesia and the Philippines. These are of course "state-focused" discussions. The processes under review, require as well, however, "M.N.C.-focused" discussions, and so the final few observations concern Del Monte's operations in Kenya, the Philippines, Mexico, and the United States (Hawaii).

INTERNATIONAL CAPITAL'S ROLE IN STATE ETHNIC DESIGN

In the last decade Malaysian state-building elites have altered their perceptions of what sort of ethnic structure best supports the state. In so doing, they provide us with an unusual opportunity not only to clarify the ethnic structure concept but also to see the role of international capital in consolidating the state on top of an ethnic structure. However, highlighting the Malaysian case does not mean that Malaysia is unique either in its state reliance on a particular ethnic structure or in the utilization of foreign investment to consolidate and reconsolidate that relationship. Rather, this brief examination of Malaysia should suggest avenues for extended fruitful political analysis of Indonesia, the Philippines, Kenya, Canada, South Africa, Brazil, Zaire, and other countries where today international capitalist penetration is the key dynamic in expansion of the world system.

Malaysia typically is discussed by students of ethnic pluralism because its several ethnic groups seem so clearly "ethnic"; they have collective identities, communal structures, distinguishable cultural packages (not just racial distinctions) to mark intergroup boundaries. Furthermore, the politics of interethnic relations seem to have played determinant roles in the politics of precolonial, colonial, and postcolonial state-building.

The ethnic structure of any country has at least two important dimensions: (1) the patterns of interaction between groups differentiated by subjectively acknowledged, culturally-derived collective identities; (2) the patterns of interaction within each of the given ethnic groups (sex, class, region, language dialect all can shape such intraethnic patterns). Along the first dimension, the sorts of interaction are differentiated by frequency and intensity of intergroup activities and also by levels of status and power stratification. A standing cliché in Malaysian studies was that the peninsular (Sabah and Sarawak, the two Borneo states are usually omitted) ethnic structure was such that in Malaysia there were three ethnic groups: Chinese, Malay, and Indian. Each had not only subjectively salient cultural differentiations that were not captured by simply noting their racial distinctions, but each also had significant degrees of intragroup social organization. Each group, according to the standard portrait, associated with the other two reluctantly and distrustingly, mainly when pushed into such interaction by foreign actors—colonial administrators, plantation managers. Aboriginal ethnic groups on the peninsula were ignored; they were beyond the "frontier," becoming salient only during wartime. By the time of political decolonization in 1957, the three acknowledged ethnic groups were stratified, but in a dual structure of stratification. Convention had it that Chinese "controlled the economy"; Malays "controlled the political system"; Indians either were at the bottom rung of both economic and political ladders, as rubber estate workers, or were perched close to the top of the ladders, discreetly as professionals, and rarely as powerful civil servants, cabinet members, bankers, or plantation owners.

Class stratification occurred inside as well as between ethnic groups in Malaysia. And it has been intraethnic class relations that have been especially important in shaping state building strategies and state-international capital relationships in the last twenty years. Ethnographic works revealed, for instance, that it wasn't the "Chinese" who "controlled the economy"; it was a group of powerful Chinese entrepreneurs to whom poorer Chinese deferred but also often resented. Chinese tin miners, rubber tappers, and small shopowners did not "control the economy." Likewise, within the Malay community it was clear that there was, and for generations had been, notable class stratification. Malay class stratification was even more ideologically explicit than that among Malaysian Chinese because it was justified in terms of the special protective role of the royal families of the peninsula's nine Malay sultans who had been bolstered by the British and thus survived to occupy the highest position in the intra-Malay class stratification.[5] Indian intragroup differentiations were hard to miss because of the unmistakeable structure of the rubber plantations and the persistence of some caste sensitivities among Hindu Indians. The British colonial state and the international capital (chiefly in tin and rubber) that it fostered and protected utilized these intraethnic class division as well as intergroup ethnic divisions to create the structure most amenable to political order and economic profit.

The postcolonial state was in part a continuation of the British colonial apparatus. It was not dismantled by either the Japanese occupation or a nationalist war; in fact the colonial state on the eve of independence expanded in order to suppress an insurgency by Malaysian Chinese-led Communists. The Malaysian state in the 1950s had a civil service with considerable training and social status and a special access accorded at the top to Malays. It had a military and police that were institutionally separate and equal (thanks to the police role fostered by the British strategists during the 1948-1960 emergency), which also gave a special access, in ranks and officer corps, for Malays. It had a federal structure derived from the British practice of bolstering and using Malay sultans for rule on the peninsula. What the postindependence Malaysia political leaders added to this was a party system dominated by a tri-communal alliance led by politicians with close ties either to the civil service and military or to local business, whose common English education enabled them to deal with each other (and British business, which remained) while keeping their respective party rank and files separated. This state was bureaucratic, only mildly expansive, based on a legitimizing ideology of cultural pluralism, with Malays as "first among equals."

May 13, 1969 changed both the political leaders' notion of the country's ethnic structure and their prognosis for what a state would have to be in the future. For on May 13, shortly after the national parliamentary elections which saw a serious challenge to each of the three communal parties in the alliance, intercommunal violence flared in the capital, Kuala Lumpur, on a scale more alarming than any since independence. Moreover, it seemed to postriot state analysts that the riots were sparked by urban Malays who were at least as disaffected from their own political elite who spoke for them in state matters through the United Malay National Organization (U.M.N.O.), as they were from the Malaysian Chinese and Indians who appeared to dominate the economic life in the urban sectors of the country. What the riots of May 1969 revealed was that the interethnic structure was not only comprised of interethnic relations, but at least as importantly of intraethnic class relations and ethnic group-state relations. That is, *ethnicity* was having the effect of politicizing class and state relations.

In the decade since those riots the Malaysian state elite has taken deliberate steps to re-entrench the state by (1) expanding the state's own institutional capacities, (2) reordering class relations among the Malays, and (3) altering interethnic (esp. Malay-Chinese) relations in such a way that Malays would believe their conditions were vastly improving, while Chinese would not feel so alienated as to mobilize against the state. All three elements in this state strategy called for increased but transformed international capitalist penetration. Foreign loans and investments would have to provide more income and more modern sector employment to Malays. At the same time, the capitalist penetration would be transformed so that more than in the past could be channeled by Malaysian state officials in ways that complemented their own statist needs. These goals and strategies to achieve those ends were incorporated into the Second and Third Malaysia Plans (the latter covers 1976-1980). By 1990, so the Malaysian—mainly Malay—state elites pledged to Malaysians, especially to their crucial Malay constituents (45% of the population), there would be a new ethnic structure in the country; it would restabilize the state so shaken by the interethnic riots of May 1969.[6]

By 1979 the ethnic structure and the state structure, and the relationship between them, did look different. But these differences are essentially of degree; the post-1969 changes in the ethnic and state structures extend certain tendencies already present in earlier state-ethnic patterns. First, the post-1969 ethnic structure never was one in which the Chinese (35% of the population), the entire community *or* its business class, controlled the Malaysian economy. At the launching of the New Economic Plan with the Second Malaysia Plan, foreign companies already owned 60% of capital shares in Malaysia. Certainly Chinese household income averages were significantly above the Malay household average and while the great majority of Malaysian households officially categorized as poor were ethnically Malay; still, the only sector of the productive economy controlled by Chinese interests was construction. Tin, rubber, import-export trading, banking, timber sectors, all contained Chinese companies, but as a whole were foreign controlled by companies some of which had been in Malaysia since the beginning of British rule (Snodgrass, 1979; Lim, 1977; Rowley, 1977; Edwards, 1977). Thus what changed in the country's ethnic structure between 1969 and 1979 was how it was perceived by Malay state leaders.

Less and less did the Malay leadership of U.M.N.O. see the necessity of courting the Chinese. They could give to Malays some of those important cabinet portfolios formerly reserved to Chinese leaders with close ties to the Chinese business community. One of the most important portfolios taken from the Chinese and given to a Malay was the Ministry of Finance. Furthermore, splits along class lines within the Chinese community were newly appreciated by Malay state elites. Rather than presuming that the former Chinese partner in the alliance, the Malayan Chinese Association (M.C.A.), could control the Chinese community on its own through its connections with large Chinese business interests, the Malay leadership coopted another previously rival Chinese bourgeois-led party (Gerakan) into the now broadened ruling party (renamed the National Front). The Indians were more peripheralized than ever. Economically, rubber estate workers lost jobs as federal land schemes spread; politically, the Indian party in the National Front was powerless.

The relations *within* the Malay community were a topic of intense concern for post-1969 leaders. The ethnic structure able to restabilize the state would have to accommodate new potentials for political mobilization among Malays and the new sense of intra-Malay class awareness. Political discontent mobilized by appeals to Islam were briefly diffused by the same tactic of ruling party cooptation. U.M.N.O.'s rival for Malay loyalties, the Parti Islam, was brought into the embrace of the National Front. But by the time of the 1978 parliamentary elections, the P.I. had once more become independent, though its leadership had become too corrupt to compete effectively against U.M.N.O.

More importantly, intra-Malay dissaffection from the regime was dealt with by distributing more state rewards to Malays, particularly in the form of land on newly opened federal rubber and oil palm schemes (which placed Malay small farmers under tighter state supervision than ever), places in the expanded government-controlled university system, posts in the growing government bureaucracy, licenses and contracts to newly emergent Malay businessmen. Malays, formerly mobilized by U.M.N.O., now were being tied ever more closely to the state itself. Chinese and

Indians had fewer avenues for state access yet were increasingly subject to supervision by the state security apparatus.

To accomplish this adjustment the state has had to be greatly expanded. The senior civil service has grown in size and policy influence. Its members are disproportionately Malay. Many have risen from rural, lower-class backgrounds but will enjoy an urban, upper middle-class lifestyle and close ties with the Malay political elite of U.M.N.O. Malaysia's military and police have grown not only in budgetary resources, but in technical sophistication and in organizational missions. The state has spawned powerful new state and parastatal corporations such as PERNAS, PETRONAS, MARA, Bank Bumiputera, all directed by Malay U.M.N.O. loyalists. State economic planning, centralized in the powerful Economic Planning Unit (under the Prime Minister) and the Treasury, has become far more ambitious than in the 1950s and 1960s when state security was conceived of by planners largely in terms of simple growth and suppression of the remnants of the Malaysian Communist Party guerrillas concentrated around the northern border with Thailand.

By contrast with the earlier phase of state-building, today's Malaysian state is directly involved in major land schemes, which not only are meant to diffuse Malay disaffection, but to integrate aboriginal ethnic groups in the peninsular and Borneo interior more tightly into the ethnic and state structures. The state is a direct participant in a growing number of joint ventures with foreign corporations. One of the most important is Sime Darby, Malaysia's largest private plantation and trading company. Traditionally British-controlled, it is now directed by Tan Siew Sin, former M.C.A. leader and Finance Minister; 25% of its shares are owned by PERNAS. Sime Darby is one of a new breed of Third World-based multinational corporations, many of which are state joint ventures.[7]

The state's military, police, and civil bureaucracies are far more active in interstate negotiations. They are building commodity organizations to press for better deals in the pricing of tin and rubber, creating more effective counterinsurgency networks of mutual benefit to states in the region, or exchanging information on contract formulas with other A.S.E.A.N. (Thailand, Singapore, Indonesia, the Philippines) state bureaucracies. While civil servants thus are becoming more powerful in Malaysian policy-making because all decisions are weighed in light of their effects on ethnic-state relations, it is also true that Malays now see the private economic sector as attractive and possible for personal mobility where, even ten years ago, ambitious Malays were oriented overwhelmingly toward the state sector for employment. Many of the Malays being recruited by politically sensitive M.N.C.'s are in fact midcareer civil servants who bring with them not only administrative skills and the right ethnic background, but state connections valuable to foreign firms doing business in Malaysia (Puthucheary, 1978).

What have been the consequences of the post-1969 changes for the relationship between the Malaysian ethnic structure and state structure and for the stabilization of the central state? The Malaysian state is more than ever thoroughly integrated into the international capitalist system. Although it has tried to offset the resultant vulnerability with commodity diversification and creation of international commodity groups, the international capitalist market structure remains beyond the control of the Malay state leadership. Light industries will move their factories from Penang industrial park when another country site looks more attractive. Presently, thanks especially to the high world prices for tin and rubber, Malaysia's export-dependent economy is very healthy. The radial tire requires natural rubber, not synthetics, and has helped to offset the competition from the synthetic side of the rubber industry, as has the high price of petroleum, a chief ingredient in synthetics. But Malaysia doesn't control the technology which led to the radial tire or to its future replacement (Edwards, 1977).[8] Tin is experiencing such a high world demand that the main problem for the Malaysian state (Malaysia is the largest single supplier of both tin and natural rubber) is to reform its own tax laws so as to provide greater incentives for both its local Chinese and British tin companies to produce tin at higher rates so that foreign consumers won't seek alternative materials (Rowley, 1977).

The earlier ethnic division of labor has been modified. Chinese and Indians have become more alienated from the Malaysian state. Testimony to this is the outward migration—for education and jobs—by those non-Malays who possess the resources. Some of these actual and potential emmigrants have precisely the sorts of skills which the industrializing economy and expanding state needs now more than ever. In recognition of this, Prime Minister Hussein Onn in 1979 made strategic senior bureaucratic appointments to publically demonstrate that under the New Economic Plan there was a place for loyal non-Malays. But such gestures have their limitations since Hussein Onn must tend to his own U.M.N.O. party Malay rank and file. Furthermore, such a handful of ministerial promotions may not convince the average Chinese tin workers or Indian rubber tapper that the state deserves his or her allegiance, many Chinese tin workers and Indian rubber tappers being women. In the July 1978 national parliamentary elections, the National Front won handily; its U.M.N.O. member came away with more parliamentary seats than ever before. But between the Chinese parties within the National Front—M.C.A. and Gerakan—there was notable tension rather than state-supportive cooperation. Chinese politicians in Gerakan (whose base is Penang, the single peninsular state with a non-Malay chief minister) accused M.C.A. leaders of not defending ordinary Chinese interests but instead (as in Indonesia, the Philippines, and Thailand) lining their own pockets with receipts from business deals worked out with the new Malay state elite. Class stratification among Chinese has not widened, as it has among Malays, but the intracommunal frictions are real.[9] Many ordinary Chinese feel trapped, with little political alternative. A few do "go inside," that is, join with the still active Communist guerrilla movement in the interior. U.M.N.O. leaders are aware of its partners' inability fully to satisfy their Chinese constituents as they were previously expected to do and recognize that the insurgency still has the organizational resources to attract some of the disaffected, which has in turn made U.M.N.O. leaders in government increasingly security conscious. Wide-ranging security laws and increased police operations extend the state. But they also threaten to scare away M.N.C.'s for whom "security" and "stability" are critical criteria for economic investment and loan decisions. Tightened state security also threatens to further alienate Chinese and Indians, who remain important components in the state-ethnic structural linkage despite their waning political leverage.

No longer do Malaysian government planners conceptualize the Chinese as holding sway over the economy, while Malays simply control the civil service, the military, and state symbolism. Still, that structural portrait is used by officials in public to muster support among the Malay public. For expansion of the state has been rationalized as equipping the Malay community with the means of both influencing and deriving greater rewards from the economy. But there has been a subtle and potentially contradictory change in interpretation. As it has appeared more and more difficult to achieve the goal of Malay ownership of one-third of the capital shares by 1990, the government has decided to define *state* ownership of capital shares as equivalent to *Malay* ownership. One analyst concludes that, "Malaysia now has the unique distinction of 'a private sector' dominated more by disguised public investment than by genuine private investors" (Ho, 1979a). Will ordinary Malays feel so identified with, and confident in the state that they will see PERNAS, PETRONAS, and MARA ownership as their own? This raises an even more serious question about the ethnic structure-state structure relationship—that of class tensions within the Malay community.

Intra-Malay stratification, while centuries old, is now being exacerbated by governmental economic policies. Even the Malay upper class is not unified. There are signs—mainly seen in struggles over policy within U.M.N.O.—that those Malay elites identified with the private sector are becoming wary of the encroachment of the new class of powerful state bureaucrats and technocratic politicians who wield influence through the regular ministries as well as through state corporations such as PERNAS.[10] Secondly, the Malay sultans, once thought to be a politically dying breed, supported only by British scaffolding, wield potent economic influence today due to their constitutional authority over land. For instance, the sultan of the state of Trengganu and his son and heir have reaped significant rewards from Exxon's growing operations in the South China Sea off the Trengganu coast. Other sultans have begun to assert new claims over lands on which the central government presumed it could build roads, open logging areas, settle Malays in oil palm or rubber schemes. Such new economic assertiveness has political ramifications. It limits the central regime's maneuverability and posits another party with whom M.N.C.'s can negotiate. Moreover, should tension between the Malay sultans and the Malay central state leaders become public, the Malay communal unity on which the state now depends could be seriously jeopardized not just vertically between Malay classes, but horizontally between rival factions at the top of the Malay communal structure.

Data collected over the last fifteen years indicate that, as the economy has grown and as the state apparatus has expanded, there has been a widening of class differences among Malays (Grace, 1976; Grove, 1979). While the Malay-based party opposition has been relatively ineffective, this intra-Malay class stratification, traditionally accepted because of the legitimized role of royalty, may be losing its legitimacy. One of the most talked about—always *sotto voce*—phenomena in Malaysian politics in the late 1970s is the rise of a Muslim evangelical movement referred to as *Dakwah* (literally meaning "missionary," but used in Malaysia specifically to refer to this movement). *Dakwah* is not monolithic, and only one off-shoot of it, *Angkatan Belia Islam Malaysia* (A.B.I.M.) is explicitly political. But it has the capacity to channel lower class and petty-bourgeois discontent among Malays against their own ethnic state and new commercial elites. Not only are Dakwah followers critical of the benefits being garnered from these privileged groups, whose positions are justified in terms of the post-1969 dedication to general Malay uplift. They criticize these Malay elites for assimilating all too easily into the non-Muslim lifestyles of the American, Japanese, or West German consultants and corporate executives with whom they drink whiskey at the Kuala Lumpur Hilton or dine and swim at the exclusive Selangor Golf Club.[11]

Whether the state's New Economic Policy can succeed in bringing more Malays into the modern sector is also in doubt. First, the Third Malaysia Plan and subsequent official reassurances to businessmen (in the form of a new "one-stop" agency to service possible foreign investors) hint that state planners realize that they cannot hope to compete with the Philippines, Indonesia, or Singapore for foreign investment if they stick to their Malay-preference criteria too stringently. They need this infusion of foreign capital to achieve at least minimally the 1969 promises to their prime ethnic constituency, yet they will lose that capital if they push too hard.

Opening up land schemes under federal sponsorship does not lean so much on foreign financing, but it has not proved successful in closing the gap between Chinese and Malays.

Those Malays that are getting jobs in the modern, i.e., manufacturing sector, are being hired especially by the multinational electronics, garment, food processing, and shoe industries. These firms, now a prominent feature in the Petaling Jaya suburb of Kuala Lumpur, in Penang, and Malacca, are attracted to Malaysia by the lure of cheap labor. Ministerial planners are well aware of this and make clear in their advertisements that Malaysian workers are not only satisfied with lower wages than their counterparts in California and Glasgow, but are educated in English, physically adept and unlikely to cause any organized challenge to managers. In other words, this awaiting work force is female. More specifically, it is in addition young (high turnover keeps company costs down), usually raised in the countryside, and largely ethnically Malay. Malay girls between the ages of seventeen and twenty-one are perhaps the most prominent sector of the Malay community being absorbed into the state-M.N.C. jointly promoted industrial sector.[12] Young female labor is the main attraction held out to M.N.C.s in all of the free trade zones being created by eager governments in Southeast Asia. In 1979 there are an estimated 300,000 workers in electronics firms in Asian free trade zones, and the majority of them are females under thirty.[13] In Malaysia, then, the state is counting on not just a particular modified ethnic structure, but a complementary sex-ethnic structure.

This may fit the needs of foreign capital, but in the long run it could cause problems for the central Malay state leadership. Its Malay constituents may not find this pattern fits their post-1969 modernizing expectations. Adherents to Dakwah may come to see the nineteen-year-old Malay girl working in a Motorola or Phillips transistor plant, wearing tight jeans, attending cosmetic classes (company sponsored), and living in dormitories away from family supervision as a manifestation of all that they find so disturbing about the new state-ethnic structural relationship.

* * *

Indonesia and the Philippines also reveal how state entrenchment, ethnic structure adjustment, and international capital go hand in hand. Since the establishment of the post-1965 "New Order," Indonesian state-building has been directed by the military, under General Suharto, in alliance with civilian technocrats and certain Indonesian Chinese businessmen. In the Philippines state-building reached a new stage of acceleration when President Ferdinand Marcos declared martial law and launched his "New Society" in 1972. In both countries the state has utilized international capital to an increasing extent to blur the ethnic basis of state expansion ideologically, while simultaneously entrenching an ethnic-state structure in practice. In Indonesia and the Philippines the state's stability and expansion depend on its being perceived of as a national state, not just the captive of a particular ethnic group. Thus there are no blatant symbolic identifications of the Indonesian state with Javanese or the Philippine state with Christian ethnic groups or with Marcos's own ethnic group, the Ilocano. On the other hand, strategically cultivated ethnic linkages are critical in the processes by which Indonesian and Philippine state institutions currently are being developed (Parker et al., 1977).

The most prominent new state institution in Indonesia's New Order is Pertamina, the state petroleum corporation. Until recent scandals forced its reorganization, Pertamina was a corrupt off-shoot of the military command, the chief pillar of the post-1965 state. In both the military and Pertamina, ethnic Javanese have been predominant. (Not all inhabitants of the main island, Java, are ethnically Javanese.) Each is deeply imbedded in international relations of aid, loans training, and marketing. The Javanese orientation of these critical and externally oriented state institutions is neither random nor unrecognized by other Indonesian ethnic communities.[14] But the Javanese character of the military and Pertamina, while providing the state with a solid corps of loyalists and an implicit set of symbols, does not mean that all Javanese benefit from such a state-ethnic linkage. Indeed one sector of Indonesian society, suffering most from the military-state corporate encouragement of foreign financed electronics industries, tourism, and green revolution-inspired agriculture, is the Javanese lower class. In the future it may well be that this class stratification will gain special political saliency precisely because it is occurring within a single ethnic group, that ethnic communalism will be the basis for a growing sense of betrayal and disaffection between mass and elite Javanese.

The New Order was not just to have reinforced Javanese political dominance; supposedly, it was to have altered the country's ethnic structure. The ethnic group officially branded the target of the New Order state's expansion was Indonesia's Chinese minority. Though only 2% of the country's population, the Chinese (many of them assimilated to the extent of having taken Indonesian names) were singled out after the coup and countercoup of 1965—in which they allegedly provided access to Peking operatives—as the group whose economic leverage would be reduced for the sake of indigenous Indonesians' economic advancement. In the case of the Chinese, then, state alliance with international capital—at first multinational banking consortia to cover the high level of debt left from the Sukarno period (which in 1979 in fact is higher than ever)—was explicitly justified in ethnic terms: international loans and investments would enable the new regime to utilize the state to replace Chinese economic domination with indigenous Indonesian (i.e., not just Javanese) economic control.

More than a decade after the launching of the New Order, this has not been the ethnic structural consequence of the state's alliance with foreign capital. Currently, while local Chinese are still officially held up as a pariah group, high-ranking state military officers, mostly Javanese, are entering into lucrative business partnerships, albeit discreetly, with wealthy local Chinese entrepreneurs (Kamm, 1979; Weinstein, 1976; Manglapus, 1976: 63-69; Crouch, 1978).[15] The relationships between Javanese senior officials, local ethnic Chinese big business, and multinational banks and corporations (Japanese, American, increasingly West German) presently provide the basis for Indonesian state maintenance and expansion. Intra-Javanese class stratification is being fueled by alliances with a certain class of ethnic Chinese. That alliance, in turn, is dependent on an expanding state apparatus, Javanese controlled, and a rising influx of capital, foreign controlled.

In post-1972 martial law Philippines the ethnic structure-state structure dynamic shares many of the features evident in Indonesia: rapid proliferation of state institutions during the 1970s; state pledges to reduce local Chinese economic influence, while at the same time alliances are formed between senior state officials and Chinese and Mestizo (Chinese-Filipino) entrepreneurs; utilization of international capital to solidify central state support and to expand state authority into regions formerly left largely to the control of localist officials and minority ethnic communal structures; decline in the real standards of well-being among the lower classes of those several ethnic groups in whose name the state is being expanded.[16]

Not only Del Monte, but Dole, Goodyear, and Japanese corporations are serving as valuable handmaidens of the Philippine Constabulary (paramilitary), Army, and Navy in their efforts to exert full control over Mindanao and the other formerly Muslim-dominated islands of the southern Philippines. In one sense the present extension of the central state, controlled by elites from several (not just one as in the Indonesian case) ethnic groups, all Christian, is the latest chapter in a state-building effort that began in 1900. Eighty years ago, the U.S. military (commanded by American officers who had learned their profession by "opening" the American West and subduing various Indian ethnic groups), followed shortly by more adventurous plantation companies, launched the process of imposing a central Philippine state over the local Muslims (Gowing, 1977). But the process had never reached completion. In the late 1970s the independent state-expanding regime of Ferdinand Marcos is aiming to complete that process in the south. But it requires foreign capital's assistance to push back the frontier.

"Frontiers" are not territorial phenomena. They mark a particular kind of interethnic, and usually ethnic-state interaction (Swift, 1978). Siberia, Amazonia, Canada's Northwest territories, the Australian "outback," the American West and Pacific islands, Japan's northern island of Hokkaido were, and to some extent still are, "frontiers." That is, they represent limits on state expansion. The limitation posed is usually not geographical; it is ethnic. On one side of the frontier is a state, controlled by certain classes of one or several ethnic groups. On the other side of the frontier is an ethnic group which has sufficient political self-consciousness and communal structure to defy the authority of that expansive state. In many instances, the state, in search of security (safer borders to defend) or new resources (natural gas, uranium, fertile land) calls on international capital as an ally in "pushing back the frontier," regardless of the state's ideological stance vis-á-vis capital.[17]

Frontiers in the Philippines, consequently, are one of the most revealing sites for watching transformations in the ethnic structure-state structure relationship and the roles of international capital in those transformations. Not only is Mindanao being consolidated within the grip of Manila, but Marcos—in the name of development of new energy resources to *lessen* international vulnerability—has sought World Bank loans for construction of a massive hydroelectric dam complex in an area which analytically should be conceived of as a "frontier" for the state. For the ethnic group which until recently controlled this region 300 miles north of Manila on Luzon (though at a marginal level of well-being for themselves) is the Kalinga, a group which has been able for generations to remain relatively outside the operational jurisdiction of the central state (Wideman, 1978). Such relative autonomy is no longer deemed tolerable by the Marcos regime. Under martial law the Philippine state has become more centralized (undermining older localist patronage systems and concentrating clientelism in the office of the presidency, and reducing localist ethnic power bases even among the dominant Christian groups), more coercive, more territorially expansive. But the new pressures on Kalinga on Luzon and Muslims on Mindanao to be integrated as marginalized groups within the Philippine ethnic structure for the sake of a more powerful Philippine state structure would not be feasible without foreign penetration from M.N.C.s, the World Bank, and the I.M.F.

INTERNATIONAL CAPITAL'S ROLE IN STATE ETHNIC DESIGN

In 1979, Del Monte, one of the international capitalist system's most powerful agribusinesses, has plantation operations in the United States, Mexico, the Philippines, and Kenya. Its plantations are not located randomly. In the United States, its original base, it is most prominent in

Hawaii; in Mexico, its winter vegetable operations are concentrated in the north; in the Philippines, Del Monte pineapple plantations are in the southern island of Mindanao; in Kenya, its pineapple plantation and canning factory are just north of Nairobi.[18]

Each of these regions in which Del Monte food production investments are concentrated is ethnically distinctive (Mexico is a bit less clear, but that in itself is a reflection of the de-Indianization policies that long have undergirded Mexican state-building). Furthermore, and especially pertinent to our argument, each of these region's ethnic group composition is deemed salient to state expansion and state maintenance by central policy-makers. The states have assisted Del Monte's global search for land, labor, and profits by sanctioning land titles or small-holder leases that almost amount to corporate control (in the Philippines, the Marcos regime has found ways to circumvent the law which prohibits new land alienation to foreigners). Each state elite with which Del Monte has dealt has also aided the corporation by providing infrastructure, loans, tax holidays and, in the case of Hawaii, immigration laws that facilitated importation of the sort of cheap labor which could insure plantation profitability.

In return, Del Monte offered the state elites opportunities to create or sustain those sorts of ethnic-state relationships which would secure the state or even expand it. First, as in Hawaii and Mindanao, the state was anxious for a vehicle to "open up" territories nominally within its jurisdiction that until then were so ethnically alienated from the central authorities that they resisted easy state incorporation. Plantations helped bring in new social controls and usually new pools of manpower from different ethnic groups and thus reduce the barriers to state penetration. In the case of Kenya, Del Monte held out the promise to provide livelihoods to Kikuyu small farmers, a group on whom the Kenyatta-led Kenyan state depended for political support and thus could not afford to see go bankrupt (Swainson, 1979).

In other words, Del Monte may be expanding its food producing activities internationally, as are so many capitalist agrobusinesses. Its corporate expansion with its accompanying international division of labor is a critical ingredient in the making and maintenance of what we term "the world-system." But to understand how Del Monte obtains the sites it does for its plantations, one needs to go beyond geographic variables and beyond those technocratic ideologies that lead certain state economic planners to put their trust in multinational corporations. One must ask whether the appeal of Del Monte to certain welcoming state elites is rooted partly in perceptions of the extent to which those states need foreign investors to insure their control over, or the support of particularly salient ethnic groups, challengers (as in Hawaii and Mindanao) or supporters (as in Kenya's Kikuyu regions).

State-building is an ongoing process. Either the maintenance of state sovereignty demands ever greater state capacities for resource accumulation, or those classes and ethnic groups subordinated or coopted remain still capable of later disaffection and perhaps mobilization against the state. Consequently state-ethnicity-international system relationships in allegedly established states are instructive. We cannot limit our investigation of the integration and reproduction of the world-system merely to the Third World, where such relationships may be more visible since the state itself is so fragile and because neo-colonialism is so rampant. More developed states do have an admitted advantage in attempting to solve their ethnic structural problems via international penetration. By definition, they should be more able to control and monitor the conditions under which foreign investors operate and thus surrender less state integrity on the road to state reconsolidation.

Thus in the United Kingdom in the late 1970s we are witnessing the central government consciously utilizing multinational corporations to reduce unemployment among three ethnic groups which have been part of the U.K. state's ethnic foundation for over 200 years but which are now threatening by their mobilized disaffection to weaken that state precisely at a time when it is rivaling Italy as the "sick man of Europe": ethnic Scots in Scotland; Protestants as well as Catholics in Ulster. Labour's Minister for Northern Ireland, Roy Mason, traveled to the United States twice during 1978-1979, luring American businesses—with loans, direct government grants, and liberal tax policies—to set up manufacturing plants in Northern Ireland. Among those M.N.C.s promising either expansion of existing plants or creation of new operations in Ulster have been General Motors, Goodyear, Ford, Hughes Tool, Dupont, and De Lorean Motor Company. The latter, producer of a controversial new sports car, pledged to create 2,000 new jobs in West Belfast by 1984 (Borders, 1979; "Renewed American Investment Interest in Northern Ireland," 1978). In addition, in 1979 the French tire manufacturer Michelin agreed to establish a plant in a mixed Catholic-Protestant area of Ulster (Arthur, 1979).

In Scotland it has been Chrysler, the oil corporations, and electronics firms that Whitehall has turned to in order to dampen the pro-S.N.P. enthusiasm. The Chrysler case suggests that the British state can lose as much (even more) than it gains by depending on international capital to sustain the existing state-ethnic structure.

Chrysler had had auto production plants in the Glasgow area before the 1960s escalation of Scottish nationalism. But with that political challenge to the unity of Britain (more immediately to the ruling Labour Party after 1974), as well as the decline of Scotland's ship-building industry (nationalized in a state salvage effort), Chrysler's continuation took on new importance in London. Chrysler's American directors, however, had less stake in

British state unity than in global rationalization and thus decided to close down their Scottish factories. But they left open a loophole; they might be able to justify maintaining those plants if assisted by British government grants. In 1976 the Labour government, after heated cabinet-level debate, decided that unemployment and S.N.P. voting success were positively correlated. The government thus presented a "massive subsidy" to Chrysler, on the condition that it keep producing cars in Glasgow. It did so for three years. In 1979, Chrysler decided to shut down its operations anyway.[19]

If reputedly developed states, such as Britain, Canada, or France, take a risk in relying on foreign capital to resolve basic contradictions in the relationship between the country's interethnic structure and its state structure, politically less developed states take an even greater gamble in such reliance. Yet those risks are being taken today in at least a dozen multiethnic countries. State elites there must satisfy a primary ethnic community which has special expectations regarding state benefits, while they demobilize other ethnic groups that are (1) alienated from the state, or (2) resistant to new state expansion, or (3) competing with them to control the growing state apparatus. Foreign capital is wooed, therefore, in order to insure just the right "mix" of mobilization and demobilization that will produce ethnic structures which entrench the state.

Regionalism and class alone are not sufficient for understanding why and when state elites woo or welcome foreign corporations, the World Bank, I.M.F. or multinational bank consortia. What is peculiarly *ethnic* about this process of international penetration is the collective presumptions about the identity of the state in any given period of its evolution (growth or decay) and the vehicle that state elites use to mobilize selective support while delegitimizing other forms of political mobilization.

CONCLUSION

World-system expansion is in significant part a *political* process. It occurs not just because of imperatives of capital and markets, but because persons placed at strategic junctures make deliberate calculations and use public authority and resources in ways that increase international capital's penetration into more and more sectors of more and more societies. The question to ask is why and when do political actors make such calculations. Often their choices are tinged with ambivalence.

It has long been recognized that state-building has an ambivalent relationship to international capital. On the one hand, the very notion of state-building presumes that authority structures are being created and institutionalized that bolster a given society's capacity for delineating choices, mobilizing resources, and dealing with other actors. In this sense, state-building is a process that should inhibit free-wheeling foreign capital penetration. On the other hand, state-building rarely is a process in which all sectors of that society have an equal hand or derive equal benefits. Those sectors which have greatest access to and control over the state's apparatus may find international capital as a most attractive ally in fending off domestic rivals and as a lucrative partner in translating state power into economic rewards for those in office. Usually social class analysis has been utilized to determine the inclination of a particular state in this ambivalent situation. The foregoing discussion suggests that ethnic relationships to international capital are also important. Class structure *and* ethnic structure are the objects of ongoing state strategic cultivation.

What does one *miss* in the state-international capital relationship, then, if one ignores state structure-ethnic structure relationships?

(1) Some incentives state elites may have for pursuing foreign investments and loans;
(2) the fragility of a state's legitimizing claims to being a "nation-state";
(3) an attractive "bargaining chip" that foreign firms can offer those state planners who are wary of external penetration;
(4) a basis for a foreign firm's division of labor within its own factory or plantation operation;
(5) the political significance of the creation of new state enterprises that deal directly with foreign capital;
(6) a potential source of saliency for lower-class disaffection and even mobilization against a state-controlling elite, that is, the sense of betrayal by their "own" communal leadership; and
(7) a potential base for collective protest against state policy or even state claims of authority outside the group wielding greatest state influence.

Ethnic structures are not always as clearly delineated as they are in Malaysia. Yet scores of contemporary states are built on top of structured relationships within and between ethnically identifying groups. Furthermore, elites in most of those states take quite deliberate steps in order to preserve or adjust those ethnic structural conditions in ways that seem to them to enhance or extend state authority. This strategy often leads them to enlist the aid of foreign firms, banks, the World Bank, or the I.M.F. But developing states will be taking a greater risk since their state capacities are, by definition, more limited and fragile. In the end, such a state strategy for insuring ethnic structural symmetry may undermine state-building, even in states presumed to be "developed."

NOTES

1. An earlier effort to think through the relationships between ethnic groups and the international capitalist system stressed the effects of multinational corporations on ethnic groups (see Enloe, 1979a; see also Stack, 1980). I am indebted to Sidney Mintz and Hashim Hussin Yaacob for their helpful critiques of the original version of this chapter.

2. See, for example, a special issue of *Publius* exploring the relationships of ethnic groups to states in federal systems. It was published in fall 1977. Another special issue devoted to the multiethnic state systems is *Annals* of September 1977.

3. Articles by Kenneth McRoberts and Jack Reese examine the applicability of the internal colonial model to Canada and France, respectively, and these appear in Hechter and Stone (1979).

4. Additional considerations of ethnic regionalism are contained in a special issue of the *Review of Radical Political Economy* published in the fall of 1978 and called "Uneven Regional Development." Also, on France, see Coulon and Morin (1979).

5. An analysis which concludes that Malays themselves have a relatively low sense of class consciousness is Nagata (1976).

6. Among the interesting analyses of Malaysia's political economy are Amin and Caldwell (1977), Lim (1979, 1977), Snodgrass (1979), Bedlington (1978), Bach (1976), and Hirschmann (1971).

7. On the politics of PERNAS, the state trading corporation, and Sime Darby, the formerly London-based plantation company, see Davenport (1976).

8. For an analysis of global trends in the rubber industry, see a three-part series called "Rubber: The Multinationals," in the Washington *Post* of March 4-6, 1979. A study concluding that the Malaysian government's extensive rubber small-holding schemes are not closing the income gap between Malays and non-Malays is Benjamin (1978).

9. Two studies of nonelite Malaysian Chinese attitudes toward the opposition DAP and toward the National Front's Gerakan and M.C.A. and the Chinese elite's role within the Malay-dominated regime are Strauch (1978, forthcoming).

10. A privately circulated study intended for prospective foreign investors in Malaysia makes this intra-U.M.N.O. elite tension its theme. It is called "Malaysia to 1980: Economic and Political Outlook for Business Planners," and is an unpublished manuscript from Business International in Hong Kong, written in 1977. Warnings to businessmen about uncertainties in Malaysia were reported in the April 30, 1979, issue of the *Asian Wall Street Journal Weekly*.

11. A perceptive analysis of Islam's role in Malaysian politics is Kessler (1978). A preliminary analysis of the Dakwah movement is Nagata (1978).

12. The reliance of foreign electronics firms on cheap female labor and their growing presence in Southeast Asia are described in L. Lim (1978), Grossman (1978-1979: 2-17), Lee (1978), Ariffin (1978), and Snow (1977).

13. This figure comes from a report assessing Asian free trade zones and the move of electronics, garment, and food-processing M.N.C.s from Singapore, the Philippines, and Malaysia to the even cheaper sources of labor (again female) in Sri Lanka, India, Indonesia, and the People's Republic of China (Ho, 1979b).

14. See Ann Gregory's analysis of Javanese dominance in the Indonesian military in a special issues of the *Journal of Asian Affairs* on ethnicity in Asian militaries (Spring 1979). See also Crouch (1978) and Jenkins (1978: 22-24).

15. For a review of the political and legal status of Chinese in Southeast Asia, see "The Overseas Chinese" (1978).

16. On Chinese entrepreneurs in the Philippines, see Lockard (1978), McBeath (1978). For more general articles on the tendencies within the post-1972 Philippine political economy, see Grace (1977), R. Lim (1978), and Dimasupil (1978). The growing strength of Chinese-Filipinos in Philippine banking is reported in Gonzaga (1979: 76-77).

17. For a case study of the Australian state's economic relationship with its "frontier" ethnic groups, see Roberts (1978). The recently established Anthropology Resource Center has been devoting particular attention to state-M.N.C.-ethnic group relations on "frontiers"; on Brazil, see, for example, Davis (1978), Jorgenson et al. (1978), and Davis et al. (1977).

18. See "Del Monte: Bitter Fruits" (1976). Nicola Swainson includes a study of Del Monte in Kenya in Swainson (1979).

19. See Rawkins (1979) and Rasmussen (1978: 4-5). Grenada TV has filmed a documentary on the British Cabinet's Chrysler subsidy decision. For an analysis of the impact of British state-petroleum M.N.C.'s relationships on the Shetland Islands, see O'Connor (1979).

REFERENCES

AMIN, M. and M. CALDWELL (1977) Malaya: The Making of a Neo-Colony. Nottingham, England: Spokesman.

ARIFFIN, J. (1978) "Industrial development in peninsular Malaysia and rural-urban migration of women workers: impact and implications." Presented at the Tenth International Congress of Anthropological and Ethnographical Sciences, New Delhi, December.

ARTHUR, P. (1979) Communication with the author, Oxford University, March 27.

BACH, R. L. (1976) "Historical patterns of capitalist penetration in Malaysia." Journal of Contemporary Asia 6, 4: 458-476.

BEDLINGTON, S. (1978) Malaysia and Singapore. Ithaca, NY: Cornell University Press.

BENJAMIN, N. (1978) "The role of land settlement in the economic development of West Malaysia, 1957-1970." Development and Change 9 (October): 581-598.

BORDERS, W. (1979) "Ulster luring U.S. companies." New York Times (March 10).

COULON, C. and F. MORIN (1979) "Occitan ethnicity and politics." Presented at the First International Political Science Association Roundtable on Ethnicity and Politics, Oxford University, March 26-28.

CROUCH, H. (1978) The Army and Politics in Indonesia. Ithaca, NY: Cornell University Press.

DAVENPORT, A. (1976) "Battle for Sime Darby." Far Eastern Economic Review (December 3): 38-42.

DAVIS, S. (1978) Victims of the Miracle. New York: Columbia University Press.

--- et al. (1977) Geological Imperative. Cambridge, MA: Anthropology Resource Center.

"Del Monte: Bitter Fruits." (1976) NACLA Latin America and Empire Report 10 (September).

DIMASUPIL, L. (1978) "Neo-colonialism and the Filipino industrial workers." AMPO: Japan-Asia Quarterly Review 10 (October-December): 34-43.

EDWARDS, C. (1977) "Rubber in the world economy." Pacific Research 3 (September/October).

ENLOE, C. H. (1979a) "Multinational corporations in the making and unmaking of ethnic groups," in R. Grant and E. S. Wellhofer (eds.) Ethno-Nationalism, Multinational Corporations, and the Modern State. Denver: University of Denver Monograph Series in World Affairs.

――― (1980) Ethnic Soldiers: State Security in Divided Societies. London: Penguin.

――― (1979b) Police, Military and Ethnicity: Foundations of State Power. New Brunswick, NJ: Transaction.

GONZAGA, L. (1979) "The favorite heads for home." Far Eastern Economic Review (March 30).

GOWING, P. G. (1977) Mandate in Moroland: The American Government of Muslim Filipinos, 1899-1920. Quezon City: Philippine Center for Advanced Studies.

GRACE, B. (1976) "The politics of income distribution in Malaysia." Asia: Fieldstaff Reports 24, 9.

――― (1977) "The politics of income distribution in the Philippines." Asia: Fieldstaff Reports 25, 8.

GROSSMAN, R. (1978-1979) "Women's place in the integrated circuit." Southeast Asia Chronicle 66; Pacific Research 9, 5-6.

GROVE, D. J. (1979) "Does economic development create a more equitable ethnic distribution?" Presented at the International Political Science Association First Round Table on Ethnicity and Politics, Oxford University, March 26-28.

HECHTER, M. and J. STONE (1979) Special issue on internal colonialism. Ethnic and Racial Studies (Fall).

HIRSCHMANN, C. (1971) "Ownership and control in the manufacturing sector of West Malaysia." UMBC Economic Review 7, 1.

HO, K. P. (1979a) "Savoring the sweet smell of oil." Far Eastern Economic Review (April 13).

――― (1979b) "Birth of the second generation." Far Eastern Economic Review (May 18).

JORGENSON, J. et al. (1978) Native Americans and Energy Development. Cambridge, MA: Anthropology Resource Center.

KAMM, H. (1979) "Indonesia's Chinese: 'real rulers' or 'harried minority.'" New York Times (May 31).

KESSLER, C. (1978) Islam and Politics in a Malay State: Kelantan 1838-1969. Ithaca, NY: Cornell University Press.

LEE, S. A. (1978) "Industrial conflict in Malaysia: a case study of rural Malay female workers." (unpublished)

LIM, L.Y.C. (1978) "Women workers in multinational corporations: the case of the electronics industry in Malaysia and Singapore." University of Michigan occasional paper 9, Ann Arbor.

LIM, M. H. (1977) "Some effects of foreign investments: the case of Malaysia." Bulletin of Concerned Asian Scholars 9 (October-December).

――― (1979) Ownership and Control of the One Hundred Largest Corporations in Malaysia. London: Oxford University Press.

LIM, R. (1978) "The Philippines and the 'dependency debate.'" Journal of Contemporary Asia 8, 2: 196-209.

LOCKARD, C. A. (1978) "Patterns of social development in modern Southeast Asian cities." Journal of Urban History 5 (November): 41-68.

McBEATH, G. A. (1978) "Political behavior of ethnic leaders." Comparative Politics 10 (April): 393-418.

MANGLAPUS, R. S. (1976) Japan in Southeast Asia: Collision Course. Washington, DC: Carnegie Endowment for International Peace.

NAGATA, J. (1976) "The status of ethnicity and the ethnicity of status: class and

ethnic identity in Malaysia and Latin America." International Journal of Comparative Sociology 17, 3-4: 241-260.
——— (1978) "Ethnic and religious aspects of Malay religious revitalisation." Southeast Asia Ethnicity and Development Newsletter (Singapore) 2 (September): 28-33.
O'CONNOR, J. (1979) "British rule in Shetland." Monthly Review 30 (April): 20-29.
"The Overseas Chinese." (1978) Far Eastern Economic Review (June 16): 17-24.
PARKER, G., F. GOLAY, and C. H. ENLOE (1977) Diversity and Development in Southeast Asia. New York: McGraw-Hill.
PUTHUCHEARY, M. (1978) The Politics of Administration: The Malaysian Experience. London: Oxford University Press.
RASMUSSEN, J. (1978) "New Grenada TV productions on policy-making: a review." British Politics Group Newsletter 11 (Winter).
RAWKINS, P. M. (1979) "The global corporation, ethno-nationalism and the changing face of the Western European state," in R. Grant and E. S. Wellhofer (eds.) Ethno-Nationalism, Multi-national Corporations, and the Modern State. Denver: University of Denver Monograph Series in World Affairs.
"Renewed American investment interest in Northern Ireland." (1978) British Politics Group Newsletter 11 (Winter): 8-9.
ROBERTS, J. (1978) From Massacres to Mining: The Colonization of Aboriginal Australia. London: War on Want.
ROWLEY, A. (1977) "Tin crisis message sinks in." Far Eastern Economic Review (September 23): 110-115.
SNODGRASS, D. (1979) Inequality and Economic Development in Malaysia. London: Oxford University Press.
SNOW, R. T. (1977) "Dependent development and the new industrial worker: the case of the export processing zone in the Philippines." Ph.D. dissertation, Harvard University.
STACK, J. [ed.] (1980) Ethnic Identities in a Transnational World. Westport, CT: Greenwood.
STRAUCH, J. (1978) "Tactical success and failure in grassroots politics: the MCA and DAP in rural Malaysia." Asian Survey 18 (December): 1280-1294.
——— (forthcoming) "General elections at the grass roots: perspectives from a Chinese new village," in K. H. Lee and M. Ong (eds.) 1978 Elections in Malaysia. London: Oxford University Press.
SWAINSON, N. (1979) Corporate Capitalism in Kenya. London: Heineman.
SWIFT, J. [ed.] (1978) "Societies at the frontier: vulnerable peoples in Asia and the Arctic." Special issue of Development and Change 9 (January).
WEINSTEIN, F. B. (1976) "Multinational corporations and the Third World: the case of Japan and Southeast Asia." International Organization 30 (Summer): 373-406.
WIDEMAN, B. (1978) "Philippines mt. people declare war on Chico Dam Project." AMPO: Japan-Asia Quarterly Review 10, 3: 24-29.

PART 3
WORLD-SYSTEMS ANALYSIS: PROBLEMS OF METHOD

Chapter 14

ON THE HOLISM OF A WORLD-SYSTEMS PERSPECTIVE

Robert L. Bach

> There is a great big something wanting, I don't quite know what it is. Please walk thirty yards, so that I can get a perspective on the thing.... Now, then, your head's right—everything's right! And yet the fact remains, the aggregate's wrong. The account don't balance.
> —Mark Twain

This essay is an attempt to gain some perspective on the methodological issues of a world-systems approach. Of particular concern is how to proceed analytically given the theoretical insistence that social action takes place at the level of a world-system as a social whole—"not 'society' in the abstract, but a definite 'world,' *a spatio-temporal whole*" (Hopkins and Wallerstein, 1977: 112). For some (Rubinson, 1977; Chase-Dunn, 1978, 1979), the theoretical issues derived from the challenge to developmentalism do not suggest and certainly do not require a reconsideration of methodological traditions. I disagree. While many of their techniques may be useful, for instance, relational network analysis (cf. Snyder and Kick, 1979), few are sufficiently grounded in the "logic of inquiry" suggested by a world-systems approach. My intent in this chapter is to clarify the basis for rethinking methodological rules by reviewing the varying conceptions of a social whole and their implications for method.

AUTHOR'S NOTE: I want to acknowledge the invaluable contributions of Terence K. Hopkins and Dale Tomich to the formulation of this chapter.

The argument is modest. Following a long-standing methodological tradition, the discussion focuses on *how* we make the connection between theoretical questions and research strategies to answer them. In this task, I merely attempt to provide some background support to methodological insights advanced by others (cf. Hopkins, 1978). Three categories of issues are pursued under this general goal. A connection is made between three broad approaches to "development" and their implied conception of the part-whole relationship. Several issues of method are then analyzed, focusing particularly on concept-formation and the selection of a unit of analysis. Finally, the use of space and time is reviewed. This final section includes a brief discussion of the alternative approaches to analyzing cycles of the world-economy.

I. SOCIAL WHOLES

In his classic essay on the meaning of part-whole relations Nagel (1957) argues that although sociologists have long claimed that "the whole is more than the sum of its parts"—an entity "sui generis" (Durkheim, 1964)—the meaning of the whole, its parts and the properties of each has often been vague and metaphorical. Since it is precisely the insistence on the "holism" of the world-system that separates it from other perspectives (Wallerstein, 1976), we must clarify what is meant by the whole and its parts and how they vary over perspectives.

A. MODERNIZATION PERSPECTIVE

That the construction of a world-systems perspective occurred in conjunction with and in opposition to the theoretical and methodological traditions of modernization theory is by now common knowledge (Wallerstein, 1974). Although a list of theoretical objections would be unmercifully redundant, several methodological issues need to be recalled. Skocpol (1977: 1075) summarizes four: (a) the tendency to reify the nation-state as the sole unit of analysis; (b) the assumption that all countries follow a similar path of growth; (c) the disregard of transnational structures; and, (d) the method of explanation based on ahistorical ideal types.

The basis for this criticism was primarily the assumption of modernization theorists that nation-states were *independent units* whose level of development was determined by the presence or absence of certain conditions. Two general categories of conditions were considered important, attributes of individuals (e.g., Inkeles, 1969) and attributes of the national society or economy (e.g., Kuznets, 1955). To the extent that a world-order was discussed, relationships found at the individual or national level were used to develop by analogy the mechanisms of the world whole.

The clearest and most important example was the neo-classical conception of the world-market and, particularly, its relationship to national development. Nation-states were viewed as independent buyers and sellers of "factors of production" which were unevenly distributed throughout the world—i.e., over nation-states. Through unrestricted, independent access to the world-market (trade, technological transfers, migration, etc.) each country could maximize its own national production and income as a result of the maximization of world production and income. As long as nation-states could enter into unfettered competition with other nation-states, then we could determine world levels of demand and supply by summing the production and consumption schedules of each independent national participant.

Given these mechanisms, the degree of inequality between nations, in the "world-order," was due to the assumed unequal distribution of natural resources (the presence or absence of certain conditions) or the *temporary* advantage of one participant. To the extent that the independence of each nation was limited by an established relationship (e.g., colonial monopoly), then an organization was imposed on the world-order and some nation-states would be disadvantaged as a result of these "distorting" influences.

The meaning of the social whole and its parts follows directly from this example. Whether we are talking about a world-order or a nation-state, the whole in this instance is nothing more than the sum of its individual parts. That is, although one could estimate a world level of supply and demand, this estimate would not represent a unique property but would necessarily be of the same type as its parts and so be broken down into them.

The social whole as a simple aggregate can mean at least three things:

(1) The whole consists of a defined geographical scope which has as its parts smaller, inclusive spatial units. A *spatial* whole could possess a nonspatial property of a type similar to the same kind of nonspatial property of any part.
(2) The whole consists of temporally extended objects with inclusive temporal units. Again, nontemporal properties may be possessed by the whole and parts.
(3) The whole consists merely of a collection of its members.

It seems clear that to the extent one would formulate a "spatio-temporal world" as a social whole it would merely consist of the sum of all spatial and temporal units and their properties. No procedural problems would be created by insisting upon analysis beginning at the level of the whole. The simple aggregation meaning of "sum" means we could translate from whole to part and back again quite easily. Therefore, there is no special meaning given to the social whole.

B. INTERSTATE DEPENDENCE PERSPECTIVE[1]

The theoretical challenge to the neo-classical and modernization perspectives was based fundamentally on an alternative view of the world order and, thus, the social whole of interest here. Politically and economically, the concern was to identify those relations between nations which blocked national development and established a *dependence* among nations. The basic insight was that such nation-state was part of a larger structure or organization which worked to the advantage of some and not others. These advantaged ("core") and disadvantaged ("peripheral") nations (United Nations, 1950) or metropole and satellite (Frank, 1969) were linked by mechanisms similar to those identified above (trade, capital flows, migration) but now these served to maintain the unequal returns to the different nations within this world structure. Each nation-state, therefore, could not be studied as an independent unit but only as a part of a larger organization—a larger whole. Chase-Dunn describes the difference as follows:

> The focus on national societies as the independent unit of analysis which characterized modernization theories has been replaced by an elaboration of the transnational, international and world-context relations which affect development [1979: 1].

Although this distinction speaks only to relations "outside" the nation-state, there is nothing preventing this international organization from affecting "internal" relations also. Indeed, Dos Santos's definition of dependence as an internal structure (1970) is entirely consistent with such a view.

Recognition of a larger organization which conditioned nation-states added additional complexity to the conceptualization of a world-order. Nation-states were not only subunits but were *political* structures contained within a larger *economic* structure (Rubinson, 1977: 818). Although these political and economic structures are often seen as hierarchically organized this is not a requirement. Consequently, Skocpol's plea for a method of analyzing the "world-system" takes a compatible form to those described above:

> The alternative picture of world capitalism that is likely to emerge from historical analyses pursued along these lines will probably pertain to intersecting structures (e.g., class structures, trade networks, state structures, and geopolitical systems) involving varying and autonomous logics and different, though overlapping, historical times, rather than a single, all-encompassing system that comes into being in one stage and then remains constant in its essential patterns until capitalism meets its demise [1977: 1087-1088].

The conception of the whole implied in these theoretical claims is apparently distinct from modernization theory. Whereas before we could obtain the whole by simply summing the parts, now there is a supra-nation-state organization which is not derived simply from its parts and, indeed, represents a unique entity. The principle of uniqueness derives from the "central tenet" of sociology (Coleman, 1964) that the simple aggregation appropriate to the former meaning of summing from part to whole denies that social behavior is patterned. By extension to the current argument, aggregating properties of nation-states as parts ignores a basic tenet that international relations are patterned.

Hopkins and Wallerstein summarized the significance of this "new" conceptualization of the part-whole relationship in discussing the "international studies" approach to national development:

> For it suggests, along with the *grouping of cases* it implies, an important theoretical hypothesis; namely, that a necessary condition of a society's modernization is its incorporation into the historically unique network of societies [1967: 39; italics added].

For our purposes, this network of societies becomes the social whole which is not reducible to each part (nation-state). That is, it is true that the whole is greater than the sum of its parts.

However, two possible meanings of this statement are compatible with this "international studies" approach. The first is that the alternative conception simply placed an *ordering* to the nations. Instead of independent nations all running a race, there are developed and *under*-developed nations. This "grouping of cases" (Hopkins and Wallerstein, 1967: 39) refers, then, to a particular configuration of nation-states where if we discuss one part (nation-state or "structure") we are obliged to talk about its "position" (ordering) in this pattern.

Theoretically, this ordering is an important step. However, an ordered network does not represent a fundamentally different conception of the part-whole relation. For such an *ordered* network "it is perfectly true though trivial (to say) that the whole is more than the sum of its parts" (Nagel, 1957: 525). There is nothing in the ordering that precludes the possibility of analyzing the whole into its elements provided they are related to each other in definite ways. The parts *remain the same* regardless of their ordering—regardless of their position in the larger social whole. *That is, we can identify the parts independently of their occurrence in the organization.*

Similarly, any conception of parts as "autonomous" (Skocpol, 1977) or "contradictory" (Wright, 1976; Sjoberg, 1976) structures necessarily makes use of a notion of an ordered sum or configuration. Structures are assumed to remain the same and only change positions as the result of changes in the relationships (ordering) among structures; a new "whole" is formed by shifts in positions.

It is quite correct to say that no methodological problem is raised by this conception of the whole. We can maintain the same conception of the part used by modernization theorists and "sum" the parts by establishing their correct order. The innovation in this conceptualization is, therefore, only "theoretical."

However, this perspective limits our conception of the whole, the international order, to merely a set of relationships among its parts. It is quite possible and more consistent with the emphasis on a world-system to claim that the whole possesses properties of its own. But in order to evaluate this sense of the statement "the whole is greater than the sum" we must be able to establish both the whole and the sum. Nagel notes:

> Most people who are inclined to assert such a statement do not specify what that sum is supposed to be; and there is therefore a basis for the supposition that they either are not clear about what they mean, or do not mean anything whatever [1957: 524].

Here we know what is meant by the sum but the whole is left unspecified. On the one hand it may be *assumed* that the whole is different from the structured sum of its parts. If so, we may identify properties of the whole, so-called "global" properties, that are not reducible either to relations among the parts (structural properties) or to the parts themselves (analytical properties) (Lazarsfeld and Menzel, 1964). Chase-Dunn (1979) offers such a conception as a remedy to the problems of analyzing a spatial whole. The world-system is assumed to be a spatial whole and is examined over time. This does not remedy, of course, the problem of establishing a spatial-*temporal* whole but merely diverts the issue to temporal rather than spatial parts. The implication is that to establish a world-system as a spatio-temporal whole using this conception of the part-whole relation we must talk about *all* space and all *time* and nonspatial and nontemporal properties of that whole. Even here, however, the whole is assumed and becomes a *context* for parts within the whole.

C. WORLD-SYSTEMS PERSPECTIVE

Although a world-systems perspective emerged as part of the critique of modernization theory, it has come to mean more than just an awareness that nation-states (or any other "structures" for that matter) are part of an international organization which conditions national development (Cardoso, 1977: 12). The key conceptual innovation is that a world-system consists of a set of singular processes (Hopkins, 1979: 24). That this conception is fundamentally different from the one described above is suggested by Cardoso (1977). In specific reference to the latter view, Cardoso writes:

> To compare what ECLA predicted as the outcome of industrialization with what was in fact happening was easy. It was more difficult to propose an alternative that could not be limited to a methodological formal critique; one that, *starting from the analysis of historical-social processes,* would be able to define an alternative problematic [1977: 10; italics added].

The focus on a set of processes singular in time and space is essential since it lays emphasis on the formation and development *of* the system itself and not merely on patterned relations among its elements. According to this view, capitalism arose only once; it was a "world" system from its inception and theoretically "global" in its projected scope. Processes extended not only beyond state boundaries but, as often as not, irrespective of them. This is in contrast to feudalism where once the constituent processes forming feudal relations were established over the broad areas of Europe they were reproduced in each locus independently of their reproduction in other places or times. It is the singularity of the processes which constitutes the world capitalist system and distinguishes it as a social whole. This is clearly the intention of Hopkins and Wallerstein's description of the whole:

> a system of social action that not only is comprehensive and singular in scope, forming a spatial "world" within its expanding, geopolitical boundaries, but is also comprehensive and singular in time, forming a temporal "world" [1977: 123].

The implication here is that the "structures" we normally use, to organize our thinking and observation and which are said to form the parts of the whole are no longer useful as a way *of proceeding* analytically.

> If there is one thing which distinguishes a world-system perspective from any other, it is its insistence that the unit of analysis is a *world*-system defined in terms of *economic* processes and links, and not any units defined in terms of juridical, political, cultural, geological, etc., criteria [Hopkins and Wallerstein, 1977: 123].

For the world-systems perspective, then, the whole consists of singular processes which *form* and *reform* the relations that express patterns or structures. Parts are "pieces" of a process, not independent of the remainder of the process but located within a specific time-place coordinate. To "sum" the parts means to bring them together successively as each produces the particular time- and place-bound relations and traits. Lenin, for example, gives us this movement as the initial task of research, to show "the connection between, and interdependence of, the various aspects of *the process* taking place in all spheres of the social economy" (1974: 26; italics added).

Because the parts of the processes *cannot be assumed to be independent* (although they may be), the patterned relations or "structures" they produce must not be abstracted—as a research strategy—from their time-place-object coordinates. That is, in opposition to the former conceptualization, the parts defined as structures may not be identified independently of their occurrence in the whole. This is certainly *not* a denial that social life is patterned or that "structures" may be identified. It is, however, a recognition that structures must be constructed in relation to (not necessarily as relationships between) each other as dependent occurrences. Clearly, then, the "parts" of modernization theorists and of those taking an "international studies" approach are not the parts said to sum to the world-system as the whole. Instead, each of the parts of which they speak is an *outcome* of the partial processes that are linked together ("summed") to reach the whole.

Two important implications are obtained from this discussion. If "structures" are not the beginning point of analysis but instead are outcomes, then the structure of the world-system is similarly not given but is constructed by its processes—and, retrospectively and prospectively, as an outcome of research. "Global" properties may exist, but unless they are constructed as an outcome of linking processes together, the entity they refer to remains abstract and unspecified.

Secondly, the emphasis on these processes leads directly to a discussion of change of the world-economy prior to the changing position of structures within the world-economy. That is, the focus of research must always be on the transformations of structures and relations as they are continually reformed by these processes. Our research strategy then must not only be able to answer why there is the present alignment of structures and relationships but also what will become of these structures. An even more difficult requirement is that such an approach must also be able to account for the changes in the categories or concepts used to capture any specific set of structures, relations, and traits.

The significance of these three conceptualizations of the part-whole relationship does not lie solely in how we define the world-economy. Instead, each implies a strategy of research, even a "logic of inquiry" that is different from the others. However, the major difference between the "international studies" approach and the modernization approach is mostly procedural—how to analyze the parts and maintain their ordering. The two perspectives do not differ substantially in their conception of the whole and its relations to the parts.

The world-system perspective as formulated does present a fundamentally different image. Long-held strategies of concept formation and comparative analysis are challenged by the insistence upon singular processes as the starting point for inquiry. Perhaps the clearest impact is on the necessity to pursue the construction of structures in their time-place coordinates and in relation to the construction of structures elsewhere. To do this requires some rethinking of the way we use theories, concepts, and data.

II. UNITS OF ANALYSIS

A. MODERNIZATION AND INTERSTATE DEPENDENCY PERSPECTIVES

The research of many modernization theorists took the form of selecting an object or unit for study and then identifying universal attributes which could be assumed to have similar meaning in each context of occurrence. That is, following the anthropological work of Radcliffe-Brown and Malinowski, the attempt was to discover and isolate the universal, functional prerequisites for the *existence* of each unit—here a nation-state or national society.

The research consisted of a search for dichotomous classifications of types of societies. Given the preoccupation of many classical theorists with the emergence of industrial society, these typologies were formed as polar ends in an evolutionary path from an immature to a mature form: preindustrial to industrial, traditional to modern, folk to urban, etc. These types of societies formed the ground for comparative analysis. Whatever was common to developed societies but absent in the undeveloped areas became a functional prerequisite for development.

In retrospect, the key methodological challenge to modernization theory predated the theory's formulation, or at least its U.S. version, namely the "introduction" of probability into the relations between concept and indicator and theory and data. For unlike Durkheim, who emphasized the definition of phenomena under study by a set of common external characteristics, the Weberian tradition adopted a more approximate or probabilistic approach to the nature of generalizing concepts (Lazarsfeld, 1959). Rules of probability thus became key research tools for evaluating the empirical usefulness of general concepts and propositions.

These rules became particularly useful in reformulating the grounds for comparative research (Zelditch, 1971). Instead of the *empirical* universals presumed by modernization theorists and limited in their capacity to explain variation, the probabilistic approach to comparisons made use of variables in *theories,* logical possibilities. In addition, all traits did not have to have an invariant point of reference; the same meaning in *every* context.

Points of reference could and did vary according to the theory being examined.

One of the important consequences of such a reformulation is that the unit of analysis does not have to "exist" as a commonly perceived object but may be selected for the purpose of relating a set of concepts to the observed data to test the approximate value of those concepts. How, then, does one select a unit of analysis? Zelditch identifies four criteria:

> The most commonly used criteria seem to be criteria of convenience, such as ease of sampling or identification. But there are more stringent criteria than these, the most important of which are: (a) theoretical relevance, (b) independence, and (c) indivisibility [1971: 282].

A unit of analysis in this formulation takes on two defining features. First, a unit is a *replicate instance* of a particular process, an abstract entity which is said to possess certain attributes according to a particular theory. Secondly, to be a replicate instance, the unit must be *independent* of other instances of that process. Otherwise no new information is added to test the theory. A third criterion, indivisibility, follows directly. If a supraunit organization is made up of several independent instances of a process, then to get additional information on that process we need to divide and "isolate" the units.

It is important to note here the significance of this rule for the "interstate dependence" approach to development and how it follows from that particular conception of the part-whole relation. Although nation-states (or any similar "structure") are part of an international order and have a particular position within it, since each nation-state is an independent occurrence of the process which forms each nation-state (and may be identified independent of its position—see above), then the international order may be divided and isolated into each unit to gain additional information on the process of interest. The only qualification is that the positioning or ordering of the unit must be maintained. This is easily done by making the position into an attribute of a unit and classifying units according to this attribute. The legitimacy of such a procedure is, of course, dependent upon a theory which provides for repeatable and independent instances of the central process, "nation-state"-building.

To determine when units are independent or indivisible is not always easy. Zelditch notes the problem this criterion poses in deciding, for example, whether northern and southern Italy are two different units to be compared:

> [A] study of dual economies, of economies in which modernized and traditional sectors are mixed, would clearly count Italy as one

unit. *To treat it as two units would be to destroy the phenomenon it was the purpose of the study to investigate* [1971: 285-286; italics added].

The point is not limited, of course, to regional or nation-state units. For example, in Snyder and Kick's (1979) useful attempt to reclassify nation-states on the basis of their position in political and trade relations, the units ("core" and "periphery") constructed by the ordering of these relations stand as independent, repeatable instances of the same process. This unit formation allows them to compare the economic development of core and periphery over time.

Another example is important here. As noted before, Chase-Dunn (1979) has suggested that one line of inquiry into the world-system as a whole is to trace it over time. Following the comparative logic just described, each time period is turned into a unit of analysis representing the repetition and independence of the time units. The theoretical basis permitting this strategy is described as follows:

> The capitalist world-system is understood to be a set of structured economic, political and social relations which have expanded and deepened, but remain analytically similar since their emergence [Chase-Dunn, 1978: 2].

In general, then, whether we examine structures over space or the same structure over time, the logic of inquiry remains the same—comparison of repeated, independent instances of the same process. In addition, it is the *theoretical concern* of the researcher which guides the selection of these units.

B. WORLD-SYSTEMS PERSPECTIVE

For a world-systems perspective, the above logic of comparative inquiry assumes what is fundamentally in question. The theoretical claim is that processes are singular and each structure is produced as a part of a larger process. It thus can not be assumed that any collection of "structures"— *including the structure of the world-system at several points in time* —represents repeatable and independent replicates of a phenomenon. Wallerstein draws the basic contrast this way:

> The key difference between a developmentalist and a world-system perspective is in the point of departure, the unit of analysis. A developmentalist perspective assumes that the unit within which social action principally occurs is a politico-cultural unit—the state, or nation, or people—and seeks to explain differences between these units, including why their economies are different. A world-system

perspective assumes, by contrast, that social action takes place in an entity within which there is an ongoing division of labour, and seeks to discover *empirically* whether such an entity is or is not unified politically or culturally, asking *theoretically* what are the consequences of the existence or nonexistence of such unity [1976: 345].

Hopkins highlights the methodological implication of this conceptualization:

> I think the methodological directive with which we work is that our acting units or agencies can only be thought of as *formed* and continually reformed, by the relations between them. Perversely, we often think of the relations as only going between the end points, the units or the acting agencies, as if the latter made the relations instead of the relations making the units [1978: 204-205].

The problem of method is arrived at straightforwardly. Unless we allow the tradition of comparative method to impose upon our theoretical formulations (and then to "distort" them), we cannot assume the appropriateness of existing units of comparative analysis. Instead, the methodological question is how can we research the formation of structures which would then allow us, if appropriate, to make comparisons following the above logic.

To raise the issue in this manner, however, creates additional problems. According to Zelditch, a unit of analysis is not something that exists "out there" but is a conceptualization. The selection of a unit of analysis, then, is fundamentally an issue of concept-formation. But for the research question at hand, the logic of comparative analysis offers little help.

Three considerations are used in selecting a unit of analysis; the purpose of comparison, theoretical analysis, and "subject-matter knowledge" (Zelditch, 1971: 287). Theoretical analysis is, of course, the most important consideration as it *defines* the structures of interest in a study of, for example, economic development. However, in order for comparisons to be sound, we must have "some knowledge of the instances to be compared."

His example is important. In comparing West Germany and China on a defined criteria of development, "it is because we know that the value of the GNP (for the two countries) arose in different ways that we question their comparability." But how do we know they arose in different ways and how do we determine what impact this "subject-matter knowledge" will have on our comparisons? The answer is simply that we must inquire into the *particular* construction of GNP in *each* country before we are satisfied the comparison is legitimate. This simple answer, however, only restates the problem—how do we form the concept to be used in the comparison. It does not reveal for us how we come by the knowledge of the particular case. The problem, it seems to me, lies more fundamentally in the particular type of concept-formation on which this tradition of comparative analysis is based.

III. CONCEPT-FORMATION

A. MODERNIZATION AND INTERSTATE DEPENDENCY PERSPECTIVES

The basic purpose of these two perspectives is summarized clearly by Sjoberg:

> The fundamental premise of this work is that social science in general, and sociology in particular, to fulfill the requirements of a science, must seek to isolate the common elements in societies and cultures. It is only by abstracting out the universal, or near-universal, traits ... that one really discovers and explicates what is unique [1976: 43].

This generalizing goal is said to separate social science from history, which is conceived of as the mere detailing of causal sequences leading to a particular event. Scientific research, then, proceeds through the formation of generalizing concepts and their application to historical data from other times and places.

Generalizing concept-formation begins with the observation of the historically specific and proceeds by extracting isolated, contingent elements into combinations revealing a pure or ideal type. In the process, these traits are abstracted from their historical context in order to make them applicable to more general instances. These concepts are "put together" in the form of an hypothesized association. An explanation for this association is sought by forming an additional concept (an "intervening trait") which is constructed by observing the conditions under which certain traits of the object of study vary. Theory is built by proposing a functional relationship between the concepts (a hypothesis). The logical format for these hypotheses is well known. As restated by Hopkins, "If a exists, and we have a proposed functional relationship 'if a then b,' then b exists" (1978: 209). This logical criterion is used then to test the theory. We observe and evaluate in a probabilistic manner whether the general concepts measured in another time and place fit this logically consistent relationship.

A review of this methodology suggests several points where it would fail to address the concerns of a world-systems analyst. The most obvious is that the applicability of a concept and, therefore, the unit beyond its particular historical context is assumed by the nature of the concept-formation. The problem with this is that the concept is formed *in order to* be general not because it is *established* as general (Mukherjee, 1978). As such, the method *assumes* that the contingent elements observed as part of the phenomena are the same over time and space. That is, the meaning of the historically specific is *given* by direct observation.

Yet it is important to realize that the historically "specific" is already *abstract* in the sense that a particular theory is "allowing" us to observe the phenomena. The fact that we form a concept by "abstracting" even further by synthesizing the predesigned parts means we have already accepted the theory which we think we test.

For a world-systems analyst, this assumption is critical. Since units of analysis and, therefore, a particular conceptualization are thought of as being formed and reformed by historical processes, we must be able to examine as part of the research strategy how these concepts are formed and how they are to change (see Mukherjee, 1978: ch. 5).

It is this realization, in part, that moves us toward an alternative formulation of concept-formation (Hopkins, 1978). The key insight is that just as processes produce "structure," concepts are equally an outcome of piecing together theoretical processes to interpret the empirical complexity and detail in each "historically specific" observation. Of course, this claim appears quite strange to the former methodology. As Stinchombe observes:

> The infinitely branching tree of causal sequences, rendered unified in a narrative of a sequence giving a unique explanation for each concrete historical entity, looks queer from the point of view of generalizing social science theory [1978: 13].

The alternative method of concept-formation is a "radically critical" (Cardoso, 1977) movement in the sense that what is observed or assumed must be constantly challenged and reconstructed. That is, the "abstract" historical events must be reconstructed to where their contingent elements no longer appear as isolated traits but form part of a theoretically and empirically constructed unit. It is only by establishing the historically specific as a "concrete" whole that we can appreciate the transformation of the elements and the concept as a whole.

This alternative concept-formation may be elaborated upon by examining the familiar passage on the "Method of Political Economy" from Marx's *Grundrisse*. The passage is of use here because it specifically marks a contrast to a "generalizing social science" approach.

Marx writes: "When we consider a given country politico-economically, we begin with its population, its distribution among classes, town, country, etc." (1973: 100). We begin, then, by identifying the contingent elements of the observation "country." However, these elements are not considered historically specific and synthesized into general concepts. Instead, Marx continues,

> It seems to be correct to begin with the real and the concrete.... However, on closer examination this proves false. The population is an abstraction if I leave out, for example, the classes of which it is composed.... These latter in turn presuppose exchange, division of labour, prices, etc.... Thus, if I were to begin with the population, this would be a chaotic conception of the whole, and I would then ... move analytically ... from the imagined concrete towards ever thinner abstractions.... From there the journey would be retraced until I had finally arrived at the population again, but not as a chaotic conception of a whole.

In this passage, then, the point of departure and observation is the same for this and the former methodological approach. However, in the present method, this initial point is already the result, an outcome, of diverse processes. Our understanding of that observation—the *particular* in the former conception—does not depend on the general concept formed by synthesizing the contingent facts but is revealed at the time of reconstruction.

Now let us return to Wallerstein's (1976) objection to the nation-state as a unit of analysis. It is possible, of course, to imagine or observe nation-states in several areas of the world. However, the nation-state as a structure presupposes not only other relations, administrative, juridical, social, cultural, etc., but the processes which constitute the development of capitalism as a spatially and temporally extended system. The nation-state is thus constructed by these simpler, more abstract processes of world capitalism. In this sense, the path of analysis from the abstract (processes) to the complex, detailed concrete corresponds to the real historical movement of the system. This is, I take it, what Cardoso (1977) means when he talks of concepts and units containing within them the movement and contradictions of historical struggles.

Given the conceptualization of the world-system, it is only with the above "grass roots movement" (Mukherjee, 1978) that we can discuss transformations *of* the unit of interest, including the world-system itself. Otherwise, the question of transformation and transition is limited to the predesigned elements of a given structure. But this fails to represent the movement which characterizes the world-economy as a social whole.

Questions of method remain of course. For example, how are we to make comparisons using this method? In fact, what this method accomplishes is a research strategy for constructing units which if not comparable in the formal sense may be usefully related to other similar instances by developing "analogies" for the purpose of clarifying particular features of any particular structure (see both Stinchombe, 1978; Hopkins, 1978).

One may also wonder if we are still in the "theory-testing" game. The answer is yes but in a different sense than is normally accepted. Instead of building theory by piecing together general, formal statements and applying them outside their intended range of application (Cardoso, 1977: 14-15), theory is tested for its "relative efficiency" in moving beyond the specific time, place, and object coordinates in forming new concepts and constructing concrete historical experiences (Mukherjee, 1978). It is in this sense that one of the intended goals of a world-systems perspective is accomplished—history and social science coming together to say something general about the mechanisms of world capitalism.

IV. SPACE AND TIME

Perhaps the most appropriate comment on the use of space and time in studies of development is that they have rarely entered into the analysis in a significant manner. For the most part, they have been pushed into the background as researchers focus on nonspatial and nontemporal properties of spatial and temporal units. That space and time should enter explicitly into the formulation of a world-systems perspective (as a spatio-temporal whole) once again points to the perspective's significant departure from both theoretical and methodological traditions.

With the increasing reawakening of interests in cycles, particularly so-called Kondratieff cycles, interest in time and space has also been kindled. However, each theoretical-methodological tradition has approached cycles from its own premises, leading to some confusion over what cycles actually involve. Therefore, consistent with the general purpose of this chapter, it may be of some use to clarify the basis upon which we pursue the analysis of cycles of the world-economy.

A. MODERNIZATION PERSPECTIVE

Time and space are used in this tradition in two ways; as a context for observing nonspatial and nontemporal properties and as a property of the unit of interest. The former use follows directly from the conception of the part-whole relations. Nation-states are independent structures which have a certain territory or geography and a particular chronology or "history." The spatial nature of the unit merely refers to that geography demarcated by nation-state (or any other) boundaries. The assumption is that society takes places *within* these spatial borders and *over* the particular geography.

Time refers to chronology or the sequences of events (nontemporal properties) which happen to the unit. Time can also refer to duration—the number of years to which a nontemporal attribute refers.

In this sense of space and time, each is considered a physical quantity which permits the observation of a unit and the organization of observations once made. Neither, however, enters into the analysis explicitly but slips away into the background as a context for the study of national units.

On occasion, geography and/or years are transformed into attributes of a nation-state. A notable example is the transformation of space as physical geography into distance and, then, into a measure of a particular theoretical concept, "transportation costs...." This measure then enters into the calculus of individual decisions which are expressed in the form of market prices.

Time can also become an attribute of the nation-state. States enter a developmental race at unequal times (chronology) then develop over a number of years (duration). Chronology becomes an attribute as it represents the occurrence of an event like national independence. Duration becomes the "experiences" or "traditions" which newly emerging states supposedly lack as they struggle to create the stable institutions that the West has built "over the years."

Since neither a temporal nor a spatial whole represents a different conceptualization than the temporal or spatial parts, analysis of the whole may take place at the level of the nation-state. Cycles of the world-economy are thus equivalent to cycles of each nation-state. Indeed, world cycles merely represent the simple aggregation of the "movement" of independent nation-states as they "catch up" or "slow down." The balance and unbalance of Rostow's (1978) world-economy, for example, merely represents these independent movements of nation-states. Theoretically, whatever factors play a role in developing a specific national economy may be said to operate at the level of the world-economy also. As Rostow writes:

> This notion of normal or optimum requirements for balance in the world economy (*and within national economies*) must now be generalized, as we turn to examine certain major phases in the evolution of the world economy [1978: 103; italics added].

Space and time are both obscured by this conception of cycles. Only time is used in any particularly meaningful way, and this is only as a measure of change. A cycle is like a *length* in a horse race. It measures how long the race has gone on and how far one horse is from another but otherwise is completely external to the running of the race. In this sense, a Kondratieff cycle represents no particularly new concept other than a time period longer than one year.

B. INTERSTATE DEPENDENCE PERSPECTIVE

The conceptual innovation of this approach outlined previoulsy applies directly to the use of space and time. Since nation-states are in a particular ordering or position within a larger structure, the issue is whether we discuss properties of the structure as a whole, the relation between structures or the smaller subunits, the nation-state in this instance. The major analytical problem from this point of view is how to translate between the different levels and their properties. The safest method for handling such problems of aggregation and disaggregation is to use traits which are simple mathematical transformations of values of microlevel variables. Hannan offers this suggestion:

> I am particularly interested in those cases in which the units of aggregation are *areal* or *temporal.* That is, I want to investigate those cases where the macro-variables are simple transformations of micro-level properties for all units in a specified area ... or for values of a single unit or groups of units measured at several points in time [1970: 35].

As in the modernization approach, space and time are used solely as an "environment" (Dogan and Rokkan, 1969: 3-4) in which we identify the traits of a repeated and independent process. The significance of space and time refers merely to the context it provides for social action, whether the context of theoretical importance is national, regional, local, urban-rural, etc. Spatial units may be modified, enlarged, or reduced according to the theoretical interests of the researcher.

The only difference with modernization theory is the scope of the spatial unit. Once we have a conception of relations linking units together, the space "expands" to take in the entire order. The space now comes to represent the environment for the whole order and not simply the sum of all the individual environments. However, nothing obstructs the analysis from identifying each environment independently of the whole organization. The unique understanding of the space of the international organization is derived not from the space per se but from the nonspatial properties observed over that space.

The use of time is very similar. The key question is one of length of time, basically how long should it take for the change of theoretical interest to occur? Most of our theories claim that the mechanisms of development take at least several years to generate significant social change. This means there is a pattern of relations among time units (years for example) which form a unique block of time (a new temporal-level equivalent to the international spatial level) which is said to possess nontemporal properties which may not be reduced to smaller time units, yearly occurrences, for example.

Cycles of the world-economy (the spatial whole) would thus represent organized networks of time units. Following the logic of comparative inquiry, each cycle could be compared with any other cycle organized on the basis of similar time networks. Each cycle would be a repeated and independent instance of that process causing fluctuations in world-level nontemporal properties. It is a major question of research from this perspective to determine whether or not the fluctuations (cycles) occur at seven, twelve, sixty, or one hundred fifty years. These blocks of time are said to represent processes of theoretical importance.

These cycles may also be transformed into attributes of the temporal units as indicators of the ordering of the unit. This ordering or temporal position could then be used as an independent variable to explain associations among other traits characterizing other temporal units. For example, we may want to talk about an "A-phase" as a context for the expansion of particular productive activities or for the changing hegemonic role in the world-system. Here there is no problem of analysis as the procedures follow directly from previous discussions.

It is important to note that in this use of cycles, time is used to organize and measure our observations. That is, it remains time as duration. As such, it does not enter into the processes of the world-economy itself but is merely an arbitrarily selected measuring instrument describing the structure of the world-economy.

C. WORLD-SYSTEMS PERSPECTIVE

While the use of time and space as measuring devices or environments of particular structures may be useful, neither use is *sufficiently* representative of the theoretical interest in time and space from a world-systems approach. As before, the former methods *assume* what is fundamentally in question, processes *of* the world-economy which form these cyclical movements. Moreover, the assumption of repeated and independent instances represented by blocks of time may "distort" the very phenomenon we wish to investigate. This certainly would be a reasonable premise if we take Hopkins's description of the subject-matter:

> system of social action that is comprehensive and singular not only in scope—and so forms a spatial "world" with its own changing geopolitical boundaries—but also in time—and so forms a temporal "world" with its own irreversible sequences and nonarbitrary periodicities [1978: 203].

This conception of temporal movements, cycles, leads us again to an emphasis on processes forming and reforming the world-economy in continually alternating relational arrangements. The repeatable cycles *in the world-economy* focused upon by the former method are here replaced by transformations and recompositions *of the world-economy*.

But perhaps the most significant implication of this methodological approach to space and time is that they are liberated from the constraints of merely representing physical quantities and arbitrary standards of measure. Space and time need to be incorporated into the processes of the world-system itself; that is, we need to think of spatial and temporal processes.

Spatial processes have become increasingly a concern of political economy. There is now a substantial literature in urban sociology which gives us clues on how to think about these spatial processes (e.g., Harvey, 1973). For example, the town-country division inherent in capitalism has come to be treated not as two separate units, one developed and the other underdeveloped. Instead, segmented spatial processes which are constitutive of capitalism, continually form and reform structures which we label as town and country. Town and country are, therefore, not only in opposition to each other as "areas" of differential development but are joined relationally. To talk about one is to talk about the other.

Discussion of temporal processes is still much more difficult. To talk of spatial processes *forming* town and country is, of course, also to talk about a temporal process. This movement is not so much over time, for this would return us to the time of arbitrary durations. Instead, there is a "speed" or "velocity" intrinsic to the movement of capitalist relations. Hopkins and Wallerstein write, for example:

> Time in the forms of its trends and cycles is constitutive of it as a system, not merely a coordinate of the variations of its properties. It does not have a history or a set of histories so much as it constitutes a history or a set of histories [1977: 124].

I must admit that this is a difficult conceptualization and, for me at least, it is not at all clear how this would affect the research process. However, it is quite evident that we cannot allow the former methods to dominate the conceptualization or methodology for studying cycles of the world-system. Here, as elsewhere, the task is to seek continually to highlight the processes leading up to and beyond the structures and elements on which the other methods focus.

NOTE

1. By "interstate dependence theory" I refer specifically to that body of dependency literature which Cardoso (1977) criticizes under the title, "The Consumption of Dependency Theory in the United States."

REFERENCES

CARDOSO, F. H. (1977) "Consumption of dependency theory in the United States." Latin American Research Review 12: 7-24.

CHASE-DUNN, C. K. (1978) "Problems of comparative research on world-system characteristics." Department of Social Relations, Johns Hopkins University. (mimeo)
——— (1979) "The uses of formal comparative research on dependency theory and the world-system perspective." Presented at the International Sociological Association Conference, Bellagio, Italy, April 24-28.
COLEMAN, J. S. (1964) "Relational analysis: the study of social organizations with survey methods," pp. 441-452 in A. Etzioni (ed.) Complex Organizations. New York: Holt, Rinehart & Winston.
DOGAN, M. and S. ROKKAN (1969) "Introduction," pp. 1-16 in M. Dogan and S. Rokkan (eds.) Quantitative Ecological Analysis in the Social Sciences. Cambridge, MA: M.I.T. Press.
DOS SANTOS, T. (1970) "The structure of dependence." American Economic Review 60: 231-36.
DURKHEIM, E. (1964) The Rules of Sociological Method. New York: Free Press.
FRANK, A. G. (1969) "The development of underdevelopment," pp. 3-94 in Latin America: Underdevelopment or Revolution. New York: Monthly Review Press.
HANNAN, M. T. (1970) Problems of Aggregation and Disaggregation in Sociological Research. Chapel Hill: Institute for Research in Social Science.
HARVEY, D. (1973) Social Justice and the City. Baltimore: Johns Hopkins University Press.
HOPKINS, T. K. (1978) "World system analysis: methodological issues," pp. 199-217 in Barbara Hockey Kaplan (ed.) Social Change in the Capitalist World Economy. Beverly Hills: Sage Publications.
——— (1979) "The study of the capitalist world-economy: some introductory considerations," pp. 21-52 in W. L. Goldfrank (ed.) The World-System of Capitalism: Past and Present. Beverly Hills: Sage Publications.
——— and I. WALLERSTEIN (1967) "The comparative study of national societies." Social Science Information 6: 25-58.
——— (1977) "Patterns of development of the modern world-system." Review 1: 111-145.
INKELES, A. (1969) "Making men modern: on the causes and consequences of individual change in six countries." American Journal of Sociology 75: 208-225.
KULA, W. (1976) An Economic Theory of the Feudal System: Towards a Model of the Polish Economy 1500-1800. London: New Left Books.
KUZNETS, S. (1955) "Problems in comparisons of economic trends," pp. 3-28 in S. Kuznets, W. Moore, and J. J. Spengler (eds.) Economic Growth: Brazil, India, Japan. Durham, NC: Duke University Press.
LAZARSFELD, P. F. (1959) "Evidence and inference in social research," in D. Lerner (ed.) Evidence and Inference. New York: Free Press.
——— and H. MENZEL (1964) "On the relation between individual and collective properties," pp. 422-440 in A. Etzioni (ed.) Complex Organizations. New York: Holt, Rinehart & Winston.
LENIN, V. I. (1974) The Development of Capitalism in Russia. Moscow: Progress Publishers.
MARX, K. (1973) Grundrisse: Foundations of the Critique of Political Economy. New York: Vintage.
MUKHERJEE, R. (1978) What Will It Be? Explorations in Inductive Sociology. Durham, NC: Carolina Academic Press.
NAGEL, E. (1957) "On the statement 'the whole is more than the sum of its parts'," pp. 519-526 in P. F. Lazarsfeld and M. Rosenberg (eds.) The Language of Social

Research: A Reader in the Methodology of Social Research. New York: Free Press.
ROSTOW, W. W. (1978) The World Economy: History and Prospect. Austin: University of Texas Press.
RUBINSON, R. (1977) "Reply to Bach and Irwin." American Sociological Review 42: 817-821.
SJOBERG, G. (1976) "The nature of the pre-industrial city," pp. 43-52 in P. Clark (eds.) The Early Modern Town. New York: Longman.
SKOCPOL, T. (1977) "Wallerstein's world capitalist system: a theoretical and historical critique." American Journal of Sociology 82: 1075-1089.
SNYDER, D. and E. KICK (1979) "Structural position in the world-system and economic growth, 1955-1970: a multiple network analysis of transnational interactions." American Journal of Sociology 84: 1096-1126.
STINCHOMBE, A. L. (1978) Theoretical Methods in Social History. New York: Academic Press.
United Nations (1950) The Economic Development of Latin America and Its Principal Problems. New York: United Nations.
WALLERSTEIN, I. (1974) "Rise and future demise of the world capitalist system." Comparative Studies in Society and History 16: 387-415.
――― (1976) "A world-system perspective on the social sciences." British Journal of Sociology 27: 343-352.
WRIGHT, E. O. (1978) Class, Crisis and the State. London: New Left Books.
ZELDITCH, M. (1971) "Intelligible comparisons," pp. 267-308 in I. Vallier (ed.) Comparative Methods in Sociology: Essays on Trends and Applications. Berkeley: University of California Press.

COMMENTARY

Christopher Chase-Dunn

Robert Bach has convincingly argued that we should rethink our methodological and epistemological assumptions in connection with our focus on world-systems. His call for the development of new methods more appropriate for interpreting events and for building a theory of the movement of the capitalist world-economy should be taken seriously. My concern is that we not become bogged down in a sterile debate between "historicists" and "social scientists" or between quantitative and qualitative researchers. These "ethnic" boundaries may provide us with much material for spirited dialogue, but a real understanding of the world-system will require that we transcend methodological sectarianism. My comments are designed to promote the integration of Bach's proposed interpretative research strategy with a direct assault on the specification of the logic of the capitalist world-economy. This second task can only be carried out in connection with a research effort which can distinguish between different models of the processes which move the system, and thus I will argue for the use of the methods of nonexperimental research design and model-testing, albeit with some suggestions for improving their applicability to the task at hand.[1]

Bach develops two main ideas in his argument for a new method: the "singular process" and the "spatio-temporal whole." The notion of "a set of singular processes" refers to features of the capitalist world-economy as a whole which cannot be understood by analyzing its parts. It seems to me that what is meant here is that capitalism as a system has certain laws of motion, a certain logic of development, which can best be understood by observing that unit of analysis in which these processes operate. I fully agree with this theoretical position but, as I have argued elsewhere (Chase-Dunn, 1979a), I think that, rather than assuming it is true and then building a new methodology based on that assumption, we should rather think about how this contention could itself be studied. In order to do this, we must engage in the formidable task of specifying alternative theories of world-system development. This means that we must have concepts which can capture features of the world-system as a whole, and it is here that Bach's proposed method of interpretation has borne the most fruit. The interpretative works of Immanuel Wallerstein and his colleagues and students have been the medium for the elaboration of a conceptual apparatus which can be used to reformulate the theory of capitalist development.

There are three levels at which we might specify models of the capitalist world-economy. The first is what I call a descriptive model. This specifies the relationships in time between the various cycles and trends which are features of the larger world-economy itself. This can be done without saying much about the causal relations between these cycles and trends or their relationship with processes operating within subsystems. Versions of this type of model are proposed by Chase-Dunn and Rubinson (1977, 1979) and by Hopkins and Wallerstein (1977). The second level is to specify causal relations between variables which are features of the world-system as a whole and variables which are features of its parts. A model of this kind is suggested by Chase-Dunn (1978) to explain the observed relationship between cycles of core competition and changes in the structure of core-periphery relations. Research based on this type of model may be useful in answering questions about the relative strengths of world-system variables and variables which are features of subsystems, and thus provide an avenue for the resolution of some of the problems raised by critics of the world-system perspective (e.g., Skocpol, 1977; Brenner, 1977).[2]

The third level of theoretical specification is implied by Bach's discussion of a "set of singular processes" which operate at the level of the world-economy as a whole. This suggests an axiomatic theory in which the main motors and tendencies of capitalist development are conceptualized and their relations are specified in propositional form. My own hunch is that this type of "deep structure" theory can best be constructed by revising Marx's (1967) accumulation model as outlined in *Capital*. Marx's focus on core capitalism rather than on the whole system, and his abstraction from the state and class relations in his analytic model can now be overcome in the light of our insights about the systemic regularities of the accumulation process at the world level and its systematic interaction with state formation, class formation, and nation-building.

This last discussion raises a number of issues about historicity, systemness, determinism, and transformation which I will soon discuss. But first let us consider Bach's second main theoretical notion, that of the "spatio-temporal whole." Bach is saying the capitalist world-system has a feature which makes it difficult to apply the standard tools of comparative research. It is not simply that there are processes which operate at the level of the whole system (as discussed above), but that these processes are of a certain kind. Time and space are claimed to be actual features of these processes rather than simply dimensions for arraying instances of processes. My problem is this. Time and space are features of all social processes in the sense that they enter into the determination of outcomes. And so I am not clear in what sense this feature asserted to be true of this whole system is not equally true of other units of analysis. It may be meant that the *social meaning* of time and space is an important feature of the cultural structure of capitalism. This is undoubtedly true, but I fail to see how this supports the claim that quantitative methods are inappropriate for world-system analysis. Another possible interpretation of this notion is that the timing or spatial location (or both) of causal processes may vary in systematic ways. In the case of the time dimension, this may only point to the existence of distributed time-lags, in which the effects of one variable on another differ depending on the time-lag between the variables. If time-lags themselves vary in a systematic way, we can build this into our model. If the time dimension is totally stochastic, we don't have a system and must content ourselves with description.[3] But Bach's notion of a spatio-temporal whole does not appear to amount to a claim that the world-system is unsystematic. The idea of a spatio-temporal whole may indeed be a fruitful one but it needs further clarification in order to be a source of insights about the nature of the world-system or a justification for excluding methodological approaches.

My suggestion that we should attempt to formulate and test theories about the underlying dynamics of the world-system raises a number of issues. I have addressed the issues of dialectical modeling, deterministic vs. voluntaristic theories, and the rigidity or flexibility of conceptual definitions and operationalization in an earlier paper (Chase-Dunn, 1979b). I would like to use my remaining space to address the question of the scope and level of abstraction of theory. Many world-system scholars rightly criticize the level of abstraction at which the French structuralists carry on their theoretical debates. On the other hand the structuralists do address questions of the underlying logic of capitalism. I will argue that these questions are important for scientific and political reasons and should not be left to those whose main recourse to evidence consists of rereading classical texts.

The term "ahistorical" was used by Marx to refer to the generalizations of classical political economy which ignored the unique qualities of different modes of production. Assumptions about timeless human nature obscured the social origins of institutions and the qualitative transformations which occurred in the development of human societies. But Marx did not deny the possibility of constructing a theoretical model of the underlying laws of a particular mode of production. On the contrary, his main work was devoted to this task.

Wallerstein has argued that the capitalist mode of production is a feature of the whole world-system, not of its parts. This involves a reformulation of Marx's conception of the capitalist mode of production which incorporates core and peripheral capitalism and the logic of geo-politics, state formation, class formation, and nation-building into a single model. This is a tall order. The Althusserians prefer to leave much of this to the realm of the less abstract "social formation" on the basis of the voluntaristic nature of politics and class struggle. While it should be made clear that any concrete political situation involves intention and human intelligence, this should not prevent us from trying to specify the tendencies of the capitalist mode of production. If the modern world-system is really a system rather than a series of indeterminate events, or a continually changing causal structure, we should be able to model its logic, and therefore to distinguish between new forms which reproduce the system and emergent forms which contribute to its transformation.

As I see it, the main use of a theory of the logic of the capitalist world-economy would be its ability to help us distinguish between social changes and political forces which reproduce capitalism and those which contribute to its transformation. The boundary question as formulated by the scholars of the Fernand Braudel Center has so far been concerned to identify the spatial and organizational boundaries of the expanding capitalist world-economy (Fernand Braudel Center, 1976), but an even more important question is the logical boundaries of capitalism as a system. If, as Immanuel Wallerstein has suggested, the twentieth century is the beginning of a period of transition to a socialist world-system, but the extant "socialist" states are functional parts of the capitalist world-economy, we need a clear theory of capitalist logic to help us distinguish newly emerging forms which contribute to the transformation of the system from those which reproduce and further expand and deepen it. This task is attempted using the "descriptive model" approach in Chase-Dunn and Rubinson (1979), but here I would propose that a clear model of the developmental logic of the capitalist world-system would be of much greater use.

The formulation of this theoretical model can proceed to a certain extent by the application of the interpretative method proposed by Bach as well as by the use of the kinds of abstraction used by Marx to create his accumulation model and by the French structuralists. But formal comparative research should also be employed to help distinguish between different versions of the theory.

NOTES

1. These ideas are developed at greater length in Chase-Dunn (1979a, 1979b).
2. A method for simultaneously estimating the causal relationships between the variable characteristics of the world-system, its zones, states, classes, firms, etc. (multilevel analysis) is proposed by Chase-Dunn (1979b).
3. I have elsewhere discussed the problem of the "width of a time point" (Chase-Dunn, 1979a) in which measurement error due to the use of events as indicators of unobserved structural variables may lead to false inferences regarding

the direction of causation. But this is unrelated to Bach's concept of "spatio-temporal whole."

REFERENCES

BACH, R. L. (1979) "On the holism of a world-systems perspective," this volume.
BRENNER, R. (1977) "The origins of capitalist development: a critique of neo-Smithian Marxism." New Left Review 104 (July-August): 25-92.
CHASE-DUNN, C. (1978) "Core-periphery relations: the effects of core competition," pp. 159-176 in B. H. Kaplan (ed.) Social Change in the Capitalist World Economy. Beverly Hills: Sage Publications.
——— (1979a) "Comparative research on world-system characteristics." International Studies Quarterly (December).
——— (1979b) "The uses of formal comparative research on dependency theory and the world-system perspective." Presented at the International Sociological Association Conference on "The Social and Political Challenges of the New International Economic Order in Comparative Perspective," Bellagio, Italy (April 24-28).
——— and R. RUBINSON (1977) "Toward a structural perspective on the world-system." Politics and Society 7, 4: 453-476.
——— (1979) "Cycles, trends and new departures in world-system development," pp. 276-295 in J. W. Meyer and M. T. Hannan (eds.) National Development in the World System 1950-1970. Chicago: University of Chicago Press.
Fernand Braudel Center (1976) Proposed Research Programs. Binghamton, NY: Fernand Braudel Center.
HOPKINS, T. K. and I. WALLERSTEIN (1977) "Patterns of world-system development: a research proposal." Review I, 2: 111-145.
MARX, K. (1967) (1867) Capital, Vols. 1-3. New York: International Publishers.
SKOCPOL, T. (1977) "Wallerstein's world capitalist system: a theoretical and historical critique." American Journal of Sociology 82 (March): 1075-1090.

Ramkrishna Mukherjee

I am rushing into those areas where angels fear to tread, because I know so little about the world-system, and not that much about the developmentalists or those who deal with the international "order." I have a feeling from what I read and hear of this paper that while talking of the methodology of world-systems analysis, it is essentially trying to clarify certain concepts: methodology has yet to come. Now the question is from which point of departure is a distinctive methodology required.

Perhaps we should clarify that point here. I think that Bach is a little too hard on the developmentalists and those internationalists who "order" the nation-states when he is discussing the unit of analysis. We should bear in mind that a unit of analysis is predicated by the level of analysis and the level of comprehension; it is not something you just pick up. Now, might we consider the proposition that to the developmentalists, the internationalists, and the world-systemists, to all of them, the world remains as the universe of study. However, certain configurations of world society are taken in abstract and studied intensively by the developmentalists because they assume that the social forces working within and beyond these configurations have relative magnitudes. But they are not yet sure how to systematize these forces and come to a definite conclusion on the manner in which that systematization should take place. They don't deny the relevance of some forces being of primary importance and in fact there are a lot of polemics on that. Whether you denote a nation-state to be the unit of analysis or a variable with which to study the world society is, to my mind, a very small difference in conceptualization.

The important point perhaps, is that in the world-systems perspective we are not concerned with a series of variables. We are concerned rather with a set of variates in the sense that their predictability is subsumed in the model, in the theory. The variables thus take the character of variates, and we categorize them as core, periphery, and semiperiphery. Now, I don't see any harm in doing it: the question is how to prove it? Just by formal inspection and picking up some as belonging to the core or the periphery or the semiperiphery? Or through a rigorous course of analysis which inductively leads me to the identification of the core, the semiperiphery, and the periphery. I think that herein comes world-systems methodology, but how do we go about it?

I can assume a singular process of social change because I have certain empirical knowledge of periodicity, of cycles and trends. Now do I just fit in the variates in that process in terms of beautiful curves? We are all fond of curves, but the question is whether the curves have substance or we just prop them up with certain external aids. So methodology comes there, but what does it signify?

Does it mean that the approach of the world-systemist is totally different from the approach of the developmentalist? that there is no point at which they can meet? I don't think so, because I know so little of both. I would have thought, however, that in the world-system approach the underlying assumption is that certain systemic forces are of greater importance than the forces working within various configurations of society. And this is why we can have a very clear typology of the core and the periphery. Here the forces are unidirectional. But the moment we talk of semiperiphery, we are conceiving of counteracting forces which lead to a change from periphery to semiperiphery. So with reference to the space-time coordinates (of which the gradation is a matter of rigorous analysis and not of assumption), we need a methodology to appraise the relative importance of the forces working through the identification of certain configurations of world society which are usually considered nation-states.

I don't think any developmentalist will disagree that nation-states rise and disappear, that they change. And the very changeability of the nation-states shows different social forces are working in differential alignments. Now, are these alignments determined primarily by the systemic forces or not? Here I think the methodology question comes in. And this methodology needs, I think, consideration not on one plane of operation of the variates, especially when we conceive of a countermove from periphery to semiperiphery. This is where the systemic model requires a new methodology because we are not conceiving of all the forces working on one plane; we are presuming dialectical changes from quantity to quality. We are conceiving of at least two different planes, and once we talk of different planes, we can conceive of very many planes of operation of social forces.

While, therefore, we can conceive that capitalism rose once and evolved into a systemic force, we can also rephrase it by saying that capitalism has been manifested in a particular manner at or over a given period of time in the world perspective. Because if we do that, it would be of some help to conceive of the countermovement from periphery to semiperiphery. But countermovement could also conceive of breaking an entity off from the system, of breaking the system itself. If not, then the disintegration of the system has to be conceived of as some social courses working from some other plane.

Either way, a system will have to consider itself in the context of other systems; otherwise the concept of system would have no meaning. And, therefore, the methodology which has to be developed would be rather complicated. It would neither mean mere correlation analysis nor the constitution of sequential but segmental acts. I hope Bach will accept these suggestions.

Terence K. Hopkins

Robert Bach ends with a programmatic plea: that in our inquiries we should "seek continually" to examine "processes leading up to *and beyond*" the patterned arrangements which, in other kinds of inquiries into modern social change, are taken as the givens. I emphasize the adverbial additive, "and beyond," because it is that notion I wish to consider in this brief commentary. I might note at the outset of these comments that it makes no procedural difference at all whether these "givens" for others are presented or read as "data" or as "parameters." By data, I mean here factually restricted "values" of either variates (ordered "qualitative" descriptions) or variables (ordered "quantitative" descriptions) in claims of the form, "for any s, if a, then b," where (a) and (b) are variates or variables and (s) is the presumably "constant" unit. By parameters, I mean processes—or, derivatively, defining "properties" constitutive of (s)—which in such inquiries are tacitly or explicitly construed as invariant or "constant" (within categories or ranges), but which in other inquiries (here, notably those of the "world-system" variety) are construed as capable of taking historically any of the *full* range of forms-contents (qualitative) or scales-magnitudes (quantitative) that, in their general theoretical formulations, the constitutive processes (or defining properties) are said to be capable of taking.

This notion of "beyond-present-arrangements" recurs, it seems to me, throughout Bach's paper but is not itself an object of attention in the paper—which is why it may be useful to comment on it. But first let me justify the claim that the notion is recurrent. In the first section, Bach examines three understandings of the concept of "social wholes," distinguishing among "developmentalist," "internationalist," and "world-historical" understandings. In his observations on the last of these, he notes that "our research strategy must ... be able" to address itself, inter alia, to the question of "what will become of these structures," i.e., the ones being continually reformed by the processes under examination. That's another way of phrasing the "beyond-present-arrangements" concern.

The next section of his chapter has "units of analysis" for its apparent topic, but this, he's able to show, is "fundamentally an issue of concept-formation," which he then proceeds to discuss. There he again uses, as his form of exposition, distinctions among developmentalist, internationalist, and world-historical conceptions of modern social change. And in characterizing the last, he notes, in effect, the need in world-historical studies to work with "open" concepts—concepts capable of being adapted to the real movements of the world-economy as the social whole under examination: otherwise, he cautions, questions of "transformation and transition" will necessarily be "limited to the predesigned elements of a given structure." Also in this context, he calls attention to the tactic of developing "analogies," between or among accounts of specific instances, as a means of "clarifying particular features" of particular developmental processes.

In the final portion of his chapter he turns to "space-time." Among his key formulations is this: what appear, from other points of view, as "repeatable cycles *in* the world-economy" appear, in world-system studies, as "transformations and recom-

Commentary

positions *of* the world-economy" (my emphases). Shortly afterwards he says, "segmented spatial processes which are constitutive of capitalism continually form and reform structures *which we label* town and country" (my emphasis)—or core and periphery, or metropole and hinterland, and so forth. At each of these points, and in virtue of their strategic locations in the paper, Bach works with a double-sided methodological idea. One side is formed by the half-specified notion of the "openness" of a concept—a notion that will be familiar to readers of such analytic philosophers of science as Nagel, Hempel, Danto. The other side, however, is formed by another half-specified notion, that of "realistic historical alternatives"—a notion that, for most of us probably, has been most effectively used by Marcuse (in, especially, *One-Dimensional Man*). Together, the two notions provide *procedural principles* (*not* substantive formats) for delimiting Bach's "beyond-present-arrangements" idea; or his "outcomes" that are not prefigured in given structures; or his "recompositions" *of* the world-economy rather than repeatable cycles within it—recompositions which, after their occurrence, we label "transformations." How do the principles work?

Let me preface a reply by first collapsing our own situation and eliminating our condition as academics. Some research can proceed on material grounds similar to those underlying play-by-play descriptions of sports events. There is the conflict out there, on the field of play. There are the general spectators. And there are those in specialized booths, relaying their observations to others, for example, the broadcaster. By collapsing our situation, I mean eliminating this kind of understanding and inquiry. The game we watch has no spectators, specialized or otherwise; only participants. And everyone broadcasts, although some more articulately than others. So, we're all, first of all, participants. And our understanding of inquiry has no other more fundamental ground. We can distance ourselves from ourselves, of course. We all do it at some time, and some of us can more or less often stretch ourselves in this way to near a breaking point. But there is no way, short of kidding ourselves—or, much more seriously, schizophrenia—that we can convert this subjective tension into observer-object distance. We have no place to stand except on such ground as we make. And the very making of that ground is a part-process of our subject matter. In our work, neutral observers are epistemologically impossible.

If that's so—at least, if it's allowed as a premise—our "stance" as observers is that of participants. And our research designs are thus invariably "activist" designs. They fundamentally entail, implicitly if not otherwise, outcomes alternative to those that occur or, by a *complex* extension, that will, and in due course do, occur (see Mukherjee, cited in Bach's chapter). But, we're lucky. In academia, when by our conceptualization we omit from consideration an historically likely outcome of the processes we're writing about, all that happens is that some months or years that someone protests the omission in an article or letter in a journal. In circles seeking to change the world, the costs are higher. Be that as it may, in *such* methodological circumstances—where we have much to gain from learning from the procedures of investigative reporting—we have no choice but to work with "realistic historical alternatives"—as conditions, as working processes, or as short-run outcomes.

Let me parenthetically clear up a possible misreading. I am *not* saying that we must draw *our* understanding of a transformation from direct participants' understanding. That would be not only silly but for most inquiries an impractical procedural rule. Whether and to what extent we draw on then (or now) contemporary fears or hopes in formalizing *our* understanding of historically alternative conditions, processes, outcomes are considerations completely subsidiary to, and dependent on, the present concern, which is whether and to what extent we must engage in formulating such historical alternatives as an activity integral to our kind of inquiry.

Let me give an example or two. I choose, first, what I imagine to be a familiar formulation. "Suppose," begins Immanuel Wallerstein—and then inserts, to cover any possible embarassment, "great historical game"—"that France had been a differently shaped geographical entity, covering only the north and west... with Rouen as the capital.... Might not such a France... have been able to do what England did— respond to the emerging world-economy by creating an industrial base?"[1] The answer's irrelevant; the logic is clear. The interpretative argument had been that the capitalist development of productive forces in the sixteenth and seventeenth centuries had been less impeded by royal policies in the area under the jurisdiction of the English monarchy than in the area under the jurisdiction of the French monarchy. And the reason given had been that capitalist development in the former, compared with the latter, had led to less contradictory class-forming patterns and to less contradictory state-forming patterns and state policies. The "suppose" is precisely included to conjure up an historical alternative, a different "France," in which class-forming and state-forming patterns would have been, not as they were, but instead more like those in the area under the jurisdiction of the English crown. (True, our author backs off and answers his own query with merely, "Perhaps"; but the *logical* point cannot be so temporized.) That's an example of historically alternative "conditions." Let me give one of "processes." Take "class struggle." In the 1920s, one might have listed all manner of confrontations as "instancing" the relational process. But it would only be in the 1930s that "sit-down strike" would have been included. Why? Because it was only in the intervening decade that the movement invented that tactic.

Let me, finally, give an example about "outcomes." We ordinarily think of "proletarianization" as pertaining, concomitantly or successively, to labor-force formation, class-in-itself formation, class-for-itself formation. Then we observe the ongoing formation of South African mining labor-forces, or of Hong Kong electronics labor-forces. And we realize we must allow for labor-force formation without, in the same breath, assuming class-formation. A new *theoretical* possibility is established for us by an actual pattern in a segment of the network as a whole.

However, it is here that we face the most difficulty. For we must not only be able to *conceptualize* theoretically "new" relational activities, however "old" they may be practically. We must also be good enough *to anticipate*. In detail? No, that's out of the question. In outline? Yes, by using negations, that is, contradictions. Which brings us back to "openness" and "realistic historical alternatives." Openness is given to us by analytic philosophy. The concept, historical alternatives, remains to be specified by times-places-objects. Our route here seems clear: spell out working processes *in relation* to their oppositions and the indigenous forces (people, groups) actively opposing. Those are the "negations" we can work with.

NOTE

1. *The Modern World-System* (New York: Academic Press, 1974), 296.

NOTES ON THE CONTRIBUTORS

ROBERT L. BACH—Assistant Professor of Sociology at S.U.N.Y.—Binghamton, currently on leave at Brookings Institution, Washington. He is writing on Mexican immigration to the United States.

KENNETH BARR—Ph.D. candidate in sociology at S.U.N.Y.—Binghamton, and Research Assistant at the Fernand Braudel Center. He is conducting a comparative historical study of cotton textile enterprises during the period 1750-1850.

ALBERT BERGESEN—Associate Professor of Sociology at the University of Arizona. Editor of *Studies of the Modern World-System* (1980).

NICOLE BOUSQUET—Research Associate, Fernand Braudel Center. She is writing a book on the disintegration of the Spanish and Portuguese empires in the beginning of the nineteenth century.

CHRISTOPHER CHASE-DUNN—Assistant Professor of Sociology at Johns Hopkins University. He is studying urbanization patterns in the world division of labor, and writing a book with Volker Bornschier entitled *Core Corporations and Underdevelopment*.

JASON W. CLAY—Social Science Analyst, U.S. Department of Agriculture. He is writing a book on northeast Brazil.

JAMES E. CRONIN—Assistant Professor of History at the University of Wisconsin—Milwaukee. Author of *Industrial Conflict in Modern Britain* (1979).

MARLENE DIXON—Research Director, Institute for the Study of Labor and Economic Crisis, San Francisco. Currently engaged in labor research.

CYNTHIA H. ENLOE—Professor of Government, Clark University. Author of *Ethnic Soldiers* (1980), and *Politics, Military and Ethnicity* (1980).

EDWARD FRIEDMAN—Professor of Political Science at the University of Wisconsin—Madison. Author of *Backward Towards Revolution* (1974). Writing with others a book on *A Chinese Village in a Socialist State*.

DAVID M. GORDON—teaches economics at the Graduate Faculty of the New School for Social Research. Has written about the economic crisis and labor economics.

TERENCE K. HOPKINS—Professor of Sociology at S.U.N.Y.—Binghamton, and Member of the Executive Board, Fernand Braudel Center.

SUSANNE JONAS—Research Director, Institute for the Study of Labor and Economic Crisis, San Francisco. Has written on Latin America.

RAMKRISHNA MUKHERJEE—Distinguished Scientist, Indian Statistical Institute, Calcutta. Author most recently of *What Will It Be? An Approach to Inductive Sociology* (1978).

MARTIN J. MURRAY—Assistant Professor of Sociology, S.U.N.Y.—Binghamton. Author of *The Development of Capitalism in Colonial Indochina, 1870–1940* (1980).

CHARLES C. RAGIN—Assistant Professor of Sociology, Indiana University. He is working on a systematization of Weberian rules of social historical research.

JAMES F. TOTH—Ph.D. candidate in anthropology at S.U.N.Y.—Binghamton. He is studying the lives of casual laborers and labor recruiters in the Egyptian delta.

IMMANUEL WALLERSTEIN—Director of the Fernand Braudel Center and Distinguished Professor of Sociology of S.U.N.Y.—Binghamton. Author of *The Modern World-System* (1974, 1980) and *The Capitalist World-Economy* (1979).